ATTRACTION AND POTENTIAL

M.M. Rahman

ATLANTIC
PUBLISHERS & DISTRIBUTORS (P) LTD

Published by
ATLANTIC
PUBLISHERS & DISTRIBUTORS (P) LTD

7/22, Ansari Road, Darya Ganj, New Delhi-110002
Phones : +91-11-40775252, 23273880, 23275880, 23280451
Fax : +91-11-23285873
Web : www.atlanticbooks.com
E-mail : orders@atlanticbooks.com

Branch Office
5, Nallathambi Street, Wallajah Road, Chennai-600002
Phones : +91-44-64611085, 32413319
E-mail : chennai@atlanticbooks.com

Printed in India at Nice Printing Press, A-33/3A, Site-IV, Industrial Area, Sahibabad, Ghaziabad, U.P.

PREFACE

This book *Attraction and Potential* is intended to cover the syllabi of B.A., B.Sc. (H), M.A., and M.Sc. of all Indian Universities as well as competitive examinations of equivalent standard.

After teaching several years to the honours and postgraduate students, I have experienced that average students find most of the existing books either too difficult to comprehend or too inadequate to meet the requirements. This book is complete in the sense that it is rich in subject matter and coverage, and yet easily accessible. The stress has been given on fundamental ideas, so that students may grasp it easily. Each topic has been introduced and developed in a simple and straightforward manner as much as possible and well within the comprehension of students of all categories. Chapters are arranged in a systematic order and the fundamental principles involved have been amply illustrated by diagrams and worked-out examples given correspondingly, so that the students may understand the methods clearly and easily. Most of the questions have been taken from the question papers of various universities in the hope that they will facilitate examination preparation. I am hopeful that the book will prove extremely beneficial to the graduate and postgraduate students of Mathematics as well as aspirants of UPSC, State Public Services, and other competitive examinations.

The present book is not an outcome of my solo efforts. I have been fortunate to receive help by many people in accomplishing this great task. I am thankful to all those persons who have helped me in any form in bringing out this book. More particularly, I am grateful to my students whose constant inspiration and help insisted me to complete the present book. I also express my sincere thanks to my wife N. Jahan and sons Tauseef, Tauqeer and Ayan for their constant encouragement and cooperation without which this book would not have been possible.

Last but not least, I am thankful to Dr. K.R. Gupta, Chief Editor of Atlantic Publishers and Distributors (P) Ltd., for taking keen interest in publishing this book.

M.M. Rahman

CONTENTS

ABBREVIATIONS

L.N.M.U.	:	Lalit Narayan Mithila University
M.U.	:	Magadh University
T.M.B.U.	:	Tilka Manjhi Bhagalpur University
B.B.A.B.U.	:	Babasaheb Bhimrao Ambedkar Bihar University
R.U.	:	Ranchi University
P.U.	:	Patna University

1 ATTRACTION OF A ROD

1.1. Newtonian Law of Attraction

[M.U. 94H, 96H, 2003H; R.U. 91H, 94H, 98H]

Statement. Every particle of matter attracts every other particle of the matter with a force which is directly proportional to the product of the masses of the particles and inversely proportional to the square of the distance between them.

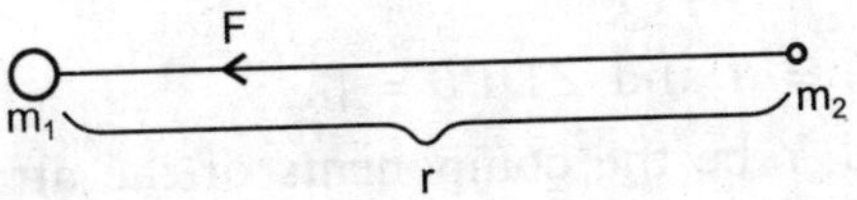

Thus if m_1, m_2 are the masses of two particles placed at a distance r, then the force F of attraction between them is $\frac{\gamma m_1 m_2}{r^2}$, where γ is a constant known as gravitational constant which is equal to the attraction between two particles each of unit mass and situated at a unit distance.

1.2. Attraction of a Rod

To find the attraction of a thin uniform rod at an external point.

[L.N.M.U. 94H; P.U. 77H, 80H, 82H; M.U. 91H, 96H, 2001H, 2003H; T.M.B.U. 95H, 98H, 2000H, 2002H, 2004H; B.B.A.B.U. 97H, 99H; R.U. 91H, 93H, 95H, 98H]

Let AB be the thin uniform rod and P the external point at which the attraction of AB is to be find out. From P we draw PD perpendicular to the line AB and PL parallel to AB. Let $PD = p$.

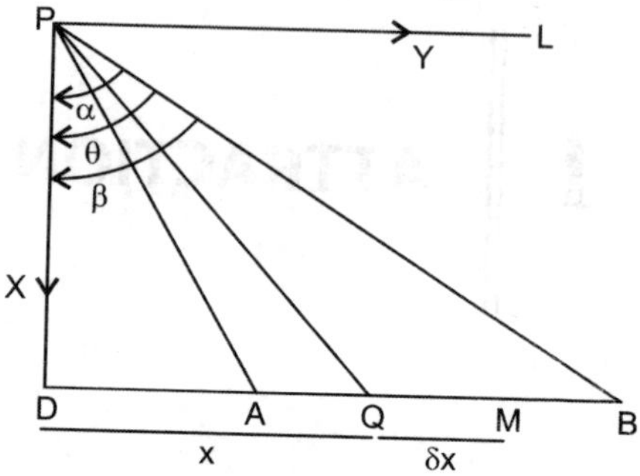

Let us take a point Q on AB, such that $DQ = x$ and $\angle DPQ = \theta$.

We consider an element QM of rod of length δx. Let K be the cross-section and ρ be the density of the rod.

Then the mass of the element $QM = K\rho\delta x$.

The attraction of the element QM on a unit mass at P = $\dfrac{\gamma K\rho\delta x}{PQ^2}$ which act in the direction of PQ, as QM is very small and the rod is very thin.

Its components along PD and PL are respectively $\dfrac{\gamma K\rho\delta x}{PQ^2}\cos\theta$ and $\dfrac{\gamma K\rho\delta x}{PQ^2}\sin\theta$

Let $\angle DPA = \alpha$ and $\angle DPB = \beta$.

Let X and Y be the components of the attraction of the whole rod AB along PD and PL respectively, then

$$X = \int_\alpha^\beta \frac{\gamma K\rho\delta x}{PQ^2}\cos\theta \text{ and } Y = \int_\alpha^\beta \frac{\gamma K\rho\delta x}{PQ^2}\sin\theta$$

In ΔPQD $\cos\theta = \dfrac{PD}{PQ} = \dfrac{p}{PQ}$

$$PQ = p\sec\theta$$

Also $\tan\theta = \dfrac{QD}{PD} = \dfrac{x}{p}$

$$x = p\tan\theta$$

$$\therefore\ dx = p\sec^2\theta\, d\theta$$

With these values X and Y becomes

$$X = \int_\alpha^\beta \frac{\gamma K\rho\, p\sec^2\theta d\theta\cos\theta}{p^2\sec^2\theta}$$

$$= \frac{\gamma K\rho}{p}\int_{\alpha}^{\beta}\cos\theta\, d\theta$$

$$= \frac{\gamma K\rho}{p}[\sin\theta]_{\alpha}^{\beta}$$

$$= \frac{\gamma K\rho}{p}(\sin\beta - \sin\alpha) \quad \ldots (1)$$

and $$Y = \int_{\alpha}^{\beta}\frac{\gamma K\rho\, p\sec^2\theta\, d\theta\sin\theta}{p^2\sec^2\theta}$$

$$= \frac{\gamma K\rho}{p}\int_{\alpha}^{\beta}\sin\theta\, d\theta$$

$$= \frac{\gamma K\rho}{p}[-\cos\theta]_{\alpha}^{\beta}$$

$$= \frac{\gamma K\rho}{p}(\cos\alpha - \cos\beta) \quad \ldots (2)$$

If R be the resultant of X and Y, and acts along a line through P making an angle ϕ with PD, we have

$$R = \sqrt{X^2 + Y^2}$$

$$= \frac{\gamma K\rho}{p}\sqrt{(\sin\beta - \sin\alpha)^2 + (\cos\alpha - \cos\beta)^2}$$

$$= \frac{\gamma K\rho}{p}\sqrt{2 - 2\cos(\beta - \alpha)}$$

$$= \frac{\gamma K\rho}{p}\sqrt{2\{1 - \cos(\beta - \alpha)\}}$$

$$= \frac{\gamma K\rho}{p}\sqrt{2\cdot 2\sin^2\frac{\beta - \alpha}{2}}$$

$$= \frac{2\gamma K\rho}{p}\sin\frac{\beta\alpha}{2}$$

$$= \frac{2\gamma K\rho}{p}\sin\frac{APB}{2}$$

$$\text{and } \tan\phi = \frac{Y}{X} = \frac{\cos\alpha - \cos\beta}{\sin\beta - \sin\alpha}$$

$$= \frac{2\sin\frac{\alpha+\beta}{2}\sin\frac{\beta-\alpha}{2}}{2\cos\frac{\alpha+\beta}{2}\sin\frac{\beta-\alpha}{2}}$$

$$= \tan\frac{\alpha+\beta}{2}$$

so that $\phi = \dfrac{\alpha+\beta}{2}$

Hence we find that

$$\text{magnitude } R = \frac{2\gamma K\rho}{p}\sin\left(\frac{APB}{2}\right) \quad \text{... (3)}$$

$$\text{and direction } \phi = \frac{\alpha+\beta}{2} \quad \text{... (4)}$$

Thus the direction of the resultant attraction bisects the angle APB.

Corollary. Attraction of an infinite rod.

Since the rod is of infinite length in both the directions

Hence $\alpha = -90°$ and $\beta = 90°$

So from (1), (2) and (4), we get

$$X = \frac{2\gamma K\rho}{p} \text{ and } Y = 0$$

$$\therefore \quad R = \frac{2\gamma K\rho}{p} \text{ and } \phi = 0$$

Hence R act along PD.

Thus the **attraction** of an infinite rod at an external point varies inversely **as** the distance of the point from the rod.

[B.B.A.B.U. 99H, 2001H, 2003H; R.U. 95H, 97H; M.U. 2005H]

1.3. Attraction of a Circular Rod

To show that the attraction of a rod AB at an external point P is the same as that of the arc of a circle of like material with centre P and radius equal to the perpendicular distance from P on AB which is intercepted by the lines PA and PB.

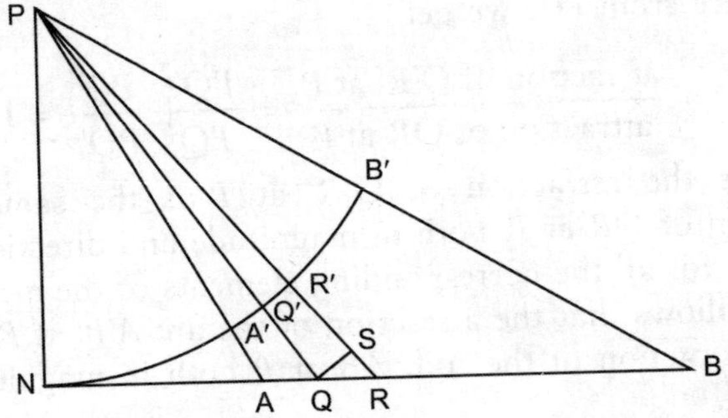

Let P be the point outside the thin straight rod AB. We draw an arc $A'B'$ of a circle with centre at P and radius PN, where N is the foot of perpendicular from P on AB, intersecting the lines PA and PB in A' and B' respectively.

We now assume that the arc $A'B'$ represents a circular rod of the same thickness, density and cross-section as the rod AB. We will show that the attraction of this circular rod $A'B'$ of P is the same as that of the rod AB.

Let QR be an element of the rod AB and $Q'R'$ the corresponding element of the circular arc $A'B'$. Then,

$$\frac{\text{attraction of } Q'R' \text{ at } P}{\text{attraction of } QR \text{ at } P} = \frac{Q'R'}{PQ'^2} \Big/ \frac{QR}{PQ^2}$$

$$= \frac{Q'R'}{QR} \frac{PQ^2}{PQ'^2} \qquad \dots (1)$$

From Q we draw QS perpendicular to PR.

From the similar figures PQS and $PQ'R'$, we have

$$\frac{Q'R'}{QS} = \frac{PQ'}{PQ}$$

Also $\quad \sin QRS = \dfrac{QS}{QR} = \dfrac{PN}{PR} = \dfrac{PQ'}{PQ}$ (Nearly)

Therefore $\quad \dfrac{Q'R'}{QR} = \dfrac{Q'R'}{QS} \dfrac{QS}{QR} = \dfrac{PQ'}{PQ} \dfrac{PQ'}{PQ}$

$$= \frac{PQ'^2}{PQ^2}$$

Hence from (1), we get

$$\frac{\text{attraction of } Q'R' \text{ at } P}{\text{attraction of } QR \text{ at } P} = \frac{PQ'^2}{PQ^2}\frac{PQ^2}{PQ'^2} = 1$$

Thus the attraction of $Q'R'$ at P is the same as the attraction of QR at P, both in magnitude and direction. Since it is true for all the corresponding elements of the arc and the rod, it follows that the attraction of the arc $A'B'$ at P is equal to the attraction of the rod. AB at P both in magnitude and direction.

2nd Method

Let $\angle QPR = \delta\theta$, then the attraction of the element $Q'R'$ at P is

$$\frac{\gamma K\rho\,(p\delta\theta)}{p^2} = \frac{\gamma K\rho\delta\theta}{p} \quad \text{where } PN = p.$$

which is also the attraction of the element QR at P.

Hence, it follows that the attraction of the rod AB at P is the same as that of the circular arc $A'B'$.

WORKED OUT EXAMPLES

1. Show that the attraction of uniform rod AB on a unit mass at P, in the direction parallel to AB, varies at $\frac{1}{PA} - \frac{1}{PB}$.

[L.N.M.U. 93H]

Solution: From P we draw PD perpendicular to AB. Let $PD = p$, $\angle APD = \alpha$ and $\angle BPD = \beta$.

We know that the attraction of the rod AB at parallel to AB

$$= \frac{\gamma K\rho}{p}(\cos\alpha - \cos\beta)$$

$$= \frac{\gamma K\rho}{p}\left(\frac{PD}{PA} - \frac{PD}{PB}\right)$$

$$= \frac{\gamma K\rho}{p}\left(\frac{p}{PA} - \frac{p}{PB}\right)$$

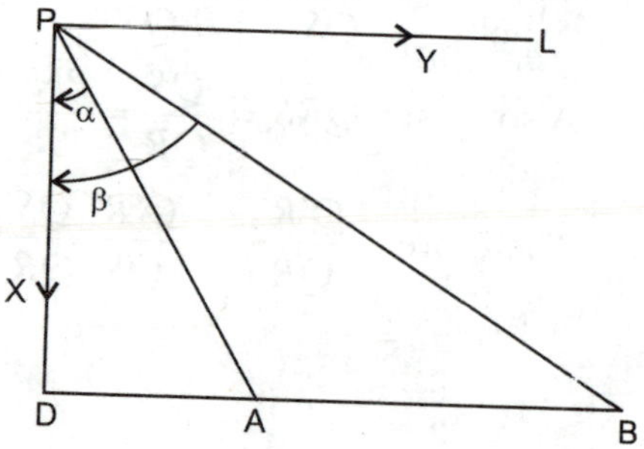

$$= \gamma K\rho\left(\frac{1}{PA} - \frac{1}{PB}\right)$$

Since $\gamma K\rho$ is constant. Hence the attraction of AB on a unit mass at P, in the direction parallel to AB, varies as $\frac{1}{PA} - \frac{1}{PB}$.

2. Two uniform rods AB and CD of length a and mass m per unit length, are placed, so that CD lies along a right bisector of AB and C and D are at distance a and $2a$ respectively from rod AB. Show that the attraction of either rod on the other is of magnitude.

$$2\gamma m^2\left[\log\left(1+\sqrt{5}\right) + \log 2 - \log\left(1+\sqrt{17}\right)\right]$$

Solution: We produce DC to meet AB in N.

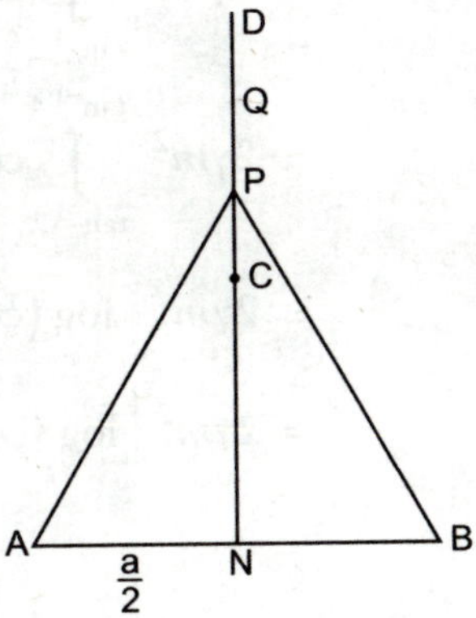

Let $NP = x$ and $NQ = x + \delta x$

$PQ = \delta x$, $AB = a$, $CD = a$, $DN = 2a$, $CN = a$

Mass of the element $PQ = m\delta x$.

Now the attraction of AB at the element PQ along PN is

$$\frac{2\gamma m}{PN}\sin\frac{APB}{2}\, m\delta x$$

$$= \frac{2\gamma m^2 \delta x}{PN}\sin APN$$

$$= \frac{2\gamma m^2 \delta x}{x}\frac{AN}{AP}$$

$$= \frac{2\gamma m^2 \delta x}{x}\frac{a}{2\sqrt{\frac{a^2}{4} + x^2}}$$

$$= \frac{\gamma m^2 \delta x a 2}{x\sqrt{a^2 + 4x^2}} = \frac{2\gamma m^2 a \delta x}{x\sqrt{4x^2 + a^2}}$$

Therefore the total attraction of AB on CD

$$= \int_a^{2a} \frac{2\gamma a m^2}{x\sqrt{4x^2 + a^2}}\, dx$$

$$= 2\gamma a m^2 \int_a^{2a} \frac{dx}{x\sqrt{a^2+4x^2}}$$

Putting $2x = a \tan\theta$.

$$2dx = a \sec^2 \theta d\theta$$

When $x = a$, $\theta = \tan^{-1}2$

and $x = 2a$, $\theta = \tan^{-1}4$

Hence required attraction

$$= \gamma a m^2 \int_{\tan^{-1}2}^{\tan^{-1}4} \frac{a \sec^2\theta d\theta}{a \sec\theta \frac{a}{2} \tan\theta}$$

$$= 2\gamma m^2 \int_{\tan^{-1}2}^{\tan^{-1}4} \sec\theta \, d\theta \cot\theta$$

$$= 2\gamma m^2 \int_{\tan^{-1}2}^{\tan^{-1}4} \operatorname{cosec}\theta d\theta$$

$$= 2\gamma m^2 \left[\log(\operatorname{cosec}\theta - \cot\theta)\right]_{\tan^{-1}2}^{\tan^{-1}4}$$

$$= 2\gamma m^2 \left[\log\left\{\operatorname{cosec}(\tan^{-1}4) - \cot(\tan^{-1}4)\right\} - \log\left\{\operatorname{cosec}(\tan^{-1}2) - \cot(\tan^{-1}2)\right\}\right]$$

$$= 2\gamma m^2 \left[\log\left\{\sqrt{1+\cot^2(\tan^{-1}4)} - \cot\left(\cot^{-1}\frac{1}{4}\right)\right\} - \log\left\{\sqrt{1+\cot^2(\tan^{-1}2)} - \cot\left(\cot^{-1}\frac{1}{2}\right)\right\}\right]$$

$$= 2\gamma m^2 \left[\log\left\{\sqrt{1+\frac{1}{16}} - \frac{1}{4}\right\} - \log\left\{\sqrt{1+\frac{1}{4}} - \frac{1}{2}\right\}\right]$$

$$= 2\gamma m^2 \left\{\log\frac{\sqrt{17}-1}{4} - \log\frac{\sqrt{5}-1}{2}\right\}$$

$$= 2\gamma m^2 \log\frac{(\sqrt{17}-1)2}{4(\sqrt{5}-1)}$$

$$= 2\gamma m^2 \log \frac{\sqrt{17}-1}{2\left(\sqrt{5}-1\right)}$$

$$= 2\gamma m^2 \log \frac{(17-1)\left(\sqrt{5}+1\right)}{2\left(\sqrt{17}+1\right)4}$$

$$= 2\gamma m^2 \log \frac{2\left(\sqrt{5}+1\right)}{\sqrt{17}+1}$$

$$= 2\gamma m^2 \left[\log\left(1+\sqrt{5}\right) + \log 2 - \log\left(1+\sqrt{17}\right)\right] \text{ Proved.}$$

3. Show that the attraction of a thin uniform straight bar of line density σ and length l on another, of line density σ^1 and length l^1, placed parallel to it and symmetrically with respect to it at a distance h is

$$\frac{Y\sigma\sigma^1}{h}\left[\sqrt{\left\{\left(l+l^1\right)^2+4h^2\right\}} - \sqrt{\left\{\left(l-l^1\right)+4h^2\right\}}\right]$$

Solution: Let $AB = l$ and $CD = l^1$ be two parallel rods placed symmetrically and let O, O^1 be their mid-points, then OO^1 is at right angles to both. So $OO^1 = h$.

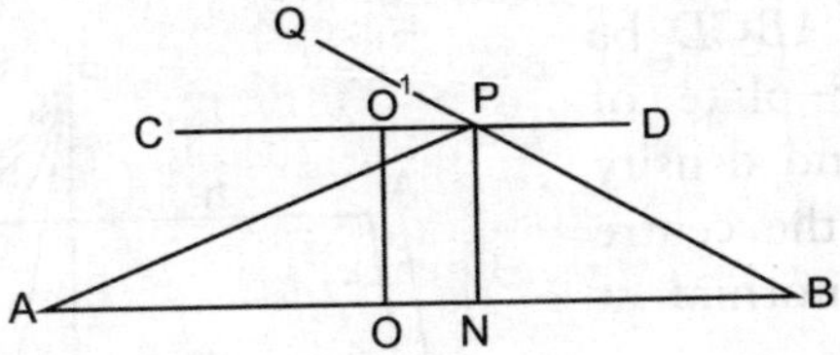

Let $O^1P = x$, then mass of the element $PQ = \delta x\sigma^1$ of the rod CD at a distance x from O^1

By symmetry the resultant attraction of the rod AB on CD will be along O^1O

The attraction of the rod AB at P along PN is

$$= \frac{\gamma\sigma\sigma^1}{h}(\sin APN + \sin BPN)$$

$$= \frac{\gamma\sigma\sigma^1}{h}\left(\frac{AN}{AP} + \frac{BN}{BP}\right)$$

$$= \frac{\gamma\sigma\sigma^1}{h}\left[\frac{\frac{l}{2}+x}{\sqrt{\left(\frac{l}{2}+x\right)^2+h^2}}+\frac{\frac{l}{2}-x}{\sqrt{\left(\frac{l}{2}-x\right)^2+h^2}}\right]$$

Hence the attraction of AB on whole of CD

$$= \frac{\gamma\sigma\sigma^1}{h}\int_{-\frac{l^1}{2}}^{\frac{l^1}{2}}\left[\frac{\frac{l}{2}+x}{\sqrt{\left(\frac{l}{2}+x\right)^2+h^2}}+\frac{\frac{l}{2}-x}{\sqrt{\left(\frac{l}{2}-x\right)^2+h^2}}\right]dx$$

$$= \frac{\gamma\sigma\sigma^1}{h}\left[\sqrt{\left(\frac{l}{2}+x\right)^2+h^2}-\sqrt{\left(\frac{l}{2}-x\right)^2+h^2}\right]_{-\frac{l^1}{2}}^{\frac{l^1}{2}}$$

$$= \frac{\gamma\sigma\sigma^1}{h}\left[\sqrt{(l+l^1)^2+4h^2}-\sqrt{(l-l^1)^2+4h^2}\right] \quad \text{Proved.}$$

4. Find the attraction of a uniform thin rectangular plate upon a unit mass situated on the normal to the plate at the centre.

[B.B.A.B.U. 98H]

Solution: Let $ABCD$ be a rectangular plate of thickness K and density ρ. Let O be the centre and OP the normal at O.

Let $AB = 2a$, $AD = 2b$ and $OP = h$.

Let H, K be the middle points of BC and CD.

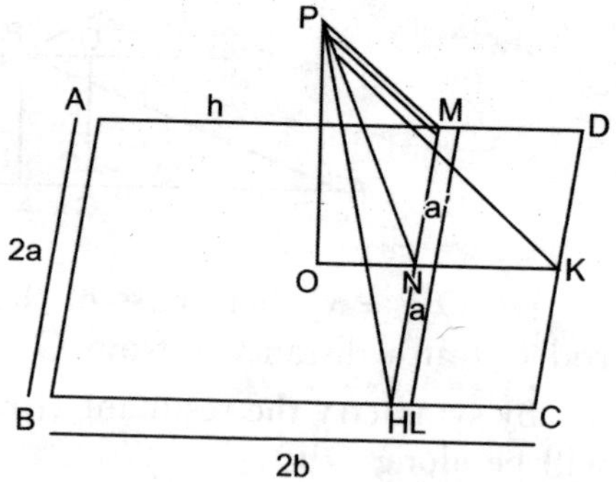

Let us divide the plate into a large number of strips parallel to AB and ML be one of these strips situated at a distance x from the centre O and whose breadth is δx.

Let N be the middle point of LM.

Hence $LN = NM = a$. Let $\angle OPN = \theta$.

$$\tan\theta = \frac{ON}{OP} = \frac{x}{h}, \sec\theta = \frac{PN}{OP} = \frac{PN}{h}$$

$x = h\tan\theta$, $PN = h\sec\theta$

Now $\quad PL = \sqrt{PN^2 + NL^2} = \sqrt{h^2\sec^2\theta + a^2}$

$$\angle MPN = \angle LPN = \frac{1}{2}\angle MPL$$

The attraction of the strip LM at P, is

$$X = \frac{2\gamma K\delta x\rho}{PN}\sin\frac{LPM}{2} \text{ along } PN$$

$$= \frac{2\gamma K\delta x\rho}{PN}\sin LPN$$

$$= \frac{2\gamma K\delta x\rho}{PN}\frac{LN}{LP}$$

$$= \frac{2\gamma K\rho a}{h\sec\theta}\frac{\delta x}{\sqrt{h^2\sec^2\theta + a^2}}$$

$$= \frac{2\gamma K\rho a\, h\sec^2\theta\delta\theta}{h\sec\theta\sqrt{h^2\sec^2\theta + a^2}}$$

Hence, the component of the attraction along PO, is

$$X\cos\theta = \frac{2\gamma K\rho a\,\theta\, d\theta}{\sqrt{h^2\sec^2\theta + a^2}}$$

$$= \frac{2\gamma K\rho a\,\delta\theta\cos\theta}{\sqrt{h^2 + a^2\cos^2\theta}}$$

By symmetry the resultant attraction of the plate at P will be along PO. Hence the total attraction R, along PO is given by

$$R = \int_{-\alpha}^{\alpha}\frac{2\gamma K\rho a\cos\theta\, d\theta}{\sqrt{h^2 + a^2\cos^2\theta}}$$

$$= 4\gamma K\rho a\int_0^{\alpha}\frac{\cos\theta\, d\theta}{\sqrt{h^2 + a^2 - a^2\sin^2\theta}}$$

$$= 4\gamma K\rho a\left[\sin^{-1}\frac{a\sin\theta}{\sqrt{h^2 + a^2}}\right]_0^{\alpha}$$

$$= 4\gamma K\rho a \sin^{-1} \frac{a \sin \alpha}{\sqrt{h^2 + a^2}}$$

$$= \frac{\gamma M}{ab} \sin^{-1} \frac{a \sin \alpha}{\sqrt{h^2 + a^2}}$$

where $\alpha = \angle OPK$, $\sin \alpha = \frac{OK}{PK} = \frac{b}{\sqrt{h^2 + b^2}}$

and M = mass of the place = $4ab\rho K$

Therefore $R = \frac{\gamma M}{ab} \sin^{-1} \frac{ab}{\sqrt{(h^2 + a^2)(h^2 + b^2)}}$

Also since $\sin OPK = \frac{b}{\sqrt{h^2 + b^2}}$

and $\sin OPH = \frac{a}{\sqrt{h^2 + a^2}}$

Then $R = \frac{\gamma M}{ab} \sin^{-1} (\sin OPH \sin OPK)$

5. Prove that the attraction of a thin uniform cylindrical shell of radius a and length l at a point on its axis at a distance b from one end and $l - b$ from the other $\left(b < \frac{l}{2}\right)$ is

$$\frac{\gamma M}{2\pi al}\left[\frac{1}{\sqrt{(a^2 + b^2)}} - \frac{1}{\sqrt{a^2 + (l-b)^2}}\right]$$

where M is the mass of the shell, the ends of the shell are open and circular.

Solution: Let P be a point on the axis where attraction is to be determined.

We divide the surface into a large number of thin rods parallel to the axis.

Let AB be one of the elementary rods on which PN is drawn perpendicular.

On account of the symmetry of the elementary rods about the point P, the attractions at right angles to the axis neutralise.

Hence we are to find the attraction at P parallel to axis i.e. parallel to AB i.e. Y.

Let $\angle APN = \alpha$ and $\angle BPN = \beta$.

Hence $$Y = \frac{\gamma K\rho}{P}(\cos\alpha - \cos\beta)$$
$$= \frac{\gamma K\rho}{PN}\left(\frac{PN}{AP} - \frac{PN}{BP}\right)$$
$$= \gamma K\rho\left(\frac{1}{AP} - \frac{1}{BP}\right)$$

Clearly $\angle POA = 90°$

$\therefore$ $$AP^2 = OA^2 + OP^2 = a^2 + b^2$$

Also $\angle BPN = 90°$

$\therefore$ $$BP^2 = PN^2 + BN^2$$
$$= a^2 + (l - b)^2$$

Hence $$Y = \gamma K\rho\left[\frac{1}{\sqrt{a^2 + b^2}} - \frac{1}{\sqrt{a^2 + (l - b)^2}}\right]$$

Also $M = (2\pi a)\, lK\rho$

Hence $$Y = \frac{\gamma M}{2\pi a l}\left[\frac{1}{\sqrt{(a^2 + b^2)}} - \frac{1}{\sqrt{\{a^2 + (l - b)^2\}}}\right]$$

6. A vertical solid cylinder of height h, radius a and density ρ bounded by plane ends perpendicular to axis is divided by a plane through the axis into two parts. Show that the horizontal attraction of one part on a particle at the centre of base O is $2\pi h\rho \log \frac{a + \sqrt{a^2 + h^2}}{h}$ and find the angle, the resultant attraction makes with the axis.

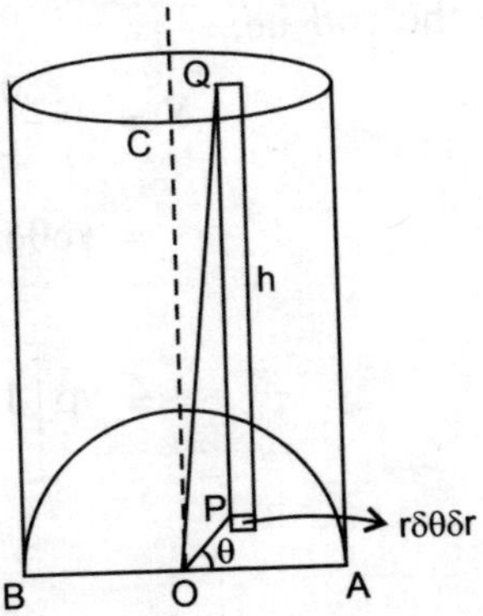

Solution: We divide the cylinder into a large number of filaments (rods) and let PQ be one of such rods standing on $r\delta\theta\delta r$.

Attraction of the elementary rod PQ at the centre O along OP which is perpendicular to it i.e. X.

$$X = \frac{\gamma r\delta\theta\delta r\rho}{r}(\sin\beta - \sin\alpha)$$

$$= \frac{\gamma r\delta\theta\delta r\rho}{r}[\sin QOP - \sin\theta]$$

$$(\because \alpha = 0, p = r = OP)$$

$$= \gamma\rho\delta\theta\delta r\left[\frac{h}{\sqrt{h^2 + r^2}}\right]$$

Its resolved part along the central radius of the base

$$= \frac{\gamma h\rho\delta\theta\delta r \sin\theta}{\sqrt{h^2 + r^2}}$$

Hence total attraction along the central radius of the base

$$= \gamma h\rho \int_0^{\pi}\int_{r=0}^{a} \frac{\sin\theta d\theta\, dr}{\sqrt{h^2 + r^2}}$$

$$= \gamma h\rho \int_0^{\pi}\left[\log\left(r + \sqrt{h^2 + r^2}\right)\right]_0^a \sin\theta d\theta$$

$$= \gamma h\rho \log\frac{a + \sqrt{h^2 + a^2}}{h}[\cos\theta]_0^{\pi}$$

$$= 2\gamma h\rho \log\frac{a + \sqrt{h^2 + a^2}}{h}$$

This gives us the horizontal attraction.

Again the attraction of the elementary rod at O, parallel to the rod i.e.

$$Y = \frac{\gamma r\delta\theta\delta r\,\rho}{r}[\cos\alpha - \cos\beta]$$

$$= \gamma\delta\theta\delta r\,\rho\left[1 - \frac{r}{\sqrt{h^2 + r^2}}\right]$$

$$= \gamma\rho\left[1 - \frac{r}{\sqrt{h^2 + r^2}}\right]\delta\theta\delta r$$

Hence total vertical attraction at O

$$= \gamma\rho \int_0^{\pi}\int_0^{a}\left[1-\frac{r}{\sqrt{h^2+r^2}}\right]d\theta dr$$

$$= \gamma\rho\left[r-\sqrt{h^2+r^2}\right]_0^a[\theta]_o^\pi$$

$$= \gamma\rho\left[a-\sqrt{h^2+a^2}+h\right]\pi$$

$$= \gamma\rho\pi\left[h+a-\sqrt{h^2+a^2}\right]$$

If ϕ be the angle which the resultant attraction makes with the axis of the cylinder i.e. vertical then

$$\phi = \tan^{-1}\frac{Y}{X}$$

7. Three equal uniform rods each of length $2a$ and of mass m per unit of length form an equilateral triangle. Show that the attraction on a particle of unit mass on straight line through the centre of the triangle at right angles to its plane and at distance z from it is

$$\frac{6\gamma maZ}{\left(Z^2+\frac{a^2}{3}\right)\left(Z^2+\frac{4a^2}{3}\right)}\frac{1}{2}$$

Solution: Let three equal rods AB, BC and CA of length $2a$ form an equilateral triangle.

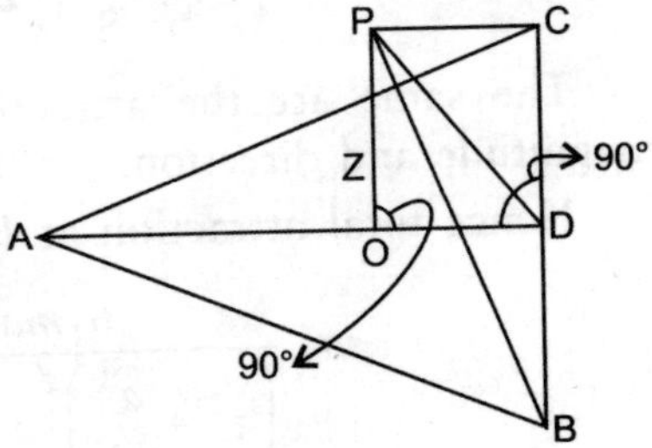

Let O be the centre of the triangle ABC and P a point on the line through O, perpendicular to the plane of the triangle ABC.

Let k be the cross-section and ρ the density of each rod.

Let D be the middle point of BC, join OD and PD. Let $OP = z$, $AB = BC = CA = 2a$.

$$OD = \frac{1}{3}AD = \frac{1}{3}2a\sin 60 = \frac{a}{\sqrt{3}}$$

$$PD^2 = OP^2 + OD^2 = z^2 + \frac{a^2}{3}$$

$$PB^2 = PD^2 + BD^2 = Z^2 + \frac{a^2}{3} + a^2$$

$$= Z^2 + \frac{4a^2}{3} = PC^2$$

Attraction of the rod BC at P

$$= \frac{2\gamma k\rho}{PD} \frac{\sin B\hat{P}C}{2} \text{ along } PD$$

$$= \frac{2\gamma k\rho}{PD} \sin DPC \cos DPO \text{ along } PO$$

$$= \frac{2\gamma k\rho}{PD} \frac{DC}{PC} \frac{OP}{PD}$$

$$= \frac{2\gamma k\rho}{PD^2} \frac{DC \cdot OP}{PC}$$

$$= \frac{2\gamma k\rho}{z^2 + \frac{a^2}{3}} \frac{az}{\sqrt{z^2 + \frac{4a^2}{3}}}$$

Replacing $k\rho$ by m, we get the attraction as

$$= \frac{2\gamma\, maz}{\left(z^2 + \frac{a^2}{3}\right)\left(z^2 + \frac{4a^2}{3}\right)} \frac{1}{2}$$

The same are the attractions of the other two rods in magnitude and direction.

Hence total attraction at P

$$= \frac{6\gamma maz}{\left(z^2 + \frac{a^2}{3}\right)\left(z^2 + \frac{4a^2}{3}\right)} \frac{1}{2}$$

8. A homogeneous prism, infinite in length, whose cross-section is an equilateral triangle ABC attracts a particle at A. Show that the resultant attraction is $\frac{4\pi\gamma M}{3a}$. Where M is the

mass of a unit length of the prism and a is the length of a side of the triangle.

Solution: We divide the prism into large number of rods of infinite length and one of them be standing on the element $r\delta\theta\delta r$. Where $AP = r$ and $\angle MAQ = \theta$.

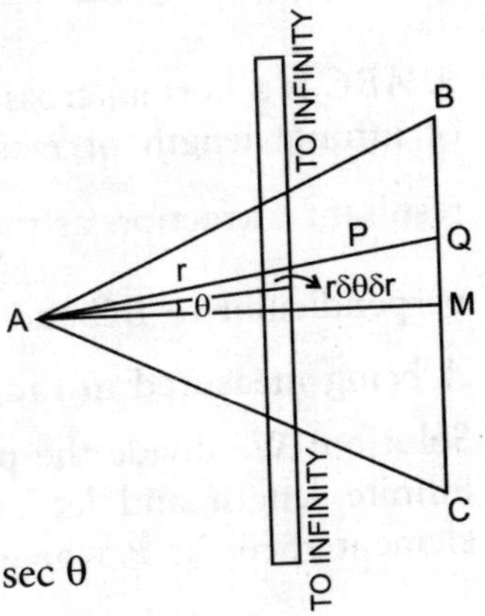

The resultant attraction of A will be along the bisector AM of $\angle CAB$, where

$$AM = AC \cos 30$$

$$= \frac{a\sqrt{3}}{2}$$

Also $\quad AM = AQ \cos\theta$

$$AQ = AM \sec\theta = \frac{a\sqrt{3}}{2}\sec\theta$$

Attraction of the infinite rod at A

$$= \frac{2\gamma\rho r\delta\theta\delta r}{r} \text{ along } AP$$

Its resolved part along $AM = 2\gamma\rho\delta\theta\delta r\cos\theta$. Hence attraction of the whole prism along AM

$$= \int_{-\pi/6}^{\pi/6}\int_{r=0}^{r=AQ} 2\gamma\rho\cos\theta d\theta\, dr$$

$$= 2\gamma\rho\int_{-\pi/6}^{\pi/6} AQ\cos\theta d\theta$$

$$= 2\gamma\rho\int_{0}^{\pi/6}\frac{a\sqrt{3}}{2}\sec\theta\cos\theta\, d\theta$$

$$= 2\gamma\rho\, a\sqrt{3}\,\frac{\pi}{6}$$

But $\quad M$ = mass of the equilateral triangle

$$= \frac{\sqrt{3}}{4}a^2\rho$$

Hence attraction

$$= 2\gamma a \sqrt{3}\frac{\pi}{6}\frac{4M}{\sqrt{3}a^2}$$

$$= \frac{4\pi\gamma M}{3a}$$

9. ABC is a normal cross-section of a uniform triangular prism of infinite length of mass m per unit length. Show that the resultant attraction at the point A is compounded of $\frac{4\gamma m A}{a}$ perpendicular to BC and $\frac{4\gamma m}{a}\log\frac{b}{c}$ parallel to BC, the angle A being measured in radians.

Solution: We divide the prism into a large number of rods of infinite length and let one of such rod be standing on the element $r\delta\theta\delta r$ at P where $AP = r$ and $\angle DAP = \theta$.

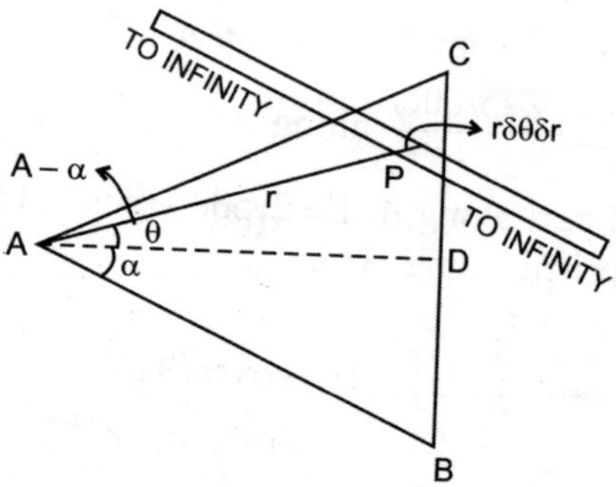

Attraction of this infinite rod at A by $\frac{2\gamma k\rho}{p}$ will be $\frac{2\gamma r\delta\theta\delta r\rho}{r}$ i.e. $2\gamma\rho\delta\theta\delta r$ along AP.

Its resolved parts along and perpendicular to BC are $2\gamma\rho\delta\theta\delta r \sin\theta$ and $2\gamma\rho\delta\theta\delta r\cos\theta$.

Hence total attraction parallel to BC is

$$= 2\gamma\rho \int_{-\alpha}^{A-\alpha}\int_{0}^{AQ} \sin\theta \, d\theta \, dr$$

$$= 2\gamma\rho \int_{-\alpha}^{A-\alpha} AQ \sin\theta \, d\theta$$

$$= 2\gamma\rho \int_{-\alpha}^{A-\alpha} AD \sec\theta \sin\theta \, d\theta$$

$$= 2\gamma\rho AD \int_{-\alpha}^{A-\alpha} \tan\theta \, d\theta$$

$$= 2\gamma\rho \, AD \left[\log \sec\theta\right]_{-\alpha}^{A-\alpha}$$

$$= 2\gamma\rho \, AD \left[\log \sec(A-\alpha) - \log \sec\alpha\right]$$

$$= 2\gamma\rho \, AD \log \frac{\sec(A-\alpha)}{\sec\alpha}$$

$$= 2\gamma\rho \, AD \log \frac{\cos\alpha}{\cos(A-\alpha)}$$

$$= 2\gamma\rho \, AD \log \frac{\cos(90-B)}{\cos(90-C)}$$

$$= 2\gamma\rho \, AD \log \frac{\sin B}{\sin C}$$

$$= 2\gamma\rho \, AD \log \frac{b}{c} \qquad \ldots (1)$$

Also $m = \frac{1}{2} aAD\rho$

Hence from (1) the attraction parallel to BC

$$= 2\gamma \frac{2m}{aAD} AD \log \frac{b}{c}$$

$$= \frac{4\gamma m}{a} \log \frac{b}{c}$$

Also total attraction perpendicular to BC

$$= 2\gamma\rho \int_{-\alpha}^{A-\alpha} \int_{0}^{AQ} \cos\theta \, d\theta \, dr$$

$$= 2\gamma \int_{-\alpha}^{A-\alpha} AQ \cos\theta \, d\theta$$

$$= 2\gamma\rho \int_{-\alpha}^{A-\alpha} AD \sec\theta \cos\theta \, d\theta$$

$$= 2\gamma\rho \, AD \int_{-\alpha}^{A-\alpha} d\theta$$

$$= 2\gamma\rho \, AD \, [\theta]_{-\alpha}^{A-\alpha}$$

$$= 2\gamma\rho \, AD \, [A - \alpha + \alpha]$$

$$= 2\gamma\rho \; AD \; A$$

$$= \frac{4\gamma m A}{a} \qquad \left(\text{since } m = \frac{1}{2} a \, AD\rho\right)$$

10. A homogeneous right elliptic cylinder is of infinite, length in one direction and on the other end the section is perpendicular to the generators. Prove that the attraction of the cylinder on the particle at the centre of this end is

$$4\gamma\rho a \left(1 - e^2\right)^{\frac{1}{2}} \int_0^{\frac{\pi}{2}} \frac{d\theta}{\sqrt{1 - e^2 \sin^2\theta}}$$

where a is the semi-major axis of the section.

Solution: Let us divide the cylinder into a large number of filaments extending to infinity in one direction. One of them is standing on $r\delta\theta\delta r$.

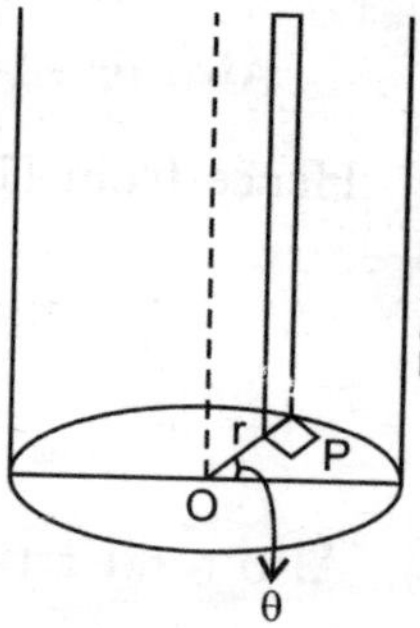

Attraction of this filament at O, along the axis of the cylinder

$$= \frac{\gamma K \rho}{p} (\cos\alpha - \cos\beta)$$

Here $K = r\delta\theta\delta r$, $p = OP = r$, $\alpha = 0$, $\beta = 90$

$$\text{Hence attraction} = \frac{\gamma r\delta\theta\delta r\rho}{r}(1 - 0)$$

$$= \gamma\rho\delta\theta\delta r$$

Hence the total attaction is

$$= \int_0^{2\pi}\int_0^{r} \gamma\rho \, \delta\theta\delta r$$

$$= \gamma\rho \int_0^{2\pi} r d\theta \qquad ...(1)$$

Let the base be an ellipse $\frac{x^2}{a^2} + \frac{y^2}{b^2} = 1$

So that

$$\frac{r^2 \cos^2\theta}{a^2} + \frac{r^2 \sin^2\theta}{b^2} = 1$$

$$\frac{r^2\left(b^2\cos^2\theta + a^2\sin^2\theta\right)}{a^2b^2} = 1$$

$$\frac{1}{r^2} = \frac{a^2\left(1-e^2\right)\cos^2\theta + a^2\sin^2\theta}{a^2b^2}$$

$$\frac{1}{r^2} = \frac{1-e^2\cos^2\theta}{a^2\left(1-e^2\right)}$$

Hence required attraction from (1)

$$= \gamma\rho \int_0^{2\pi} \frac{a\sqrt{1-e^2}\,d\theta}{\sqrt{1-e^2\cos^2\theta}}$$

$$= \gamma\rho a\sqrt{1-e^2} \int_0^{2\pi} \frac{d\theta}{\sqrt{1-e^2\cos^2\theta}}$$

$$= 4\gamma\rho a\sqrt{1-e^2} \int_0^{\frac{\pi}{2}} \frac{d\theta}{\sqrt{1-e^2\cos^2\theta}}$$

11. A solid circular cylinder of uniform density ρ stands on the xy plane and is infinite in the Z direction. Show that the Z component of its attraction at a point P of its base is $\gamma\rho l$, where l is the parameter of an ellipse having the base for the auxiliary circle and P for one focus.

Solution: Let us divide the cylinder into a large number of rods which are of infinite length in one direction.

Let one of such rod be standing on $r\delta\theta\delta r$, so its cross-section is $r\delta\theta\delta r$.

Now attraction of the elementary rod in Z direction i.e. parallel to the rod by using formula $\frac{\gamma k \rho}{p}(\cos\alpha - \cos\beta)$

Here $k = r\delta\theta\delta r$, $p = PQ = r$, $\alpha = 0°$, $\beta = 90°$

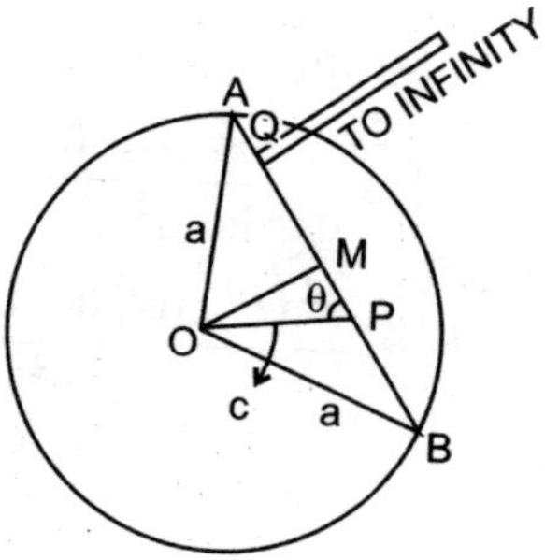

Hence the attraction of the element is

$$= \frac{\gamma r\delta\theta\delta r\,\rho}{r}(\cos 0 - \cos 90)$$

$$= \gamma\rho\delta\theta\delta r.$$

Hence total attraction

$$= \gamma\rho \int_0^{\pi} \int_{r=-PB}^{r=PB} \delta\theta\delta r$$

$$= \gamma\rho \int_0^{\pi} (PA + PB)\,\delta\theta \qquad \text{... (1)}$$

Now $OP = c$, $OM = c\sin\theta$, $MP = c\cos\theta$.

$$AM = \sqrt{OA^2 - OM^2} = \sqrt{a^2 - c^2\sin^2\theta}$$

$$PA = PM + AM = c\cos\theta + \sqrt{a^2 - c^2\sin^2\theta}$$

and $$PB = MB - MP = \sqrt{a^2 - c^2\sin^2\theta} - c\cos\theta$$

$$PA + PB = 2\sqrt{a^2 - c^2\sin^2\theta}$$

$$= 2\sqrt{a^2 - a^2e^2\sin^2\theta}$$

$$= 2a\sqrt{1 - e^2\sin^2\theta}$$

Hence from (1), we get

$$\text{Attraction} = \gamma\rho 4a \int_0^{\frac{\pi}{2}} \sqrt{1 - e^2\sin^2\theta\, d\theta} \qquad \text{... (1)}$$

Equation of the ellipse, whose auxilary circle is in the circle in the figure is $\frac{x^2}{a^2} + \frac{y^2}{b^2} = 1$

where $x = a\cos\phi,\ y = b\sin\phi$

$$\text{Now}\quad \left(\frac{ds}{d\phi}\right)^2 = \left(\frac{dx}{d\phi}\right)^2 + \left(\frac{dy}{d\phi}\right)^2$$

$$= a^2\sin^2\phi + b^2\cos^2\phi$$

$$= a^2\sin^2\phi + a^2\left(1-e^2\right)\cos^2\phi$$

$$= a^2\left(1-e^2\cos^2\phi\right)$$

The parameter l of the ellipse is

$$l = 2\int ds = 2\int_0^{\pi}\frac{ds}{d\phi}\,d\phi$$

$$= 2\int_0^{\pi} a\sqrt{1-e^2\cos^2\phi}\,d\phi$$

$$= 4a\int_0^{\frac{\pi}{2}}\sqrt{1-e^2\cos^2\phi}\,d\phi$$

$$= 4a\int_0^{\frac{\pi}{2}}\sqrt{1-e^2\sin^2\phi}\,d\phi$$

$$= 4a\int_0^{\frac{\pi}{2}}\sqrt{1-e^2\sin^2\theta}\,d\theta$$

Hence, from (2) attraction $= \gamma\rho l$.

12. The cross-section of a long uniform solid cylinder is a semicircle. Show that the direction of the resultant attraction at a point on an edge from the ends of the cylinder makes an angle $\tan^{-1}\left(\frac{2}{\pi}\right)$ with the plane face.

Solution: We divide the cylinder into a large number of rods of infinite lengths and let one of such rods be standing on $r\delta\theta\delta r$.

Attraction of this infinite rod at A along AP

$$= \frac{2\gamma r\delta\theta\delta r\,\rho}{r} = 2\gamma\delta\theta\delta r\ \rho$$

Its resolved parts along and perpendicular to diameter AB are $2\gamma\rho\delta\theta\delta r\cos\theta$ and $2\gamma\rho\delta\theta\delta r\sin\theta$.

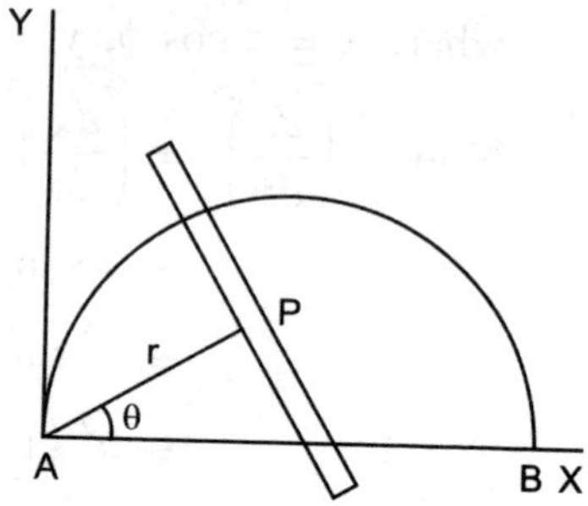

Hence if X, Y are the total attractions at A along and perpendicular to AB, then

$$X = \int_0^{\frac{\pi}{2}}\int_0^{AQ} 2\gamma\rho\cos\theta\, d\theta\, dr$$

$$= 2\gamma\rho\int_0^{\frac{\pi}{2}} AQ\cos\theta$$

$$= 2\gamma\rho\int_0^{\frac{\pi}{2}} AB\cos^2\theta\, d\theta$$

$$= 2\gamma\rho\, 2a\,\frac{1}{2}\frac{\pi}{2} = \pi\gamma\rho a$$

Also
$$Y = \int_0^{\frac{\pi}{2}}\int_0^{AQ} 2\gamma\rho\sin\theta\, d\theta\, dr$$

$$= 2\gamma\rho\int_0^{\frac{\pi}{2}} AQ\sin\theta\, d\theta$$

$$= 2\gamma\rho\int_0^{\frac{\pi}{2}} 2a\cos\theta\sin\theta\, d\theta$$

$$= -2\gamma\rho a\left[\frac{\cos 2\theta}{2}\right]_0^{\frac{\pi}{2}}$$

$$= -2\gamma\rho a[-1-1] = 2\gamma\rho a$$

Hence the required angle $= \tan^{-1}\dfrac{Y}{X}$

$$= \tan^{-1}\left(\frac{2\gamma\rho a}{\pi\gamma\rho a}\right)$$

$$= \tan^{-1}\left(\frac{2}{\pi}\right)$$

13. Two thin straight uniform rods *AB* and *CD* are pivoted together at their middle points. Show that the attraction between them reduce to a couple of moment $2\gamma mm'(AC - BC)$ cosec α. Where m and m' are their line densities and α is the angle between them.

Solution: Let the rods *AB*, *CD* be pivoted at their middle point *O*. We consider an element *PQ* of the rod *CD*, of the length δx, at a distance x from O, i.e. $OP = x$. Let $AB = 2a$, $CD = 2b$.

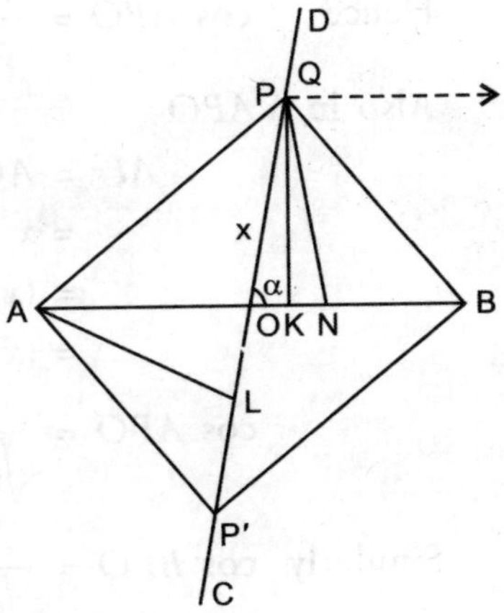

If *PN* be the perpendicular from *P* on *AB*, the attraction of *AB* on *PQ* is $\frac{2\gamma mm'\delta x}{PN}\sin\frac{APB}{2}$ acting along the bisector *PK* of the angle *APB*.

The attraction of *AB* on a similar element *P'Q'* on the other side of O, is $\frac{2\gamma mm'\delta x}{P'N'}\sin\frac{AP'B}{2}$ acting along the bisector *P'K'* of *P'N'* the angle *AP'B*.

It will be seen from the figure *APBP'A*, which is a parallelogram, that these two attractions are equal and parallel i.e. they form a couple. The moment of this couple is

$$= \frac{2\gamma mm'\delta x}{PN}\sin\frac{APB}{2}\, 2x \sin OPK$$

$$= \frac{2\gamma mm'\delta x\, x}{PN}(2\sin APK \sin OPK)$$

$$= \frac{2\gamma mm'\delta x}{PN}[\cos APO - \cos BPO] \quad \text{... (1)}$$

From A we draw AL perpendicular to CD.

$$\text{In } \Delta APL, \cos APO = \frac{PL}{AP} = \frac{PO + OL}{AP}$$

$$= \frac{x + OL}{AP}$$

$$\text{In } \Delta OAL \quad \cos \alpha = \frac{OL}{OA} = \frac{OL}{a}$$

$$\text{Hence} \quad \cos APO = \frac{x + a\cos\alpha}{AP}$$

Also in ΔAPO

$$AP^2 = AO^2 + OP^2 - 2AO\ OP\cos(\pi - \alpha)$$

$$= x^2 + a^2 + 2ax\cos\alpha$$

$$= (x + a\cos\alpha)^2 + a^2(1 - \cos^2\alpha)$$

$$= (x + a\cos\alpha)^2 + a^2\sin^2\alpha$$

$$\cos APO = \frac{x + a\cos\alpha}{\sqrt{(x + a\cos\alpha)^2 + a^2\sin^2\alpha}}$$

$$\text{Similarly} \quad \cos BPO = \frac{x - a\cos\alpha}{\sqrt{(x - a\cos\alpha)^2 + a^2\sin^2\alpha}}$$

Therefore the moment of the resultant couple from (1)

$$= \frac{2\gamma mm'}{\sin\alpha}\int_0^b\left(\frac{x + a\cos\alpha}{AP} - \frac{x - a\cos\alpha}{BP}\right)dx \quad \text{... (2)}$$

$$\text{Now} \int_0^b \frac{x + a\cos\alpha}{AP}\,dx$$

$$= \int_0^b \frac{x + a\cos\alpha}{\sqrt{(x + a\cos\alpha)^2 + a^2\sin^2\alpha}}\,dx$$

$$= \left[\sqrt{(x + a\cos\alpha)^2 + a^2\sin^2\alpha}\right]_0^b$$

$$= \sqrt{a^2 + b^2 + 2ab\cos\alpha} - a$$

$$= AC - a$$

Similarly $\displaystyle\int_0^b \frac{x - a\cos\alpha}{BP}\,dx = BC - a$

Hence the moment of the resultant couple from (2)

$$= \frac{2\gamma mm'}{\sin\alpha}\left[AC - a - (BC - a)\right]$$

$$= 2\gamma mm' \operatorname{cosec}\alpha\,(AC - BC)$$

14. An infinitely long thin rod of uniform line density m and a thin uniform rod of mass M and finite length $2a$ are placed so that the shortest distance between them is b and bisects the finite rod. Prove that the resultant attraction of either rod on the other is equivalent to a wrench of intensity $\dfrac{2\gamma m\phi}{a\sin\theta}$ and pitch $\dfrac{b\cot\theta(\tan\phi - \phi)}{\phi}$ where ϕ is the angle between the rods and $\phi = \tan^{-1}\left(\dfrac{a\sin\theta}{b}\right)$.

Solution: Let AB be the finite rod of length $2a$ whose middle point is O and its mass is M, on which we consider an element δx at P where $OP = x$ and the mass of thin element is $\dfrac{M}{2a}\delta x$.

CD is the infinite rod of line density m, passing through O' where $OO' = b$ is the shortest distance between the rods. From

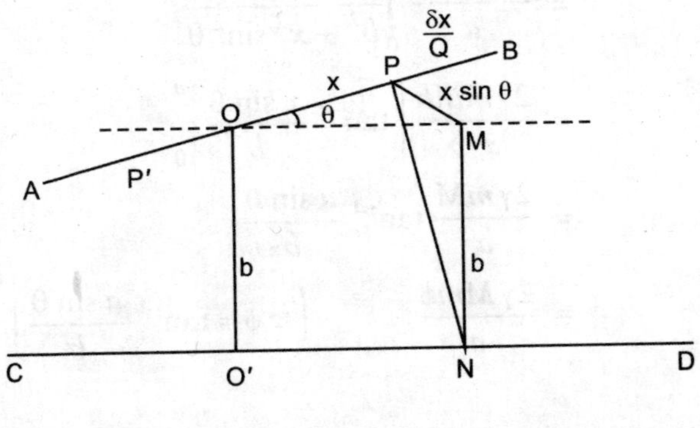

P we draw PN perpendicular to CD and from N we draw NM parallel to OO' to meet the line through O parallel to CD at M. Given $\angle POM = \theta$ and $MN = \theta$.

In $\Delta\, OPM$ $\cos\theta = \dfrac{OM}{OP} = \dfrac{OM}{x}$

$$OM = x\cos\theta$$

Also $\sin\theta = \dfrac{PM}{OP} = \dfrac{PM}{x}$

$$PM = x\sin\theta$$

From right angled triangle PMN, we have

$$PN^2 = PM^2 + MN^2 = x^2\sin^2\theta + b^2$$

Attraction of the infinite rod at P is $\dfrac{2\gamma m}{PN}\dfrac{M\delta x}{2a}$ along PN.

Its resoled part along MN

$$= \frac{2\gamma m}{PN}\frac{M\delta x}{2a}\cos PNM$$

$$= \frac{2\gamma m\, M\delta x}{2aPN}\frac{MN}{PN}$$

$$= \frac{\gamma mM\, b\delta x}{a\left(b^2 + x^2\sin^2\theta\right)}$$

The resultant attraction will be along OO' and is

$$= \frac{\gamma mMb}{a}\int_{-a}^{a}\frac{dx}{b^2 + x^2\sin^2\theta}$$

$$= \frac{2\gamma mMb}{a}\int_{0}^{a}\frac{dx}{b^2 + x^2\sin^2\theta}$$

$$= \frac{2\gamma mMb}{a\cdot b}\left[\tan^{-1}\frac{x\sin\theta}{b}\right]_0^a$$

$$= \frac{2\gamma mM}{a}\tan^{-1}\frac{a\sin\theta}{b}$$

$$= \frac{2\gamma\, Mm\phi}{a} \qquad \left(\because \phi = \tan^{-1}\frac{a\sin\theta}{b}\right)$$

Again the component of attraction along PM at P and P' are

$$\frac{2\gamma m}{PN}\frac{M\delta x}{2a}\sin PNM = \frac{2\gamma mM\cdot\delta x}{2aPN}\frac{PM}{PN} = \frac{2\gamma m\, M\delta x\, x\sin\theta}{2a\, PN\, PN}$$

$$= \frac{2\gamma m\, M\delta x\, x\sin\theta}{2a\, PN^2}$$

$$= \frac{\gamma m\, M\delta x\, x\sin\theta}{aPN^2}$$

$$= \frac{\gamma m\, M\delta x\sin\theta\, x}{a\left(b^2 + x^2\sin^2\theta\right)}$$

$$= \frac{\gamma m\, M\sin\theta}{a}\frac{x\delta x}{b^2 + x^2\sin^2\theta}$$

These two components form a couple whose arm is $2x\cos\theta$ and hence its moment is

$$= \frac{\gamma mM\sin\theta}{a}\frac{x\delta x}{b^2 + x^2\sin^2\theta}2x\cos\theta$$

$$= \frac{2\gamma mM\sin\theta\cos\theta}{a}\int_0^a \frac{x^2 dx}{b^2 + x^2\sin^2\theta}$$

$$= \frac{2\gamma mM\sin\theta\cos\theta}{a\sin^2\theta}\int_0^a \frac{x^2 dx}{x^2 + b^2\operatorname{cosec}^2\theta}$$

$$= \frac{2\gamma mM}{a}\cot\theta\int_0^a \frac{x^2 + b^2\operatorname{cosec}^2\theta - b^2\operatorname{cosec}^2\theta}{x^2 + b^2\operatorname{cosec}^2\theta}d\theta$$

$$= \frac{2\gamma mM}{a}\cot\theta\int_0^a \left[1 - \frac{b^2\operatorname{cosec}^2\theta}{x^2 + b^2\operatorname{cosec}^2\theta}\right]d\theta$$

$$= \frac{2\gamma mM}{a}\cot\theta\left[x - \frac{b^2\operatorname{cosec}^2\theta}{b\operatorname{cosec}\theta}\tan^{-1}\frac{x}{b\operatorname{cosec}\theta}\right]_0^a$$

$$= \frac{2\gamma mM}{a}\cot\theta\left[a - b\operatorname{cosec}\theta\tan^{-1}\frac{a\sin\theta}{b}\right]$$

$$= \frac{2\gamma mM}{a}\cot\theta\left[a - b\operatorname{cosec}\theta\,\phi\right]$$

$$= \frac{2\gamma mM \cot\theta\, b}{a}\left[\frac{a}{b} - \phi \operatorname{cosec}\theta\right]$$

$$= \frac{2\gamma Mm \cot\theta\, b}{a\sin\theta}\left[\frac{a}{b}\sin\theta - \phi\right]$$

$$= \frac{2\gamma Mm\, b \cot\theta}{a\sin\theta}(\tan\phi - \phi)$$

$$= \frac{2\gamma Mm \cot\theta}{\tan\phi}(\tan\phi - \phi) \qquad \left(\because \frac{b}{a\sin\theta} = \frac{1}{\tan\phi}\right)$$

$$= 2\gamma mM \cot\theta\left(\frac{\tan\phi - \phi}{\tan\phi}\right)$$

Hence the pitch of the wrench is

$$= \frac{2\gamma mM \cot\theta \dfrac{(\tan\phi - \phi)}{\tan\phi}}{\dfrac{2\gamma mM\,\phi}{a\sin\theta}}$$

$$= \frac{a\sin\theta\cot\theta(\tan\phi - \phi)}{\tan\phi}$$

$$= \frac{\cot\theta(\tan\phi - \phi)}{\tan\phi}\,\frac{a\sin\theta}{\phi}$$

$$= \frac{b\cot\theta(\tan\phi - \phi)}{\phi} \qquad \left(\because \frac{a\sin\theta}{\tan\phi} = b\right)$$

15. Two uniform rods AB and CD are of linear density λ and λ^1 and lengths $2a$ and $2c$ respectively. The middle point E of AB and F of CD are at a distance b apart and AB, CD, EF are mutually perpendicular. Show that the attraction between the rod is

$$4\gamma\lambda\lambda^1 \sin^{-1}\frac{ac}{\sqrt{(a^2+b^2)(b^2+c^2)}}$$

where γ is the gravitational constant.

Solution: Let us take a point P in CD such that $FP = x$, then element $PQ = \delta x$.

Mass of the element $PQ = \lambda^1 \delta x$

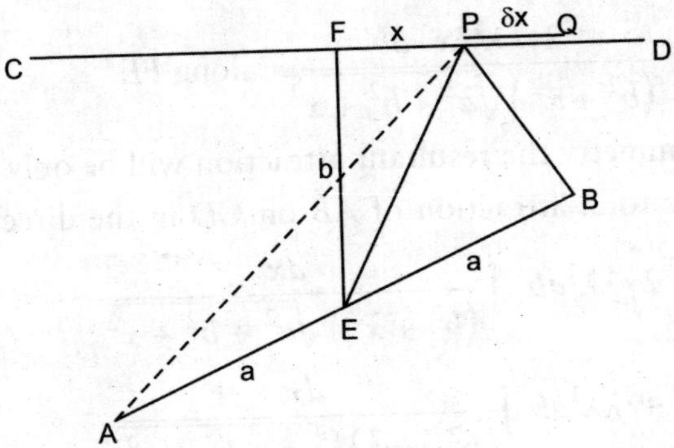

Join PE and it is clear that PE is at right angles to AB.

Attraction of AB on the element PQ

$$= \frac{2\gamma\lambda}{PE} \sin\frac{APB}{2}\, \lambda^1 \delta x \text{ along } PE$$

$$= \frac{2\gamma\lambda\lambda^1\delta x}{PE} \sin APE$$

$$= \frac{2\gamma\lambda\lambda^1\, \delta x}{\sqrt{b^2+x^2}} \frac{AE}{AP}$$

$$= \frac{2\gamma\lambda\lambda^1\, \delta x}{\sqrt{b^2+x^2}} \frac{a}{\sqrt{a^2+EP^2}}$$

$$= \frac{2\gamma\lambda\lambda^1\delta x}{\sqrt{b^2+x^2}} \frac{a}{\sqrt{a^2+b^2+x^2}} \text{ along } PE$$

Its resolved part along EF

$$= \frac{2\gamma\lambda\lambda^1\delta x}{\sqrt{b^2+x^2}} \frac{a}{\sqrt{a^2+b^2+x^2}} \cos PEF$$

$$= \frac{2\gamma\lambda\lambda^1\delta x}{\sqrt{b^2+x^2}} \frac{a}{\sqrt{a^2+b^2+x^2}} \frac{EF}{PE}$$

$$= \frac{2\gamma\lambda\lambda^1\delta x}{\sqrt{b^2+x^2}} \frac{a}{\sqrt{a^2+b^2+x^2}} \frac{b}{\sqrt{b^2+x^2}}$$

$$= \frac{2\gamma\lambda\lambda^1\delta x \cdot ab}{(b^2 + x^2)\sqrt{a^2 + b^2 + x^2}} \text{ along } FE$$

By symmetry the resultant attraction will be only along FE. Hence total attraction of AB on CD in the direction FE is

$$= 2\gamma\lambda\lambda^1 ab \int_{-c}^{c} \frac{dx}{(b^2 + x^2)\sqrt{a^2 + b^2 + x^2}}$$

$$= 4\gamma\lambda\lambda^1 ab \int_{0}^{c} \frac{dx}{(b^2 + x^2)\sqrt{a^2 + b^2 + x^2}}$$

Putting $x = b \tan \theta$

$$\therefore dx = b \sec^2 \theta \, d\theta$$

When $x = c$, $\quad \theta = \tan^{-1} \frac{c}{b}$

When $x = 0$, $\quad \theta = 0$

Hence total attraction

$$= 4\gamma\lambda\lambda^1 ab \int_{0}^{\tan^{-1}\frac{c}{b}} \frac{b \sec^2 \theta \, d\theta}{b^2 \sec^2 \theta \sqrt{a^2 + b^2 \sec^2 \theta}}$$

$$= 4\gamma\lambda\lambda^1 a \int_{0}^{\tan^{-1}\frac{c}{b}} \frac{d\theta}{\sqrt{a^2 + b^2 \sec^2 \theta}}$$

$$= 4\gamma\lambda\lambda^1 a \int_{0}^{\tan^{-1}\frac{c}{b}} \frac{d\theta \cos \theta}{\sqrt{a^2 \cos^2 \theta + b^2}}$$

$$= 4\gamma\lambda\lambda^1 a \int_{0}^{\tan^{-1}\frac{c}{b}} \frac{d\theta \cos \theta}{\sqrt{a^2 + b^2 - a^2 \sin^2 \theta}}$$

$$= \frac{4\gamma\lambda\lambda^1 a}{a} \int_{0}^{\tan^{-1}\frac{c}{b}} \frac{a \cos \theta \, d\theta}{\sqrt{a^2 + b^2 - a^2 \sin^2 \theta}}$$

$$= 4\gamma\lambda\lambda^1 \left[\sin^{-1} \frac{a \sin\theta}{\sqrt{a^2 + b^2}}\right]_0^{\tan^{-1}\frac{c}{b}}$$

$$= 4\gamma\lambda\lambda^1 \sin^{-1}\left[\frac{a}{\sqrt{a^2 + b^2}} \sin\left(\tan^{-1}\frac{c}{b}\right)\right]$$

$$= 4\gamma\lambda\lambda^1 \sin^{-1}\left[\frac{a}{\sqrt{a^2 + b^2}} \frac{c}{\sqrt{b^2 + c^2}}\right] \quad \text{Proved.}$$

16. (i) A uniform wire of infinite length attracts according to inverse nth power if the distance, show that the resulting attraction is

$$\frac{\gamma m \sqrt{m}}{c^{n-1}} \frac{\Gamma\frac{n}{2}}{\Gamma\frac{n+1}{2}}$$

where m is the mass per unit length of the wire and c is its least distance from the attracted point.

(ii) If the rod AB is of finite length, show that components of attraction at a point P parallel and perpendicular to AB are respectively

$$\frac{\gamma m}{n-1}\left[\frac{1}{(PA)^{n-1}} - \frac{1}{(PB)^{n-1}}\right] \text{ and } \frac{\gamma m}{c^{n-1}} \int_\alpha^\beta \cos^{n-1}\theta d\theta$$

Solution: (i) Let P be the point at which we are to determine the attraction of the rod AB. From P we draw PN perpendicular to the rod. Let $PN = c$. We consider an element $OS = \delta x$ at Q where $NQ = x$ and whose mass is $m\delta x$.

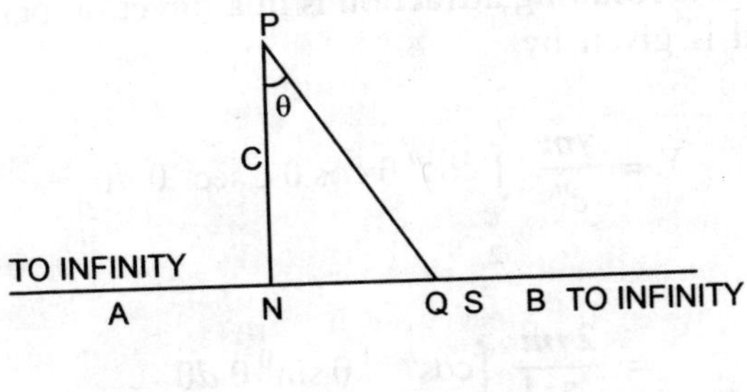

Attraction of this element at P according to given law of attraction is $\dfrac{\gamma m \delta x}{(PQ)^n}$ along PQ.

In ΔPQN $\cos\theta = \dfrac{PN}{PQ} = \dfrac{c}{PQ}$

$$PQ = \frac{c}{\cos\theta}$$

Hence components of the attraction parallel and perpendicular to the rod are $\dfrac{\gamma m \delta x}{c^n}\cos^n\theta\sin\theta$ and $\dfrac{\gamma m \delta x}{c^n}\cos^n\theta\cos\theta$.

Hence the total attraction parallel to the rod is

$$X = \frac{\gamma m}{c^n}\int_{-\infty}^{\infty}\cos^n\theta\sin\theta\,d\theta$$

Putting $x = c\tan\theta$

$$\therefore\ dx = c\sec^2\theta\,d\theta$$

$$X = \frac{\gamma m}{c^n}\int_{-\frac{\pi}{2}}^{\frac{\pi}{2}}\cos^n\theta\sin\theta\,c\sec^2\theta\,d\theta$$

$$= \frac{\gamma m}{c^{n-1}}\int_{-\frac{\pi}{2}}^{\frac{\pi}{2}}\cos^{n-2}\theta\sin\theta\,d\theta$$

$= 0$ [since $\cos^{n-2}\theta\sin\theta$ is an odd function]

Hence the resulting attraction is in a direction perpendicular to the rod is given by

$$Y = \frac{\gamma m}{c^n}\int_{-\frac{\pi}{2}}^{\frac{\pi}{2}}\cos^n\theta\cos\theta\,c\sec^2\theta\,d\theta$$

$$= \frac{2\gamma m}{c^{n-1}}\int_0^{\frac{\pi}{2}}\cos^{n-1}\theta\sin^0\theta\,d\theta$$

$$= \frac{2\gamma m}{c^{n-1}} \frac{\overline{|\frac{n}{2}}\overline{|\frac{1}{2}}}{2\overline{|\frac{n-1+0+2}{2}}}$$

$$= \frac{\gamma m}{c^{n-1}} \frac{\sqrt{\pi}\,\overline{|\frac{n}{2}}}{\overline{|\frac{n+1}{2}}}$$

(ii) In this case the rod is of finite length.

If AP and BP makes angle α and β with PN, then

$$X = \frac{\gamma m}{c^{n-1}} \int_{\alpha}^{\beta} \cos^{n-2}\theta \sin\theta \, d\theta$$

$$= \frac{\gamma m}{c^{n-1}} \left[\frac{\cos^{n-1}\theta}{n-1} \right]_{\alpha}^{\beta}$$

$$= \frac{\gamma m}{n-1} \left[\frac{1}{(c \sec\alpha)^{n-1}} - \frac{1}{(c \sec\beta)^{n-1}} \right]$$

$$= \frac{\gamma m}{n-1} \left[\frac{1}{(PA)^{n-1}} - \frac{1}{(PB)^{n-1}} \right]$$

In $\Delta\, APN$ $\cos\alpha = \frac{PN}{AP} = \frac{c}{AP}$

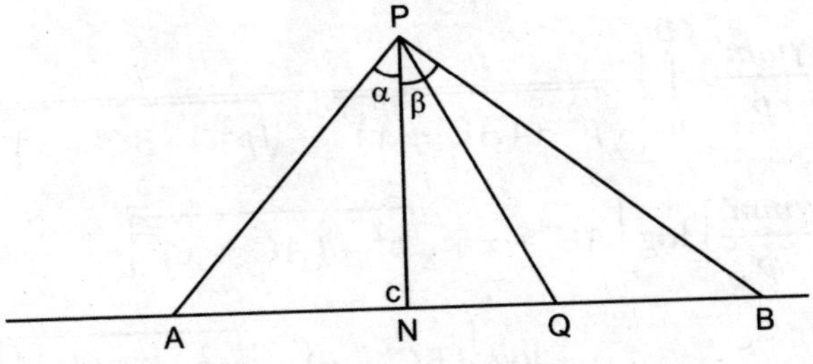

$AP = c \sec\alpha$, $BP = c \sec\beta$.

$$\text{Also } Y = \frac{\gamma m}{c^{n-1}} \int_{\alpha}^{\beta} \cos^{n-1}\theta \, d\theta$$

17. Two uniform parallel straight rods AB, CD attract each other. Show that the components of their mutual attractions perpendicular and parallel to them are

$$\frac{\gamma mm'}{p}(BC - BD - AC + AD)$$

and $$\gamma mm' \log \frac{(BD' + BD)(AD' + AD)}{(AC' + AC)(BC' + BC)}$$

where C', D' are projections of C, D on AB, p the distance between the rods and m, m' masses per unit length.

Solution: We consider an element $PQ = \delta x$ of the rod CD at P where $CP = x$ and mass of the element $= m'\delta x$.

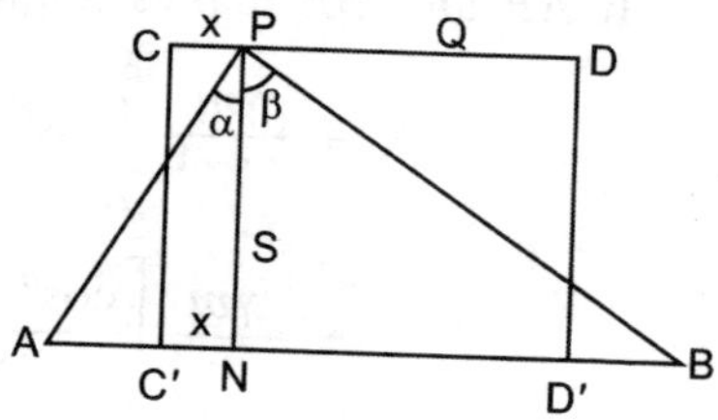

Also $PN = p$ the distance between the two rods.

Now component of attraction of rod AB at P parallel to AB

$$= \frac{\gamma m}{p}(\cos\alpha - \cos\beta)\, m'\delta x$$

Hence the total attraction of AB on whole of CD parallel to AB is

$$= \frac{\gamma m}{p}\int_0^{CD}(\cos\alpha - \cos\beta)\, m' dx$$

$$= \frac{\gamma mm'}{p}\int_0^{CD}\left\{\frac{p}{\sqrt{p^2 + (AC' + x)^2}} - \frac{p}{\sqrt{p^2 + (BC' - x)^2}}\right\} dx$$

$$= \frac{\gamma mm'}{p}\left[\log\left\{AC' + x + \sqrt{p^2 + (AC' + x)^2}\right\}\right.$$

$$\left. + \log\left\{(BC' - x) + \sqrt{p^2 + (BC' - x)^2}\right\}\right]_0^{CD}$$

$$= \gamma mm' \left[\log \frac{(AC' + CD) + \sqrt{p^2 + (AC' + CD)^2}}{AC' + \sqrt{p^2 + AC'^2}} \right.$$

$$\left. + \log \frac{(BC' - CD) + \sqrt{p^2 + (BC' - CD)^2}}{BC' + \sqrt{p^2 + BC'^2}} \right] \quad \dots (1)$$

Now

$$AC' + CD = AC' + C'D' = AD'$$

$$p^2 + AD'^2 = PN^2 + AD'^2 = DD'^2 + AD'^2 = AD^2$$

$$BC' - CD = BC' - C'D' = BD'$$

$$p^2 + BD'^2 = PN^2 + BD'^2 = DD'^2 + BD'^2 = BD^2$$

Hence the required attraction from (1) becomes

$$= \gamma mm' \log \frac{AD' + AD}{AC' + AC} + \log \frac{BD' + BD}{BC' + BC}$$

$$= \gamma mm' \log \frac{(AD' + AD)(BD' + BD)}{(AC' + AC)(BC' + BC)}$$

Again component of attraction of AB at P in a direction perpendicular to AB is

$$= \frac{\gamma m}{p} (\sin \beta + \sin \alpha)\, m' \delta x$$

Hence the total attraction of AB on whole of CD is

$$= \frac{\gamma mm'}{p} \int_0^{CD} \left\{ \frac{BC' - x}{\sqrt{p^2 + (BC' - x)^2}} + \frac{AC' + x}{\sqrt{p^2 + (AC' + x)^2}} \right\} dx$$

$$= \frac{\gamma mm'}{p} \left[-\sqrt{p^2 + (BC' - x)^2} + \sqrt{p^2 + (AC' + x)^2} \right]_0^{CD}$$

$$= \frac{\gamma mm'}{p} \left[-\sqrt{p^2 + (BC' - CD)^2} + \sqrt{p^2 + BC'^2} \right.$$

$$\left. + \sqrt{p^2 + (AC' + CD)^2} - \sqrt{p^2 + AC'^2} \right]$$

$$= \frac{\gamma mm'}{p} [- BD + AD + BC - AC]$$

18. AB, $A'B'$ are two parallel rods of line densities m and m' are placed with the line joining their middle points perpendicular to the rods and of length c. Show that the attraction between the rods is $\dfrac{2\gamma mm'}{c}(AB' - AA')$.

Solution: The rods are placed symmetrically in parallel lines and their mid-points are O and O'. Let $AB = 2a$, $A'B' = 2b$, OO' is perpendicular to AB and CD. Given $OO' = C$.

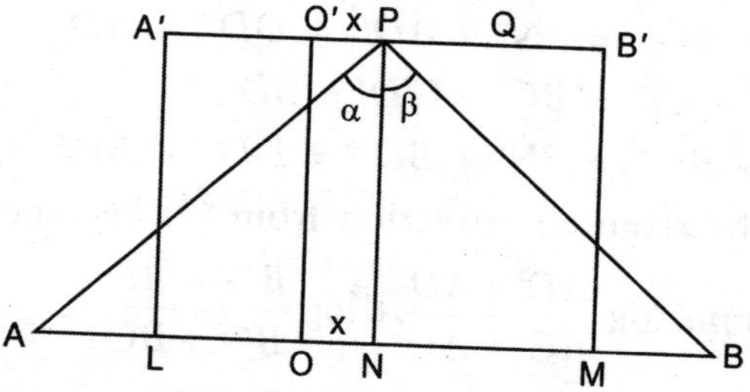

By symmetry the resultant attraction will be along OO' i.e. in a direction perpendicular to the rods. We consider an element $PQ = \delta x$ at P where $C'P = x$ and its mass is $m'\delta x$.

Attraction of AB at P is $\dfrac{\gamma m}{c}(\sin\beta + \sin\alpha)\, m'\delta x$.

Hence the attraction of AB on whole of $A'B'$

$$= \frac{\gamma mm'}{c}\int_{-b}^{b}\left[\frac{a-x}{\sqrt{c^2+(a-x)^2}} + \frac{a+x}{\sqrt{c^2+(a+x)^2}}\right]dx$$

$$= \frac{\gamma mm'}{c}\left[-\sqrt{c^2+(a-x)^2} + \sqrt{c^2+(a+x)^2}\right]_{-b}^{b}$$

$$= \frac{\gamma mm'}{c}\left[-\sqrt{c^2+(a-b)^2} + \sqrt{c^2+(a+b)^2}\right.$$

$$\left. + \sqrt{c^2+(a+b)^2} - \sqrt{c^2+(a-b)^2}\right]$$

$$= \frac{2\gamma mm'}{c}\left[\sqrt{c^2+(a+b)^2} - \sqrt{c^2+(a-b)^2}\right]$$

Also - $AM = AO + OM = a + b$

$B'M = c$

$$AB'^2 = AM^2 + MB'^2 = (a + b)^2 + c^2$$
$$AL = AO - OL = a - A'O' = a - b$$
$$AA'^2 = AL^2 + A'L^2 = (a - b)^2 + c^2$$

Hence attraction $= \dfrac{2\gamma mm'}{c}[AB' - AA']$.

19. P is the particle on the diagonal AC of a square $ABCD$ and within the square, show that the attraction of the perimeter of the square upon P is equal to $YM \dfrac{OP}{PA\,PB\,PC}$. Where M is the mass of the perimeter and O is the centre of the square.

Solution: Attraction of the rod BC at P will be $\dfrac{2\gamma k\rho}{p_2}\sin\dfrac{BPC}{2}$ along the bisector of $\angle BPC$.

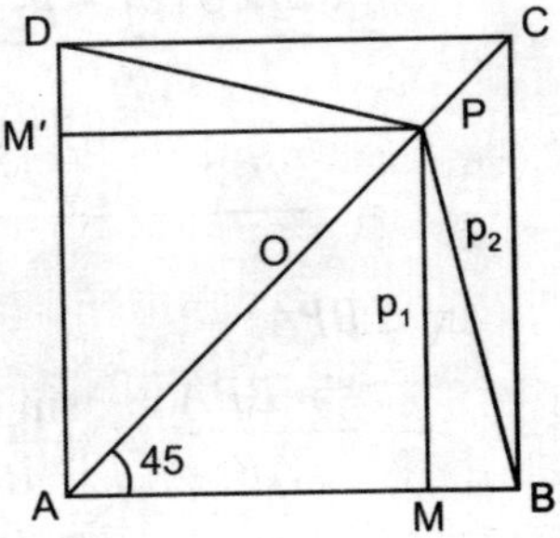

Its component along PC will be

$$\frac{2\gamma k\rho}{p_2}\sin\frac{BPC}{2}$$
$$= \frac{\gamma k\rho}{p_2}\sin BPC$$
$$= \frac{\gamma k\rho}{p_2}\sin(\pi - BPA)$$
$$= \frac{\gamma k\rho}{p_2}\sin BPA \qquad \text{... (1)}$$

Similarly attractions of CD at $P = \dfrac{2\gamma k\rho}{p_2}$ along bisector of $\angle CPD$ and its compoent along PC is

$$\frac{2\gamma k\rho}{p_2}\sin\frac{CPD}{2}\cos\frac{CPD}{2} = \frac{\gamma k\rho}{p_2}\sin CPD$$

But $\angle CPD = \angle BPC = \pi - \angle BPA$.

Hence attraction of CD along PC is

$$= \frac{\gamma k\rho}{p_2}\sin(\pi - BPA) = \frac{\gamma k\rho}{p_2}\sin BPA$$

Hence the resultant of attractions of BC and CD at P along PC is

$$\frac{2\gamma k\rho}{p_2}\sin BPA \qquad \text{... (3)}$$

Similarly the resultant of the attraction of AB and AD at P along PA will be

$$\frac{2\gamma k\rho}{p_1}\sin BPA \text{ or } \frac{-2\gamma k\rho}{p_1}\sin BPA \text{ along PC} \qquad \text{... (4)}$$

Hence the resultant attraction of all the four rods of P along PC or AC is

$$= 2\gamma k\rho\left(\frac{1}{p_2}-\frac{1}{p_1}\right)\sin BPA$$

$$= \frac{2\gamma k\rho\,(p_1-p_2)}{p_1 p_2}\sin BPA$$

$$= \frac{2\gamma k\rho\sqrt{2}\left[(OA+OP)-(OC-OP)\right]}{PA\,PC}\frac{AB}{PB}\sin 45^\circ$$

In $\Delta\, BPA$

$$\frac{\sin BPA}{AB} = \frac{\sin 45^\circ}{BP}$$

$$= \frac{2\sqrt{2}\gamma k\rho\, 2\, OP}{PAPC}\frac{AB}{PB}\cdot\frac{1}{\sqrt{2}}$$

$$= \frac{4\gamma k\rho\, OP\, AB}{PA\, PC\, PB}$$

Since M is the mass of the perimeter

$$\therefore\ M = 4\ ABk\rho$$

Hence resultant attraction $= \dfrac{\gamma MOP}{PA\,PB\,PC}$

20. An infinitely long homogeneous prism of density ρ, has a rectangular cross-section of length a and breadth b. Show that at any point on one of the edges, the components of attraction along the sides a and b of the section through the point are

$$\gamma\rho\left[2a\tan^{-1}\frac{b}{a}+b\log\frac{a^2+b^2}{b^2}\right]$$

and $$\gamma\rho\left[2b\tan^{-1}\frac{a}{b}+a\log\frac{a^2+b^2}{a^2}\right]$$

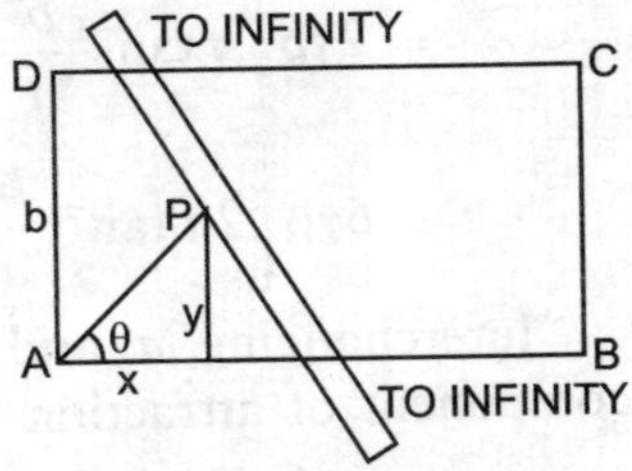

Solution: *ABCD* is the rectangular normal section of the prism with $AB = a$ and $AD = b$. Let us take *A* as origin and *AB*, *AD* as *x* axis and *y* axis.

Now we consider the prism as made up of a large number of rods of infinite length and we take an elementary rod of cross-section $\delta x\delta y$ and infinite in length in both directions.

Hence attraction at *A* due to the rod

$$= \frac{2\gamma\delta x\delta y\,\rho}{AP} \text{ in the direction } AP$$

Its component along *x* axis

$$= \frac{2\gamma\delta x\delta y\,\rho}{AP}\cos\theta$$

$$= \frac{2\gamma\delta x\delta y\,\rho}{AP}\,\frac{x}{AP}$$

Hence the total attraction at *A*, along *AB* due to whole of the prism

$$= 2\gamma\rho\int_0^a\int_0^b\frac{x\,dx\,dy}{x^2+y^2}$$

$$= 2\gamma\rho\int_0^a\frac{x}{x}\left\{\tan^{-1}\frac{y}{x}\right\}_0^b dx$$

$$= 2\gamma\rho\left[\left\{x\tan^{-1}\frac{y}{x}\right\}_0^a - \int_0^a\frac{x}{1+\dfrac{b^2}{x^2}}\left(\frac{-b}{x^2}\right)dx\right]$$

$$= 2\gamma\rho\left[a\tan^{-1}\frac{b}{a}+\frac{b}{2}\int_0^a\frac{2xdx}{x^2+b^2}\right]$$

$$= 2\gamma\rho\left[a\tan^{-1}\frac{b}{a}+\frac{b}{2}\left\{\log\left(x^2+b^2\right)\right\}_0^a\right]$$

$$= 2\gamma\rho\left[a\tan^{-1}\frac{b}{a}+\frac{b}{2}\left\{\log\left(a^2+b^2\right)-\log b^2\right\}\right]$$

$$= 6\gamma\rho\left[2a\tan^{-1}\frac{b}{a}+b\log\frac{a^2+b^2}{b^2}\right]$$

Interchanging a and b in this result, we may get the component of attraction along AD as

$$= \gamma\rho\left[2b\tan^{-1}\frac{a}{b}+a\log\frac{a^2+b^2}{a^2}\right]$$

21. A uniform solid cylinder of mass M is formed by the planes $z = 0$, $z = c$ and the cylindrical surface $x^2 + y^2 = ax$. Prove that z component of the attraction at the origin is

$$\frac{\gamma M}{\pi a^2 c}(4a+\pi c-l)$$

where $2l$ is the perimeter of an ellipse of semi axes $\sqrt{c^2+4a^2}$ and c.

Solution: The polar equation of the circle $x^2 + y^2 = 2ax$ is

$$r^2 = 2ar\cos\theta \text{ or}$$

$$r = 2a\cos\theta$$

which passes through pole O and is of radius a.

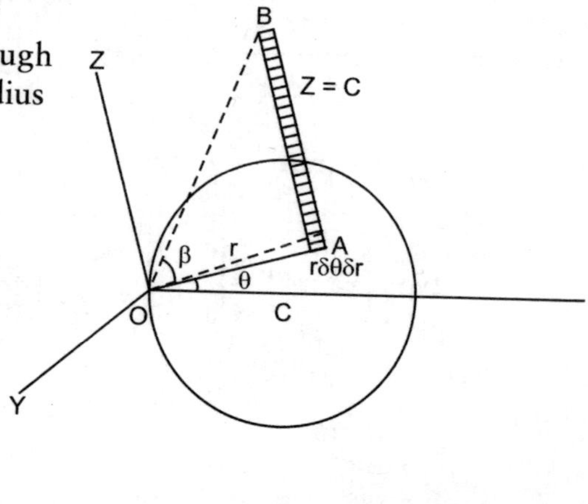

This circle is one end of the cylinder.

Let us consider the circle as made up of a large number of rods of length c parallel to the axis of the cylinder.

Let $r\delta\theta\delta r$ be the cross-section of one such elementary rod AB. Attraction at the origin O due to the elementary filament AB in a direction parallel to the filament i.e. z-component is

$$\frac{\gamma r\delta\theta\delta r\,\rho}{r}(\cos\alpha - \cos\beta)$$

Here $\alpha = 0$, $\beta = \angle AOB$, $\cos\beta = \dfrac{AO}{OB} = \dfrac{r}{\sqrt{r^2+c^2}}$

Hence z component of attraction due to the filament is

$$= \gamma\rho\,\delta\theta\delta r\left[1 - \frac{r}{\sqrt{r^2+c^2}}\right]$$

Hence the z component of the attraction due to whole cylinder is

$$= \gamma\rho\int_{-\frac{\pi}{2}}^{\frac{\pi}{2}}\int_0^{2a\cos\theta}\left[r - \frac{r}{\sqrt{r^2+c^2}}\right]d\theta dr$$

$$= \gamma\rho\int_{-\frac{\pi}{2}}^{\frac{\pi}{2}}\left[r - \sqrt{r^2+c^2}\right]_0^{2a\cos\theta}d\theta$$

$$= \gamma\rho\int_{-\frac{\pi}{2}}^{\frac{\pi}{2}}\left[2a\cos\theta - \sqrt{4a^2\cos^2\theta + c^2} + c\right]d\theta$$

$$= 2\gamma\rho\int_0^{\frac{\pi}{2}}\left[2a\cos\theta - \sqrt{4a^2\cos^2\theta + c^2} + c\right]d\theta$$

$$= 2\gamma\rho\left[\{2a\sin\theta + c\theta\}_0^{\frac{\pi}{2}} - \int_0^{\frac{\pi}{2}}\sqrt{4a^2\cos^2\theta + c^2}\,d\theta\right]$$

$$= 2\gamma\rho\left[2a + c\frac{\pi}{2} - \int_0^{\frac{\pi}{2}} \sqrt{c^2 + 4a^2 - 4a^2 \sin^2\theta\, d\theta}\right]$$

$$= \gamma\rho\left[4a + \pi c - 2\sqrt{c^2 + 4a^2}\int_0^{\frac{\pi}{2}} \sqrt{1 - \frac{4a^2}{\sqrt{c^2 + 4a^2}} \sin^2\theta\, d\theta}\right] \quad \ldots (1)$$

But we have

$$4a\int_0^{\frac{\pi}{2}} \sqrt{1 - e^2 \sin^2\theta\, d\theta} = 2l$$

Where $$e^2 = 1 - \frac{b^2}{a^2} = 1 - \frac{c^2}{c^2 + 4a^2}$$

$$= \frac{4a^2}{c^2 + 4a^2}$$

Hence

$$2l = 4\sqrt{c^2 + 4a^2}\int_0^{\frac{\pi}{2}} \sqrt{1 - \frac{4a^2}{c^2 + 4a^2} \sin^2\theta\, d\theta}$$

Hence from (1) we get the z component of attraction as

$$= \gamma\rho\left[4a + \pi c - l\right]$$

But $$M = \pi a^2 c\rho$$

Therefore attraction is $= \dfrac{M\gamma}{\pi a^2 c}(4a + \pi c - l)$

22. A uniform cube attracts according to the law of nature. Show that the attraction at a point situated at a corner consists of three components along the edges equal to

$$\gamma\rho a\left[\log\left(3 + 2\sqrt{2}\right)\left(2 - \sqrt{3}\right) + \frac{\pi}{6}\right]$$

where ρ is the density and a the length of an edge.

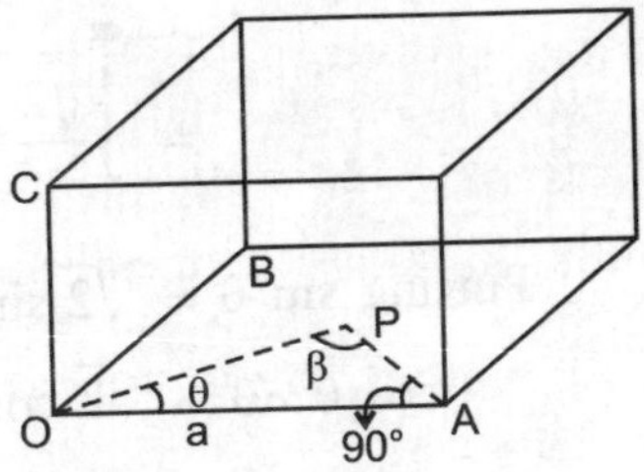

Solution: We divide the cube into a large number of filaments parallel to the edge OC of the cube. Let $r\delta\theta\delta r$ be the cross-section of one such elementary filament.

Attraction of this filament at O in a direction parallel to the rod

$$= \frac{\gamma\rho r\delta\theta\delta r}{r}(\cos\alpha - \cos\beta)$$

Here $\alpha = 0$, $\cos\beta = \dfrac{AP}{OP} = \dfrac{r}{\sqrt{r^2+a^2}}$

Hence the required attraction

$$= \gamma\,\rho\delta\theta\delta r\left(1 - \frac{r}{\sqrt{r^2+a^2}}\right)$$

Hence the total attractions at O parallel to edge OC is

$$= 2\gamma\rho\int_{\theta=0}^{\frac{\pi}{4}}\int_{r=0}^{a\sec\theta}\left[1 - \frac{r}{\sqrt{r^2+a^2}}\right]d\theta dr$$

$$= 2\gamma\rho\int_0^{\frac{\pi}{4}}\left[r - \sqrt{r^2+a^2}\right]_0^{a\sec\theta} d\theta$$

$$= 2\gamma\rho\int_0^{\frac{\pi}{4}}\left[a\sec\theta - a\sqrt{\sec^2\theta+1} + a\right]d\theta$$

$$= 2\gamma\rho a\left[\{\theta + \log(\sec\theta + \tan\theta)\}_0^{\frac{\pi}{4}} - I\right] \qquad \dots (1)$$

Where $\qquad I = \displaystyle\int_0^{\frac{\pi}{4}}\sqrt{\sec^2\theta+1}\,d\theta$

$$= \int_0^{\frac{\pi}{4}}\frac{\sqrt{1+\cos^2\theta}}{\cos\theta}\,d\theta$$

$$= \int_0^{\frac{\pi}{4}} \frac{\sqrt{2-\sin^2\theta}}{1-\sin^2\theta} \cos\theta \, d\theta$$

Putting $\sin\theta = \sqrt{2}\sin y$

$$\cos\theta \, d\theta = \sqrt{2}\cos y \, dy$$

When $\theta = \frac{\pi}{4}$, $\sin y = \frac{1}{2}, y = \frac{\pi}{6}$

and $\theta = 0$, give $y = 0$

Hence $$I = \int_0^{\frac{\pi}{6}} \frac{\sqrt{2-2\sin^2 y}}{1-2\sin^2 y} \sqrt{2}\cos y \, dy$$

$$= 2\int_0^{\frac{\pi}{6}} \frac{\cos^2 y}{1-2\sin^2 y} dy$$

$$= 2\int_0^{\frac{\pi}{6}} \frac{\cos^2 y \, dy}{\cos^2 y\left(\sec^2 y - 2\tan^2 y\right)}$$

$$= 2\int_0^{\frac{\pi}{6}} \frac{dy}{1-\tan^2 y}$$

$$= 2\int_0^{\frac{\pi}{6}} \frac{\sec^2 y \, dy}{\left(1+\tan^2 y\right)\left(1-\tan^2 y\right)}$$

Let $z = \tan y$

$$dz = \sec^2 y \, dy$$

When $y = \frac{\pi}{6}, z = \frac{1}{\sqrt{3}}$

and $y = 0$, $z = 0$

So $$I = 2\int_0^{\frac{1}{\sqrt{3}}} \frac{dz}{\left(1+z^2\right)\left(1-z^2\right)}$$

$$= \int_0^{\frac{1}{\sqrt{3}}} \left(\frac{1}{1+z^2} + \frac{1}{1-z^2} \right) dz$$

$$= \left[\tan^{1} z + \frac{1}{2} \log \frac{1+z}{1-z} \right]_0^{\frac{1}{\sqrt{3}}}$$

$$= \frac{\pi}{6} + \frac{1}{2} \log \frac{\sqrt{3}+1}{\sqrt{3}-1}$$

$$= \frac{\pi}{6} + \frac{1}{2} \log \frac{(\sqrt{3}+1)^2}{3-1}$$

$$= \frac{\pi}{6} + \frac{1}{2} \log (2+\sqrt{3})$$

$$= \frac{\pi}{6} + \frac{1}{2} \log \frac{1}{2-\sqrt{3}}$$

$$= \frac{\pi}{6} - \frac{1}{2} \log (2-\sqrt{3})$$

Hence required attraction from (1)

$$= 2\gamma\rho a \left[\frac{\pi}{4} + \log(\sqrt{2}+1) - \frac{\pi}{6} + \frac{1}{2} \log (2-\sqrt{3}) \right]$$

$$= 2\gamma\rho a \left[\frac{\pi}{12} + \log(\sqrt{2}+1) + \frac{1}{2} \log (2-\sqrt{3}) \right]$$

$$= \gamma\rho a \left[\frac{\pi}{6} + \log(\sqrt{2}+1)^2 + \log (2-\sqrt{3}) \right]$$

$$= \gamma\rho a \left[\frac{\pi}{6} + \log(3+2\sqrt{2})(2-\sqrt{3}) \right] \quad \text{Proved.}$$

23. A particle is placed at any point P on the bisector of the angle C of a triangle ABC. Show that the direction of the resultant attraction of the three sides at P, bisects the angle AB and is equal in magnitude to

$$2\gamma\rho \left(\frac{1}{p_2} - \frac{1}{p_1} \right) \sin \frac{APB}{2}$$

where p_1 and p_2 are the perpendiculars from P on AC and AB respectively.

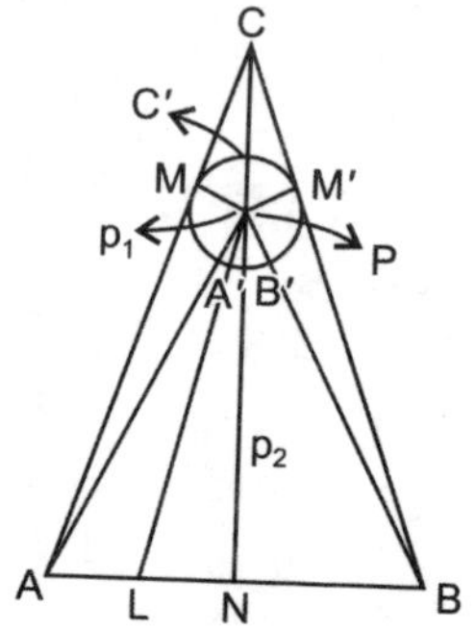

Solution: Here attraction of rod BC at P = attraction of arc $B'C'$ of the circle whose centre is at P and radius PM' the perpendicular from P on BC.

Similarly attraction of rod AC at P = attraction of arc $A'C'$ of the circle.

Hence attraction due to both the rods AC and BC at P is equal to the attraction of arcs $A'C'$ and $B'C'$ taken together. But attraction of the whole circle at P is equal to zero. Hence the attractions due to $A'C'$ and $B'C'$ taken together is equal and opposite to that of arc $A'B'$ at P, so that it bisects angle $A'PB$ and is equal to

$$\frac{-2\gamma m}{p_1}\sin\frac{A'PB'}{2}=\frac{-2\gamma m}{p_1}\sin\frac{APB}{2}$$

The attraction of the rod AB at P also bisects $\angle APB$ and is equal to $\dfrac{2\gamma m}{p_2}\sin\dfrac{APB}{2}$.

Hence the resultant of these attractions is

$$= 2\gamma m\left(\frac{1}{p_2}-\frac{1}{p_1}\right)\sin\frac{APB}{2}$$

24. A triangular framework of three rods, of uniform mass per unit of length, attracts according to the law of nature, show that the particle will be in equilibrium under their attraction if placed at the incentre of the triangle.

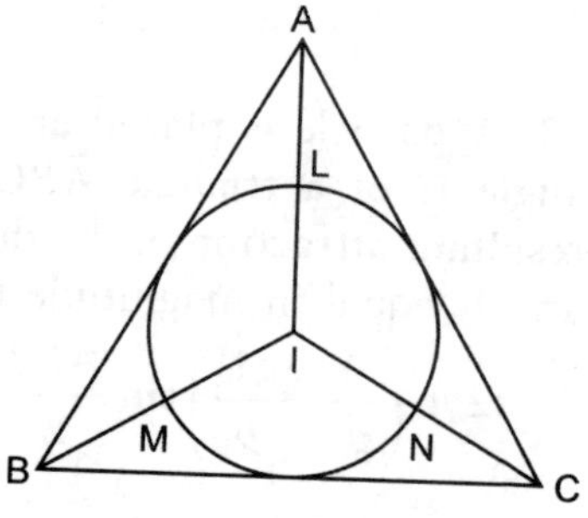

Solution: Let ABC be a triangle whose incentre is I. Join IA, IB and IC respectively.

Let L, M and N be the points at which IA, IB and IC cut the inscribed circle. Then the attraction of the rod BC at the external point I is the same as that of the arc MN of a circle, of like material with centre I. Similar results are true for the other rods CA and AB.

Hence the total attraction at I due to AB, BC and CA = the total attraction at I due to the arcs LM, MN and NL. Hence the attraction at I due to the circle LMN = O.

25. A uniform rod is bent into the form of a curve such that the direction of attraction of any arc AB at the origin O bisects the angle AOB. Show that the curve is either a straight line or a circle whose centre is O.

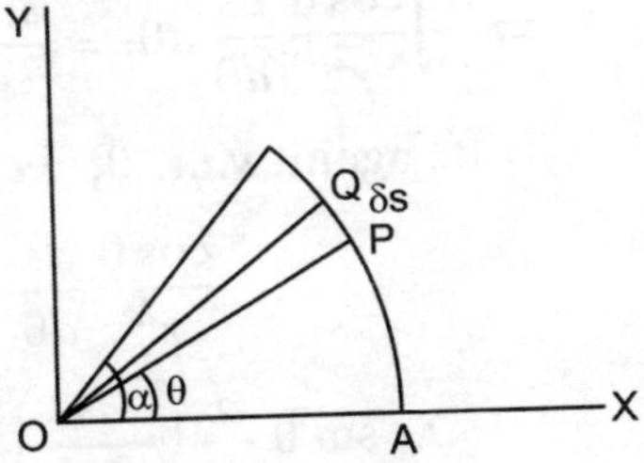

Solution: We consider an element δs of mass $\rho\delta s$ at P whose attraction at O is $\frac{\gamma\rho\delta s}{r^2}$.

Its component parallel to axes are $\frac{\gamma\rho\delta s}{r^2}\cos\theta$ and $\frac{\gamma\rho\delta s}{r^2}\sin\theta$.

Hence the total attraction parallel to the axes are

$$\int\frac{\gamma\rho}{r^2}\cos\theta\, ds \quad\text{and}\quad \int\frac{\gamma\rho}{r^2}\sin\theta\, ds.$$

It is given that the resultant attraction of any arc AB bisects the angle AOB. Hence the attraction of arc AB will bisects the angle AOP i.e. it will make an angle $\frac{\theta}{2}$ with initial line.

$$\therefore\ \tan\frac{\theta}{2} = \frac{\int\frac{\gamma\rho}{r^2}\sin\theta\, ds}{\int\frac{\gamma\rho}{r^2}\cos\theta\, ds}$$

$$\therefore\ \tan\frac{\theta}{2}\int\frac{\cos\theta}{r^2}\frac{ds}{d\theta}\,d\theta = \int\frac{\sin\theta}{r^2}\frac{ds}{d\theta}\,d\theta$$

Diff. it w.r.t. θ, we get

$$\frac{1}{2}\sec^2\frac{\theta}{2}\int\frac{\cos\theta}{r^2}\frac{ds}{d\theta}\,d\theta+\tan\frac{\theta}{2}\frac{\cos\theta}{r^2}\frac{ds}{d\theta} = \frac{\sin\theta}{r^2}\frac{ds}{d\theta}$$

$$\int\frac{\cos\theta}{r^2}\frac{ds}{d\theta}\,d\theta+2\cos^2\frac{\theta}{2}\frac{\sin\frac{\theta}{2}}{\cos\frac{\theta}{2}}\frac{\cos\theta}{r^2}\frac{ds}{d\theta}$$

$$= 2\cos^2\frac{\theta}{2}\frac{\sin\theta}{r^2}\frac{ds}{d\theta}$$

$$\Rightarrow \int\frac{\cos\theta}{r^2}\frac{ds}{d\theta}\,d\theta+\frac{\sin\theta\cos\theta}{r^2}\frac{ds}{d\theta} = \frac{\sin\theta\,(1+\cos\theta)}{r^2}\frac{ds}{d\theta}$$

$$\Rightarrow \int\frac{\cos\theta}{r^2}\frac{ds}{d\theta}\,d\theta = \frac{\sin\theta}{r^2}\frac{ds}{d\theta}$$

Diff. again w.r.t. θ, we get

$$\frac{\cos\theta}{r^2}\frac{ds}{d\theta} = \frac{\cos\theta}{r^2}\frac{ds}{d\theta}+\frac{\sin\theta\,d}{d\theta}\left(\frac{ds}{r^2d\theta}\right)$$

$$\therefore\ \sin\theta\frac{d}{d\theta}\left(\frac{ds}{r^2d\theta}\right) = 0$$

or

$$\frac{d}{d\theta}\left(\frac{ds}{r^2d\theta}\right) = 0$$

Integrating, we get

$$\frac{ds}{r^2d\theta} = \text{const} = \frac{1}{\lambda}\ (\text{Let})$$

$$\Rightarrow \frac{1}{r^2}\left[r^2+\left(\frac{dr}{d\theta}\right)^2\right]^{\frac{1}{2}} = \frac{1}{\lambda}$$

$$\Rightarrow \frac{1}{r^4}\left[r^2+\left(\frac{dr}{d\theta}\right)^2\right] = \frac{1}{\lambda^2}$$

$$\Rightarrow \frac{1}{r^2}+\frac{1}{r^4}\left(\frac{dr}{d\theta}\right)^2 = \frac{1}{\lambda^2} \qquad \text{... (1)}$$

$$\Rightarrow \qquad \frac{1}{p^2} = \frac{1}{\lambda^2}$$

$$\therefore p = \lambda$$

Hence the curve is a circle. Again if we put $u = \dfrac{1}{r}$

then $$\frac{du}{d\theta} = \frac{1}{r^2}\frac{dr}{d\theta}$$

Hence (1) becomes

$$u^2 + \left(\frac{du}{d\theta}\right)^2 = \frac{1}{\lambda^2}$$

$$\left(\frac{du}{d\theta}\right)^2 = \frac{1}{\lambda^2} - u^2$$

$$\Rightarrow \qquad \frac{du}{d\theta} = -\sqrt{\frac{1}{\lambda^2} - u^2}$$

$$\Rightarrow \qquad d\theta = \frac{-\,du}{\sqrt{\dfrac{1}{\lambda^2} - u^2}}$$

Integrating, we get

$$\cos\theta = \cos^{-1}(\lambda u)$$

$$\Rightarrow \qquad \lambda u = \cos\theta$$

$$\Rightarrow \qquad \frac{\lambda}{r} = \cos\theta$$

$$\Rightarrow \qquad \lambda = r\cos\theta$$

$$\Rightarrow \qquad \lambda = x$$

$$\Rightarrow \qquad x = \lambda$$

which represent a straight line.

EXERCISES

1. Two straight wires of length l and l' and of masses m and m' are placed so that they are in the same straight line and the distance between the nearest end is c, show that the

force of attraction between the two wires is $\frac{\gamma mm'}{ll'} \log \frac{(l+c)(l'+c)}{c(l+l'+c)}$.

2. Two equal uniform bars of masses m_1, m_2 and length l are symmetrically placed so as to be parallel and at a distance y. Show that the work done against their mutual attraction in putting one away symmetrically till it is at a distance y_2 from the other is

$$\frac{2\gamma m_1 m_2}{l^2}\left[y - \sqrt{y^2 + l^2} - l \log \frac{\sqrt{y^2 + l^2} - l}{y}\right]_{y_1}^{y_2}.$$

3. A right circular cylinder is of infinite length in one direction and is homogeneous, the finite extremity being perpendicular to generators. Prove that the attraction at the centre of this end is $\frac{2M\gamma}{a}$ where M is the mass per unit length and a the radius.

4. Two uniform rods AB, AC each of mass m and length a are freely joined at A. Show that the couple required to hold them at right angles against their mutual attraction is $\left(2 - \sqrt{2}\right)\frac{\gamma m^2}{a}$.

5. Two uniform non-intersecting straight bars, of infinite length and of line densities σ and σ^1 attract according to the Newtonian law. Show that the resultant force between the bars is $2\gamma\sigma\sigma^1$ cosec α, where α is the angle between the bars.

6. Show that for a long rod of length $2l$ and line density m, the component attraction parallel and perpendicular to the rod are $\frac{2\gamma mx}{l^2}\left(l + \frac{2x^2 - 3y^2}{2l^2}\right)$ and $\frac{2\gamma m}{y}\left(1 - \frac{y^2}{2l^2}\right)$ where the origin is at the middle point of the rod and the axis of x along it and terms of order equal to or higher than $\left(\frac{d}{l}\right)^4$

are neglected, where d is the distance from the middle point.

7. Prove that the resultant attraction at P of straight rod AB of the uniform line density m is $\dfrac{2\gamma me}{Pb}$ directed along Pb, where e is the eccentricity of the ellipse of force, A, B, passing through P and b is the point in which the normal to the ellipse at P cuts AB.

8. Every particle of three similar uniform nods of infinite length, in the same plane, attracts with a force varying inversely as the square of the distance, prove that a particle will be in equilibrium if it be placed at the centre of gravity of the triangle formed by the rods.

9. An infinite series of parallel infinite long rods of uniform line density μ are placed at equal intervals c in a plane, show that the resultant attraction at a point in the plane, whose distance from the nearest rod is a, is $\dfrac{2\gamma\mu\pi}{e}\cot\dfrac{\pi a}{c}$.

10. Prove that any closed rectilinear polygon of thin uniform attracting wire, all of whose sides touch one and the same circle, exerts no attraction at the centre of the circle.

11. Let the finite rod AB be produced both ways to infinity and let the portion beyond A attract and the portion beyond B repel P, the portion between A and B enerting no force at P. Prove that the resulting force at P bisects the angle external to APB and is equal to $\dfrac{2\gamma m}{p}\cos\dfrac{APB}{2}$.

12. A uniform wire of mass M has the form of a semi circular arc of radius a together with the diameter of the semi circle. Find the attraction of the wire upon a particle of unit mass placed at the other end of the diameter through the middle point of the arc of the semi circle.

$$\left[\textbf{Ans. } \frac{\gamma M}{a^2(\pi+2)}\left[\sqrt{2}+\log\left(\sqrt{2}+1\right)\right]\right]$$

2 ATTRACTION OF A DISC AT ANY POINT

2.1. To find the attraction of a uniform circular disc (plate) of radius *a* and small thickness *K*, at a point on the axis of the disc at a distance *p* from its centre.
[L.N.M.U. 93H; M.U. 97H, 99H, 04H; T.M.B.U. 93H, 96H, 2001H, 2003H; B.B.A.B.U. 96H, 2000H, 2002H, 2004H]

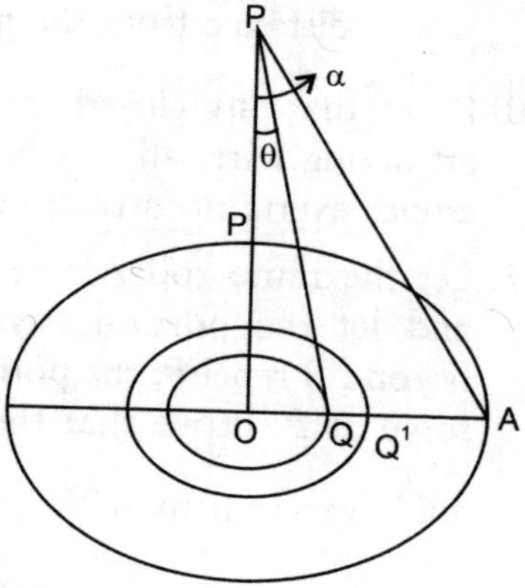

Let P be the point on the axis OP of the circular disc at a distance p from the centre O of the plate.

We divide the area of the disc into a large number of concentric circular strips and let us consider the portion of the disc included between two concentric circles of radii x and $x + \delta x$.

Let us take a point Q on this elementary strip.

Total area of this elementary circular strip

$$= \pi\ (x + \delta x)^2 - \pi x^2$$

$$= 2\pi x \delta x \quad \text{as } \delta x \text{ is very very small.}$$

Hence total mass of this elementary circular strip

$$= 2\pi x \delta x K \rho.$$

Let $\angle OPA = \alpha$

Attraction of a unit mass at Q at a unit mass at P is $\frac{\gamma}{PQ^2}$ along PQ or $\frac{\gamma}{PQ^2}\cos\theta$ along the axis PO.

Hence attraction of the annylus (area between two concentric circles) at P

$$= \frac{\gamma\cos\theta}{PQ^2}\, 2\pi x\delta x K\rho \text{ along } PO$$

$$= \frac{2\pi\gamma K\rho x\delta x}{PQ^2}\cos\theta$$

Hence attraction of the whole disc at P

$$= 2\pi\gamma K\rho \int \frac{x\cos\theta\, dx}{PQ^2} \qquad \dots (1)$$

In ΔPOQ $\quad \tan\theta = \frac{x}{p}, \qquad \cos\theta = \frac{OP}{PQ} = \frac{p}{PQ}$

$$\therefore x = p\tan\theta \qquad p = PQ\cos\theta$$

$$dx = p\sec^2\theta\, d\theta \qquad PQ = p\sec\theta$$

Hence from (1) required attraction

$$= 2\pi\gamma K\rho \int \frac{p\tan\theta\cos\theta\, p\sec^2\theta\, d\theta}{p^2\sec^2\theta}$$

$$= 2\pi\gamma K\rho \int_0^\alpha \sin\theta\, d\theta$$

$$= 2\pi\gamma K\rho\,[-\cos\theta]_0^\alpha$$

$$= 2\pi\gamma K\rho\,(1-\cos\alpha)$$

Hence attraction of a disc at a point on its axis is

$$2\pi\gamma K\rho\,(1-\cos\alpha) \qquad \dots (2)$$

Also attraction of a disc at a point on its axis is

$2\pi\gamma K\rho\left(1-\frac{p}{\sqrt{a^2+p^2}}\right)$ since in ΔOAP $\cos\alpha = \frac{p}{\sqrt{a^2+p^2}}$

Corollary I. If the disc is of infinite radius, then

$$\cos\alpha = \frac{p}{\sqrt{a^2+p^2}} = 0 \text{ i.e. } \alpha = 90^\circ$$

Hence putting $\alpha = 90°$ in (2), we get the attraction of an infinite disc $= 2\pi\gamma K\rho$.

Corollary II. If the disc is of infinite radius but the point P comes very near to the centre, then $p = O$. Hence

$$\cos\alpha = \frac{p}{\sqrt{a^2+p^2}} = 0, \text{ so } \alpha = 90°$$

and in this case attraction $= 2\pi\gamma K\rho$.

Corollary III. Change in attraction of a disc of infinite radius as the point P on its axis (close to the centre) crosses to P' on the other side.

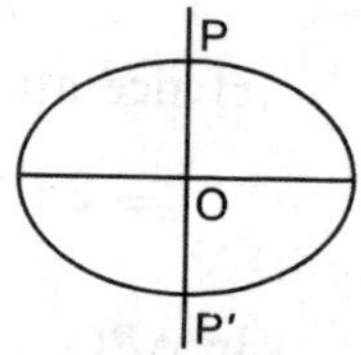

Let P and P' be two points, on opposite sides of, and indefinitely close to the surface, such that PP' is normal to the surface.

Attaction of infinite disc at $P = 2\pi\gamma K\rho$ and the attraction of the infinite disc at $P' = -2\pi\gamma K\rho$, the negative sign is taken here since its direction is opposite of that at P.

Hence, attraction at P – attraction at P'

$$= 2\pi\gamma K\rho - (-2\pi\gamma K\rho)$$
$$= 4\pi\gamma K\rho$$

Hence if a point, indefinitely close to an attracting surface, passes normally to a point indefinitely close on the other side, then the change in attraction is equal to $4\pi\gamma K\rho$.

Corollary IV. Attraction of a circular ring bounded by circles of radii a and b $(a < b)$

$$= 2\pi\gamma K\rho \int_\alpha^\beta \sin\theta\, d\theta$$

$$= 2\pi\gamma K\rho \left[-\cos\theta\right]_\alpha^\beta$$

$$= 2\pi\gamma K\rho\,(\cos\alpha - \cos\beta)$$

$$= 2\pi\gamma K\rho\left[\frac{p}{\sqrt{a^2+p^2}} - \frac{p}{\sqrt{b^2+p^2}}\right]$$

WORKED OUT EXAMPLES

1. Find the attraction of a uniform solid right circular cone of height h and vertical angle 2α at (i) the vertex, (ii) the centre of the plane base, (iii) also find the ratio of these two attractions in case of solid right circular cone.

[P.U. 82H; L.N.M.U. 93H]

Solution: Let V be the vertex and O the centre of the base of the cone.

We divide the cone into a large number of elementary discs parallel to the base of the cone. Let one of such disc be at a distance x from O and of thickness δx, whose centre is at N.

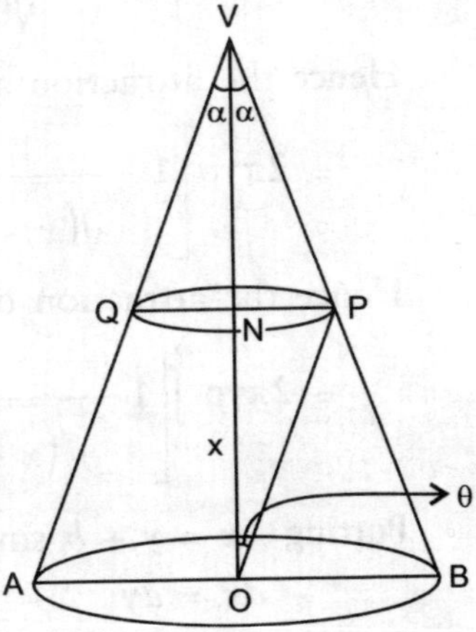

Let $\angle PON = \theta$, $\angle OVB = \alpha$.

(i) By symmetry, the attraction of the disc at V is along VN, and is equal to $2\pi\gamma\rho\,(1 - \cos\alpha)\,\delta x$.

Hence the attraction of the cone at V

$$= 2\pi\gamma\rho \int_0^h (1 - \cos\alpha)\,dx$$

$$= 2\pi\gamma\rho\,(1 - \cos\alpha)\,h$$

(ii) Attraction of the disc at the centre O of the plane base

$$= 2\pi\gamma\rho\delta x\,(1 - \cos\theta)$$

where θ is variable for different discs.

$ON = x, \qquad VN = OV - ON = h - x$

In ΔVPN $\tan\alpha = \dfrac{PN}{VN} = \dfrac{PN}{h-x}$

$$PN = (h - x)\tan\alpha$$

In ΔOPN $\cos\theta = \dfrac{ON}{OP} = \dfrac{x}{\sqrt{ON^2 + PN^2}}$

$$= \frac{x}{\sqrt{x^2 + (h-x)^2 \tan^2\alpha}}$$

$$= \frac{x \cos \alpha}{\sqrt{x^2 \cos^2 \alpha + (h - x)^2 \sin^2 \alpha}}$$

$$= \frac{x \cos \alpha}{\sqrt{x^2 - 2hx \sin^2 \alpha + h^2 \sin^2 \alpha}}$$

$$= \frac{x \cos \alpha}{\sqrt{(x - h \sin^2 \alpha)^2 + h^2 \sin^2 \alpha - h^2 \sin^4 \alpha}}$$

$$= \frac{x \cos \alpha}{\sqrt{(x - h \sin^2 \alpha)^2 + h^2 \sin^2 \alpha \cos^2 \alpha}}$$

Hence the attraction at O due to this elementary disc is

$$= 2\pi\gamma\rho \left[1 - \frac{x \cos \alpha}{\sqrt{(x - h \sin^2 \alpha)^2 + h^2 \sin^2 \alpha \cos^2 \alpha}}\right]$$

Hence the attraction of the whole cone at O

$$= 2\pi\gamma\rho \int_0^h \left[1 - \frac{x \cos \alpha}{\sqrt{(x - h \sin^2 \alpha)^2 + h^2 \sin^2 \alpha \cos^2 \alpha}}\right] dx$$

Putting $x = y + h \sin^2 \alpha$

$dx = dy$

When $x = h$, $\quad y = h \cos^2 \alpha$

and $x = 0$, $\quad y = -h \sin^2 \alpha$

Then attraction

$$= 2\pi\gamma\rho \int_{-h \sin^2 \alpha}^{h \cos^2 \alpha} \left[1 - \frac{(y + h \sin^2 \alpha) \cos \alpha}{\sqrt{y^2 + h^2 \sin^2 \alpha \cos^2 \alpha}}\right] dy$$

$$= 2\pi\gamma\rho \int_{-h \sin^2 \alpha}^{h \cos^2 \alpha} \left[1 - \frac{y \cos \alpha}{\sqrt{y^2 + h^2 \sin^2 \alpha \cos^2 \alpha}} - \frac{h \sin^2 \alpha \cos \alpha}{\sqrt{y^2 + h^2 \sin^2 \alpha \cos^2 \alpha}}\right] dy$$

$$= 2\pi\gamma\rho\Big[y - \cos\alpha\sqrt{y^2 + h^2\sin^2\alpha\cos^2\alpha}$$

$$- h\sin^2\alpha\cos\alpha\log\left\{y + \sqrt{y^2 + h^2\sin^2\alpha\cos^2\alpha}\right\}\Big]_{-h\sin^2\alpha}^{h\cos^2\alpha}$$

$$= 2\pi\gamma\rho\Big[h - \cos\alpha\,(h\cos\alpha - h\sin\alpha)$$

$$- h\sin^2\alpha\cos\alpha\log\frac{h\cos^2\alpha + h\cos\alpha}{-h\sin^2\alpha + h\sin\alpha}\Big]$$

$$= 2\pi\gamma\rho\Big[h\sin^2\alpha + h\sin\alpha\cos\alpha$$

$$- h\sin^2\alpha\cos\alpha\log\frac{\cos\alpha + \cos^2\alpha}{\sin\alpha - \sin^2\alpha}\Big]$$

$$= 2\pi\gamma\rho h\sin\alpha\Big[\cos\alpha + \cos\alpha$$

$$- \sin\alpha\cos\alpha\log\frac{\cos\alpha + \cos^2\alpha}{\sin\alpha - \sin^2\alpha}\Big]$$

(iii) When $2\alpha = \dfrac{\pi}{2}$ i.e. $\alpha = \dfrac{\pi}{4}$, the attraction at the centre of the base

$$= 2\pi\gamma\rho h\,\frac{1}{\sqrt{2}}\left[\frac{2}{\sqrt{2}} - \frac{1}{2}\log\frac{\frac{1}{\sqrt{2}} + \frac{1}{2}}{\frac{1}{\sqrt{2}} - \frac{1}{2}}\right]$$

$$= \frac{2\pi\gamma\rho h}{\sqrt{2}}\left[\sqrt{2} - \frac{1}{2}\log\frac{\sqrt{2}+1}{\sqrt{2}-1}\right]$$

$$= \frac{2\pi\gamma\rho h}{\sqrt{2}}\left[\sqrt{2} - \frac{1}{2}\log\frac{(\sqrt{2}+1)^2}{2-1}\right]$$

$$= \frac{2\pi\gamma\rho h}{\sqrt{2}}\left[\sqrt{2} - \log\left(\sqrt{2}+1\right)\right]$$

Also attraction at vertex

$$= 2\pi\gamma\rho h\left(1 - \frac{1}{\sqrt{2}}\right)$$

$$= \frac{2\pi\gamma\rho h\left(\sqrt{2}-1\right)}{\sqrt{2}}$$

Hence the ratio of the two attractions

$$= \frac{\sqrt{2}-1}{\sqrt{2}-\log\left(\sqrt{2}+1\right)}$$

2. A right circular cone of uniform density ρ has its axis vertical and vertex downwards show that the attraction at a point P on the axis, at a distance c above the vertex is

$$2\pi\gamma\rho c \sin\alpha\cos\alpha\left\{\frac{\cos\beta-\cos\alpha}{\sin\beta}-\sin\alpha\log\left(\tan\frac{\alpha}{2}\cot\frac{\beta}{2}\right)\right\}$$

where 2α is the vertical angle of the cone and $\alpha-\beta$ the angle which the radius of its base subtends at P.

Solution: We consider an elementary disc of the cone bounded by the planes parallel to the base at distances x and $x+\delta x$ from the vertex, and let the radius of this disc subtend an angle θ at P.

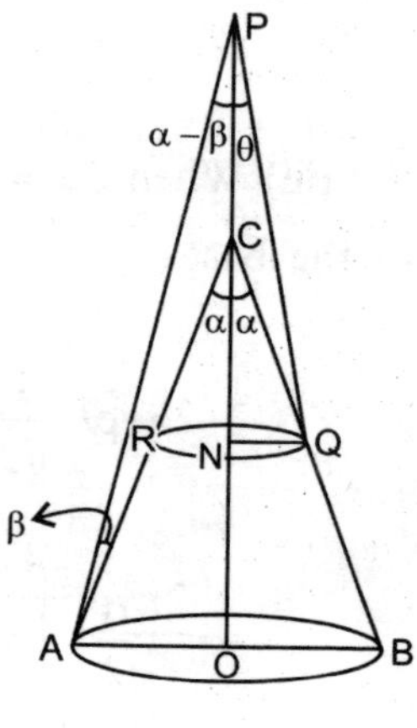

In ΔPQN

$$\tan\theta = \frac{QN}{PN} = \frac{QN}{PC+CN} = \frac{QN}{c+x}$$

In ΔCQN

$$\tan\alpha = \frac{QN}{CN} = \frac{QN}{x}$$

$$QN = x\tan\alpha$$

$$\tan\theta = \frac{x\tan\alpha}{c+x}$$

or $$\frac{x}{\tan\theta} = \frac{c+x}{\tan\alpha} = \frac{c+x-x}{\tan\alpha-\tan\theta}$$

$$= \frac{c}{\tan\alpha-\tan\theta}$$

$$x = \frac{c\tan\theta}{\tan\alpha-\tan\theta}$$

$$dx = \frac{c\left[\sec^2\theta\left(\tan\alpha - \tan\theta\right) + \sec^2\theta\tan\theta\right]}{\left(\tan\alpha - \tan\theta\right)^2}\,d\theta$$

$$= \frac{c\sec^2\theta\tan\alpha \cdot d\theta}{\left(\tan\alpha - \tan\theta\right)^2}$$

$$= \frac{c\sec^2\theta\sin\alpha\cos^2\alpha\cos^2\theta}{\cos\alpha\sin^2\left(\alpha - \theta\right)}\,d\theta$$

$$= c\sin\alpha\cos\alpha\,\text{cosec}^2\left(\alpha - \theta\right)d\theta$$

Also $$x = \frac{c\sin\theta\cos\alpha\cos\theta}{\cos\theta\sin\left(\alpha - \theta\right)}$$

$$= \frac{c\sin\theta\cos\alpha}{\sin\left(\alpha - \theta\right)}$$

The attraction of the disc at $P = 2\pi\gamma\rho\ (1 - \cos\theta)\ \delta x$

Therefore the attraction of the whole cone is

$$= 2\pi\gamma\rho\int\left(1 - \cos\theta\right)dx$$

$$= 2\pi\gamma\rho\int_0^{\alpha-\beta}\left(1 - \cos\theta\right)c\sin\alpha\cos\alpha\,\text{cosec}^2\left(\alpha - \theta\right)d\theta$$

Let $\alpha - \theta = \phi$

Also $d\theta = -\,d\phi$

When $\theta = \alpha - \beta,\ \phi = \beta$

$\theta = 0,\ \phi = \alpha$

Hence attraction

$$= 2\pi\gamma\rho c\int_\alpha^\beta\left[1 - \cos\left(\alpha - \phi\right)\right]\left(-\,\text{cosec}^2\phi\right)\sin\alpha\cos\alpha\,d\phi$$

$$= 2\pi\gamma\rho c\sin\alpha\cos\alpha\int_\alpha^\beta\left[-\,\text{cosec}^2\phi + \frac{\cos\alpha\cos\phi + \sin\alpha\sin\phi}{\sin^2\phi}\right]d\phi$$

$$= 2\pi\gamma\rho c \sin\alpha\cos\alpha \int_{\alpha}^{\beta} \left[-\text{cosec}^2\phi + \cos\alpha\cot\phi\,\text{cosec}\,\phi + \sin\alpha\,\text{cosec}\,\phi\right] d\phi$$

$$= 2\pi\gamma\rho c \sin\alpha\cos\alpha \left[\cot\phi - \cos\alpha\,\text{cosec}\,\phi + \sin\alpha \log\tan\frac{\phi}{2}\right]_{\alpha}^{\beta}$$

$$= 2\pi\gamma\rho c \sin\alpha\cos\alpha \left[\frac{\cos\phi - \cos\alpha}{\sin\phi} + \sin\alpha\log\tan\frac{\phi}{2}\right]_{\alpha}^{\beta}$$

$$= 2\pi\gamma\rho c \sin\alpha\cos\alpha \left[\frac{\cos\beta - \cos\alpha}{\sin\beta} + \sin\alpha\log\frac{\tan\frac{\beta}{2}}{\tan\frac{\alpha}{2}}\right]$$

$$= 2\pi\gamma\rho c \sin\alpha\cos\alpha \left[\frac{\cos\beta - \cos\alpha}{\sin\beta} - \sin\alpha\log\frac{\tan\frac{\alpha}{2}}{\tan\frac{\beta}{2}}\right]$$

3. A frustrum of a uniform thin hollow cone attracts a particle placed at the vertex, show that attraction is $2\pi\gamma\,\sigma\sin\alpha\cos\alpha \log\frac{R}{r}$, where R and r are the radii of the circular ends, α is the semivertical angle of the cone and σ is the surface density.

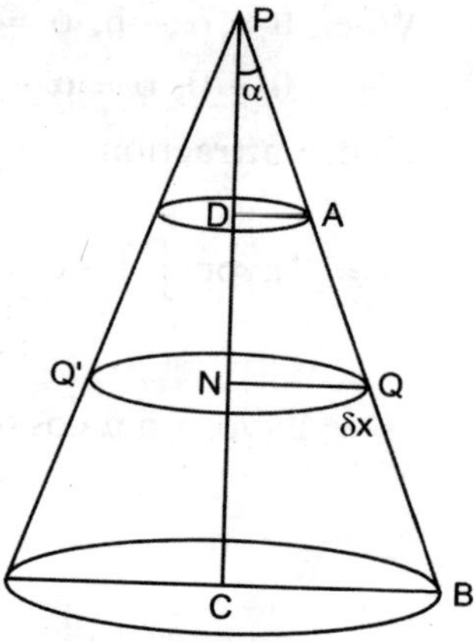

Solution: Let $ABCD$ be the frustrum of the cone whose vertex is P. We consider an elementary ring through Q of breadth δx at distance $PQ = x$.

Mass of the ring $= 2\pi\,(x\sin\alpha)\,\sigma\,\delta x$.

Attraction of the ring at P

$$= \frac{\gamma 2\pi\, x\sin\alpha\,\sigma\,\delta x}{PQ^2} \text{ along } PQ$$

$$= \frac{2\pi\gamma\,\sigma\,x\,\delta x \sin\alpha}{x^2}\cos\alpha \text{ along the axis of the cone}$$

$$= 2\pi\gamma\,\sigma \sin\alpha \cos\alpha \frac{1}{x}\delta x$$

Therefore the attraction of the whole frustrum at P

$$= 2\pi\sigma\gamma \sin\alpha \cos\alpha \int_{PD}^{PC} \frac{1}{x}\,dx$$

In ΔPAD $\quad \tan\alpha = \frac{AD}{PD} = \frac{r}{PD}$

$$PD = r\cot\alpha$$

In ΔPBC $\quad \tan\alpha = \frac{BC}{PC} = \frac{R}{PC}$

$$PC = R\cot\alpha$$

Hence the attraction

$$= 2\pi\sigma\gamma \sin\alpha \cos\alpha \int_{r\cot\alpha}^{R\cot\alpha} \frac{dx}{x}$$

$$= 2\pi\gamma\sigma \sin\alpha \cos\alpha \left[\log x\right]_{r\cot\alpha}^{R\cot\alpha}$$

$$= 2\pi\gamma\rho \sin\alpha \cos\alpha \log\frac{R\cot\alpha}{r\cot\alpha}$$

$$= 2\pi\gamma\rho \sin\alpha \cos\alpha \log\frac{R}{r}$$

4. Find the attraction of a cylinder at a point on its axis which is situated (i) outside (ii) inside at a distance c from the centre of the upper surface h the height of the cylinder. [B.B.A.B.U. 93H]

Solution: (i) Let P be a point on the axis of the cylinder at a distance c from the centre O of the upper surface. Here $OO' = h$.

We consider an elementary disc QNR of thickness δx at a distance x from P.

Let $\angle QPN = \alpha$ and $PN = x$

In ΔPQN $\quad \cos\alpha = \frac{PN}{PQ} = \frac{x}{\sqrt{a^2 + x^2}}$

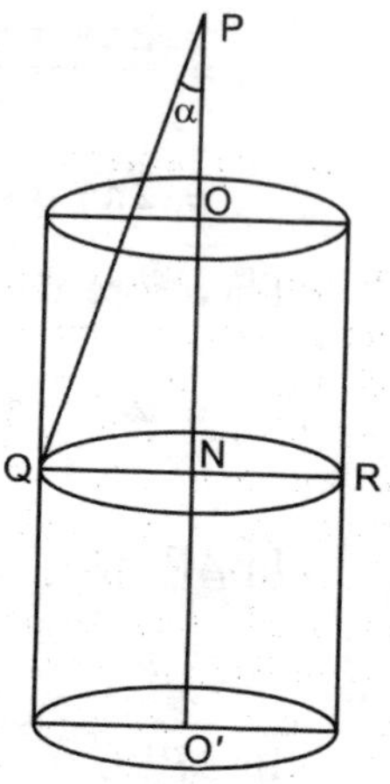

Attraction of this disc at P

$$= 2\pi\gamma\, \delta x \rho\, (1 - \cos\alpha)$$

$$= 2\pi\gamma\, \delta x \rho \left[1 - \frac{x}{\sqrt{a^2 + x^2}}\right]$$

Hence the attraction of the cylinder at P

$$= 2\pi\gamma\rho \int_c^{c+h} \left[1 - \frac{x}{\sqrt{a^2 + x^2}}\right] dx$$

$$= 2\pi\gamma\rho \left[x - \sqrt{a^2 + x^2}\right]_c^{c+h}$$

$$= 2\pi\gamma\rho \left[c + h - \sqrt{a^2 + (c+h)^2} - \left\{c - \sqrt{a^2 + c^2}\right\}\right]$$

$$= 2\pi\gamma\rho \left[h - \sqrt{a^2 + (c+h)^2} + \sqrt{a^2 + c^2}\right]$$

(ii) Here P is inside the cylinder.

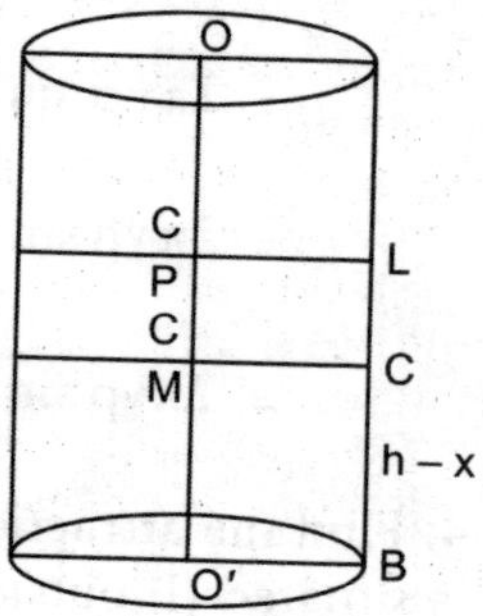

Let us take a point M on the axis such that $OP = PM = c$. The attractions at P due to the two cylinders of equal height above and below P will be equal and opposite. Hence we have to find the attraction due to the cylinder of height $h - 2c = H$ (say) at a point P on the axis outside it a distance c from M. Hence as in (i) we get the required attraction

$$= 2\pi\gamma\rho \left[x - \sqrt{a^2 + x^2}\right]_c^{c+H}$$

$$= 2\pi\gamma\rho \left[c + H - \sqrt{a^2 + (c+H)^2} - \left\{c - \sqrt{a^2 + c^2}\right\}\right]$$

$$= 2\pi\gamma\rho \left[h - 2c - \sqrt{a^2 + (h-c)^2} + \sqrt{a^2 + c^2}\right]$$

5. Find the ratio of the base of the height of a right circular cylinder of given volume so that the attraction at the centre of one of the circular ends may be the greatest possible.

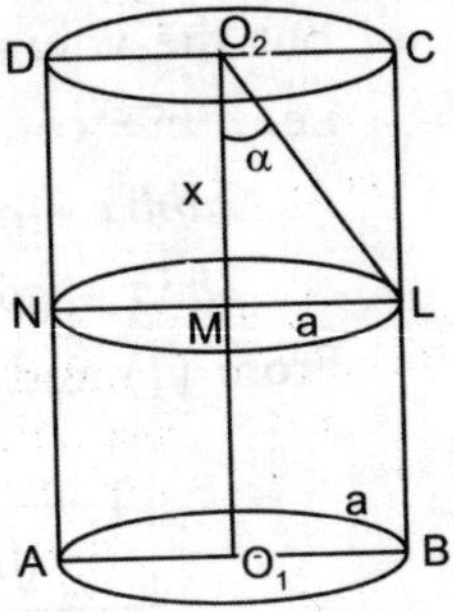

Solution: Let *ABCD* be the cylinder of radius a and height h.

We consider an elementary disc *LMN* of thickness δx at a distance x from O_2, the centre of the circular end *CD*.

Let $\angle LO_2M = \alpha$, then

$$\cos\alpha = \frac{O_2M}{O_2L} = \frac{O_2M}{\sqrt{O_2M^2 + ML^2}}$$

$$= \frac{x}{\sqrt{x^2 + a^2}}$$

Hence attraction of the elementary disc at O_2

$$= 2\pi\gamma\rho\delta x\,(1 - \cos\alpha) \text{ along } O_2M$$

$$= 2\pi\gamma\rho\left[1 - \frac{x}{\sqrt{x^2 + a^2}}\right]\delta x$$

Hence the attraction A of the cylinder at O_2, along O_2O_1 is given by

$$A = 2\pi\gamma\rho \int_{x=0}^{h}\left[1 - \frac{x}{\sqrt{x^2 + a^2}}\right]dx$$

$$= 2\pi\gamma\rho\left[x - \sqrt{x^2 + a^2}\right]_0^h$$

$$= 2\pi\gamma\rho\left[h - \sqrt{h^2 + a^2} + a\right] = f(a, h) \text{ (say)}$$

Now $\delta A = \dfrac{\partial A}{\partial a}\delta a + \dfrac{\partial A}{\partial h}\delta h$

$$= \delta a 2\pi\,\gamma\rho\left[1 - \frac{a}{\sqrt{h^2 + a^2}}\right] + \left[1 - \frac{h}{\sqrt{h^2 + a^2}}\right]\delta h$$

For maximum A, $\delta A = 0$

$$\Rightarrow \left[1 - \frac{a}{\sqrt{h^2 + a^2}}\right]\delta a + \left[1 - \frac{h}{\sqrt{h^2 + a^2}}\right]\delta h = 0 \qquad \text{... (1)}$$

But the volume of the cylinder $= \pi a^2 h$ = constant

i.e. $a^2 h$ = constant

$$2ah\delta a + a^2 \delta h = 0$$

$$2h\delta a + a\delta h = 0 \qquad \dots (2)$$

From (1) and (2), we get

$$\frac{\left[1 - \frac{a}{\sqrt{h^2 + a^2}}\right]}{2h} = \frac{1 - \frac{h}{\sqrt{h^2 + a^2}}}{a}$$

$$\Rightarrow \quad a\left[1 - \frac{a}{\sqrt{h^2 + a^2}}\right] = 2h\left[1 - \frac{h}{\sqrt{h^2 + a^2}}\right]$$

$$\Rightarrow \quad 2h - a = \frac{2h^2 - a^2}{\sqrt{h^2 + a^2}}$$

$$\Rightarrow \quad (2h - a)^2 (h^2 + a^2) = (2h^2 - a^2)^2$$

$$\Rightarrow \quad (4h^2 - 4ah + a^2)(h^2 + a^2) = 4h^4 - 4a^2h^2 + a^4$$

$$\Rightarrow \quad 4h^4 - 4ah^3 + 5a^2h^2 - 4a^3h + a^4 = 4h^4 - 4a^2h^2 + a^4$$

$$\Rightarrow \quad 9a^2h^2 - 4ah^3 - 4a^3h = 0$$

$$\Rightarrow \quad 4a^2 - 9ah + 4h^2 = 0$$

$$\Rightarrow \quad a = \frac{9h \pm \sqrt{81h^2 - 64h^2}}{2.4}$$

$$= \frac{\left(9 \pm \sqrt{17}\right)h}{8}$$

Hence $\quad \dfrac{a}{h} = \dfrac{9 - \sqrt{17}}{8} \text{ (if } a < h)$

6. Find the attraction of a uniform thin shell in the form of the portion of a circular cylinder between the planes perpendicular to the axis on a particle at the axis and prove that a particle slightly displaced on the axis from the position of equilibrium will perform small oscillations of period $2\pi M \frac{1}{2}\left(a^2 + C^2\right)^{3/4}$

where $2a$ is the length and c the radius of the cylinder and M its mass.

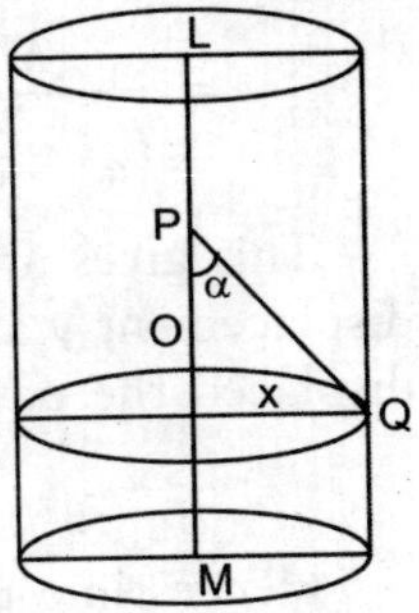

Solution: Let O be the centre of cylinder of height $2a$ and radius C and P be the particle of a distance y from O, i.e. $OP = y$ so that

$$LP = OL - OP = a - y$$

and $PM = PO + OM = a + y$

We consider a ring through Q of thickness δx at a distance x from P.

Attraction of this ring at P is

$$= \frac{2\pi c \rho \delta x}{PQ^2} \text{ along } PQ$$

$$= \frac{2\pi c \rho \delta x}{c^2 + x^2} \cos\alpha \text{ along the axis}$$

$$= \frac{2\pi c \rho \delta x}{c^2 + x^2} \frac{x}{\sqrt{c^2 + x^2}}$$

Hence the whole attraction at P

$$= 2\pi\rho c \int_{-(a-y)}^{a+y} \frac{x\,dx}{\left(c^2 + x^2\right)^{3/2}}$$

$$= 2\pi\rho c \left[-\frac{1}{\sqrt{c^2 + x^2}} \right]_{-(a-y)}^{a+y}$$

$$= 2\pi\rho c \left[\frac{1}{\sqrt{c^2 + (a-y)^2}} - \frac{1}{\sqrt{c^2 + (a+y)^2}} \right]$$

$$= \frac{2\pi\rho c}{\sqrt{a^2 + c^2}} \left[\left\{ 1 + \frac{y^2 - 2ay}{a^2 + c^2} \right\}^{-\frac{1}{2}} - \left\{ 1 + \frac{y^2 + 2ay}{a^2 + c^2} \right\}^{-\frac{1}{2}} \right]$$

$$= \frac{2\pi\rho c}{\sqrt{a^2 + c^2}} \left[1 - \frac{1}{2} \frac{y^2 - 2ay}{a^2 + c^2} + \ldots\ldots \right.$$

$$\left. - \left\{ 1 - \frac{1}{2} \frac{y^2 + 2ay}{a^2 + c^2} + \ldots\ldots \right\} \right]$$

$$= \frac{2\pi\rho c}{\sqrt{a^2+c^2}} \frac{1}{2} \frac{4ay}{a^2+c^2}$$

$$= \frac{My}{\left(a^2+c^2\right)^{3/2}} \qquad \text{since } M = 2\pi c\,(2a)\rho$$

This gives attraction. Clearly attraction is proportional to displacement y and is directed towards the centre O. So when displaced the paticle will execute smaller oscillations.

$$\text{Hence time period} = 2\pi\left[\frac{\left(a^2+c^2\right)^{3/2}}{M}\right]^{\frac{1}{2}}$$

$$= 2\pi M^{-\frac{1}{2}}\left(a^2+c^2\right)^{\frac{3}{4}}$$

7. A homogeneous right circular cylinder is of infinite length in one direction and at the other end the section is perpendicular to the generators. Prove that the attraction on a particle at the centre of this end is $\dfrac{2\gamma M}{a}$, where M is the mass of the cylinder per unit to a length.

Solution: Let P be the centre of the end of the cylinder. We are to determine the attraction at P. We consider an elementary disc QMR of thickness δx at a distance x from P.

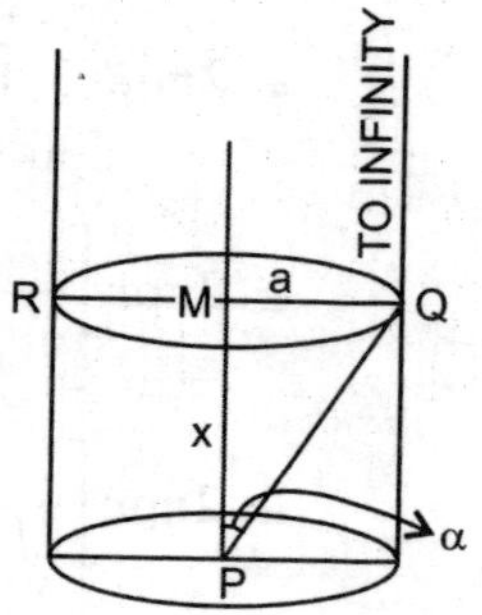

Let $\angle QPM = \alpha$

$$\therefore \cos\alpha = \frac{x}{\sqrt{a^2+x^2}}$$

Attraction at P, due to the elementary disc

$$= 2\pi\gamma\rho\delta x\,(1-\cos\alpha)$$

$$= 2\pi\gamma\rho\delta x\left[1-\frac{x}{\sqrt{a^2+x^2}}\right]$$

Therefore the total attraction at O due to cylinder is

$$= 2\pi\gamma\rho \int_0^{\alpha}\left[1-\frac{x}{\sqrt{a^2+x^2}}\right]dx$$

$$= 2\pi\gamma\rho\left[x-\sqrt{a^2+x^2}\right]_0^{\alpha}$$

$$= 2\pi\gamma\rho\left[\frac{-a^2}{x+\sqrt{a^2+x^2}}\right]_0^{\alpha}$$

$$= -2\pi\gamma\rho a^2\left[\frac{1}{x+\sqrt{a^2+x^2}}\right]_0^{\alpha}$$

$$= -2\pi\gamma\rho a^2\left[0-\frac{1}{a}\right]$$

$$= 2\pi\gamma\rho a$$

But $M = \pi a^2\rho$

Hence required attraction $= 2\pi\dfrac{\gamma a M}{\pi a^2}$

$$= \frac{2\gamma M}{a}$$

8. Show that the attraction of a spherical segment on a unit particle at its vertex is

$$2\pi\gamma\rho h\left[1-\frac{1}{3}\sqrt{\frac{2h}{a}}\right]$$

and that on a unit particle at the centre of the base is

$$\frac{2\pi\gamma\rho h}{3(a-h)^2}\left[3a^2-3ah+h^2-h^{\frac{1}{2}}(2a-h)^{\frac{3}{2}}\right]$$

where a is the radius and h the height of the segment.

Solution: Let APB be the segment of the sphere of which P is the vertex and C is the centre of the base.

Case I: To determine the attraction at the vertex P.

We divide the segment into a large number of elementary strips and let one of such elementary disc be QNR of thickness δx at a distance x from P. Let $\angle QPN = \alpha$.

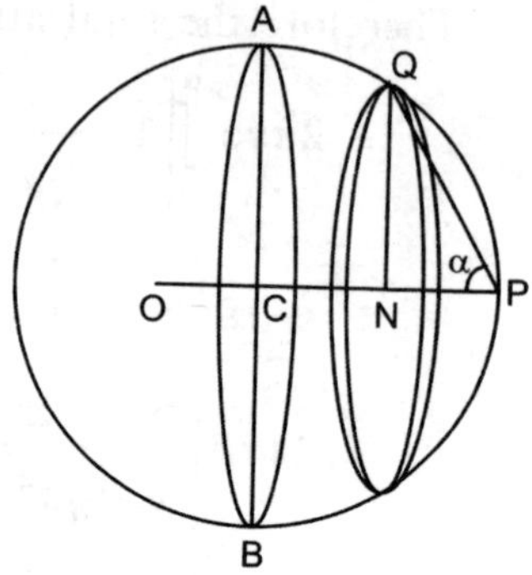

Attraction of this disc at P

$$= 2\pi\gamma\rho\delta x\ (1 - \cos\alpha)$$

In ΔPQN,

$$\cos\alpha = \frac{PN}{PQ}$$

Now $\quad PN = x$

$$PQ^2 = PN^2 + NQ^2 = x^2 + NQ^2$$

Also $\quad CQ^2 = CN^2 + QN^2$

$$a^2 = (CP - PN)^2 + QN^2$$

$$a^2 = (a - x)^2 + QN^2$$

$$a^2 - (a - x)^2 = QN^2$$

$$a^2 - (a^2 + x^2 - 2ax) = QN^2$$

$$QN^2 = 2ax - x^2$$

Hence $\quad PQ^2 = x^2 + 2ax - x^2 = 2ax$

Now $\quad \cos\alpha = \frac{PN}{PQ} = \frac{x}{\sqrt{2ax}} = \sqrt{\frac{x}{2a}}$

Hence the total attraction at P due to the whole segment

$$= 2\pi\gamma\rho \int_0^h \left(1 - \sqrt{\frac{x}{2a}}\right) dx$$

$$= 2\pi\gamma\rho \left[x - \frac{2}{3}\frac{x^{3/2}}{\sqrt{2a}}\right]_0^h$$

$$= 2\pi\gamma\rho \left[h - \frac{2}{3}\frac{h^{3/2}}{\sqrt{2a}}\right]$$

$$= 2\pi\gamma\rho h \left[1 - \frac{1}{3}\sqrt{\frac{2h}{a}}\right]$$

Case II: To determine the attraction at C (the centre of the base)

We have
$$\begin{aligned} CQ^2 &= CN^2 + NQ^2 \\ &= (CP - PN)^2 + 2ax - x^2 \\ &= (h - x)^2 + x\,(2a - x) \\ &= h^2 + x^2 - 2hx + 2ax - x^2 \\ &= h^2 + 2x\,(a - h) \end{aligned}$$

Let $\angle QCN = \beta$

$$\cos\beta = \frac{CN}{CQ} = \frac{h - x}{\sqrt{h^2 + 2x\,(a - h)}}$$

Hence attraction at C, due to the elementary disc

$$= 2\pi\gamma\rho\delta x\,(1 - \cos\beta)$$

$$= 2\pi\gamma\rho\delta x\left[1 - \frac{h - x}{\sqrt{h^2 + 2x\,(a - h)}}\right]$$

Hence the attraction at C, due to the whole segment

$$= 2\pi\gamma\rho\int_0^h\left[1 - \frac{h - x}{\sqrt{h^2 + 2x\,(a - h)}}\right]dx$$

$$= 2\pi\gamma\rho\left[\left\{x - (h - x)\frac{\sqrt{h^2 + 2x\,(a - h)}}{a - h}\right\}_0^h + \frac{1}{a - h}\int_0^h\sqrt{h^2 + 2x\,(a - h)}\,(-dx)\right]$$

$$= 2\pi\gamma\rho\left[h - 0 - \left\{0 - \frac{h^2}{a - h}\right\} - \frac{1}{2\,(a - h)^2}\,\frac{2}{3}\left[\left\{h^2 + 2x\,(a - h)\right\}^{3/2}\right]_0^h\right]$$

$$= 2\pi\gamma\rho\left[h + \frac{h^2}{a - h} - \frac{1}{3\,(a - h)^2}\left\{(2ah - h^2)^{3/2} - h^3\right\}\right]$$

$$= \frac{2\pi\gamma\rho}{3(a-h)^2}\left[3h(a-h)^2 + 3h^2(a-h) - h^{3/2}(2a-h)^{3/2} + h^3\right]$$

$$= \frac{2\pi\gamma\rho h}{3(a-h)^2}\left[3(a^2 - 2ah + h^2) + 3h(a-h) - h^{1/2}(2a-h)^{3/2} + h^2\right]$$

$$= \frac{2\pi\gamma\rho h}{3(a-h)^2}\left[3(a^2 - 2ah + h^2 + ah - h^2) - h^{1/2}(2a-h)^{3/2} + h^2\right]$$

$$= \frac{2\pi\gamma\rho h}{3(a-h)^2}\left[3a^2 - 3ah + h^2 - h^{1/2}(2a-h)^{3/2}\right]$$

Proved.

9. Prove that a solid uniform hemisphere of radius a exerts no resultant attracts at a point on its axis at a distance c from the centre given by the equation $12c^4 - 8a^3c + 3a^4 = 0$.

[P.U. 78H, 80H]

Solution: Let P be the point on the hemisphere ABC at which the attraction is zero. Given $OP = c$.

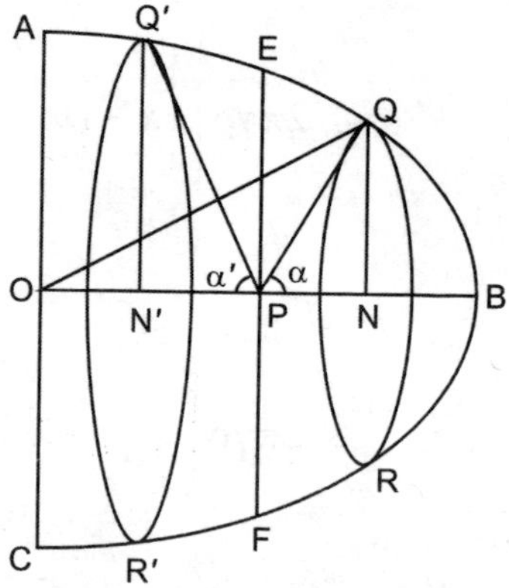

To find the attraction due to the segment EBF, we consider an elementary disc QNR of thickness δx at a distance x from P.

The attraction of this disc at $P = 2\pi\gamma\rho\delta x\,(1 - \cos\alpha)$

In ΔPNQ

$$\cos\alpha = \frac{PN}{PQ} = \frac{x}{\sqrt{PN^2 + QN^2}}$$

$$= \frac{x}{\sqrt{PN^2 + OQ^2 - ON^2}}$$

$$= \frac{x}{\sqrt{x^2 + a^2 - (x+c)^2}}$$

Thus the attraction of the elementary disc QNR at P

$$= 2\pi\gamma\rho\left[1 - \frac{x}{\sqrt{a^2 - c^2 - 2cx}}\right]\delta x$$

Hence attraction at P due to the portion EBF

$$= 2\pi\gamma\rho \int_0^{a-c}\left[1 - \frac{x}{\sqrt{a^2 - c^2 - 2cx}}\right]dx$$

$$= 2\pi\gamma\rho\left[x - x\int(a^2 - c^2 - 2cx)^{-1/2}\,dx - \frac{2}{2c}\int(a^2 - c^2 - 2cx)^{1/2}\,dx\right]$$

$$= 2\pi\gamma\rho\left[x + \frac{2x}{2c}(a^2 - c^2 - 2cx)^{1/2} + \frac{2}{3\cdot 2c^2}(a^2 - c^2 - 2cx)^{3/2}\right]_0^{a-c}$$

$$= 2\pi\gamma\rho\left[x + \frac{x\sqrt{a^2 - c^2 - 2cx}}{c} + \frac{(a^2 - c^2 - 2cx)^{3/2}}{3c^2}\right]_0^{a-c}$$

$$= 2\pi\gamma\rho\left[(a-c) + \frac{(a-c)\sqrt{a^2 - c^2 - 2c(a-c)}}{c} + \frac{\{a^2 - c^2 - 2c(a-c)\}^{3/2}}{3c^2} - \frac{(a^2 - c^2)^{3/2}}{3c^2}\right]$$

$$= 2\pi\gamma\rho\left[(a-c) + \frac{(a-c)\sqrt{(a-c)^2}}{c} + \frac{(a-c)^3}{3c^2} - \frac{(a^2-c^2)^{3/2}}{3c^2}\right]$$

$$= \frac{2\pi\gamma\rho}{3c^2}\left[3c^2(a-c) + 3c(a-c)^2 + (a-c)^3 - (a^2-c^2)^{3/2}\right]$$

$$= \frac{2\pi\gamma\rho}{3c^2}\left[(a-c)\{3c^2 + 3ca - 3c^2 + a^2 - 2ac + c^2\} - (a^2-c^2)^{3/2}\right]$$

$$= \frac{2\pi\gamma\rho}{3c^2}\left[(a-c)(a^2+c^2+ac) - (a^2-c^2)^{3/2}\right]$$

$$= \frac{2\pi\gamma\rho}{3c^2}\left[a^3 - c^3 - (a^2-c^2)^{3/2}\right]$$

Now to determine attraction of the remaining portion *AEFC* we consider an elementary disc $Q'R'$ at a distance y from P.

Then as above, attraction at P due to the portion *AEFC*

$$= 2\pi\gamma\rho\int_0^c\left[1 - \frac{y}{\sqrt{a^2-c^2+2cy}}\right]dy$$

$$= 2\pi\gamma\rho\left[y - \frac{y\sqrt{a^2-c^2+2cy}}{c} + \frac{(a^2-c^2+2cy)^{3/2}}{3c^2}\right]_0^c$$

$$= 2\pi\gamma\rho\left[c - \frac{c\sqrt{a^2+c^2}}{c} + \frac{(a^2+c^2)^{3/2}}{3c^2} - \frac{(a^2-c^2)^{3/2}}{3c^2}\right]$$

$$= 2\pi\gamma\rho\left[c - \sqrt{a^2+c^2} + \frac{(a^2+c^2)\sqrt{a^2+c^2}}{3c^2} - \frac{(a^2-c^2)^{3/2}}{3c^2}\right]$$

$$= \frac{2\pi\gamma\rho}{3c^2}\left[3c^3 - \sqrt{a^2+c^2}\,(2c^2-a^2) - (a^2-c^2)^{3/2}\right]$$

$$= \frac{2\pi\gamma\rho}{3c^2}\left[3c^3 - \sqrt{a^2+c^2}\,(2c^2-a^2) - (a^2-c^2)^{3/2}\right]$$

But these two values of attraction on P must be equal if there is to be no attraction at P.

$$a^3 - c^3 - (a^2-c^2)^{3/2} = 3c^3 - \sqrt{a^2+c^2}\,(2c^2-a^2) - (a^2-c^2)^{3/2}$$

$$\Rightarrow \quad a^3 - 4c^3 = -\sqrt{a^2+c^2}\,(2c^2-a^2)$$

$$\Rightarrow \quad 4c^3 - a^3 = \sqrt{a^2+c^2}\,(2c^2-a^2)$$

$$\Rightarrow \quad (4c^3-a^3)^2 = (a^2+c^2)(2c^2-a^2)^2$$

$$\Rightarrow \quad 16c^6 - 8a^3c^3 + a^6 = (a^2+c^2)(4c^4 - 4a^2c^2 + a^4)$$

$$\Rightarrow \quad 16c^6 - 8a^3c^3 + a^6 = 4c^4a^2 - 4a^4c^2 + a^6 + 4c^6 - 4a^2c^4 + a^4c^2$$

$$\Rightarrow \quad 12c^6 - 8a^3c^3 = -3a^4c^2$$

$$\Rightarrow \quad 12c^4 - 8a^3c + 3a^4 = 0$$

10. Show that the attraction of a solid hemisphere at the centre of its plane base is $\frac{3}{2}\gamma\frac{M}{a^2}$ where M is the mass, and a is the radius.

Solution: Let O be the centre of the hemisphere of radius a and mass M. If ρ is the density of the hemisphere, then

$$M = \frac{2}{3}\pi a^3 \rho$$

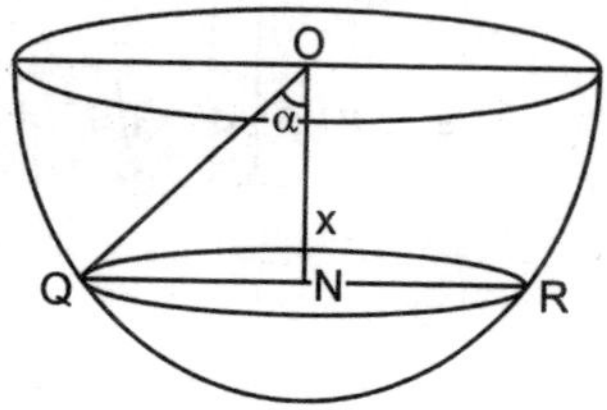

We consider an elementary disc QNR at a distance x from centre O and of thickness δx.

If $\angle QON = \alpha$, then

$$\cos\alpha = \frac{ON}{OQ} = \frac{x}{a}$$

Attraction of this elementary disc, at the centre O

$$= 2\pi\gamma\delta x\rho\,(1-\cos\alpha)$$

$$= 2\pi\gamma\delta x\rho\left(1-\frac{x}{a}\right)$$

Hence the attraction of the whole hemisphere, at the centre O

$$= 2\pi\gamma\rho\int_0^a\left(1-\frac{x}{a}\right)dx$$

$$= 2\pi\gamma\rho\left[x-\frac{x^2}{2a}\right]_0^a$$

$$= 2\pi\gamma\rho\left[a-\frac{a}{2}\right]$$

$$= \pi\gamma\rho a$$

Also mass of the hemisphere $= M = \frac{3}{2}\pi a^3\rho$

So required attraction $= \dfrac{\pi\gamma\rho\, 3M}{2\pi a^3}$

$$= \frac{3}{2}\gamma\frac{M}{a^2}$$

11. A solid uniform hemisphere is of mass M and radius a. Prove that its attraction at any point P of its axis on the convex side of the curved surface is equal to

$$\frac{\gamma M}{r^2}\left(1+\frac{R^3+2r^3-3r^2R}{a^3}\right)$$

Where r and R are the distances of P from the centre and rim of the base.

Solution: Let O be the centre of the hemisphere of radius a and mass M. If ρ be the density of the hemisphere then

$$M = \frac{2}{3}\pi a^3 \rho$$

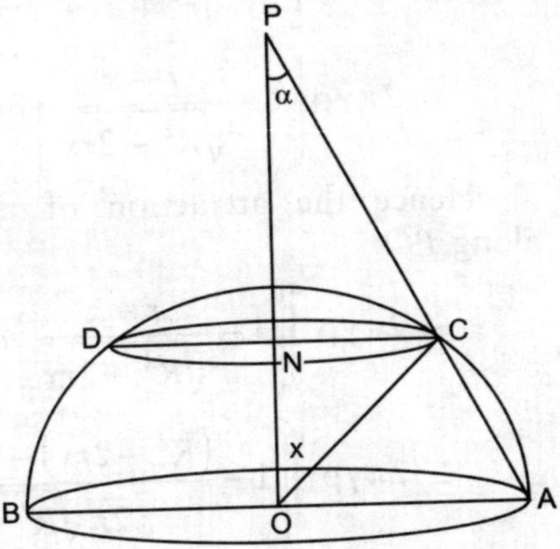

If P be the point on the axis of the hemisphere and on the convex side of the curved surface such that $OP = r$ and $AP = R$.

From ΔAOP we have

$$AP^2 = OA^2 + OP^2$$
$$R^2 = a^2 + r^2$$

We divide the hemisphere into a large number of elementary discs and let CD be one of such disc whose distance from the centre O is x, the thickness being δx.

Let $\angle CPN = \alpha$

In ΔCPN $\quad \cos\alpha = \dfrac{PN}{PC} = \dfrac{PN}{\sqrt{PN^2 + CN^2}}$

$$PN = OP - ON = r - x$$

Also $\quad OC^2 = ON^2 + CN^2$

$$OC^2 - ON^2 = CN^2$$
$$a^2 - x^2 = CN^2$$

Hence $\cos\alpha = \dfrac{r - x}{\sqrt{(r-x)^2 + a^2 - x^2}}$

Attraction of the elementary disc CND at P, along PN

$$= 2\pi\gamma\rho\delta x\,(1 - \cos\alpha)$$

$$= 2\pi\gamma\rho\left[1 - \frac{r-x}{\sqrt{(r-x)^2 + a^2 - x^2}}\right]\delta x$$

$$= 2\pi\gamma\rho\left[1 - \frac{r-x}{\sqrt{r^2 + a^2 - 2rx}}\right]\delta x$$

$$= 2\pi\gamma\rho\left[1 - \frac{r-x}{\sqrt{R^2 - 2rx}}\right]\delta x$$

Hence the attraction of the whole hemisphere at P along PO

$$= 2\pi\gamma\rho\int_0^a\left[1 - \frac{r-x}{\sqrt{R^2 - 2rx}}\right]dx$$

$$= 2\pi\gamma\rho\int_0^a\left[1 - \frac{(R^2 - 2rx) - (R^2 - 2r^2)}{2r\sqrt{R^2 - 2rx}}\right]dx$$

$$= 2\pi\gamma\rho\int_0^a\left[1 - \frac{1}{2r}\sqrt{R^2 - 2rx} + \frac{R^2 - 2r^2}{2r}\frac{1}{\sqrt{R^2 - 2rx}}\right]\delta x$$

$$= 2\pi\gamma\rho\left[x + \frac{1}{6r^2}(R^2 - 2rx)^{3/2} - \frac{R^2 - 2r^2}{2r^2}\sqrt{R^2 - 2rx}\right]_0^a$$

$$= 2\pi\gamma\rho\left[a + \frac{1}{6r^2}(R^2 - 2ar)^{3/2} - \frac{R^2 - 2r^2}{2r^2}\sqrt{R^2 - 2ar}\right.$$
$$\left. - \left\{\frac{R^3}{6r^2} - \frac{R^2(R^2 - 2r^2)}{2r^2}\right\}\right]$$

$$= 2\pi\gamma\rho\left[a + \frac{1}{6r^2}(a^2 + r^2 - 2ar)^{3/2} - \frac{R^3}{6r^2}\right.$$
$$\left. - \frac{R^2 - 2r^2}{2r^2}\sqrt{a^2 + r^2 - 2ar} + \frac{R(R^2 - 2r^2)}{2r^2}\right]$$

$$= 2\pi\gamma\rho\left[a + \frac{(r-a)^3}{6r^2} - \frac{R^3}{6r^2} - \frac{(R^2 - 2r^2)}{2r^2}(r-a)\right.$$
$$\left. + \frac{R}{2r^2}(R^2 - 2r^2)\right]$$

$$= \frac{2\pi\gamma\rho}{6r^2}\left[6ar^2 + (r-a)^3 - R^3 - 3\left(R^2 - 2r^2\right)(r-a) + 3R\left(R^2 - 2r^2\right)\right]$$

$$= \frac{\pi\gamma\rho}{3r^2}\left[6ar^2 + r^3 - 3r^2a + 3ra^2 - a^3 - R^3 - 3\left(R^2r - R^2a - 2r^3 + 2r^2a\right) + 3\left(R^3 - 2Rr^2\right)\right]$$

$$= \frac{\pi\gamma\rho}{3r^2}\left[-3r^2a + 7r^3 + 3ra^2 - a^3 + 2R^3 - 3R^2r + 3R^2a - 6Rr^2\right]$$

$$= \frac{\pi\gamma\rho}{3r^2}\left[3a\left(R^2 - r^2\right) - a^3 + 4r^3 - 3r\left(R^2 - r^2\right) + 3ra^2 + 2R^3 - 6Rr^2\right]$$

$$= \frac{\pi\gamma\rho}{3r^2}\left[3a^3 - a^3 + 4r^3 - 3ra^2 + 3ra^2 + 2R^3 - 6Rr^2\right]$$

$$= \frac{\pi\gamma\rho}{3r^2}\left[2a^3 + 4r^3 + 2R^3 - 6Rr^2\right]$$

$$= \frac{2\pi\gamma\rho}{3r^2}\left[a^3 + 2r^3 + R^3 - 3r^2R\right]$$

$$= \frac{2\pi\gamma\rho a^3}{3r^2}\left[1 + \frac{R^3 + 2r^3 - 3r^2R}{a^3}\right]$$

$$= \frac{\gamma M}{r^2}\left(1 + \frac{R^3 + 2r^3 - 3r^2R}{a^3}\right)$$

12. A uniform solid of density ρ, is in the form of finite portion of a paraboloid of revolution of latus rectum $4a$, cutoff by a plane perpendicular to the axis at a distance $2a$ from the vertex. Prove that the attraction at the centre of the circular end is

$$4\pi\gamma\rho a\left[\sqrt{2} - \log\left(1 + \sqrt{2}\right)\right]$$

Solution: The paraboloid of latus rectum $4a$ is generated by the revolution of the parabola $y^2 = 4ax$ about x-axis. Let AMB be a plane at a distance $2a$ from the ver x.

We consider an elementary disc CND perpendicular to the axis of the paraboloid at a distance x from the vertex O and of thickness δx.

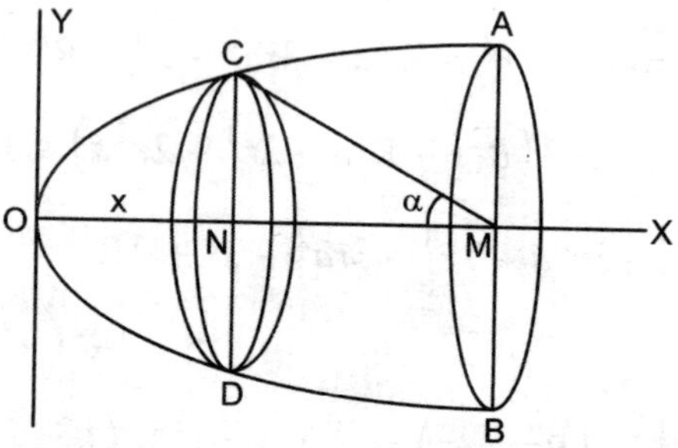

Let $\angle CMN = \alpha$, then $\cos\alpha = \dfrac{MN}{CM} = \dfrac{MN}{\sqrt{CN^2 + NM^2}}$

Since C lies on the parabola $y^2 = 4ax$

$$CN^2 = 4ax$$

Also $\quad MN = OM - ON = 2a - x$

Hence $\quad \cos\alpha = \dfrac{2a - x}{\sqrt{4ax + (2a - x)^2}}$

$$= \frac{2a - x}{\sqrt{4a^2 + x^2}}$$

Attraction of the elementary disc CND at M

$$= 2\pi\gamma\rho\delta x\,(1 - \cos\alpha)$$

$$= 2\pi\gamma\rho\left[1 - \frac{2a - x}{\sqrt{4a^2 + x^2}}\right]dx$$

Hence attraction of the given solid at M

$$= \int_0^{2a} 2\pi\gamma\rho\left[1 - \frac{2a - x}{\sqrt{4a^2 + x^2}}\right]dx$$

$$= 2\pi\gamma\rho\int_0^{2a}\left[1 - \frac{2a}{\sqrt{4a^2 + x^2}} + \frac{x}{\sqrt{4a^2 + x^2}}\right]dx$$

$$= 2\pi\gamma\rho\left[x - 2a\log\left(x + \sqrt{4a^2 + x^2}\right) + \sqrt{4a^2 + x^2}\right]_0^{2a}$$

$$= 2\pi\gamma\rho\left[2a - 2a\log\left(2a + 2\sqrt{2}a\right) + 2\sqrt{2}a - 2a + 2a\log 2a\right]$$

$$= 4\pi\gamma\rho a\left[\sqrt{2} - \log\frac{2\left(1+\sqrt{2}\right)a}{2a}\right]$$

$$= 4\pi\gamma\rho a\left[\sqrt{2} - \log\left(1+\sqrt{2}\right)\right]$$

13. A portion of a uniform solid paraboloid of revolution is cut off by a plane at right angles to the axis of x. Prove that the attraction at the focus will be zero, when $\sin\left(\frac{1}{2}PSX\right) = \frac{1}{\sqrt{e}}$, P being the point of the rim.

Solution: Let the paraboloid be generated by the revolution of $y^2 = 4ax$ about the x-axis and it being cut by the plane $x = b$.

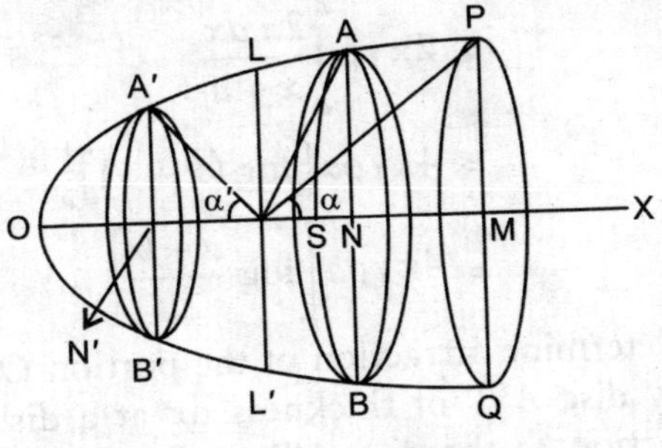

We have to find the attraction at S and the condition when it is zero.

The attraction at S will be the difference of attractions due to two portions namely $LPQL'$ and OLL'.

To determine attraction due to the portion $LPQL'$, we consider an elementary disc AB of thickness δx at a, distance x from O.

Let $\angle ASN = \alpha$, $ON = x$

In $\Delta ASN \quad \cos\alpha = \dfrac{SN}{AS} = \dfrac{ON - OS}{\sqrt{SN^2 + AN^2}}$

$$= \frac{x-a}{\sqrt{(x-a)^2 + AN^2}}$$

Since A lies on $y^2 = 4ax$

$$AN^2 = 4ax$$

Hence $\quad \cos\alpha = \dfrac{x-a}{\sqrt{(x-a)^2 + 4ax}} = \dfrac{x-a}{x+a}$

Attraction of the disc at S

$$= 2\pi\gamma\rho\delta x\,(1 - \cos\alpha)$$

$$= 2\pi\gamma\rho\delta x\left[1 - \frac{x-a}{x+a}\right]$$

$$= 2\gamma\rho\delta x\,\frac{2a}{x+a}$$

Hence attraction at S, due to the portion $\angle PQL'$

$$= 2\pi\gamma\rho\int_a^b \frac{2a\,dx}{x+a}$$

$$= 4\pi\gamma\rho a\Big[\log(x+a)\Big]_a^b$$

$$= 4\pi\gamma\rho a\left[\log\frac{a+b}{2a}\right] \qquad \text{... (1)}$$

Now to determine attraction of the portion OLL', we take an elementary disc $A'B'$ of thickness dx at a distance x from O, then attraction of the disc $A'B'$ at S

$$= 2\pi\gamma\rho\delta x\,(1 - \cos\alpha')$$

where $\angle ASO = \alpha'$

In $\Delta A'SN' \cos\alpha' = \dfrac{N'S}{A'S}$

$$N'S = OS - ON' = a - x$$

Since A' lies on the parabola

$$A'N^2 = 4ax'$$

$$A'S^2 = A'N'^2 + N'S^2$$
$$= 4ax + (a - x)^2$$
$$= (a + x)^2$$
$$A'S = a + x$$

Hence $\quad \cos \alpha' = \dfrac{a - x}{a + x}$

Hence attraction of the disc $A'B'$ at S

$$= 2\pi\gamma\rho\delta x \left(1 - \frac{a - x}{a + x}\right)$$

Thus attraction of the portion LOL' at S

$$= 2\pi\gamma\rho \int_0^a \frac{2x\, dx}{a + x}$$
$$= 4\pi\gamma\rho \int_0^a \left(1 - \frac{a}{a + x}\right) dx$$
$$= 4\pi\gamma\rho \left[x - a \log (a + x)\right]_0^a$$
$$= 4\pi\gamma\rho \left[a - a \log 2a + a \log a\right]$$
$$= 4\pi\gamma\rho a \left[\log \frac{ae}{2a}\right] \qquad \dots (2)$$

The attraction at S will be zero if (1) and (2) are equal.

i.e. if $\quad 4\pi\gamma\rho a \log \dfrac{a + b}{2a} = 4\pi\gamma\rho a \log \dfrac{ae}{2a}$

$\Rightarrow \quad a + b = ae \qquad \dots (3)$

Now $\quad 2 \sin^2\left(\dfrac{1}{2} PSX\right) = 1 - \cos (PSX)$

$$= 1 - \frac{SM}{PS}$$
$$= 1 - \frac{b - a}{b + a}$$
$$= \frac{2a}{a + b} = \frac{2a}{ae}$$

$$= \frac{2}{e} \text{ from (3)}$$

Hence $$\sin\left(\frac{1}{2} PSX\right) = \frac{1}{\sqrt{e}}$$

14. Prove that of the uniform density of a circular disc at any point distant r from the centre is λr, then the attraction at a point on the axis at a distance d is

$$\pi\gamma\lambda d\left[\log\frac{\sqrt{a^2+d^2}+a}{\sqrt{a^2+d^2}-a} - \frac{2a}{\sqrt{a^2+d^2}}\right]$$

Solution: We consider an elementary disc of radius x and width δx.

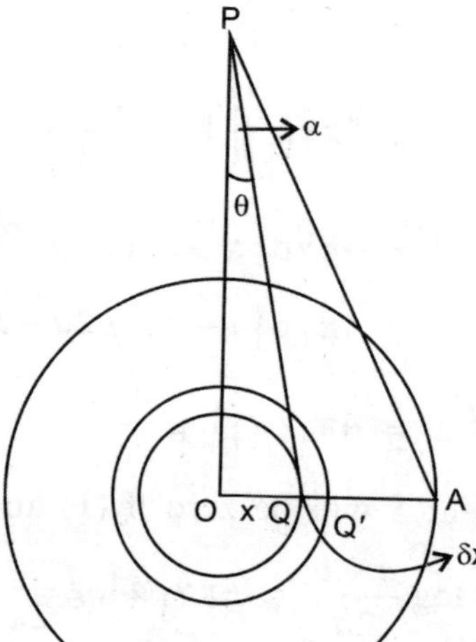

Let P be a point at a distance d from O on the axis. Let $\angle OPQ = \theta$, $\angle OPA = \alpha$, attraction at P due to the elementary ring $= \dfrac{\gamma\, 2\pi x\, d\delta x\, \lambda x}{PQ^2}$ along PQ

$$= \frac{\gamma 2\pi x\delta x\lambda x}{x^2+d^2}\cos\theta \text{ along the axis } OP$$

$$= \frac{2\pi\gamma\lambda x^2\delta x}{x^2+d^2}\frac{d}{\sqrt{x^2+d^2}}$$

Hence the attraction at P due to the whole disc

$$= 2\pi\gamma\lambda d \int_0^a \frac{x^2 dx}{\left(x^2 + d^2\right)^{3/2}}$$

Let $x = d \tan y$

$dx = d \sec^2 y dy$

Hence attraction

$$= 2\pi\gamma\lambda d \int_0^a \frac{d^2 \tan^2 y \, d \sec^2 y dy}{d^3 \sec^3 y}$$

$$= 2\pi\gamma\lambda d \int_0^a \frac{\sin^2 y}{\cos y} dy$$

$$= 2\pi\gamma\lambda d \int_0^a \frac{1 - \cos^2 y}{\cos y} dy$$

$$= 2\pi\gamma\lambda d \int_0^a (\sec y - \cos y) \, dy$$

$$= 2\pi\gamma\lambda d \left[\log(\sec y + \tan y) - \sin y\right]_0^a$$

$$= 2\pi\gamma\lambda d \left[\log\left(\sqrt{\frac{1 + x^2}{d^2}} + \frac{x}{d}\right) - \frac{x}{\sqrt{x^2 + d^2}}\right]_0^a$$

$$= 2\pi\gamma\lambda d \left[\log \frac{\sqrt{x^2 + d^2} + x}{d} - \frac{x}{\sqrt{x^2 + d^2}}\right]_0^a$$

$$= 2\pi\gamma\lambda d \left[\log \frac{\sqrt{a^2 + d^2} + a}{d} - \frac{a}{\sqrt{a^2 + d^2}}\right]$$

$$= \pi\gamma\lambda d \left[\log \frac{\left\{\sqrt{a^2 + d^2} + a\right\}^2}{d^2} - \frac{2a}{\sqrt{a^2 + d^2}}\right]$$

$$= \pi\gamma\lambda d\left[\log \frac{\left\{\sqrt{a^2+d^2}+a\right\}^2\left\{\sqrt{a^2+d^2}-a\right\}}{d^2\left\{\sqrt{a^2+d^2}-a\right\}} - \frac{2a}{\sqrt{a^2+d^2}}\right]$$

$$= \pi\gamma\lambda d\left[\log \frac{\sqrt{a^2+d^2}+a^2}{\sqrt{a^2+d^2}-a} - \frac{2a}{\sqrt{a^2+d^2}}\right]$$

15. Show that the attraction at the origin due to the homogeneous solid of density ρ bounded by the surface obtained by revolving one loop of the curve $r^2 = a^2 \cos^2 \theta$ about the initial line is $\frac{\pi\gamma\rho a}{3}$.

Solution: The equation of the revolving curve is $r^2 = a^2 \cos 2\theta$. We consider an elementary area $r\delta\theta\delta r$ at P.

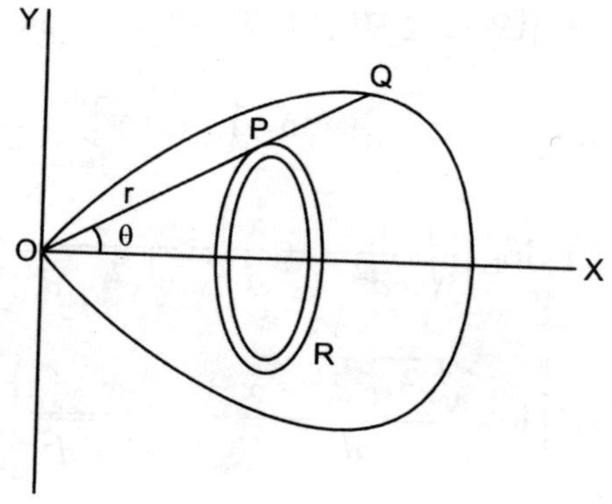

The mass of the ring generated by the revolution of this elementary area about the initial line $OX = \rho r\delta\theta\delta r\ 2\pi r \sin\theta$.

Attraction at O, due to a unit mass at P

$$= \frac{\gamma}{r^2} \text{ along } OP$$

$$= \frac{\gamma}{r^2} \cos\theta \text{ along } OX$$

Hence the attraction at O due to the ring

$$= \frac{\gamma}{r^2} \cos\theta\, \rho r \delta\theta \delta r\, 2\pi r \sin\theta \text{ along } OX$$

$$= 2\pi\gamma\rho \sin\theta \cos\theta\, \delta\theta \delta r \text{ along } OX$$

Therefore attraction at O, due to the whole solid

$$= 2\pi\gamma\rho \int_{\theta=0}^{\frac{\pi}{4}} \int_{r=0}^{a\sqrt{\cos^2\theta}} \sin\theta \cos\theta \, d\theta \, dr \text{ along } OX$$

$$= 2\pi\gamma\rho \int_0^{\frac{\pi}{4}} a\sqrt{\cos 2\theta} \sin\theta \cos\theta \, d\theta$$

$$= \pi\gamma\rho a \int_0^{\frac{\pi}{4}} \sqrt{\cos 2\theta} \sin 2\theta \, d\theta$$

$$= -\frac{\pi\gamma\rho a}{2} \frac{2}{3} \left[(\cos 2\theta)^{\frac{3}{2}} \right]_0^{\frac{\pi}{4}}$$

$$= -\frac{\pi\gamma\rho a}{3} [0 - 1]$$

$$= \frac{1}{3} \pi\gamma\rho a$$

16. A uniform circular lamina is divided into two segments by a chord which subtends an angle 2α ($\angle\, \pi$) at the centre. Prove that attraction at the centre of the circle due to the minor segment is $2\gamma\sigma\left[\log\tan\left(\frac{\pi}{2}+\frac{\alpha}{2}\right) - \sin\alpha\right]$, σ being the surface density of the lamina.

[L.N.M.U. 93H]

Solution: Let O be the centre of the circle and AB a chord dividing the circle into two segments, the minor one being ABC, whose attraction at O is to be determined. AB subtends an angle 2α at O. Let $\angle AOD = \alpha$, $\angle MOD = \theta$.

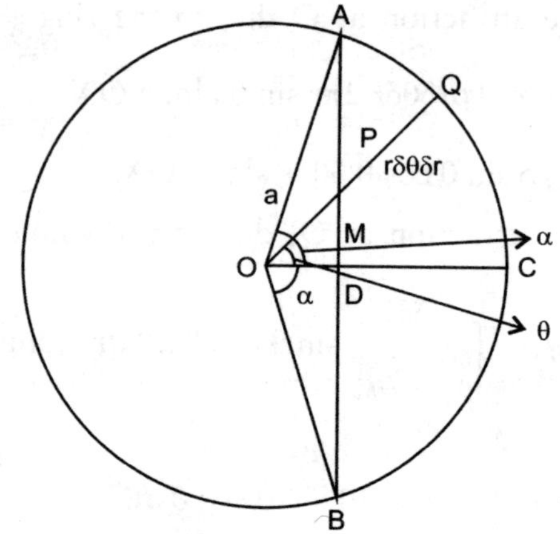

We consider a small element $r\delta\theta\delta r$ at P of the small segment ABC.

Mass of this element $= r\delta\theta\delta r\sigma$

Its attraction at O

$$= \frac{\gamma r\ \delta\theta\ \delta r\sigma}{r^2} \text{ along } OP$$

$$= \frac{\gamma\sigma\delta\theta\delta r}{r} \cos\theta \text{ along the central radius } OC.$$

Hence attraction of the minor segment ABC, at O

$$= \gamma\sigma \int_{-\alpha}^{\alpha} \int_{OM}^{OQ} \frac{\cos\theta}{r}\, d\theta\, dr$$

$$= 2\gamma\sigma \int_{0}^{\alpha} \int_{OM}^{OQ} \frac{\cos\theta}{r}\, d\theta\, dr$$

In ΔOAD $\cos\alpha = \dfrac{OD}{OA} = \dfrac{OD}{a}$

$$OD = a\cos\alpha$$

In ΔOMD $\cos\theta = \dfrac{OD}{OM}$

$$OM = OD\sec\theta = a\cos\alpha\sec\theta$$

Hence required attraction

$$= 2\gamma\sigma \int_0^{\alpha} \cos\theta \left[\log r\right]_{a\cos\alpha\sec\theta}^{a} d\theta$$

$$= 2\gamma\sigma \int_0^{\alpha} \cos\theta \log \frac{a}{(a\cos\alpha\sec\theta)} d\theta$$

$$= 2\gamma\sigma \int_0^{\alpha} \log(\sec\alpha\cos\theta)\cos\theta\, d\theta$$

$$= 2\gamma\sigma \left[\left\{\sin\theta \log(\sec\alpha\cos\theta)\right\}_0^{\alpha} - \int_0^{\alpha} \frac{\sin\theta}{\sec\alpha\cos\theta}(-\sec\alpha\sin\theta)\, d\theta\right]$$

$$= 2\gamma\sigma \left[0 + \int_0^{\alpha} \frac{\sin^2\theta}{\cos\theta} d\theta\right]$$

$$= 2\gamma\sigma \int_0^{\alpha} \frac{1-\cos^2\theta}{\cos\theta} d\theta$$

$$= 2\gamma\sigma \int_0^{\alpha} (\sec\theta - \cos\theta)\, d\theta$$

$$= 2\gamma\sigma \left[\log\tan\left(\frac{\pi}{4}+\frac{\theta}{2}\right) - \sin\theta\right]_0^{\alpha}$$

$$= 2\gamma\sigma \left[\log\tan\left(\frac{\pi}{4}+\frac{\alpha}{2}\right) - \sin\alpha\right]$$

17. Prove that a thin triangular lamina ABC of uniform surface density σ exerts at a point on the line through A perpendicular to the plane of the triangle and at a distance K from A an attraction the intensity of whose component perpendicular to the lamina is

$$\gamma\sigma\left[A - \sin^{-1}\frac{K\cos B}{\sqrt{K^2-p^2}} - \sin^{-1}\frac{K\cos C}{\sqrt{K^2+p^2}}\right]$$

where p is the perpendicular distance of A from BC.

Solution: From A we draw AD perpendicular to BC.

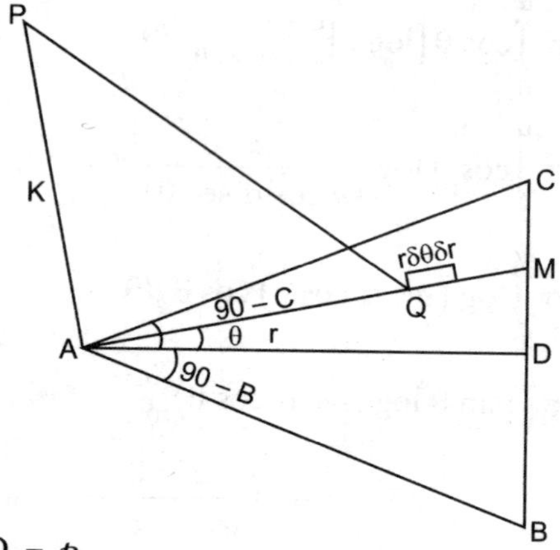

Given $AD = p$

We consider an element $r\delta\theta\delta r$ at Q referred to A as pole and AD as initial line.

Mass of this element $= \sigma r\delta\theta\delta r$

Attraction at P, due to this elementary mass

$$= \frac{\gamma\sigma r\delta\theta\delta r}{PQ^2} \text{ along } PQ$$

$$= \frac{\gamma\sigma r\delta\theta\delta r}{PQ^2} \cos\alpha \text{ along } PA$$

$$= \frac{\gamma\sigma r\delta\theta\delta r}{K^2 + r^2} \frac{K}{\sqrt{K^2 + r^2}} \text{ along } PA$$

Hence the total attraction at P along PA

$$= \gamma K\sigma \int_{-(90-B)}^{90-C} \int_{O}^{AM} \frac{rd\theta dr}{(K^2 + r^2)^{3/2}}$$

In ΔADM $\quad \cos\theta = \dfrac{AD}{AM} = \dfrac{p}{AM}$

$$AM = p \sec\theta$$

$$\text{Hence attraction} = \gamma K\sigma \int_{-(90-B)}^{90-C} \int_{O}^{p\sec\theta} \frac{rd\theta\, dr}{(K^2 + r^2)^{3/2}}$$

$$= \gamma K\sigma \int_{-(90-B)}^{90-C} \left[-\frac{1}{\sqrt{K^2 + r^2}} \right]_0^{p \sec\theta} d\theta$$

$$= \gamma K\sigma \int_{-(90-B)}^{90-C} \left[\frac{1}{K} - \frac{1}{\sqrt{K^2 + p^2 \sec^2\theta}} \right] d\theta$$

$$= \gamma\sigma \int_{-(90-B)}^{90-C} \left[1 - \frac{K\cos\theta}{\sqrt{K^2 + p^2 - K^2\sin^2\theta}} \right] d\theta$$

$$= \gamma\sigma \left[\theta - \sin^{-1} \frac{K\sin\theta}{\sqrt{K^2 + p^2}} \right]_{-(90-B)}^{90-C}$$

$$= \gamma\sigma \left[180 - B - C - \sin^{-1} \frac{K\cos C}{\sqrt{K^2 + p^2}} - \sin^{-1} \frac{K\cos B}{\sqrt{K^2 + p^2}} \right]$$

$$= \gamma\sigma \left[A - \sin^{-1} \frac{K\cos C}{\sqrt{K^2 + p^2}} - \sin^{-1} \frac{K\cos B}{\sqrt{K^2 + p^2}} \right]$$

18. Show that the attraction of a thin elliptic disc of uniform thickness K and uniform density ρ, at the focus is

$$2\pi\gamma K\rho \sqrt{\frac{a-b}{a+b}}$$

where a and b are its semi axes or $2\pi K\rho \dfrac{1-\sqrt{1-e^2}}{e}$ where e is the eccentricity.

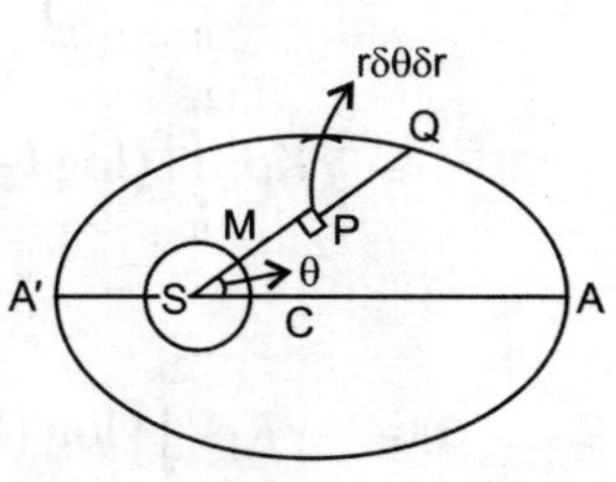

Solution: The polar equation of the ellipse referred to S as pole and SA as initial line is

$$\frac{l}{r} = 1 - e\cos\theta$$

We consider an elementary area $r\delta\theta\delta r$ at a distance r from the focus S. By symmetry the attraction acts along the major axis SA.

Attraction of the elementary area $r\delta\theta\delta r$ at S

$$= \frac{\gamma r\delta\theta\delta r\, K\rho}{r^2} \text{ along } SP$$

$$= \frac{\gamma r\delta\theta\delta r\, K\rho}{r^2} \cos\theta \text{ along } SA$$

Hence the attraction of the whole disc, at S

$$= \gamma K\rho \int_0^{2\pi} \int_0^{\frac{1}{1-e\cos\theta}} \frac{\cos\theta}{r}\, d\theta\, dr$$

On integrating w.r.t. r, we shall have $\log r$, which will be infintite for $r = 0$.

To get rid of this we draw a circle of radius λ about S, such that this circle lies entirely within the lamina i.e. $\lambda \angle SA'$

or $\lambda \angle CA' - CS$

or $\lambda \angle a - a \cdot e$

The attraction of this circle at the focus, its centre is zero.

The limit of r will now be from $SM = \lambda$ to $\dfrac{l}{1-e\cos\theta}$.

Hence the attraction of the disc at S

$$= \gamma K\rho \int_0^{2\pi} \int_\lambda^{\frac{l}{1-e\cos\theta}} \frac{\cos\theta}{r}\, d\theta\, dr$$

$$= \gamma K\rho \int_0^{2\pi} \left[\log \frac{l}{1-e\cos\theta} - \log\lambda\right] \cos\theta\, d\theta$$

$$= \gamma K\rho \int_0^{2\pi} \Big[(\log l - \log\lambda)\cos\theta - \{\log(1-e\cos\theta)\}\cos\theta\Big]\, d\theta$$

$$= -\gamma K\rho \int_0^{2\pi} \left[\log(1-e\cos\theta)\right]\cos\theta\, d\theta$$

$$= -\gamma K\rho \left[\{\sin\theta \log(1-e\cos\theta)\}_0^{2\pi} - \int_0^{2\pi} \frac{e\sin^2\theta}{1-e\cos\theta}\, d\theta\right]$$

$$= \gamma K\rho \int_0^{2\pi} \frac{e - e\cos^2\theta}{1 - e\cos\theta}\, d\theta$$

$$= \gamma K\rho \int_0^{2\pi} \left[\cos\theta + \frac{1}{e} - \frac{1-e^2}{e} \cdot \frac{1}{1 - e\cos\theta}\right] d\theta$$

$$= \gamma K\rho \left[0 + \frac{2\pi}{e} - \frac{1-e^2}{e} \frac{2\pi}{\sqrt{1-e^2}}\right]$$

$$= \frac{\gamma K\rho 2\pi}{e}\left[1 - \sqrt{1-e^2}\right]$$

$$= \frac{\gamma K\rho 2\pi}{e}\left[1 - \frac{b}{a}\right] \left(\because e^2 = 1 - \frac{b^2}{a^2}\right)$$

$$= \frac{2\pi\gamma K\rho a}{\sqrt{a^2 - b^2}} \frac{a-b}{a}$$

$$= 2\pi\gamma K\rho \sqrt{\frac{a-b}{a+b}}$$

19. Show that the attraction of a circular disc of radius a, whose law of attraction is

$$\frac{\mu}{(\text{distance})^3}, \text{ is } \frac{M\mu}{c\left(c^2 - a^2\right)} \text{ or } \frac{M\mu c}{a^2\left(a^2 - c^2\right)}$$

according as $c >$ or $< a$, where M is the mass of the disc and c the distance from the centre of the attracted point which is in the plane of the disc.

Solution: Let O be the centre of the disc and P the attracted point, so that $OP = c$. From O we draw ON perpendicular to AB on a line through P which intersects the disc at A and B.

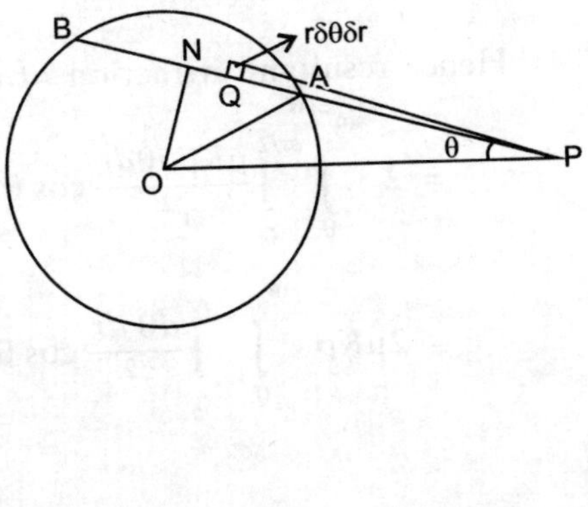

Case I: When $c > a$ i.e. P is an external point.

We consider an elementary area $r\delta\theta\delta r$ at Q, a point on PAB, referred to P as pole and PO as initial line. By symmetry the resultant attraction of the disc is along PO.

Let $$PA = r_1,\ PB = r_2$$

$$r_1 = PA = PN - AN$$

$$= PN - \sqrt{OA^2 - ON^2}$$

In ΔOPN $$\sin\theta = \frac{ON}{OP} = \frac{ON}{c}$$

$$ON = c\sin\theta$$

$$\cos\theta = \frac{PN}{OP} = \frac{PN}{c}$$

$$PN = c\cos\theta$$

Hence $$PA = r_1 = c\cos\theta - \sqrt{a^2 - c^2\sin^2\theta}$$

Also $$r_2 = PB = PN + NB$$

$$= c\cos\theta + AN$$

$$= c\cos\theta + \sqrt{OA^2 - ON^2}$$

$$= c\cos\theta + \sqrt{a^2 - c^2\sin^2\theta}$$

Attraction of the elementary element $r\delta\theta\delta rK\rho$ is $\dfrac{\mu K\rho r\delta\theta\delta r}{r^3}$ along PQ according to given law.

Hence attraction along PO

$$= \frac{\mu K\rho\,\delta\theta\delta r}{r^2}\cos\theta$$

Hence resultant attraction of the disc along PO is

$$= 2\int_0^{\sin^{-1}\frac{a}{c}}\int_{r_1}^{r_2}\frac{\mu K\rho\, d\theta dr}{r^2}\cos\theta$$

$$= 2\mu K\rho\int_0^{\sin^{-1}\frac{a}{c}}\int_{r_1}^{r_2}\frac{d\theta\, dr}{r^2}\cos\theta$$

$$= 2\mu K\rho \int_0^{\sin^{-1}\frac{a}{c}} \cos\theta \left[-\frac{1}{r}\right]_{r_1}^{r_2} d\theta$$

$$= 2\mu K\rho \int_0^{\sin^{-1}\frac{a}{c}} \left[\frac{1}{r_1} - \frac{1}{r_2}\right] \cos\theta \, d\theta$$

$$= 2\mu K\rho \int_0^{\sin^{-1}\frac{a}{c}} \left[\frac{1}{c\cos\theta - \sqrt{a^2 - c^2\sin^2\theta}} - \frac{1}{c\cos\theta + \sqrt{a^2 - c^2\sin^2\theta}}\right] \cos d\theta$$

$$= 2\mu K\rho \int_0^{\sin^{-1}\frac{a}{c}} \frac{2\sqrt{a^2 - c^2\sin^2\theta}}{c^2 - a^2} \cos\theta \, d\theta$$

$$= 4\mu K\rho \int_0^{\sin^{-1}\frac{a}{c}} \frac{\sqrt{a^2 - c^2\sin^2\theta}}{c^2 - a^2} \cos\theta \, d\theta$$

Putting $c \sin\theta = a \sin\phi$

$\therefore c\cos\theta \, d\theta = a\cos\phi \, d\phi$

When $\theta = \sin^{-1}\dfrac{a}{c}$

then $\sin\phi = 1$ i.e. $\phi = \dfrac{\pi}{2}$

When $\theta = 0$, $\phi = \dfrac{\pi}{2}$

Hence required attraction

$$= \frac{4\mu K\rho}{c^2 - a^2} \int_0^{\frac{\pi}{2}} \frac{a\cos\phi \, a\cos\phi}{c} d\phi$$

$$= \frac{4\mu K\rho}{c^2 - a^2} \frac{a^2}{c} \int_0^{\frac{\pi}{2}} \cos^2\phi \, d\phi$$

$$= \frac{4\mu K\rho\, a^2}{c\left(c^2 - a^2\right)} \frac{1}{2} \frac{\pi}{2}$$

$$= \frac{\mu K\rho\, a^2}{c\left(c^2 - a^2\right)} = \frac{M\mu}{c\left(c^2 - a^2\right)}$$

Since $M = \pi a^2 K\rho$

Case II: When $c < a$ i.e. P is an internal point.

In this case resultant attraction of the disc

$$= 2\mu K\rho \int_o^{\pi} \int_0^{r_2} \frac{1}{r^2} \cos\theta \, d\theta dr$$

where $PB = r_2 = c\cos\theta + \sqrt{a^2 - c^2\sin^2\theta}$

In the above integral we get the factor $\frac{1}{r}$ which for $r = 0$ becomes meaningless. To avoid this we take a small circle of radius $\lambda < (a - c)$ with P as centre and observe that the attraction of this circle at P is zero by symmetry.

Therefore the required attraction

$$= 2\mu K\rho \int_0^{\pi} \int_{\lambda}^{r_2} \frac{\cos\theta}{r^2} \, d\theta \, dr$$

$$= 2\mu K\rho \int_0^{\pi} \left[-\frac{1}{r^2}\right]_{\lambda}^{r_2} \cos\theta \, d\theta$$

$$= 2\mu K\rho \int_0^{\pi} \left[\frac{1}{\lambda} - \frac{1}{c\cos\theta + \sqrt{a^2 - c^2\sin^2\theta}}\right] \cos\theta \, d\theta$$

$$= 2\mu K\rho \left[\{\sin\theta\}_0^{\pi} - \int_0^{\pi} \frac{\cos\theta \, d\theta}{c\cos\theta + \sqrt{a^2 - c^2\sin^2\theta}}\right]$$

$$= -2\mu K\rho \int_0^{\pi} \frac{\cos\theta \, d\theta \left[c\cos\theta - \sqrt{a^2 - c^2\sin^2\theta}\right]}{c^2\cos^2\theta - \left(a^2 - c^2\sin^2\theta\right)}$$

$$= -2\mu K\rho \int_0^{\pi} \frac{\left[c\cos\theta - \sqrt{a^2 - c^2\sin^2\theta}\right]}{a^2 - c^2} \cos\theta \, d\theta$$

$$= \frac{2\mu K\rho}{a^2 - c^2} \int_0^{\pi} \left[c\cos^2\theta - \sqrt{a^2 - c^2\sin^2\theta}\cos\theta \right] d\theta$$

Let $I_1 = \int_0^{\pi} \sqrt{a^2 - c^2\sin^2\theta}\cos\theta\, d\theta$

Let $y = c\sin\theta$

$dy = c\cos\theta\, d\theta$

$$I_1 = \int_0^{\pi} \sqrt{a^2 - y^2}\,\frac{dy}{c}$$

$$= \frac{1}{c}\left[\frac{y\sqrt{a^2 - y^2}}{2} + \frac{a^2}{2}\sin^{-1}\frac{y}{a} \right]_0^{\pi}$$

$$= \frac{1}{2c}\left[c\sin\theta\sqrt{a^2 - c^2\sin^2\theta} + a^2\sin^{-1}\frac{c\sin\theta}{a} \right]_0^{\pi}$$

$= 0$

Hence required attraction

$$= \frac{4\mu K\rho c}{a^2 - c^2} \int_0^{\frac{\pi}{2}} \cos^2\theta\, d\theta$$

$$= \frac{4\mu K\rho c}{a^2 - c^2} \cdot \frac{1}{2} \cdot \frac{\pi}{2} = \frac{\mu K\rho c\pi}{a^2 - c^2}$$

$$= \frac{Mc\mu}{a^2\left(a^2 - c^2\right)} \quad \text{since } M = \pi a^2 K\rho$$

20. A lamina bounded internally and externally by concentric circles of radii b and a respectively is formed of material attraction according to the law (distance)$^{-5}$. Show that the resultant attraction vanishes at a point distance

$$a^{\frac{1}{3}} b^{\frac{1}{3}} \sqrt{\frac{a^{\frac{4}{3}} + b^{\frac{4}{3}}}{a^{\frac{2}{3}} - b^{\frac{2}{3}}}} \text{ from its centre.}$$

Solution: To find the attraction of the annulus bounded by two concentric circles we will first find the attraction of the complete disc at an external and an internal point according to given law.

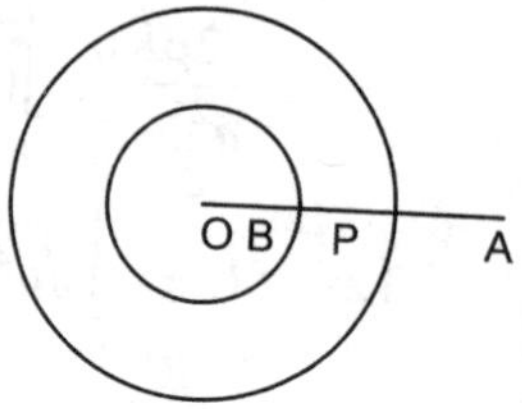

We assume that the resultant attraction vanishes at a point P where $OP = c$.

Case I: We first find the attraction at an external point P.

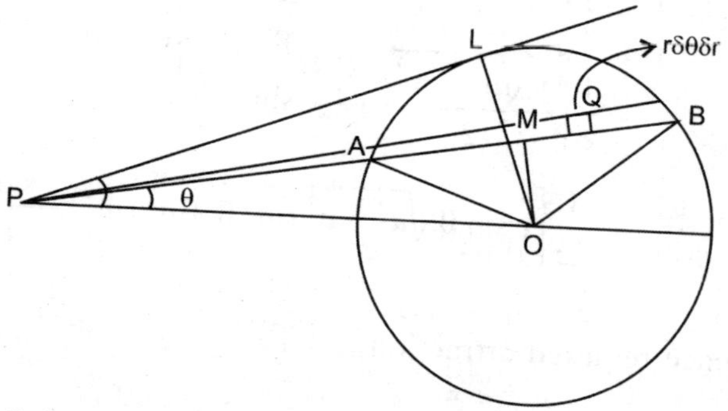

Let O be the centre of the disc and P the attracted point so that $OP = c$. From O we draw OM perpendicular to AB on a line through P which intersects the disc at A and B.

We consider an elementary area $r\delta\theta\delta r$ at Q, a point on PAB referred to P as pole and PO as initial line. By symmetry the resultant attraction of the disc is along PO.

Let $$PA = r_1, \; PB = r_2$$

$$r_1 = PA = PM - AM = PM - \sqrt{OA^2 - OM^2}$$

In ΔOPM $$\sin\theta = \frac{OM}{OP} = \frac{OM}{c}, \; \cos\theta = \frac{PM}{OP} = \frac{PM}{c}$$

$$OM = c\sin\theta, \; PM = c\cos\theta$$

Hence $$PA = r_1 = c\cos\theta - \sqrt{a^2 - c^2\sin^2\theta}$$

$$PB = r_2 = PM + MB = PM + AM$$

$$= c\cos\theta + \sqrt{a^2 - c^2\sin^2\theta}$$

Attraction of the elementary element $r\delta\theta\delta r K\rho$ is $\dfrac{\mu K\rho r\delta\theta\delta r}{r^5}$ along PQ according to given law.

Hence attraction along $PO = \dfrac{\mu K\rho\delta\theta\delta r}{r^4}\cos\theta$

Hence the total attraction of the disc along PO

$$= \mu K\rho \int_{0=-\alpha}^{\alpha} \int_{r=PA=r_1}^{PB=r_2} \frac{\cos\theta \, d\theta \, dr}{r^4}$$

where r_1, r_2 are the roots of the equation

$$r^2 - 2cr\cos\theta + c^2 = a^2$$

Hence $r_1 + r_2 = 2c\cos\theta$, $r_1 r_2 = c^2 - a^2$

Now
$$r_2 - r_1 = \sqrt{4c^2\cos^2\theta - 4\left(c^2 - a^2\right)}$$
$$= 2\sqrt{a^2 - c^2\sin^2\theta}$$

and
$$r_1^2 + r_1 r_2 + r_2^2 = \left(r_1 + r_2\right)^2 - r_1 r_2$$
$$= 4c^2\cos^2\theta - \left(c^2 - a^2\right)$$
$$= 3c^2 + a^2 - 4c^2\sin^2\theta$$

Hence the required attraction

$$= \mu K\rho \int_{-\alpha}^{\alpha} \left[-\frac{1}{3r^3}\right]_{r_1}^{r_2} \cos\theta \, d\theta$$

$$= \frac{\mu K\rho}{3} \int_{-\alpha}^{\alpha} \left(\frac{1}{r_1^3} - \frac{1}{r_2^3}\right) \cos\theta \, d\theta$$

$$= \frac{2\mu K\rho}{3} \int_0^{\alpha} \frac{r_2^2 - r_1^3}{r_1^3 \, r_2^3} \cos\theta \, d\theta$$

($\because$ r_1 and r_2 are even functions of θ)

$$= \frac{2\mu K\rho}{3} \int_0^{\alpha} \frac{2\sqrt{a^2 - c^2\sin^2\theta}\left(3c^2 + a^2 - 4c^2\sin^2\theta\right) d\theta \cos\theta \, d\theta}{\left(c^2 - a^2\right)^3}$$

$$= \frac{4\mu K\rho}{3\left(c^2 - a^2\right)^3} \int_0^\alpha \sqrt{a^2 - c^2 \sin^2\theta}\left(3c^2 + a^2 - 4c^2\sin^2\theta\right)\cos\theta\, d\theta$$

Let $c \sin\theta = a \sin\phi$

$$c \cos\theta\, d\theta = a \cos\phi\, d\phi$$

When $\theta = \alpha$, $\sin\theta = \sin\alpha = \frac{a}{c}$

$$\sin\phi = 1$$

$$\phi = \frac{\pi}{2}$$

$$\theta = 0, \phi = 0$$

Hence required attraction

$$= \frac{4\mu K\rho}{3\left(c^2 - a^2\right)^3} \int_0^{\frac{\pi}{2}} \frac{c^2\cos^2\phi}{c}\left(3c^2 + a^2 - 4a^2\sin^2\phi\right) d\phi$$

$$= \frac{4\mu K\rho}{3\left(c^2 - a^2\right)^3} \frac{a^2}{c} \int_0^{\frac{\pi}{2}} \left\{\left(3c^2 + a^2\right)\cos^2\phi - 4a^2\sin^2\phi\cos^2\phi\right\} d\phi$$

$$= \frac{4\mu K\rho}{3\left(c^2 - a^2\right)^3} \frac{a^2}{c}\left[\left(3c^2 + a^2\right)\frac{1}{2}\frac{\pi}{2} - 4a^2\frac{1}{4.2}\frac{\pi}{2}\right]$$

$$= \frac{4\mu K\rho a^2}{3c\left(c^2 - a^2\right)^3}\frac{\pi}{4}\left[3c^2 + a^2 - a^2\right]$$

$$= \frac{\mu K\rho a^2\pi}{3c\left(c^2 - a^2\right)^3} 3c^2$$

$$= \frac{\mu K\rho a^2\pi c}{\left(c^2 - a^2\right)^3} \qquad \dots (1)$$

From the figure, point P is external with respect to circular lamina of radius b and hence replacing a by b in (1) we get attraction as

$$\frac{\mu K \rho b^2 \pi c}{\left(c^2 - b^2\right)^3} \quad \text{... (2)}$$

Case II: Now we find the attraction at internal point P.

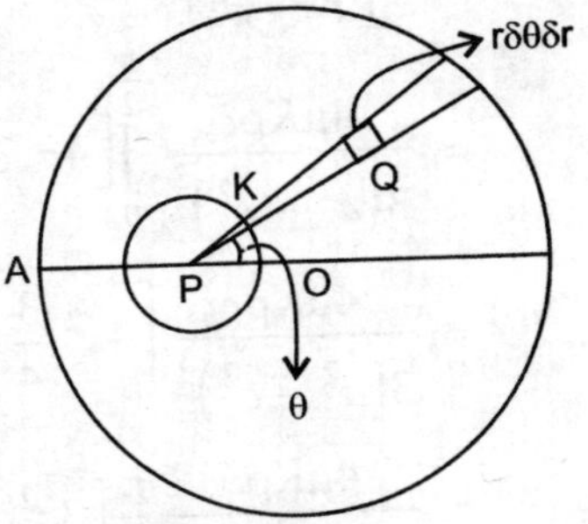

In this case resultant attraction of the disc

$$= \mu K \rho \int_0^{\pi} \int_0^{r_2} \frac{\cos\theta}{r^4}\, d\theta\, dr$$

In the above integral we get the factor $\frac{1}{r}$ which for $r = 0$ becomes meaningless. To avoid this we take a small circle of radius $r < a - c$ with P as centre and deserve that the attraction of this circle at P is zero by symmetry.

Hence the required attraction

$$= \mu K \rho \int_0^{\pi} \int_{-r_1}^{r_2} \frac{\cos\theta}{r^4}\, d\theta\, dr$$

$$= \mu K \rho \int_0^{\pi} \left[-\frac{1}{3r^3}\right]_{-r_1}^{r_2} \cos\theta\, d\theta$$

$$= \frac{-\mu K \rho}{3} \int_0^{\pi} \left[\frac{1}{r_1^3} + \frac{1}{r_2^3}\right] \cos\theta\, d\theta$$

$$= \frac{-\mu K \rho}{3} \int_0^{\pi} \frac{r_1^3 + r_2^3}{r_1^3\, r_2^3} \cos\theta\, d\theta$$

Again $r_1 + r_2 = 2c\cos\theta$,

$$r_1 r_2 = -(a^2 - c^2)$$

Now $r_1^2 - r_1 r_2 + r_2^2 = \left(r_1 + r_2\right)^2 - 3r_1 r_2$

$$= 4c^2\cos^2\theta + 3\left(a^2 - c^2\right)$$

Thus required attraction

$$= \frac{-\mu K\rho}{3}\int_0^{\pi}\frac{2c\cos\theta\left[4c^2\cos^2\theta+3\left(a^2-c^2\right)\right]}{-\left(a^2-c^2\right)^3}\cos\theta\, d\theta$$

$$= \frac{\mu K\rho c}{3\left(a^2-c^2\right)^3}\int_0^{\pi}\cos^2\theta\left[4c^2\cos^2\theta+3\left(a^2-c^2\right)\right]d\theta$$

$$= \frac{4\mu K\rho c}{3\left(a^2-c^2\right)^3}\int_0^{\frac{\pi}{2}}\left[4c^2\cos^4\theta+3\left(a^2-c^2\right)\cos^2\theta\right]d\theta$$

$$= \frac{4\mu K\rho c}{3\left(a^2-c^2\right)^3}\left[4c^2\,\frac{3}{4}\cdot\frac{1}{2}\cdot\frac{\pi}{2}+3\left(a^2-c^2\right)\frac{1}{2}\frac{\pi}{2}\right]$$

$$= \frac{4\mu K\rho c}{3\left(a^2-c^2\right)^3}\,\frac{\pi}{4}\left[3c^2+3a^2-3c^2\right]$$

$$= \frac{\mu K\rho c}{3\left(a^2-c^2\right)^3}\,\pi\cdot 3a^2$$

$$= \frac{\mu K\rho c\pi a^2}{\left(a^2-c^2\right)^3} \qquad \ldots (3)$$

The attraction at P will be zero if the attractions given by (2) and (3) are equal

$$\frac{\mu K\rho b^2\pi c}{\left(c^2-b^2\right)^3} = \frac{\mu K\rho c\pi a^2}{\left(a^2-c^2\right)^3}$$

or $$b^{2/3}\left(a^2-c^2\right) = a^{2/3}\left(c^2-b^2\right)$$

or $$c^2\left(a^{2/3}+b^{2/3}\right) = a^2b^{2/3}+b^2a^{2/3}$$

or $$c^2\left(a^{2/3}+b^{2/3}\right) = a^{2/3}b^{2/3}\left(a^{4/3}+b^{4/3}\right)$$

or $$c = a^{1/3}b^{1/3}\sqrt{\frac{\left(a^{4/3}+b^{4/3}\right)}{a^{2/3}+b^{2/3}}}$$

21. An elliptic disc of mass M and semi axes a and b, attraction according to the law $\dfrac{\mu}{\text{distance}}$, show that its component attractions at an external point (x, y) in the directions parallel to the axes are $\dfrac{2\mu M}{a+b}\dfrac{x}{a}$ and $\dfrac{2\mu M}{a+b}\dfrac{y}{b}$.

Deduce that in the case of an infinite cylinder of density ρ which attracts according to the law of nature, the components are $\dfrac{4\gamma\pi\rho ab}{a+b}\dfrac{x}{a}$ and $\dfrac{4\gamma\pi\rho ab}{a+b}\dfrac{y}{b}$ where a and b are the semi axes of its cross-section.

Solution: Let the equation of the ellipse be $\dfrac{X^2}{a^2}+\dfrac{Y^2}{b^2}=1$ referred to centre C as origin, where X, Y denote the current coordinates.

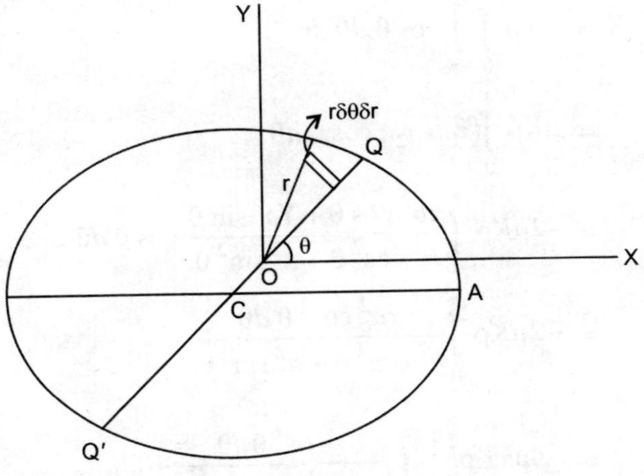

Let coordintes of O be (x, y), transferring the origin to O (x, y) and changing to polars the equation of the ellipse is

$$\frac{(r\cos\theta+x)^2}{a^2}+\frac{(r\sin\theta+y)^2}{b^2}=1$$

i.e. $(b^2\cos^2\theta + a^2\sin^2\theta)\, r^2$

$$+ 2r\,(xb^2\cos\theta + ya^2\sin\theta)$$

$$+ b^2x^2 + a^2y^2 - a^2b^2 = 0$$

This is a quadratic equation in r. Let r_1 and r_2 be its roots, then

$$r_1 + r_2 = \frac{-2\left(xb^2 \cos\theta + ya^2 \sin\theta\right)}{b^2\cos^2\theta + a^2\sin^2\theta} \qquad \text{... (1)}$$

Now we consider an elementary area $r\delta\theta\delta r$ at a distance r from O.

Attraction of this element at O, according to the given law

$$= \frac{\mu r\delta\theta\delta r K\rho}{r} \text{ along } OP$$

$$= \mu K\rho\delta\theta\delta r$$

Its resolved part parallel to the axes are $\mu K\rho\delta\theta\delta r \cos\theta$ and $\mu K\rho\delta\theta\delta r \sin\theta$.

If X, Y denote the total attractions at O along the axes, we have

$$X = \mu K\rho \int_0^{\pi}\int_{-r_1}^{r_2} \cos\theta \, d\theta \, dr$$

$$= \mu K\rho \int_0^{\pi} (r_1 + r_2)\cos\theta \, d\theta$$

$$= -2\mu K\rho \int_0^{\pi} \frac{xb^2\cos\theta + Ya^2\sin\theta}{b^2\cos^2\theta + a^2\sin^2\theta}\cos\theta \, d\theta$$

$$= -2\mu K\rho \int_0^{\pi} \frac{xb^2\cos^2\theta \, d\theta}{b^2\cos^2\theta + a^2\sin^2\theta}$$

$$= -4\mu x K\rho b^2 \int_0^{\frac{\pi}{2}} \frac{\cos^2\theta \, d\theta}{b^2\cos^2\theta + a^2\sin^2\theta}$$

$$= -4\mu x K\rho b^2 \int_0^{\frac{\pi}{2}} \frac{d\theta}{b^2 + a^2\tan^2\theta} \frac{\sec^2\theta}{1 + \tan^2\theta}$$

Putting $t = \tan\theta$

$$dt = \sec^2\theta \, d\theta$$

$$= -4\mu x K\rho b^2 \int_0^\infty \frac{dt}{(b^2 + a^2t^2)(1+t^2)}$$

$$= \frac{-4\mu x K\rho b^2}{b^2 - a^2} \int_0^\infty \left[\frac{1}{1+t^2} - \frac{a^2}{b^2 + a^2t^2}\right]$$

$$= \frac{-4\mu x K\rho b^2}{b^2 - a^2}\left[\tan^{-1} t - \frac{a}{b}\tan^{-1}\left(\frac{ta}{b}\right)\right]_0^0$$

$$= \frac{-4\mu x K\rho b^2}{b^2 - a^2}\left[\frac{\pi}{2} - \frac{a}{b}\frac{\pi}{2}\right]$$

$$= \frac{-4\mu K\rho x b^2}{b^2 - a^2}\frac{\pi}{2}\frac{b-a}{b}$$

$$= \frac{-2\mu K\rho x b\pi}{(b+a)} = -2\mu$$

$$= \frac{-2\mu M}{a+b}\frac{x}{a} \text{ since } \mu = \pi ab K\rho$$

Here negative sign shows the direction of attraction.

Similarly,

$$Y = \mu K\rho \int_0^\pi \frac{-2\left(xb^2 + ya^2\sin\theta\right)}{b^2\cos^2\theta + a^2\sin^2\theta}\sin\theta\, d\theta$$

$$= -2\mu K\rho \int_0^\pi \frac{ya^2\sin^2\theta\, d\theta}{b^2\cos^2\theta + a^2\sin^2\theta}$$

$$= -4\mu K\rho y a^2 \int_0^{\frac{\pi}{2}} \frac{\sin^2\theta\, d\theta}{b^2\cos^2\theta + a^2\sin^2\theta}$$

$$= -4\mu K\rho a^2 y \int_0^{\frac{\pi}{2}} \frac{\cos^2\theta\, d\theta}{b^2\sin^2\theta + a^2\cos^2\theta}$$

$$= \frac{-4\mu K\rho a^2 y}{b^2 - a^2}\frac{\pi}{2}\frac{-b+a}{a} \text{ as for } X$$

$$= \frac{-2\mu K\rho a^2 y\pi}{a(b+a)}$$

$$= \frac{-2\mu y\,(K\rho a\pi)}{a+b}$$

$$= \frac{-2\mu y M}{b\,(a+b)}.$$

Attraction of an infinite elliptic cylinder

We divide the elliptic cylinder into elementary rods of infinite length and let one of these be standing on the element $r\delta\theta\delta r$.

Attraction of this element at O $= \dfrac{2\gamma r\delta\theta\delta r\rho}{r} = 2\gamma\,\rho\delta\theta\delta r$

Its resolved part parallel to x-axis $= 2\gamma\rho\delta\theta\delta r\cos\theta$.

Hence the total attraction along the x-axis

$$= 2\gamma\rho\int_0^{\pi}\int_{-r_1}^{r_2}\cos\theta\, d\theta dr$$

$$= 2\gamma\rho\frac{X}{\mu K\rho} \text{ as for } X$$

$$= \frac{2\gamma}{\mu K}\left(\frac{-2\mu M}{a+b}\right)\frac{x}{a}$$

$$= \frac{-4\gamma}{K\,(a+b)}\pi ab K\rho\frac{x}{a}$$

$$= \frac{-4\gamma\,\pi\rho ab}{a+b}\frac{x}{a}$$

Similarly the attraction of infinite cylinder parallel to y-axis

$$= \frac{-4\gamma\,\pi\rho ab}{a+b}\frac{y}{b}.$$

22. Show that uniform, thin square lamina of mass M whose side is of length l exerts an attraction at a point on the perpendicular to the lamina through one corner whose component parallel to the lamina is

$$\frac{\sqrt{2}\gamma M}{l^2}\log\left[\frac{\left(h^2+l^2\right)^{\frac{1}{2}}\left\{l+\left(h^2+l^2\right)^{\frac{1}{2}}\right\}}{h\left\{l+\left(h^2+2l^2\right)^{\frac{1}{2}}\right\}}\right]$$

where h is the distance from P to the lamina.

Solution: Let $ABCD$ be a square lamina of mass M. Let AP be the perpendicular to the lamina through the corner A and P be a point on it such that $AP = h$. We consider an element $\delta x\delta y$ at Q. The attraction of the element at P

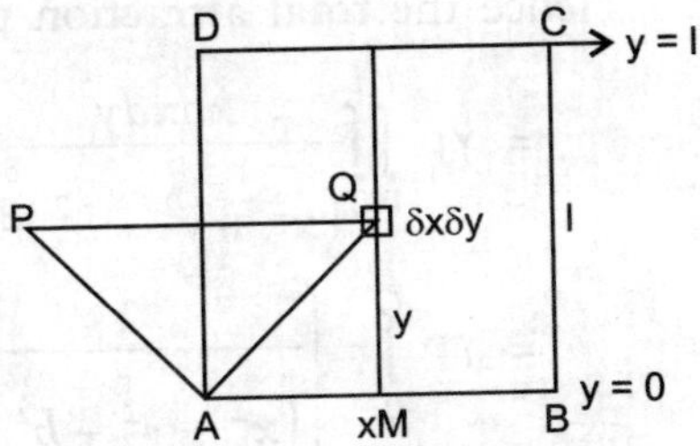

$$= \frac{\gamma\,\delta x\delta y\,\rho}{PQ^2} \text{ along } PQ.$$

Its resolved part in the direction AQ

$$= \frac{\gamma\,\delta x\delta y\,\rho}{PQ^2}\cos AQP$$

$$= \frac{\gamma\,\delta x\delta y\,\rho}{PQ^2}\sin APQ$$

$$= \frac{\gamma\,\delta x\delta y\,\rho}{PQ^2}\frac{AQ}{PQ}$$

$$= \frac{\gamma\,\delta x\delta y\,\rho}{PQ^3} AQ \text{ along } AQ$$

Also resolved part of the attraction of the element along AB

$$= \frac{\gamma\,\delta x\delta y\,\rho}{PQ^3} AQ\cos QAM$$

$$= \frac{\gamma\,\delta x\delta y\,\rho}{PQ^3} AQ\frac{x}{AQ}$$

$$= \frac{\gamma \rho x \delta x \delta y}{PQ^3}$$

$$= \frac{\gamma \rho x \, \delta x \delta y}{\left(x^2 + y^2 + h^2\right)^{\frac{3}{2}}}$$

Hence the total attraction parallel to AB

$$= \gamma\rho \int_0^l \int_0^l \frac{x dx dy}{\left(x^2 + y^2 + h^2\right)^{\frac{3}{2}}}$$

$$= \gamma\rho \int_0^l - \left\{ \frac{1}{\left(x^2 + y^2 + h^2\right)^{\frac{1}{2}}} \right\}_0^l dy$$

$$= \gamma\rho \int_0^l \left[\frac{1}{\sqrt{y^2 + h^2}} - \frac{1}{\sqrt{y^2 + h^2 + l^2}} \right] dy$$

$$= \gamma\rho \left[\log \frac{y + \sqrt{y^2 + h^2}}{y + \sqrt{y^2 + h^2 + l^2}} \right]_0^l$$

$$= \gamma\rho \log \left\{ \frac{l + \sqrt{l^2 + h^2}}{l + \sqrt{2l^2 + h^2}} \cdot \frac{\sqrt{h^2 + l^2}}{h} \right\}$$

$$= \frac{\gamma M}{l^2} \log \frac{\left(l^2 + h^2\right)^{\frac{1}{2}} \left\{ l + \left(l^2 + h^2\right)^{\frac{1}{2}} \right\}}{h \left\{ l + \left(2l^2 + h^2\right)^{\frac{1}{2}} \right\}}.$$

23. Show that the attraction at a pole of solid prolate spheroid due to the matter on the four sides of the equatorial plane is

$$2\pi\gamma\rho a \left[1 - \frac{1}{e^2} \left\{ 2 - \sqrt{2 - e^2} \right\} + \frac{1 - e^2}{e^3} \log \frac{(1 + e)^2}{1 + e\sqrt{2 - e^2}} \right]$$

where a is the semi-axis, e the eccentricity of meridian and ρ is the density.

Solution: We know that prolate spheroid is obtained by revolution of ellipse $\frac{x^2}{a^2}+\frac{y^2}{b^2}=1$ about major axis $AA' = 2a$.

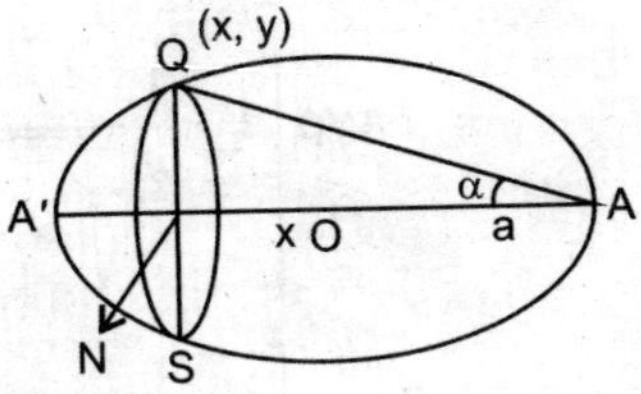

A is the pole of spheroid at which we are to find the attraction due to one half of the spheroid towards the left of O. We divide the spheroid into a large number of circular discs and *QS* be one of such elementary disc of width δx at a distance x from O.

Attraction of the disc at *A*

$$= 2\pi\gamma\rho\delta x\,(1-\cos\alpha)$$

$$= 2\pi\gamma\rho\,\delta x\left(1-\frac{AN}{AQ}\right)$$

$$= 2\pi\gamma\rho\left[1-\frac{a+x}{\sqrt{AN^2+QN^2}}\right]\delta x$$

$$= 2\pi\gamma\rho\left[1-\frac{a+x}{\sqrt{(a+x)^2+y^2}}\right]\delta x$$

$$= 2\pi\gamma\rho\left[1-\frac{a+x}{\sqrt{(a+x)^2+\frac{b^2}{a^2}\left(a^2-x^2\right)}}\right]\delta x$$

$$= 2\pi\gamma\rho\left[1\frac{a+x}{\sqrt{(a+x)^2+\left(1-e^2\right)\left(a^2-x^2\right)}}\right]\delta x$$

$$= 2\pi\gamma\rho\left[1-\frac{a+x}{\sqrt{a^2\left(1+1-e^2\right)+2ax+x^2\left(1-1+e^2\right)}}\right]\delta x$$

$$= 2\pi\gamma\rho\left[1-\frac{a+x}{\sqrt{a^2\left(2-e^2\right)+2ax+e^2x^2}}\right]\delta x$$

$$= 2\pi\gamma\rho\left[1-\frac{1}{e}\frac{a+x}{\sqrt{x^2+\frac{2a}{e^2}x+a^2\left(\frac{2}{e^2}-1\right)}}\right]\delta x$$

$$= 2\pi\gamma\rho\left[1-\frac{1}{e}\frac{a+x}{\sqrt{\left(x+\frac{a}{e^2}\right)^2-\frac{a^2}{e^4}+\frac{2a^2}{e^2}-a^2}}\right]\delta x$$

$$= 2\pi\gamma\rho\left[1-\frac{1}{e}\frac{a+x}{\sqrt{\left(x+\frac{a}{e^2}\right)^2-\frac{a^2}{e^4}\left(1-2a^2e^2+e^4\right)}}\right]\delta x$$

$$= 2\pi\gamma\rho\left[1-\frac{1}{e}\frac{a+x}{\sqrt{\left(x+\frac{a}{e^2}\right)^2-\frac{a^2}{e^4}\left(1-e^2\right)^2}}\right]\delta x$$

Hence the required attraction at B

$$= 2\pi\rho\gamma\int_0^a\left[1-\frac{1}{e}\frac{x+\frac{a}{e^2}-\frac{a}{e^2}+a}{\sqrt{\left(x+\frac{a}{e^2}\right)^2-\frac{a^2}{e^4}\left(1-e^2\right)^2}}\right]\delta x$$

$$= 2\pi\gamma\rho\int_0^a\left[1-\frac{1}{e}\frac{x+\frac{a}{e^2}}{\sqrt{\left(x+\frac{a}{e^2}\right)^2-\frac{a^2}{e^4}\left(1-e^2\right)^2}}\right.$$

$$\left.+\frac{a\left(1-e^2\right)}{e^3\sqrt{\left(x+\frac{a}{e^2}\right)^2-\frac{a^2}{e^4}\left(1-e^2\right)^2}}\right]\delta x$$

$$= 2\pi\gamma\rho\left[x-\frac{1}{e}\left\{\sqrt{\left(x+\frac{a}{e^2}\right)^2-\frac{a^2}{e^4}\left(1-e^2\right)^2}\right\}\right.$$

$$+\frac{a\left(1-e^2\right)}{e^3}\log\left\{x+\frac{a}{e^2}+\sqrt{\left(x+\frac{a}{e^2}\right)^2-\frac{a^2}{e^4}\left(1-e^2\right)^2}\right\}\Bigg]_0^a$$

$$= 2\pi\gamma\rho\left[a-\frac{1}{e}\left\{a\sqrt{\left(1+\frac{1}{e^2}\right)^2-\left(\frac{1}{e^2}-1\right)^2}-\sqrt{\frac{a^2}{e^4}-\frac{a^2}{e^4}\left(1-e^2\right)^2}\right\}+\frac{a\left(1-e^2\right)}{e^3}\log\frac{a+\frac{a}{e^2}+\sqrt{\left(a+\frac{a}{e^2}\right)^2-\frac{a^2}{e^4}\left(1-e^2\right)^2}}{\frac{a}{e^2}+\sqrt{\frac{a^2}{e^4}-\frac{a^2}{e^4}\left(1-e^2\right)^2}}\right]$$

$$= 2\pi\gamma\rho\left[a-\frac{1}{e}\left\{a\frac{2}{e^2}-\frac{a}{e^2}e\sqrt{2-e^2}\right\}+\frac{a\left(1-e^2\right)}{e^3}\log\frac{a+\frac{a}{e^2}+\frac{a}{e^2}\sqrt{4e^2}}{\frac{a}{e^2}\left\{1+e\sqrt{2-e^2}\right\}}\right]$$

$$= 2\pi\gamma\rho a\left[1-\frac{1}{e^2}\left\{2-\sqrt{2-e^2}\right\}+\frac{\left(1-e^2\right)}{e^3}\log\frac{e^2+1+2e}{1+e\sqrt{2-e^2}}\right]$$

$$= 2\pi\gamma\rho a\left[1-\frac{2-\sqrt{2-e^2}}{e^2}+\frac{1-e^2}{e^3}\log\frac{(1+e)^2}{1+e\sqrt{2-e^2}}\right]$$

24. If the law of force be the inverse fifth power of the distance, show that the attraction of a uniform solid sphere of density ρ and radius a at an external point distance c from the centre is

$$\frac{\gamma\pi\rho}{4c^2}\left\{\frac{2ca\left(c^2+a^2\right)}{\left(c^2-a^2\right)^2}+\log\frac{c-a}{c+a}\right\}$$

Solution: First we shall determine the attraction of a circular plate of radius r at a point P distant p from the centre of the axis when the law of attraction is that of inverse fifth power of the distance.

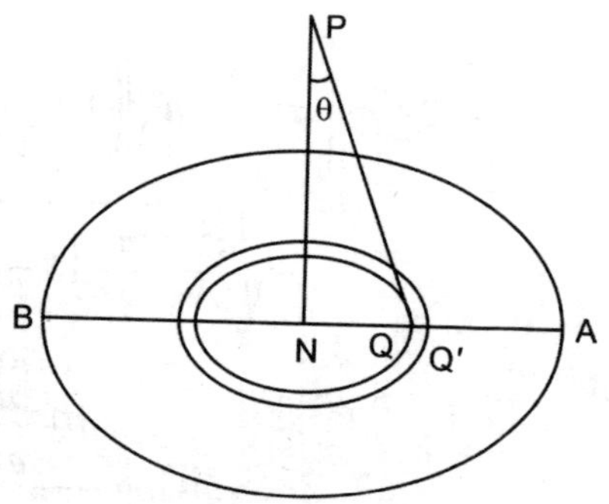

We consider an elementary disc of radius x and width δx.

Hence mass of the elementary disc $= 2\pi x\delta x K\rho$

Hence its attraction at P under given law

$$= \frac{\gamma 2\pi x\delta x K\rho}{PQ^5} \text{ along } PQ$$

$$= \frac{\gamma 2\pi x\delta x K\rho}{PQ^5} \cos QPN \text{ along the axis}$$

$$= \frac{\gamma 2\pi x\delta x K\rho}{PQ^5}\,\frac{p}{PQ}$$

$$= \frac{\gamma 2\pi x\delta x K\rho p}{\left(x^2+p^2\right)^3}$$

Hence the attraction due to the circular disc of radius r

$$= \gamma K\pi\rho p\int_0^r \frac{2xdx}{\left(x^2+p^2\right)^3}$$

$$= \gamma\pi K\rho p\left[-\frac{1}{2\left(x^2+p^2\right)^2}\right]_0^r$$

$$= \frac{\gamma \pi K \rho p}{2} \left[\frac{1}{p^4} - \frac{1}{\left(p^2 + r^2\right)^2} \right]$$

$$= \frac{\gamma \pi K \rho}{2} \left[\frac{1}{p^3} - \frac{p}{\left(p^2 + r^2\right)^2} \right] \qquad \dots (1)$$

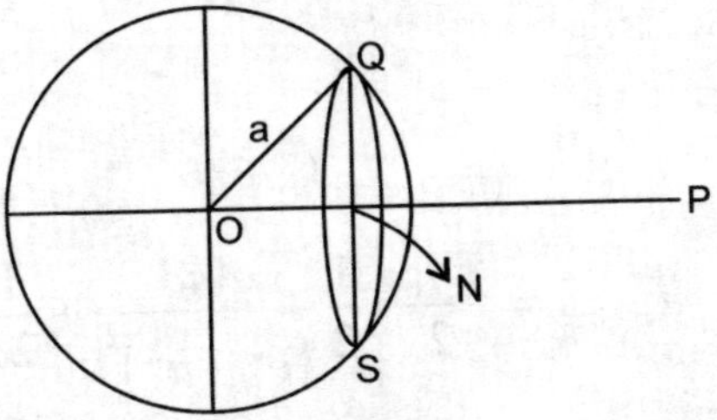

Let O be the centre of the sphere in the question and P an external point such that $OP = c$.

The radius of the sphere $= a$.

We divide the sphere into a large number of circular disc which are at right angles to OP. Let one of such disc be QS at a distance x from P and width δx. Radius of this disc $= \sqrt{a^2 - (c-x)^2}$

Hence attraction of the disc from (1) at P

$$= \frac{\gamma \pi \rho \delta x}{2} \left[\frac{1}{x^3} - \frac{x}{\left\{x^2 + a^2 - (c-x)^2\right\}^2} \right]$$

$$= \frac{\pi \gamma \rho}{2} \left[\frac{1}{x^3} - \frac{x}{\left(a^2 - e^2 + 2cx\right)^2} \right] \delta x$$

Hence attraction at P due to the given sphere

$$= \frac{\pi \gamma \rho}{2} \int_{c-a}^{c+a} \left[\frac{1}{x^3} - \frac{x}{\left(a^2 - e^2 + 2cx\right)^2} \right] dx$$

$$= \frac{\pi \gamma \rho}{2} \left[-\frac{1}{2x^2} - \left\{ \frac{x\,(-1)}{2c\left(a^2 - c^2 + 2cx\right)} + \frac{1}{2c} \int \frac{dx}{a^2 - c^2 + 2cx} \right\} \right]$$

$$= \frac{\pi\gamma\rho}{2}\left[-\frac{1}{2x^2}+\frac{x}{2c\left(a^2-c^2+2cx\right)} - \frac{1}{4c^2}\log\left(a^2-c^2+2cx\right)\right]_{c-a}^{c+a}$$

$$= \frac{\pi\gamma\rho}{2}\left[-\frac{1}{2}\left\{\frac{1}{(c+a)^2}-\frac{1}{(c-a)^2}\right\}+\frac{1}{2c}\left\{\frac{a+c}{(c+a)^2} - \frac{c-a}{(c-a)^2}\right\}-\frac{1}{4c^2}\log\frac{(a+c)^2}{(c-a)^2}\right]$$

$$= \frac{\pi\gamma\rho}{2}\left[\frac{1}{2}\frac{4ac}{\left(c^2-a^2\right)^2}+\frac{1}{2c}\frac{(-2a)}{c^2-a^2}-\frac{1}{2c^2}\log\frac{a+c}{c-a}\right]$$

$$= \frac{\pi\gamma\rho}{2}\left[\frac{2ac}{\left(c^2-a^2\right)^2}-\frac{a}{c\left(c^2-a^2\right)}+\frac{1}{2c^2}\log\frac{c-a}{c+a}\right]$$

$$= \frac{\pi\gamma\rho}{2}\left[\frac{2ac^2-a\left(c^2-a^2\right)}{c\left(c^2-a^2\right)^2}+\frac{1}{2c^2}\log\frac{c-a}{c+a}\right]$$

$$= \frac{\pi\gamma\rho}{2}\left[\frac{a\left(c^2+a^2\right)}{c\left(c^2-a^2\right)^2}+\frac{1}{2c^2}\log\frac{c-a}{c+a}\right]$$

$$= \frac{\pi\gamma\rho}{4c^2}\left[\frac{2ca\left(c^2+a^2\right)}{\left(c^2-a^2\right)^2}+\log\frac{c-a}{c+a}\right]$$

EXERCISES

1. Show that the attraction of a uniform solid circular cylinder of radius a and density ρ at an external point on the axis of the cylinder is $2\pi\gamma\rho a\left[\tan\frac{\theta}{2}-\tan\frac{\phi}{2}\right]$ where θ and ϕ are the angles subtended at P by the radii of the nearer and farther ends of the cylinder.

2. P is a point on a uniform sphere of mass M and radius a. The sphere is divided into two parts by a plane

perpendicular to the diameter through P. Show that if the radius of the section of a plane subtends an angle α at P the attraction at P of the portion of the sphere which contains P is $\frac{3\gamma M}{a^2}\cos^2\alpha\left(1-\frac{2}{3}\cos\alpha\right)$.

3. A finite solid of uniform density ρ is bounded by the paraboloid $x^2 + y^2 = 4az$ and the plane $z = a$, prove that the intensity of the attraction at the origin is $2\pi\gamma\rho a\left[1-\sqrt{5}+4\log\frac{1}{2}\left(1+\sqrt{5}\right)\right]$.

4. Show that the attraction at the focus S of a segment of a paraboloid of revolution bounded by a plane perpendicular to the axis of at a distance b from the vertex is $4\pi\gamma\rho a\log\left(\frac{a+b}{ae}\right)$ where $4a$ is the latus rectum of the generating parabola. [I.A.S. 77]

5. A quantity of homogeneous matter of density ρ is in the form of a paraboloid of revolution bounded by a plane perpendicular to the axis. Prove that its attraction at its vertex tends as c, the length of the axis increases to the limit $4\pi\gamma\rho a\log\left(\frac{c}{ae}\right)$ where $4a$ is the length of the latus rectum of the generating parabola.

6. The law of attraction being that of the inverse distance, find the attraction of a uniform circular disc or an external point in its own plane. Deduce the attraction of an infinite circular cylinder, attracting according to the law of nature. [M.U. 92H, 2000H]

[**Ans.** Attraction of the uniform circular disc at an external point $= \frac{\gamma M}{c}$ where M is the total mass and c the distance of P from centre. Attraction of the infinite cylinder at an external point $= \frac{2\pi\gamma\rho a^2}{c}$ where ρ is the density, γ is the gravitational constant and a is the radius of the disc.]

7. A solid of density ρ is formed by the revolution about the axis of x of the part cut off from the paraboloid $y^2 = 4ax$ by its evolute $27ay^2 = 4(x - 2a)^3$. Show that the attraction at the cusp of the evolute is $\pi\gamma\rho a\left[4 \sin \lambda^{-1} 4 + 5\sqrt{17} - 27\right]$.

8. A thin area of uniform thickness and uniform density is bounded by two ellipses whose equations are $\frac{l}{r} = 1 - \frac{1}{2}\cos\theta$ and $\frac{2}{r} = 1 - \frac{1}{2}\cos\theta$. Find the attraction at the pole due to the area.

[**Ans.** Zero]

9. A uniform solid cylinder of mass M is formed by the planes $z = 0$, $z = c$ and the cylindrical surface $x^2 + y^2 = 2ax$. Prove that the z component of the attraction at the origin is $\frac{\gamma M}{\pi a^2 c}(4a + \pi c - 1)$ where $2l$ is the perimeter of an ellipse of semi-axes $\sqrt{c^2 + 4a^2}$ and c.

10. Show that the resultant attractions of one of a solid homogeneous oblate spheroid cutoff by an equatorial plane, at a point on the rim of the base, is inclined to the plane of the base at an angle whose tangent is

$$\frac{4c\left\{\tan h^{-1}(e) - e\right\}}{\left\{a \sin^{-1}(e) - ce\right\}}$$

where a and c are the semi-axes and e the eccentricity of the meridian section.

11. The density of an infinite circular cylinder of radius a at a distance r from its axis is proportional to $\sqrt{a^2 - r^2}$. Show that the attraction at an internal point distant r from axis is $\frac{2\gamma M}{a^3 r}\left\{a^3 - \left(a^2 - r^2\right)^{\frac{3}{2}}\right\}$ where M is the mass of a unit length of cylinder, and γ is the gravitational constant.

12. Two rigid and equal semi-circular arcs of matter with uniform section and density are hinged together at both extremities. The matter attracts according to law of nature.

If equal and opposite forces applied along the line joining the mid-points of the semi circles kept them apart with their planes at right angles, prove that the magnitude of each force will be $4\gamma m^2 \log\left(\sqrt{2}+1\right)$ where m is the line density of the arcs.

3 ATTRACTION OF A SPHERICAL SHELL AND A SOLID SPHERE

3.1. To find the attraction of a thin uniform spherical shell at an external or internal point.

[L.N.M.U. 93H, 94H; M.U. 92H, 98H; T.M.B.U. 93H, 96H]

Let O be the centre of a thin spherical shell of radius a, thickness K and density ρ.

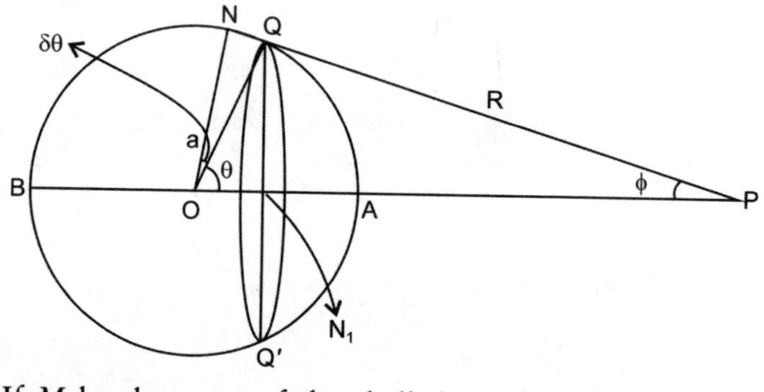

If M be the mass of the shell then $M = 4\pi a^2 K\rho$. Let P be the point at which the attraction of the shell is to be found out. Let $OP = c$.

From any point Q of the shell we draw ON_1 perpendicular to OP.

Let $\angle POQ = \theta$, $\angle OPQ = \phi$ and $PQ = R$.

The shell is generated by the revolution of semi-circumference AQB about the diameter AB. Let arc $QN = a\delta\theta$.

A circular ring of cross-section $Ka\delta\theta$ and radius QN_1 is generated by the revolution of this element $a\delta\theta$ about the diameter AB.

Every point of the strip QQ' is at the same distance R from the point P.

Mass of the strip $= K\rho\ (2\pi a \sin\theta)\ a\delta\theta$.

Attraction at P due to a unit mass of the strip QQ'

$$= \frac{\gamma}{PQ^2} \text{ along } PQ$$

$$= \frac{\gamma}{PQ^2} \cos\phi \text{ along } PO$$

Hence the attraction at P due to the circular strip QQ'

$$= \frac{\gamma}{PQ^2} \cos\phi\ K\rho\,(2\pi a \sin\theta)\ a\delta\theta \text{ along } PQ$$

Therefore total attraction at P along PO due to the whole spherical shell

$$= \int \frac{\gamma \cos\phi}{PQ^2} K\rho\,(2\pi\ a \sin\theta)\ a d\theta \qquad \ldots (1)$$

In ΔOPQ

$$PQ^2 = OQ^2 + OP^2 - 2OPOQ \cos\theta$$

$$R^2 = a^2 + c^2 - 2ac \cos\theta$$

$$\therefore \quad 2RdR = 2ac \sin\theta\ d\theta$$

In ΔOPQ, again

$$\cos\phi = \frac{OP^2 + PQ^2 - OQ^2}{2OPPQ}$$

$$= \frac{c^2 + R^2 - a^2}{2cR}$$

Hence from (1) the required attraction

$$= \gamma K\rho 2\pi a \int \frac{1}{R^2} \frac{R^2 + c^2 - a^2}{2cR} \frac{RdR}{c}$$

$$= \frac{\gamma K\rho\,\pi a}{c^2} \int_{PA}^{PB} \frac{R^2 + c^2 - a^2}{R^2} dR$$

$$= \frac{\gamma K\rho\pi a}{c^2} \int_{PA}^{PB} \left[1 + \frac{c^2 - a^2}{R^2}\right] dR$$

$$= \frac{\gamma K \rho \pi a}{c^2}\left[R - \frac{c^2 - a^2}{R}\right]_{PA}^{PB} \qquad \ldots (2)$$

Case I: When P is an external point, then

$$PA = OP - OA = c - a$$

and $\quad PB = PO + OB = c + a$

Hence from (2), the attraction becomes

$$= \frac{\gamma K \rho \pi a}{c^2}\left[R - \frac{c^2 - a^2}{R}\right]_{c-a}^{c+a}$$

$$= \frac{\gamma K \rho \pi a}{c^2}\left[c + a - (c - a) - \left(c^2 - a^2\right)\left\{\frac{1}{c+a} - \frac{1}{c-a}\right\}\right]$$

$$= \frac{\gamma K \rho \pi a}{c^2}\left[2a - \frac{\left(c^2 - a^2\right)(-2a)}{c^2 - a^2}\right]$$

$$= \frac{\gamma K \rho \pi a}{c^2}[2a + 2a]$$

$$= \frac{\gamma K \rho \pi a\, 4a}{c^2}$$

$$= \frac{\gamma\, 4K\rho\pi a^2}{c^2} = \frac{\gamma M}{c^2} = \frac{\gamma \cdot \text{Mass of the shell}}{OP^2}$$

which is the same as would be of whole mass M of the shell were concentrated at the centre O.

Hence attraction of a uniform spherical shell at an external point P is equal to $\dfrac{\gamma M}{OP^2}$.

Case II: When P is an internal point, then

$$PA = OA - OP = a - c$$

and $\quad PB = OB + OP = a + c$

Hence from (2) the attraction of a spherical shell at an internal point P at a distance c from the centre

$$= \frac{\gamma K\rho\pi a}{c^2}\left[R - \frac{c^2 - a^2}{R}\right]_{a-c}^{a+c}$$

$$= \frac{\gamma K\rho\pi a}{c^2}\left[(a+c)-(a-c) - (c^2 - a^2)\left\{\frac{1}{a+c} - \frac{1}{a-c}\right\}\right]$$

$$= \frac{\gamma K\rho\pi a}{c^2}\left[2c - \frac{c^2 - a^2}{a^2 - c^2}(-2c)\right]$$

$$= \frac{2\gamma K\rho\pi a}{c^2}[2c - 2c]$$

$$= 0$$

Hence the attraction of a spherical shell at an internal point is zero.

Case III: When P is a point on the surface of the shell, then $PA = 0$ and $PB = 2a$ and $c = a$.

Hence from (2), attraction of the shell at P

$$= \frac{\gamma K\rho\pi a}{a^2}[R - 0]_0^{2a}$$

$$= \frac{\gamma K\rho\pi a}{a^2} 2a$$

$$= 2\gamma K\rho\pi$$

$$= \frac{1}{2}\gamma\frac{4\pi a^2 K\rho}{a^2} = \frac{1}{2}\frac{\gamma M}{a^2}$$

Hence the attraction of a thin uniform shperical shell at a point on its surface is equal to $\frac{1}{2}\frac{\gamma M}{a^2}$.

3.2. To find the attraction of a uniform solid sphere at an external or internal point

[M.U. 93H, 95H, 97H, 98H, 99H, 02H; T.M.B.U. 94H]

Let O be the centre of a uniform solid sphere of radius a and density ρ. If M be the mass of the sphere, then

$$M = \frac{4}{3}\pi a^3\rho$$

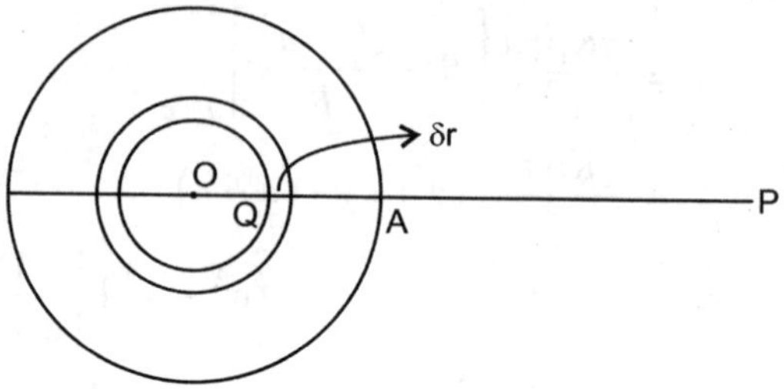

Let P be the point at a distance c from the centre of the sphere at which attraction is to be found out.

We divide the sphere into an infinite number of concentric shells each of indefinitely small thickness and let one of them be of radius r and thickness δr.

So mass of this shell

$$= \frac{\rho 4\pi}{3}\left[(r+\delta r)^3 - r^3\right]$$

$$= \frac{4\pi\rho}{3}[3r^2\delta r]$$

Neglecting higher powers of δr as δr is very very small

$$= 4\pi\rho r^2\delta r$$

Case I: When P is an external point.

The attraction at P due to an elementary shell

$$= \frac{\gamma 4\pi r^2 \delta r \rho}{OP^2} = \frac{\gamma 4\pi r^2 \delta r \rho}{c^2}$$

Hence the attraction of the whole sphere at P

$$= \frac{\gamma 4\pi\rho}{c^2}\int_0^a r^2 dr$$

$$= \frac{4\pi\rho\gamma}{c^2}\frac{a^3}{3}$$

$$= \frac{\gamma}{c^2}\frac{4}{3}\pi a^3\rho$$

$$= \frac{\gamma M}{OP^2} = \frac{\gamma \cdot \text{Mass of the sphere}}{OP^2}$$

This shows that the attraction of a uniform solid sphere at an external point is the same as that of a mass M, equal to the mass of the sphere, concentrated at the centre of the sphere.

[P.U. 79H, M.U. 74H, 76H, 79H, 80H; T.M.B.U. 91H]

Case II: When P is an internal point.

In this case we also divide the sphere into a large number of concentric shells, each of indefinitely small thickness.

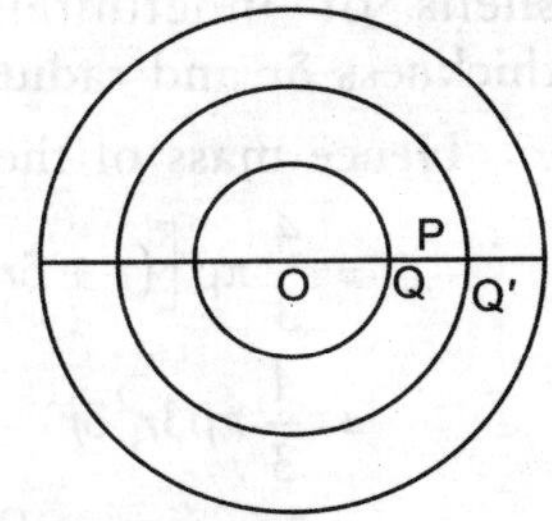

Thus we get some shells whose radii are greater than OP and P is, therefore an internal point for such shells.

Hence the attraction of all such shells is zero.

We need only therefore consider shells of a radius r which is less than c.

For any such shell P is an external point and its attraction at P

$$= \frac{\gamma \cdot \text{Mass of the shell}}{OP^2}$$

$$= \frac{\gamma \cdot 4\pi r^2 \delta r \rho}{c^2}$$

Hence the attraction at P, due to the matter of the sphere enclosed within the sphere of radius c is

$$= \frac{\gamma \pi 4\rho}{c^2} \int_0^c r^2\, dr$$

$$= \frac{\gamma \pi 4\rho}{c^2} \frac{c^3}{3} = \frac{4}{3} \pi \gamma \rho c$$

Case III: When P is on the surface of the shpere.

In this case $c = a$. Hence the required attraction by case I or II

$$= \frac{4}{3} \pi \rho \gamma a = \frac{4}{3} \frac{\pi \rho \gamma a^3}{a} = \frac{\gamma M}{a^2}$$

3.3. To find the attraction of a spherical shell of external and internal radii *a* and *b* respectively at a point *P*.

Case I: When P is an external point i.e. $P = P_1$.

We divide the shell into an infinite number of concentric shells of indefinitely small thickness δr and radius r.

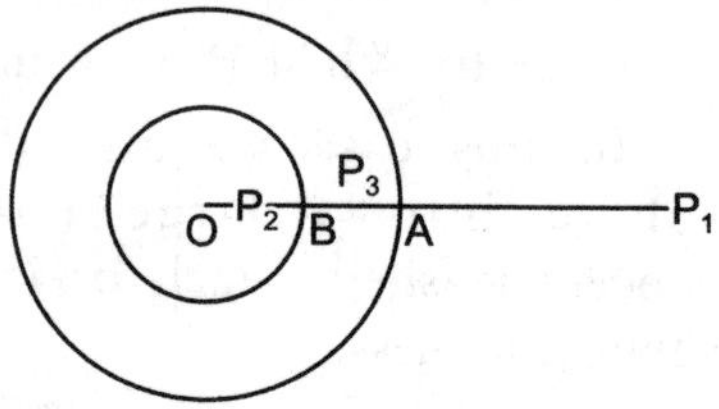

Hence mass of the shell

$$= \frac{4}{3}\pi\rho\left[(r+\delta r)^3 - r^3\right]$$

$$= \frac{4}{3}\pi\rho 3r^2\delta r$$

$$= 4\pi r^2\delta r\rho$$ [Neglecting higher power than δr as δr is very very small]

Hence attraction of the shell at P_1

$$= \frac{\gamma \cdot 4\pi r^2 \delta r\, \rho}{c^2}$$

Thus total attraction at P_1

$$= \frac{\gamma \cdot 4\pi\rho}{c^2}\int_b^a r^2\,dr$$

$$= \frac{\gamma\, 4\pi\rho\left(a^3 - b^3\right)}{c^2}$$

Case II: P is a point internal to sphere of radius b i.e. $P = P_2$

In this case P_2 is an internal point for all such elementary shell into which the given shell is divided. Hence its attraction at P is zero.

Case III: P is a point inside the given shell i.e. $P = P_3$.

We divide the given shell into an infinite number of shells of very small thickness. For all those shells whose radius is greater than $OP_3 = c$, P_3 will be an internal point and as such their attraction will be zero and for all those whose radii are less than OP_3, P_3 is an external point and attraction of one elementary shell of radius r and mass

$$4\pi r^2 \delta r \rho = \frac{\gamma 4\pi r^2 \delta r \rho}{OP_3^2} = \frac{\gamma 4\pi r^2 dr \rho}{c^2} = \frac{4\pi\gamma\rho}{c^2} r^2 \delta r$$

Hence the total attraction

$$= \frac{4\pi\gamma\rho}{c^2}\int_b^c r^2 dr$$

$$= \frac{4\pi\gamma\rho}{c^2}\left[\frac{r^3}{3}\right]_b^c$$

$$= \frac{4\pi\gamma\rho}{c^2}\frac{\left(c^3 - b^3\right)}{3}$$

$$= \frac{4}{3}\pi\gamma\rho\,\frac{c^3 - b^3}{c^2}.$$

WORKED OUT EXAMPLES

1. Show that the attraction of a uniform thin hemispherical shell of mass M and radius a, at a point on the diameter perpendicular to the plane of the rim of the shell at a distance x from its centre is $\frac{\gamma M}{x^2}\left[1 - \frac{a}{\sqrt{a^2 + x^2}}\right]$.

Solution:

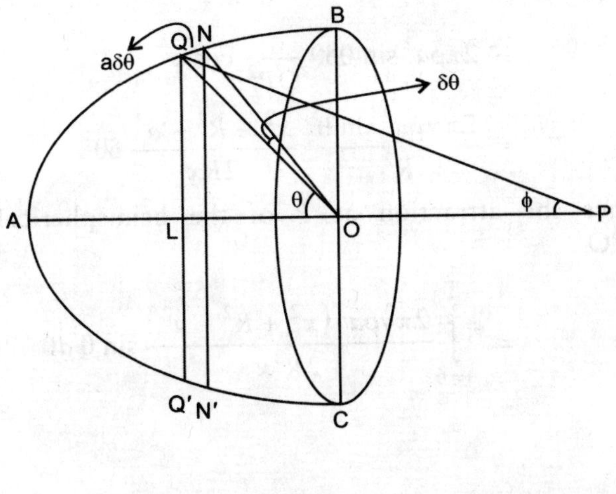

Let O be the centre of the base of the hemispherical shell of mass M and radius a, and let P be the point on the diameter AO produced perpendicular to the plane BC of the rim of the shell. Hence $M = 2\pi a^2 \rho$.

Let $a\delta\theta$ be an elementary arc of the shell at Q. This arc generates a circular ring of thickness $a\delta\theta$ and radius $QL = a \sin\theta$ when revolve about the diameter OA.

Mass of the elementary ring $= 2\pi\rho a \; a \sin\theta\delta\theta$

Let $OP = x$, $PQ = R$ and $\angle OPQ = \phi$ then in ΔPOQ

$$\cos\phi = \frac{x^2 + R^2 - a^2}{2Rx}$$

Also $PQ^2 = OP^2 + OQ^2 - 2OPOQ \cos(\pi - \theta)$

$$R^2 = x^2 + a^2 + 2ax\cos\theta$$

Differentiating we get

$$2RdR = -2ax\sin\theta\, d\theta$$

or $\quad RdR = -ax\sin\theta\, d\theta$

Now attraction at P due to a unit mass of the ring at Q

$$= \frac{\gamma}{QP^2} \text{ along } PQ$$

$$= \frac{\gamma}{QP^2}\cos\phi \text{ along } PO$$

Hence attraction of the elementary ring $QNN'Q'$ along PO

$$= 2\pi\rho a^2 \sin\theta\delta\theta \frac{\gamma}{QP^2}\cos\phi$$

$$= \frac{2\pi\gamma\rho a^2\sin\theta}{R^2}\cdot\frac{x^2 + R^2 - a^2}{2Rx}\delta\theta$$

Hence the attraction at P of the hemispherical shell along PO

$$= \int_{\theta=0}^{\frac{\pi}{2}} \frac{2\pi\gamma\rho a^2\left(x^2 + R^2 - a^2\right)}{2R^3 x}\sin\theta\, d\theta$$

$$= \int_{R=PA}^{PB} \frac{2\pi\gamma\rho a^2 \left(x^2 + R^2 - a^2\right)}{2R^3 x}\left(\frac{-R}{ax}\right) dR$$

$$= \frac{-\pi\gamma\rho a}{x^2} \int_{a+x}^{\sqrt{a^2+x^2}} \frac{x^2 + R^2 - a^2}{R^2}\, dR$$

$$= \frac{-\pi\gamma\rho a}{x^2} \int_{a+x}^{\sqrt{a^2+x^2}} \left(\frac{x^2 - a^2}{R^2} + 1\right) dR$$

$$= \frac{-\pi\gamma\rho a}{x^2} \left[-\frac{x^2 - a^2}{R} + R\right]_{a+x}^{\sqrt{a^2+x^2}}$$

$$= \frac{-\pi\gamma\rho a}{x^2} \left[-\left(x^2 - a^2\right)\left\{\frac{1}{\sqrt{a^2+x^2}} - \frac{1}{a+x}\right\} + \sqrt{a^2+x^2} - (a+x)\right]$$

$$= \frac{-\pi\gamma\rho a}{x^2} \left[\frac{-\left(x^2 - a^2\right) + a^2 + x^2}{\sqrt{a^2+x^2}} + \frac{x^2 - a^2 - (a+x)^2}{a+x}\right]$$

$$= \frac{-\pi\gamma\rho a}{x^2} \left[\frac{2a^2}{\sqrt{a^2+x^2}} + \frac{x^2 - a^2 - \left(a^2 + x^2 + 2ax\right)}{a+x}\right]$$

$$= \frac{-\pi\gamma\rho a}{x^2} \left[\frac{2a^2}{\sqrt{a^2+x^2}} - \frac{2a(a+x)}{a+x}\right]$$

$$= \frac{-2\pi\gamma\rho a^2}{x^2} \left[\frac{a}{\sqrt{a^2+x^2}} - 1\right]$$

$$= \frac{\gamma M}{x^2} \left[1 - \frac{a}{\sqrt{x^2+a^2}}\right]$$

2. A thin spherical shell of radius a attracts an internal point P at a distance r from the centre. If the shell be divided into two parts by a plane through P perpendicular to the radius, the resultant attraction of each part at P is

$$\frac{2\pi\gamma ma}{r^2}\left\{a - \sqrt{a^2 - r^2}\right\}$$

where m is the surface density.

Solution: Let O be the centre of the thin spherical shell of radius a and P be an internal point such that $OP = r$.

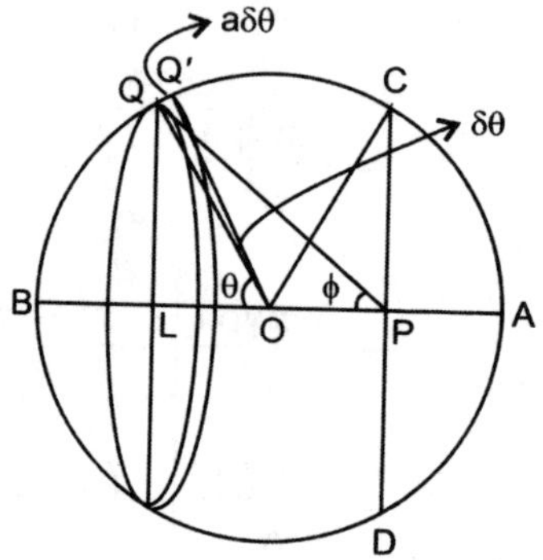

Let the sphere be divided into two parts by the plane CD through P perpendicular to the radius OPA.

We have to find the attractions of the two parts CAD and CBD at the point P.

To find the attraction of the part CBD at the point P.

We consider an arc $a\delta\theta$ of the shell at Q. This arc when revolved about the diameter AB will generate a circular ring of radius $QL = a \sin\theta$ and thickness $a\delta\theta$.

Mass of this elementary ring $= 2\pi ma \sin\theta\; a\delta\theta$

Let $PQ = R$ and $\angle OPQ = \phi$

In ΔOPQ we have

$$\cos\phi = \frac{r^2 + R^2 - a^2}{2rR}$$

and $$\cos(\pi - \theta) = \frac{OQ^2 + OP^2 - PQ^2}{2OPOQ}$$

$$-\cos\theta = \frac{a^2 + r^2 - R^2}{2ar}$$

Differentiating we get

$$\sin\theta\, d\theta = -\frac{R}{ar}\, dR$$

Attraction of the elementary ring, at the point P along PL

$$= \gamma \frac{2\pi ma \sin\theta \, a\delta\theta}{R^2} \cos\phi$$

$$= \frac{2\pi\gamma ma^2}{R^2} \cos\phi \sin\theta \, \delta\theta$$

Hence the attraction of the part CBD at the point P along PB

$$= \int \frac{2\pi\gamma\, ma^2}{R^2} \cos\phi \sin\theta \, d\theta$$

$$= 2\pi\, \gamma ma^2 \int_{R=PB}^{PC} \frac{1}{R^2} \frac{r^2 + R^2 - a^2}{2rR} \left(\frac{-R}{ar}\right) dR$$

$$= \frac{\pi\gamma ma}{r^2} \int_{r+a}^{\sqrt{a^2-r^2}} \left(\frac{a^2 - r^2}{R^2} - 1\right) dR$$

$$= \frac{\pi\gamma ma}{r^2} \left[-\frac{a^2 - r^2}{R} - R \right]_{r+a}^{\sqrt{a^2-r^2}}$$

$$= \frac{\pi\gamma ma}{r^2} \left[-(a^2 - r^2)\left\{ \frac{1}{\sqrt{a^2 - r^2}} - \frac{1}{r+a} \right\} - \left\{ \sqrt{a^2 - r^2} - (r+a) \right\} \right]$$

$$= \frac{\pi\gamma ma}{r^2} \left[a - r + r + a - 2\sqrt{a^2 - r^2} \right]$$

$$= \frac{2\pi\gamma ma}{r^2} \left[a - \sqrt{a^2 - r^2} \right] \qquad \text{... (1)}$$

For the part CAD, the limits of R are from PC to PA i.e. from $\sqrt{a^2 - r^2}$ to $a - r$.

Hence the attraction of the part CAD at the point P can be obtained from (1) by replacing r by $-r$ in (1) and it becomes

$$= \frac{2\pi\gamma ma}{r^2} \left[a - \sqrt{a^2 - r^2} \right]$$ which is same as (1).

Hence the two parts have the same attraction at P.

3. The matter of a spherical shell attracts with a force varying as the inverse fifth power of the distance. Show that the attraction on an external point P is $\dfrac{\gamma M \cdot CP}{PT^2}$ where M is the mass of the shell, C its centre and PT is the tangent from P.

Solution: Let $CP = c$. We consider an elementary arc $a\delta\theta$ at Q. This arc when revolved about the diameter AB will generate a circular strip of length $2\pi a \sin\theta$ and width $a\delta\theta$. Every point of this strip will be at the same distance R from P.

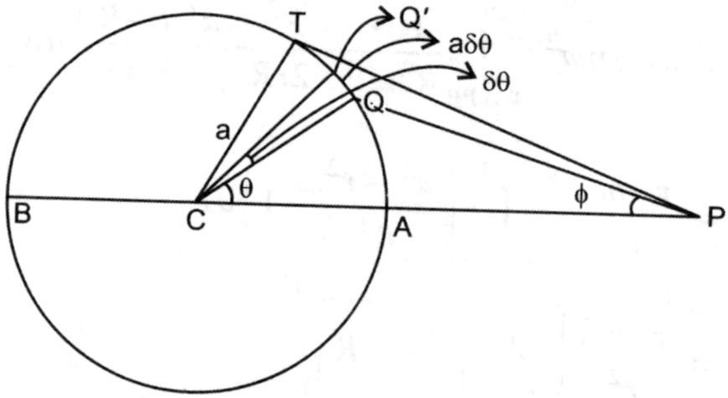

The whole shell is generated by the revolution of semicircular arc ATB about AB.

According to the given law the attraction due to the circular strip at P will be

$$= \frac{\gamma}{PQ^5}\rho\,(2\pi a \sin\theta)\, a\delta\theta \text{ along } PQ$$

$$= 2\pi\gamma\rho\,\frac{a\sin\theta}{R^5}\cdot a\delta\theta\cos\phi \text{ along } PA$$

Let $PQ = R$

In $\Delta\, CPQ$ $\quad \cos\phi = \dfrac{CP^2 + PQ^2 - CQ^2}{CP\,PQ}$

$$= \frac{R^2 + c^2 - a^2}{2cR}$$

Also $\quad \cos\theta = \dfrac{CP^2 + CQ^2 - PQ^2}{2CP\,CQ}$

$$= \frac{c^2 + a^2 - R^2}{2ca}$$

$$\therefore \quad -\sin\theta\, d\theta = \frac{-2R}{2ca}\, dR$$

or $$a \sin\theta\, d\theta = \frac{R dR}{c}$$

Hence attraction at P due to whole surface of the shell

$$= 2\pi\gamma\rho a^2 \int_{R=PA}^{PB} \frac{\sin\theta}{R^5} \cos\phi\, d\theta$$

$$= 2\pi\gamma\rho a^2 \int_{R=PA}^{PB} \frac{R dR}{R^5 ac} \frac{R^2 + c^2 - a^2}{2Rc}$$

$$= \frac{\pi\gamma\rho a}{c^2} \int_{R=PA}^{PB} \frac{R^2 + c^2 - a^2}{R^5}\, dR$$

$$= \frac{\pi\gamma\rho a}{c^2} \int_{c-a}^{c+a} \left(\frac{1}{R^3} + \frac{c^2 - a^2}{R^5}\right) dR$$

$$= \frac{\pi\gamma\rho a}{c^2} \left[-\frac{1}{2R^2} - \frac{c^2 - a^2}{4R^4}\right]_{c-a}^{c+a}$$

$$= \frac{\pi\gamma\rho a}{c^2} \left[-\frac{1}{2}\left\{\frac{1}{(c+a)^2} - \frac{1}{(c-a)^2}\right\} - \frac{c^2 - a^2}{4}\left\{\frac{1}{(c+a)^4} - \frac{1}{(c-a)^4}\right\}\right]$$

$$= \frac{\pi\gamma\rho a}{c^2} \left[-\frac{1}{2} \frac{(-4ca)}{(c^2 - a^2)^2} - \frac{c^2 - a^2}{4} \frac{\left\{(c-a)^4 - (c+a)^4\right\}}{(c^2 - a^2)^4}\right]$$

$$= \frac{\pi\gamma\rho a}{c^2} \left[\frac{2ca}{(c^2 - a^2)^2} - \frac{\left\{(c-a)^4 - (c+a)^4\right\}}{4(c^2 - a^2)^3}\right]$$

$$= \frac{\pi\gamma\rho a}{c^2}\left[\frac{2ca}{\left(c^2-a^2\right)^2} - \frac{\left\{(c-a)^2+(c+a)^2\right\}\left\{(c-a)^2-(c+a)^2\right\}}{4\left(c^2-a^2\right)^3}\right]$$

$$= \frac{\pi\gamma\rho a}{c^2}\left[\frac{2ca}{\left(c^2-a^2\right)^2} - \frac{2\left(c^2+a^2\right)(-4ac)}{4\left(c^2-a^2\right)^3}\right]$$

$$= \frac{\pi\gamma\rho a}{c^2}\left[\frac{2ca}{\left(c^2-a^2\right)^2} + \frac{2\left(c^2+a^2\right)ac}{\left(c^2-a^2\right)^3}\right]$$

$$= \frac{2\pi\gamma\rho aca}{c^2\left(c^2-a^2\right)^2}\left[1+\frac{c^2+a^2}{c^2-a^2}\right]$$

$$= \frac{2\pi\gamma\rho a^2 c}{c^2\left(c^2-a^2\right)^2}\frac{2c^2}{c^2-a^2}$$

$$= \frac{4\pi\gamma\rho a^2 c}{\left(c^2-a^2\right)^3} = \frac{\gamma M\cdot CP}{PT^6}$$

Since $M = 4\pi a^2\rho$

and $CP^2 = CT^2 + PT^2$

$PT^2 = CP^2 - CT^2$

$= c^2 - a^2$

4. Find if there is any law of attraction in addition to that of the inverse square of the distance, by which the attraction of a thin uniform spherical shell would be zero at an internal point.

Solution: Let the law of attraction be $\frac{f(r)}{r^2}$ under which the attraction of a thin uniform spherical shell would be zero at an internal point.

Let Q be any point of the shell. From Q we draw QN perpendicular to OP. Let $\angle POQ = \theta$, then all the points on a

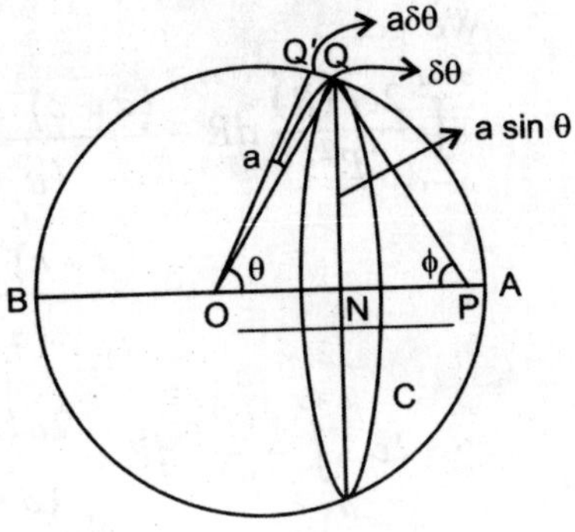

circle with $NQ = a \sin\theta$ as radius are at equal distances from P, and the attraction of each on P resolved along PO

$$= \frac{f(R)}{R^2}\cos\theta \text{ where } PQ = R.$$

Hence the resultant attraction of the portion of the shell generated by the arc $a\delta\theta$

$$= \gamma K\rho \frac{a\delta\theta\, 2\pi a \sin\theta}{R^2} f(R)\cos\phi$$

In ΔOPQ

$$PQ^2 = OP^2 + OQ^2 - 2OP\ OQ\cos\theta$$

$$R^2 = c^2 + a^2 - 2ca\cos\theta$$

$$\therefore \quad 2R\delta R = 2ac\sin\theta\delta\theta$$

Hence attraction of this elementary portion

$$= 2\pi\gamma K\rho \frac{a}{c}\frac{f(R)}{R}\cos\phi\,\delta R$$

$$= 2\pi\gamma K\rho \frac{a}{c}\frac{c^2 + R^2 - a^2}{2cR}\frac{f(R)}{R}\delta R$$

$$= \frac{\pi\gamma K\rho a}{c^2}\frac{R^2 + c^2 - a^2}{R^2} f(R)\delta R$$

Hence the resultant attraction at P

$$= \frac{\pi\gamma K\rho a}{c^2}\int_{a-c}^{a+c}\frac{R^2 + c^2 - a^2}{R^2} f(R)\,dR \qquad \ldots (1)$$

for all values of c less than a, by question.

Differentiating (1) with respect to c and using the result, if

$$u = \int_a^b f(x, \alpha)\,dx \text{ then}$$

$$\frac{dy}{d\alpha} = \int_a^b \frac{d}{d\alpha}[f(x,\alpha)]\,dx + f(b,\alpha)\frac{db}{d\alpha} - f(a,\alpha)\frac{da}{d\alpha}$$

We get

$$\int_{a-c}^{a+c} \frac{2cf(R)}{R^2}\, dR + \frac{(a+c)^2 + c^2 - a^2}{(a+c)^2} f(a+c) \frac{d}{dc}(a+c) - \frac{(a-c)^2 + c^2 - a^2}{(a-c)^2} f(a-c) \frac{d}{dc}(a-c) = 0$$

$$\Rightarrow \quad 2c \int_{a-c}^{a+c} \frac{f(R)}{R^2}\, dR + \frac{2c(c+a)}{(a+c)^2} f(a+c) + \frac{2c(c-a)}{(a-c)^2} f(a-c) = 0$$

$$\Rightarrow \quad \int_{a-c}^{a+c} \frac{f(R)}{R^2}\, dR = \frac{f(a-c)}{a-c} - \frac{f(a+c)}{a+c} \qquad \dots (2)$$

Again similarly differentiating (1) with respect to '*a*' we get

$$\int_{a-c}^{a+c} \frac{-2af(R)}{R^2}\, dR + \frac{(a+c)^2 + c^2 - a^2}{(a+c)^2} f(a+c) \frac{d}{da}(a+c) - \frac{(a-c)^2 + c^2 - a^2}{(a-c)^2} f(a-c) \frac{d}{da}(a-c) = 0$$

$$\Rightarrow \quad -2a \int_{a-c}^{a+c} \frac{f(R)}{R^2}\, dR + \frac{2c(c+a)}{(a+c)^2} f(a+c) + \frac{2c(a-c)}{(a-c)^2} f(a-c) = 0$$

$$\Rightarrow \quad \int \frac{f(R)}{R^2}\, dR = \frac{c}{a} \frac{f(a-c)}{a-c} + \frac{c}{a} \frac{f(a+c)}{a+c} \qquad \dots (3)$$

From (2) and (3), we get

$$\frac{f(a-c)}{a-c} - \frac{f(a+c)}{a+c} = \frac{c}{a} \frac{f(a+c)}{a+c} + \frac{c}{a} \frac{f(a-c)}{a-c}$$

$$\Rightarrow \quad \frac{f(a-c)}{a-c}\left[1 - \frac{c}{a}\right] = \frac{f(a+c)}{a+c}\left[1 + \frac{c}{a}\right]$$

$\Rightarrow f(a - c) = f(a + a)$

This relation is true for all values of a and for all values of c less than a. It follows that $f(r)$ is the same for all values of r, that is, $f(r)$ is constant $= A$ (say).

Hence the only law of attraction admissible $= \dfrac{f(r)}{r^2} = \dfrac{A}{r^2}$ which is inverse square of distance.

5. Find if there is any other law of attraction in addition to that of the inverse square of the distance by which the attraction of a thin uniform shell of radius a would be the same at all external points as if its mass were collected at its centre. [I.A.S. 75; M.U. 81H]

Solution: Let the law of attraction be $\dfrac{f(r)}{r^2}$ under which the attraction of a thin uniform spherical shell at an external point is $\dfrac{\gamma M}{c^2}$ which is same as that of a mass M of the shell concentrated at the centre whose distance from P is c.

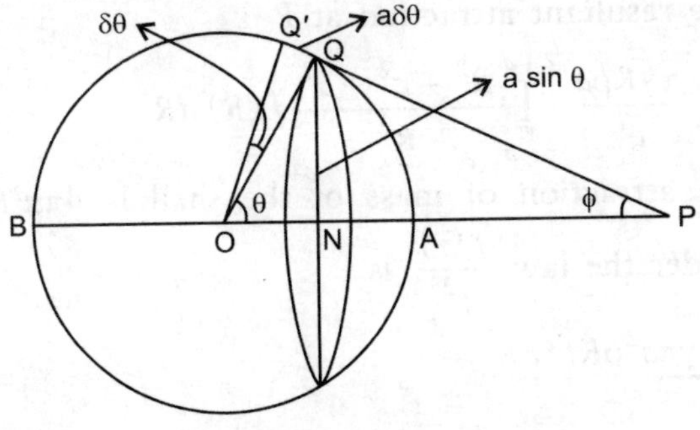

Let Q be any point of the shell. From Q we draw QN perpendicular to OP. Let $\angle POQ = \theta$, then all the points on a circle with $NQ = a \sin\theta$ as radius are at equal distance from P, and the attraction of each on P resolved along $PO =$

$\dfrac{f(R)}{R^2}\cos\phi$

where $PQ = R$.

Hence the resultant attraction of the portion of the shell generated by arc $a\delta\theta$

$$= \frac{\gamma K\rho a\,\delta\theta\,2\pi a \sin\theta}{R^2} f(R)\cos\phi$$

In ΔOPQ

$$PQ^2 = OP^2 + OQ^2 - 2OP\,OQ\cos\theta$$

$$\Rightarrow \quad R^2 = c^2 + a^2 - 2ac\cos\theta$$

$$\therefore \quad 2R\delta R = 2ac\sin\theta\delta\theta.$$

Also $\cos\phi = \dfrac{c^2 + R^2 - a^2}{2cR}$

Hence attraction of this elementary portion

$$= \frac{2\pi\gamma K\rho a}{c}\frac{f(R)}{R}\cos\phi\,\delta R$$

$$= \frac{2\pi\gamma K\rho a}{c}\frac{c^2 + R^2 - a^2}{2cR}\frac{f(R)}{R}\delta R$$

$$= \frac{\pi\gamma K\rho a}{c^2}\frac{R^2 + c^2 - a^2}{R^2} f(R)\,\delta R$$

Hence resultant attraction at P

$$= \frac{\pi\gamma K\rho a}{c^2}\int_{c-a}^{c+a}\frac{R^2 + c^2 - a^2}{R^2} f(R)\,dR \qquad \text{... (1)}$$

Again attraction of mass of the shell is $4\pi a^2 K\rho$ at the centre under the law $\dfrac{f(r)}{r^2}$ is

$$\frac{4\gamma\pi a^2\rho K f(c)}{c^2} \qquad \text{... (2)}$$

By the given condition (1) and (2) are same.

Hence

$$\frac{\pi\gamma K\rho a}{c^2}\int_{c-a}^{c+a}\frac{R^2 + c^2 - a^2}{R^2} f(R)dR = \frac{4\gamma\pi a^2 K\rho f(c)}{c^2}$$

or $$\frac{1}{a}\int_{c-a}^{c+a}\frac{R^2 + c^2 - a^2}{R^2} f(R)dR = 4f(c) \qquad \text{... (3)}$$

This is true for all values of a and all values of c greater than a.

Differentiating (3) w.r.t. a and using the result if

$u = \int_a^b f(x, \alpha)$ then

$$\frac{du}{d\alpha} = \int_a^b \frac{d}{d\alpha}\left[f(x, \alpha)\right]dx + f(b, \alpha)\frac{db}{d\alpha} - f(a, \alpha)\frac{da}{d\alpha}$$

We get

$$-\frac{1}{a^2}\int_{c-a}^{c+a} \frac{R^2 + c^2 - a^2}{R^2} f(R)dR + \frac{1}{a}\left[\frac{2c}{c+a} f(c+a) + \frac{2c}{c-a} f(c-a) - 2a\int \frac{f(R)}{R^2} dR\right] = 0$$

$$\Rightarrow \quad -\frac{1}{a^2}\int_{c-a}^{c+a} \frac{f(R)}{R^2}\left\{R^2 + c^2 - a^2 + 2a^2\right\} dR = -\frac{2c}{a}\left[\frac{f(c+a)}{c+a} + \frac{f(c-a)}{c-a}\right]$$

$$\Rightarrow \quad \int_{c-a}^{c+a} \frac{f(R)}{R^2}\left(R^2 + c^2 + a^2\right) dR = 2ca\left[\frac{f(c+a)}{c+a} + \frac{f(c-a)}{c-a}\right] \qquad \ldots (4)$$

Differentiating (4) with respect to 'c' we get

$$\int_{c-a}^{c+a} \frac{2c}{R^2} f(R)dR + \frac{(c+a)^2 + c^2 + a^2}{(c+a)^2} f(c+a)\cdot 1 - \frac{(c-a)^2 + c^2 + a^2}{(c-a)^2} f(c-a)\cdot 1 = 2a\left[\frac{f(c+a)}{c+a} + \frac{f(c-a)}{c-a}\right]$$

$$+ 2ca\left[\frac{f'(c+a)}{c+a} - \frac{f(c+a)}{(c+a)^2} + \frac{f'(c-a)}{c-a} - \frac{f(c-a)}{(c-a)^2}\right]$$

$$\Rightarrow \int_{c-a}^{c+a} \frac{2cf(R)}{R^2}\,dR = f(c+a)\left[\frac{2a}{c+a} - \frac{2ac}{(c+a)^2} - 1 - \frac{c^2+a^2}{(c+a)^2}\right] + f(c-a)\left[\frac{2a}{c-a} - \frac{2ac}{(c-a)^2} + 1 + \frac{c^2+a^2}{(c-a)^2}\right] + 2ac\left[\frac{f'(c+a)}{c+a} + \frac{f'(c-a)}{c-a}\right]$$

$$\Rightarrow \int_{c-a}^{c+a} \frac{2cf(R)dR}{R^2} = f(a+c)\left[\frac{a-c}{c+a} - 1\right] + f(c-a)\left[\frac{a+c}{c-a} + 1\right] + 2ac\left[\frac{f'(c+a)}{c+a} + \frac{f'(c-a)}{c-a}\right]$$

$$\Rightarrow \int_{c-a}^{c+a} \frac{2cf(R)}{R^2}\,dR = 2c\left[-\frac{f(c+a)}{c+a} + \frac{f(c-a)}{c-a}\right] + 2ac\left[\frac{f'(c+a)}{c+a} + \frac{f'(c-a)}{c-a}\right] \quad \ldots (5)$$

Similarly differentiating (4) with respect to a we get

$$\int_{c-a}^{c+a} \frac{2af(R)}{R^2}\,dR = 2a\left[\frac{-f(c+a)}{c+a} + \frac{f(c-a)}{c-a}\right] + 2ac\left[\frac{f'(c+a)}{c+a} - \frac{f'(c-a)}{c-a}\right] \quad \ldots (6)$$

Now (5) × a – (6) × c gives

$$O = 2a^2c\left[\frac{f'(c+a)}{c+a}+\frac{f'(c-a)}{c-a}\right]$$

$$-2ac^2\left[\frac{f'(c+a)}{c+a}-\frac{f'(c-a)}{c-a}\right]$$

$$\Rightarrow \quad \frac{f'(c+a)}{c+a}(a-c) = \frac{-f'(c-a)}{c-a}(c+a)$$

$$\therefore \quad \frac{f'(c+a)}{(c+a)^2} = \frac{f'(c-a)}{(c-a)^2}$$

Above relation shows that $\frac{f(r)}{r^2}$ is same for all values of c and a.

i.e. $\frac{f'(r)}{r^2}$ is constant = A (say)

Hence $f'(r) = Ar^2$

Integrating we get

$$f(r) = \frac{Ar^3}{3} + B$$

$$\Rightarrow \quad \frac{f(r)}{r^2} = \frac{Ar}{3} + \frac{B}{r^2}$$

$$\frac{f(r)}{r^2} = cr + \frac{B}{r^2} \qquad \text{... (7)}$$

In case $B = 0$, then $\frac{f(r)}{r^2} = cr$ ... (8)

i.e. directly as distance.

In case $c = 0$ then $\frac{f(r)}{r^2} = \frac{B}{r^2}$ ... (9)

i.e. inverse square of distance.

Therefore the required law is either of (7), (8) or (9).

6. If a mountain in the form of an enveloping cone of semi-vertical angle α were added to a sphere of uniform density, then gravity at its summit would be

$$g\,\frac{1+\sin^3\alpha-\cos^3\alpha}{2\sin\alpha}$$

where g is the value of gravity at all points of the surface of the sphere and the mountain is supposed to be of the same density as the sphere.

Solution: Let C be the centre of the sphere of radius a, O is the vertex of the inveloping cone, OCD is the diameter of the sphere through O. Since the densities of the sphere and the cone are same, the combination may be regarded as a single solid obtained by revolving the area $OADCO$ about the diameter OCD. Let $\angle AOD = \alpha$, $OC = c$.

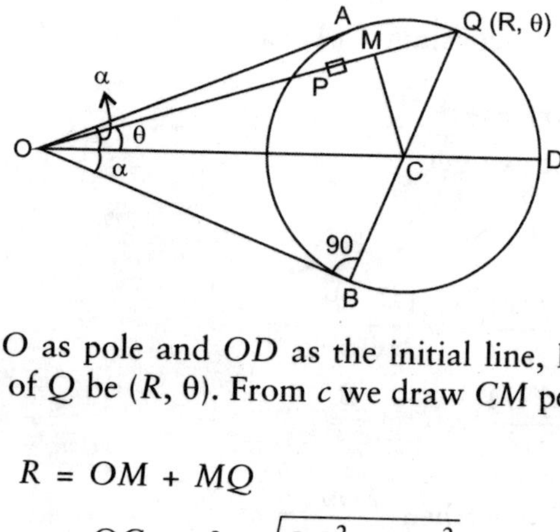

Taking O as pole and OD as the initial line, let the polar coordinates of Q be (R, θ). From c we draw CM perpendicular to OQ

Then $\quad R = OM + MQ$

$$= OC\cos\theta + \sqrt{QC^2 - CM^2}$$

$$= c\cos\theta + \sqrt{a^2 - OC^2\sin^2\theta}$$

$$= c\cos\theta + \sqrt{a^2 - c^2\sin^2\theta} \qquad \text{... (1)}$$

We consider an elementary area $r\delta\theta\delta r$ at P which when revolved about OD will generate a ring of radius $r\sin\theta$.

Mass of the elementary ring $= (2\pi\, r\sin\theta)\, r\delta\theta\delta r\rho$

Attracting of the ring at $O = \dfrac{\gamma(2\pi r\sin\theta)\,r\delta\theta\,\delta r\rho}{r^2}$

Its resolved part along OC

$$= \frac{\gamma(2\pi r\sin\theta)\,r\delta\theta\,\delta r\rho}{r^2}\cos\theta$$

$$= 2\pi\gamma\rho\sin\theta\cos\theta\,\delta\theta\,\delta r$$

Therefore the attraction of the whole solid

$$= 2\pi\gamma\rho\int_{\theta=0}^{\alpha}\int_{r=0}^{R}\sin\theta\cos\theta\,d\theta\,dr$$

$$= 2\pi\gamma\rho\int_{0}^{\alpha}R\sin\theta\cos\theta\,d\theta$$

$$= 2\pi\gamma\rho\int_{0}^{\alpha}\left[c\cos\theta+\sqrt{a^2-c^2\sin^2\theta}\right]\sin\theta\cos\theta\,d\theta$$

from (1)

$$= 2\pi\gamma\rho\left[-\frac{c\cos^3\theta}{3}-\frac{1}{2c^2}\,\frac{2}{3}\left(a^2-c^2\sin^2\theta\right)^{\frac{3}{2}}\right]_0^{\alpha}$$

$$= 2\pi\gamma\rho\left[-\frac{c}{3}\left(\cos^3\alpha-1\right)-\frac{1}{3c^2}\left\{\left(a^2-c^2\frac{a^2}{c^2}\right)^{\frac{3}{2}}-a^3\right\}\right]$$

Since $\sin\alpha = \dfrac{a}{c}$

$$= 2\pi\gamma\rho c\left[\frac{1}{3}\left(1-\cos^3\alpha\right)+\frac{a^3}{3c^3}\right]$$

$$= \frac{2\pi\gamma\rho c}{3}\left[1-\cos^3\alpha+\sin^3\alpha\right]$$

$$= \frac{4\pi\gamma\rho c}{3}\sin\alpha\left[\frac{1-\cos^3\alpha+\sin^3\alpha}{2\sin\alpha}\right]$$

$$= \frac{4\pi\gamma\rho c}{3}\,\frac{a}{c}\left[\frac{1-\cos^3\alpha+\sin^3\alpha}{2\sin\alpha}\right]$$

$$= g\left[\frac{1-\cos^3\alpha+\sin^3\alpha}{2\sin\alpha}\right]$$

Since g = attraction of the earth at a point on its surface

$$= \frac{4}{3}\pi\gamma\rho a$$

7. If O is the centre of a solid uniform sphere and P an external point, show that the sphere on OP as diameter cut off portion whose attraction at P is equal to $\frac{1}{2}\frac{\gamma M}{OP^2}$ where M is the whole mass.

Solution: Let $OA = a$ be the radius of the sphere whose centre is O. Let $OP = c$.

A sphere is described on OP as diameter, which cuts off a portion $OBACO$ of the first sphere whose attraction is to be determined at P. The above portion of the sphere is generated by revolving the area $OBAO$ about OA. We consider an elementary area $r\delta\theta\delta r$. This area when revolved about OA will generate a circular solid ring of radius $r\sin\theta$ and cross-section $r\delta\theta\delta r$.

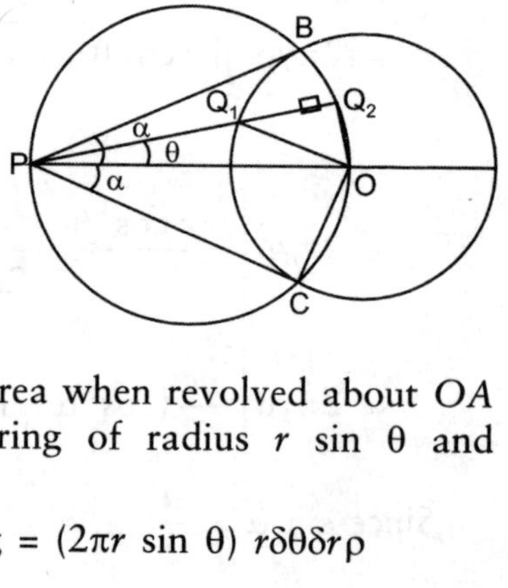

Mass of this elementary ring $= (2\pi r\sin\theta)\, r\delta\theta\delta r\rho$

Attraction of this ring at P

$$= \frac{\gamma\,(2\pi r\sin\theta)\, r\delta\theta\delta r\,\rho}{r^2} = 2\pi\gamma\rho\sin\theta\,\delta\theta\,\delta r$$

Its resolved part along PQ

$$= (2\pi\gamma\rho\sin\theta\,\delta\theta\,\delta r)\cos\theta$$

Now

$$PQ_1 = PQ_2 - Q_1Q_2$$

$$= c\cos\theta - \sqrt{OQ_1^2 - OQ_2^2}$$

$$= c\cos\theta - \sqrt{a^2 - c^2\sin^2\theta}$$

and $PQ_2 = c\cos\theta$

Hence attraction of the solid $OBACO$ at P, in the direction PO

$$= 2\pi\gamma\rho \int_{\theta=0}^{\alpha} \int_{r=PQ_1}^{r=PQ_2} \sin\theta\cos\theta\, d\theta\, dr$$

$$= 2\pi\gamma\rho \int_0^{\alpha} \sin\theta\cos\theta\,(PQ_2 - PQ_1)\, d\theta$$

$$= 2\pi\gamma\rho \int_0^{\alpha} \left[c\cos\theta - \left\{c\cos\theta - \sqrt{a^2 - c^2\sin^2\theta}\right\}\right] \times \sin\theta\cos\theta\, d\theta$$

$$= 2\pi\gamma\rho \int_0^{\alpha} \sqrt{a^2 - c^2\sin^2\theta}\, \sin\theta\cos\theta\, d\theta$$

Putting $c\sin\theta = a\sin\phi$

$$c\cos\theta\, d\theta = a\cos\phi\, d\phi$$

When $\theta = \alpha$, $c\sin\alpha = a\sin\phi$

or $$c\frac{a}{c} = a\sin\phi$$

or $$\sin\phi = 1$$

$$\phi = \frac{\pi}{2}$$

when $\theta = 0$, $\phi = 0$

Hence required attraction

$$= 2\pi\gamma\rho \int_0^{\frac{\pi}{2}} \sqrt{a^2 - a^2\sin^2\phi}\, \frac{a\sin\phi}{c} \frac{a}{c}\cos\phi\, d\phi$$

$$= 2\pi\gamma\rho \int_0^{\frac{\pi}{2}} \frac{a^3}{c^2}\cos^2\phi\sin\phi\, d\phi$$

$$= \frac{2\pi\gamma\rho a^3}{c^2}\left[-\frac{\cos^3\phi}{3}\right]_0^{\frac{\pi}{2}}$$

$$= \frac{2\pi\gamma\rho a^3}{c^2}$$

$$= \frac{1}{2}\gamma \frac{\frac{4}{3}\pi a^3\rho}{c^2}$$

$$= \frac{1}{2}\gamma \frac{M}{OP^2} \quad \text{since } M = \frac{4}{3}\pi a^3\rho$$

8. Two uniform solid spheres are of density ρ and radius a and the distance between their centres is c (> $2a$). Prove that they attract each other with a force $\frac{16\gamma\pi^2\rho^2 a^6}{9c^2}$ where γ is the constant of gravitation.

Solution: Let O and O′ be the centres of two equal spheres of the same density ρ, the radius of each being a.

Given $OO' = c$.

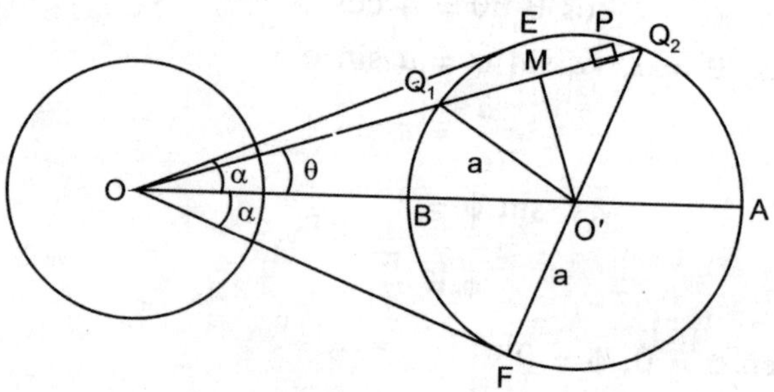

If M be the mass of the sphere then

$$M = \frac{4}{3}\pi a^3\rho$$

Let the tangent from O to the second sphere make an aıgle α with OO' then $\sin\alpha = \frac{a}{c}$ or $\alpha = \sin^{-1}\frac{a}{c}$. Taking O as ɔole and OO' as initial line, let coordinates of P be (r, θ).

Attraction of the first sphere at any point P in the seɛond sphere $= \frac{\gamma M}{r^2}$.

Now we consider an element $r\delta\theta\delta r$ at P. The second sphere is obtained by the revolution of the area $AEBA$ about AB. This element when revolved about AB will generate a circular ring of radius $r \sin \theta$.

Mass of the ring $= \rho(2\pi r \sin \theta)\, r\delta\theta\,\delta r$

Hence the attraction of the first sphere on the element

$$= \frac{\gamma M}{r^2}(r\delta\theta\delta r)(2\pi r \sin \theta)\, \rho \text{ along } OP$$

Its resolved part along OO^1

$$= \gamma M \cdot 2\pi\rho\,(\sin \theta\, \delta\theta\delta r) \cos \theta$$

Also $\quad OQ_1 = OM - MQ_1 = c \cos \theta - \sqrt{OQ_1^2 - OM^2}$

$$= c \cos \theta - \sqrt{a^2 - c^2 \sin^2 \theta}$$

and $\quad OQ_2 = OM + MQ_2 = c \cos \theta + \sqrt{CQ_2^2 - OM^2}$

$$= c \cos \theta + \sqrt{a^2 - c^2 \sin^2 \theta}$$

Hence the required attraction

$$= 2\pi\gamma M\rho \int_0^{\alpha} \int_{OQ_1}^{OQ_2} \sin \theta \cos \theta \, d\theta \, dr$$

$$= 2\pi\gamma M\rho \int_0^{\alpha} (OQ_2 - OQ_1) \sin \theta \cos \theta \, d\theta$$

$$= 2\pi\gamma M\rho \int_0^{\alpha} 2\sqrt{a^2 - c^2 \sin^2 \theta} \sin \theta \cos \theta \, d\theta$$

Putting $c \sin \theta = a \sin \phi$

$$c \cos \theta \, d\theta = a \cos \phi \, d\phi$$

Where $a = \sin^{-1} \dfrac{a}{c}$

then $\quad c\dfrac{a}{c} = a \sin \phi$

Hence $\quad \phi = \dfrac{\pi}{2}$

When $\theta = 0, \phi = 0$

$$= 4\pi\gamma M\rho \int_0^{\frac{\pi}{2}} a\cos\phi \frac{a}{c}\sin\phi \frac{a\cos\phi}{c}\,d\phi$$

$$= \frac{4\pi\gamma M\rho a^3}{c^2}\int_0^{\frac{\pi}{2}} \cos^2\phi \sin\theta\,d\phi$$

$$= \frac{4\pi\gamma M\rho a^3}{c^2}\left[-\frac{1}{3}\cos^3\phi\right]_0^{\frac{\pi}{2}}$$

$$= \frac{4\pi\gamma M\rho a^3}{3c^2}$$

$$= \frac{4}{3c^2}\pi\gamma\rho a^3\left(\frac{4}{3}\pi a^3\rho\right)$$

$$= \frac{16\gamma\pi^2 a^6\rho^2}{9c^2}$$

9. If a self-attracting shell of mass M bounded by concentric spheres of radii a and b be cut by a plane through the centre, prove that the pressure between the halves is

$$\frac{3\gamma M^2}{16}\cdot\frac{a^2+2ab+3b^2}{\left(a^2+ab+b^2\right)^2}$$

Solution: Let O be the centre of the shell whose external and internal radii are a and b.

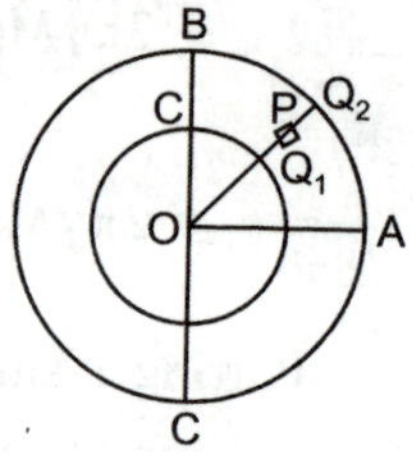

The mass of the shell is

$$M = \frac{4}{3}\pi\left(a^3 - b^3\right)\rho \qquad \dots (1)$$

The shell is divided into two halves by a plane through the centre.

Now attraction of one half on itself is zero as it forms pairs of equal and opposite forces. Therefore attraction of one half on the other half is the same as that of the whole on that half. So we are to determine here attraction of the whole shell on the half portion BAC.

Now attraction of the whole shell at a point P within the shell

= Attraction of the sphere of radius a at an internal point P

= Attraction of the sphere of radius b at an external point P

$$= \frac{4}{3}\pi\gamma\rho r - \frac{\gamma \frac{4}{3}\pi b^3 \rho}{r^3}$$

$$= \frac{4}{3}\pi\gamma\rho\left(r - \frac{b^3}{r^3}\right)$$

Now we consider an elementary area $r\delta\theta\delta r$ at P which when revolved about OA will generate a circular ring of radius $r \sin\theta$ whose mass $= (2\pi r \sin\theta)\, r\, \delta\theta\delta r\rho$.

Hence the attraction on this element resolved along OA

$$= \frac{4}{3}\pi\gamma\rho\left(r - \frac{b^3}{r^2}\right)(2\pi\, r \sin\theta)\, r\delta\theta\delta r\, \rho \cos\theta$$

$$= \frac{8}{3}\pi^2\rho^2\gamma\left(r^3 - b^3\right)\sin\theta\cos\theta\,\delta\theta\,\delta r$$

Thus total attraction $\frac{\pi}{2}$

$$= \frac{8}{3}\pi^2\rho^2\gamma \int_0^{\frac{\pi}{2}}\int_b^a \left(r^3 - b^3\right)\sin\theta\cos\theta\, d\theta\, dr$$

$$= \frac{8}{3}\pi^2\rho^2\gamma \int_0^{\frac{\pi}{2}}\left[\frac{r^4}{4} - b^3 r\right]_b^a \sin\theta\cos\theta\, d\theta$$

$$= \frac{8}{3}\pi^2\rho^2\gamma\left[\frac{a^4 - b^4}{4} - b^3(a - b)\right]\int_0^{\frac{\pi}{2}}\sin\theta\cos\theta\, d\theta$$

$$= \frac{8}{3}\pi^2\rho^2\gamma\left[\frac{(a-b)(a+b)(a^2+b^2)}{4} - b^3(a-b)\right]\left[\frac{\sin^2\theta}{2}\right]_0^{\frac{\pi}{2}}$$

$$= \frac{8}{3}\pi^2\rho^2\gamma\,\frac{(a-b)}{8}\left[a^3+a^2b+ab^2+b^3-4b^3\right]$$

$$= \frac{1}{3}\pi^2\rho^2\gamma\,(a-b)\left[a^3-a^2b+2a^2b-2ab^2+3ab^2-3b^3\right]$$

$$= \frac{1}{3}\pi^2\rho^2\gamma\,(a-b)\left[a^2(a-b)+2ab(a-b)+3b^2(a-b)\right]$$

$$= \frac{1}{3}\pi^2\rho^2\gamma\,(a-b)^2(a^2+2ab+3b^2)$$

$$= \frac{1}{3}\frac{\pi^2\gamma 9M^2}{16\pi^2}\frac{(a-b)^2(a^2+2ab+3b^2)}{(a^3-b^3)^2} \quad \text{from (1)}$$

$$= \frac{3\gamma M^2}{16}\frac{(a^2+2ab+3b^2)}{(a^2+ab+b^2)^2}$$

10. **A uniform solid sphere of mass M is cut in two by a diametral plane. Show that the resultant attraction between the halves is $\frac{3\gamma M^2}{16a^2}$, where a is the radius of the sphere and γ is the constant of gravitation.**

[T.M.B.U. 01H; B.B.A.B.U. 96H]

Solution: Let O be the centre of the sphere and $BACOB$ be its one half

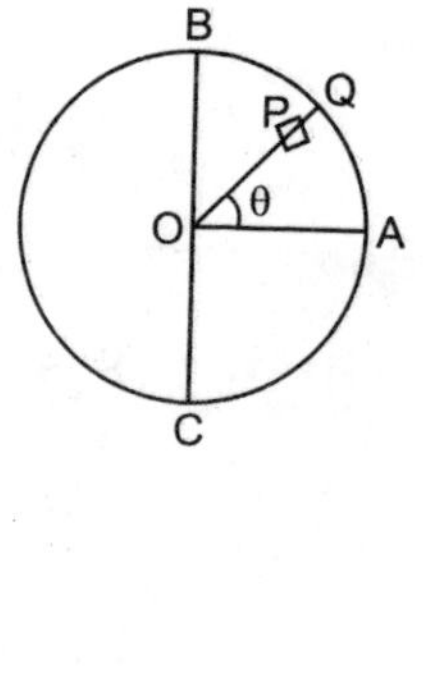

$$\text{Mass } M = \frac{4}{3}\pi a^3\rho \qquad \dots (1)$$

We have to find the attraction between the halves. Now the attraction of one half on itself is zero as it will form a pair of equal and opposite forces.

Hence we can say that the attraction of one half on the other half is the same as the attraction of whole on that half.

Attraction of a sphere of uniform density at an internal point P distance r from the centre $= \frac{4}{3}\pi\gamma\rho r$.

We consider an elementary area $r\delta\theta\delta r$ at P which when revolved about OA will generate a circular ring of radius $r \sin \theta$ and hence its mass $= (2\pi\, r \sin\theta)\, r\delta\theta\delta r\rho$.

Hence the attraction of the element along OA

$$= \frac{4}{3}\pi\gamma\rho r\,(2\pi r \sin\theta)\, r\delta\theta\,\delta r\,\rho\cos\theta$$

Therefore the attraction of the whole sphere along OA

$$= \int_0^{\frac{\pi}{2}}\int_0^{a} \frac{4}{3}\pi\gamma\rho r\, 2\pi r \sin\theta\cos\theta\,\rho r\, d\theta\, dr$$

$$= \frac{8}{3}\pi^2\rho^2\gamma \int_0^{\frac{\pi}{2}}\int_0^{a} r^3 \cos\theta\sin\theta\, d\theta\, dr$$

$$= \frac{8}{3}\pi^2\rho^2\gamma \left[\frac{r^4}{4}\right]_0^a \left[\frac{\sin^2\theta}{2}\right]_0^{\frac{\pi}{2}}$$

$$= \frac{8}{3}\pi^2\rho^2\gamma\,\frac{a^4}{4}\,\frac{1}{2}$$

$$= \frac{\gamma}{3}\pi^2\rho^2 a^4$$

$$= \frac{\gamma a^4}{3}\,\frac{9M^2}{16a^6} \quad \text{from (1)}$$

$$= \frac{3M^2\gamma}{16a^2}$$

11. Prove that if a solid sphere of uniform density ρ is divided into two parts by a plane which cuts the surface in a circle of radius b, the attraction between the two parts is $\frac{1}{3}\gamma\pi^2\rho^2 b^4$.

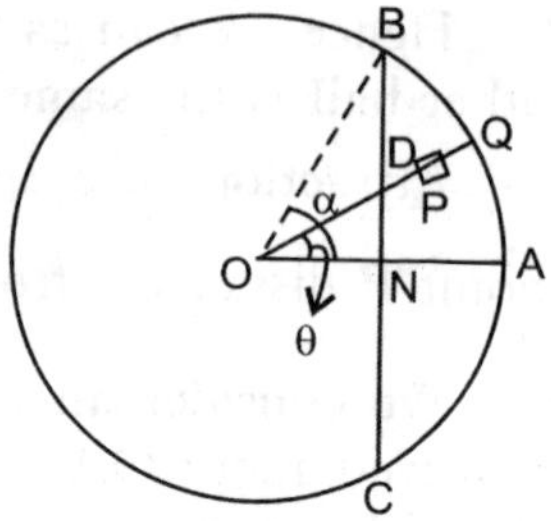

Solution: Let O be the centre of the sphere of radius R.

The dividing plane is BNC. This plane is a circle of radius b so that $BN = NC = b$. Let $\angle BON = \alpha$.

If a is the radius of the sphere then angular distance of B or C from $OA = \alpha = \sin^{-1}\dfrac{b}{a}$.

Since attraction of the one part on itself is zero, therefore attraction of the one part upon the other part is the same as that of the whole on that part. So we are to find the attraction of the whole sphere on one part, say upon the part on right side of the dividing plane BC.

In ΔOBN
$$OB^2 = ON^2 + BN^2$$
$$a^2 = ON^2 + b^2$$
$$a^2 - b^2 = ON^2$$
$$\therefore \quad ON = \sqrt{a^2 - b^2}$$

In ΔODN
$$\cos\theta = \frac{ON}{OD}$$
$$OD = ON \sec\theta$$
$$= \sqrt{a^2 - b^2}\sec\theta$$

Also $OQ = a$

In ΔBON
$$\sin\alpha = \frac{BN}{OB} = \frac{b}{a}$$

Since attraction of the one part on itself is zero, therefore attraction of the one part upon the other part is the same as that of the whole on that part. Hence we are to find the attraction of the whole sphere on one part say upon the part on the right side of the dividing plane.

We consider an elementary area $r\delta\theta\delta r$ at $P\ (r, \theta)$ which when revolved about OA will generate a circular ring of radius $r \sin\theta$.

Mass of the elementary area $= (2\pi\ r \sin\theta)\ r\delta\theta\ \delta r\rho$

Also attraction of the sphere an internal point P at a distance r from the centre $= \frac{4}{3}\pi\gamma\rho r$.

Hence the attraction of this element resolved along OA

$$= \frac{4}{3}\pi\gamma\rho r\,(2\pi r \sin\theta)\, r\delta\theta\delta r\, \rho\cos\theta$$

Hence attraction of the sphere on one part, resolved along OA

$$= \int_{\theta=0}^{\alpha} \int_{r=\sqrt{a^2-b^2}\sec\theta}^{a} \frac{4}{3}\pi\gamma\rho r\,(2\pi r\sin\theta) r d\theta dr\, \rho\cos\theta$$

$$= \frac{8}{3}\pi^2\rho^2\gamma \int_{\theta=0}^{\alpha} \int_{\sqrt{a^2-b^2}\sec\theta}^{a} r^3 dr \sin\theta\cos\theta\, d\theta$$

$$= \frac{8}{3}\pi^2\rho^2\gamma \int_0^{\alpha} \sin\theta\cos\theta\, d\theta \left[\frac{r^4}{4}\right]_{\sqrt{a^2-b^2}\sec\theta}^{a}$$

$$= \frac{8}{3}\pi^2\rho^2\gamma^2 \int_0^{\alpha} \sin\theta\cos\theta\, d\theta \left\{a^4 - \left(a^2-b^2\right)^2 \sec^2\theta\right\}$$

$$= \frac{2}{3}\pi^2\rho^2\gamma \int_0^{\alpha} \left[a^4 \sin\theta\cos\theta - \left(a^2-b^2\right)^2 \tan\theta\sec^2\theta\right] d\theta$$

$$= \frac{2}{3}\pi^2\rho^2\gamma \left[a^4\frac{\sin^2\theta}{2} - \left(a^2-b^2\right)^2\frac{\tan^2\theta}{2}\right]_0^{\alpha}$$

Since $\sin\alpha = \frac{b}{a}$

Hence $\tan\alpha = \frac{b}{\sqrt{a^2-b^2}}$

Therefore required attraction

$$= \frac{1}{3}\pi^2\rho^2\gamma \left[\frac{b^2a^4}{a^2} - \left(a^2-b^2\right)^2 \frac{b^2}{\left(a^2-b^2\right)}\right]$$

$$= \frac{1}{3}\pi^2\rho^2\gamma \left[a^2b^2 - \left(a^2-b^2\right)b^2\right]$$

$$= \frac{1}{3}\pi^2\rho^2\gamma b^2 b^2$$

$$= \frac{1}{3}\gamma\pi^2\rho^2 b^4$$

12. Prove that the force required to separate the two parts of a solid uniform sphere divided in any manner is

$$\gamma\frac{MM'}{a^3}GG'$$

where M, M' are the masses and G, G' the centres of gravity of the two parts and a is the radius of the sphere.

Solution: Let O be the centre of the sphere which is divided into two parts by a plane BDC at a distance c from the centre O, so that $OD = c$.

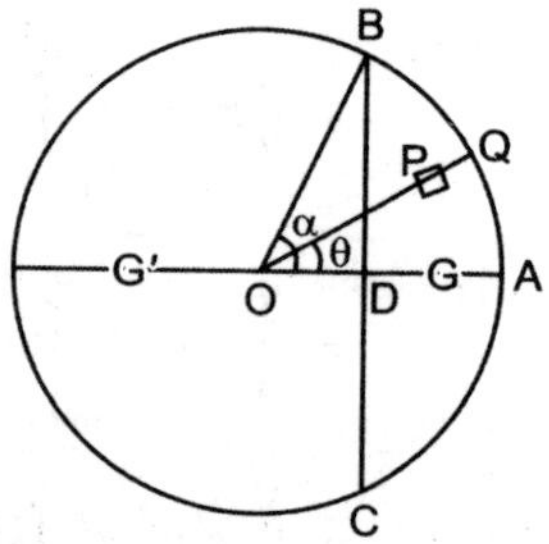

The figure is the section of the sphere through the centres of gravity G and G′.

In ΔOBD $\cos\alpha = \frac{OD}{OB} = \frac{c}{a}$

Equation of the circle is $x^2 + y^2 = a^2$

Applying the general formula to determine the centre of gravity, we have

$$OG = \frac{\int_c^a x\rho\pi y^2 dx}{\int_c^a \rho\pi y^2 dx} = \frac{\pi\rho\int_c^a x\left(a^2 - x^2\right)dx}{M}$$

$$= \frac{\pi\rho}{M}\int_c^a\left(a^2x - x^3\right)dx$$

$$= \frac{\pi\rho}{M}\left[\frac{a^2x^2}{2} - \frac{x^4}{4}\right]_c^a$$

$$= \frac{\pi\rho}{M}\left[\left(\frac{a^4}{2} - \frac{a^4}{4}\right) - \left(\frac{a^2c^2}{2} - \frac{c^4}{4}\right)\right]$$

$$= \frac{\pi\rho}{M}\left[\frac{\left(a^2 - c^2\right)^2}{4}\right]$$

$$= \frac{\pi\rho}{4M}\left(a^2 - c^2\right)^2$$

$$\text{Also} \quad OG' = \frac{\int_{-a}^{c} x\pi\rho y^2 dx}{\int_{-a}^{c} \rho\pi y^2 dx}$$

$$= \frac{\pi\rho \int_{-a}^{c} x\left(a^2 - x^2\right) dx}{M'}$$

$$= \frac{\pi\rho}{M'}\left[-\frac{1}{4}\left(a^2 - x^2\right)^2\right]_{-a}^{c}$$

$$= \frac{-\pi\rho}{4M'}\left(a^2 - c^2\right)^2$$

The negative sign shows that G' is on the other side of O.

$$\text{Hence} \quad |OG'| = \frac{\pi\rho}{4M'}\left(a^2 - c^2\right)^2$$

$$\therefore GG' = GO + OG' = \frac{\pi\rho\left(a^2 - c^2\right)^2}{4}\left[\frac{1}{M} + \frac{1}{M'}\right]$$

$$= \frac{\pi\rho\left(a^2 - c^2\right)^2}{4}\,\frac{M + M'}{MM'}$$

$$= \frac{\pi\rho}{4}\left(a^2 - c^2\right)^2 \frac{\frac{4}{3}\pi a^3\rho}{MM'}$$

$$\text{Since} \quad M + M' = \frac{4}{3}\pi a^3\rho$$

$$\text{or} \quad GG' = \frac{\pi^2\rho^2 a^3}{3MM'}\left(a^2 - c^2\right)^2$$

$$\text{i.e.} \quad GG' \cdot MM' = \frac{1}{3}\pi^2\rho^2 a^3\left(a^2 - c^2\right)^2 \qquad \dots (1)$$

Since attraction of the one part upon itself is zero, therefore attraction of the one part upon the other part is the same as that of the whole on that part. Thus we are to find the attraction of the whole sphere on one part, whose centre of gravity is G.

Attraction of the sphere at an internal point P at a distance r from the centre $= \frac{4}{3}\pi\gamma\rho r$.

We consider an elementary area $r\delta\theta\delta r$ at $P\ (r, \theta)$ which when revolved about OA will generate a circular ring of radius $r \sin \theta$.

Mass of the elementary area $= (2\pi\ r \sin \theta)\ r\delta\theta\delta r\rho$

Hence the attraction of this element resolved along OA

$$= \frac{4}{3}\pi\gamma\rho r\,(2\pi r \sin\theta)\, r\delta\theta\delta r\ \rho \cos\theta$$

Therefore the attraction of the sphere on one part, resolved along OA

$$= \int_{\theta=0}^{\alpha} \int_{r=c\sec\theta}^{a} \frac{4}{3}\pi\gamma\rho r\,(2\pi r \sin\theta)\, r d\theta\, dr\, \rho\cos\theta$$

$$= \frac{8}{3}\pi^2\rho^2\gamma \int_0^{\alpha} \sin\theta\cos\theta \left[\frac{r^4}{4}\right]_{c\sec\theta}^{a} d\theta$$

$$= \frac{2}{3}\pi^2\rho^2\gamma \int_0^{\alpha} \sin\theta\cos\theta\left(a^4 - c^4\sec^4\theta\right) d\theta$$

$$= \frac{2}{3}\gamma\pi^2\rho^2\left[\frac{a^4}{2}\sin^2\theta - \frac{c^4}{2}\tan^2\theta\right]_0^{\alpha}$$

$$= \frac{1}{3}\gamma\pi^2\rho^2\left[a^4\left(1-\cos^2\theta\right) - c^4\left(\sec^2\theta - 1\right)\right]_0^{\alpha}$$

$$= \frac{1}{3}\gamma\pi^2\rho^2\left[a^4\left(1-\frac{c^2}{a^2}\right) - c^4\left(\frac{a^2}{c^2} - 1\right)\right] \quad \left[\because \cos\alpha = \frac{c}{a}\right]$$

$$= \frac{1}{3}\gamma\pi^2\rho^2\left[a^2\left(a^2 - c^2\right) - c^2\left(a^2 - c^2\right)\right]$$

$$= \frac{1}{3}\gamma\pi^2\rho^2\left(a^2 - c^2\right)^2$$

$$= \frac{\gamma MM'}{a^3} \cdot GG' \qquad \text{from (1)}$$

13. A homogeneous sphere of radius a and mass M_1 is in contact with the centre of the plane face of a homogeneous hemisphere of radius a and mass M_2. Show that the pressure between them due to their mutual attraction is $\frac{\gamma M_1 M_2}{a^2}\left(\sqrt{2} - 1\right)$.

Solution: Let C be the centre of the sphere and A be the centre of the base of the hemisphere. Let A be the point of contact of the two bodies.

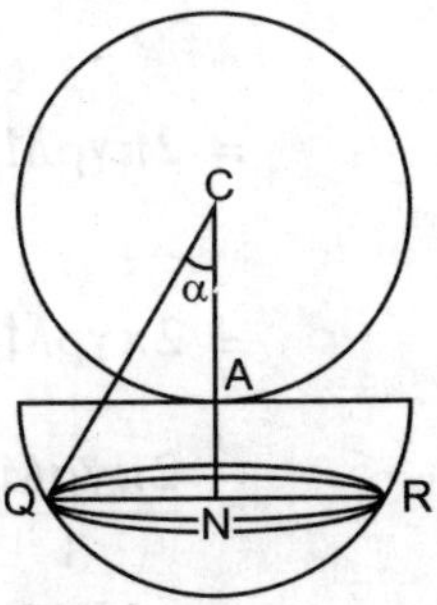

Every point of the hemisphere is external to the sphere, hence attraction of the sphere at the hemisphere will be the same as that of the hemisphere on a particle of mass M_1 equal to the mass of the sphere supposed to be placed at the centre C. Hence it follows that their mutual attraction will be the same as attraction of the hemisphere at a particle of mass M_1 supposed to be placed at C.

We consider an elementary disc QR at a distance x from A, so that $AN = x$, $CN = CA + AN = a + x$.

In ΔQCN $\quad QC^2 = QN^2 + CN^2$

$$= a^2 - x^2 + (a + x)^2$$

$$= 2a^2 + 2ax$$

$$= 2a\,(a + x)$$

Let $\angle QCN = \alpha$

$$\therefore \qquad QC = \sqrt{2a\,(a + x)}$$

Attraction of the elementary disc QR at a particle of mass M_1 placed at C

$$= 2\pi\gamma\delta x\rho\,(1 - \cos\alpha)M_1$$

$$= 2\pi\gamma\delta x\rho\left[1 - \frac{a+x}{\sqrt{2a(a+x)}}\right]M_1$$

$$= 2\pi\gamma\rho\left[1 - \frac{\sqrt{a+x}}{\sqrt{2a}}\right]M_1\delta x$$

Hence attraction of the hemisphere upon a mass M_1 at C

$$= 2\pi\gamma\rho M_1 \int_0^a \left[1 - \frac{1}{\sqrt{2a}}(a+x)^{\frac{1}{2}}\right]dx$$

$$= 2\pi\gamma\rho M_1 \left[x - \frac{1}{\sqrt{2a}}(a+x)^{\frac{3}{2}}\frac{2}{3}\right]_0^a$$

$$= 2\pi\gamma\rho M_1 \left[a - \frac{1}{\sqrt{2a}}\frac{2.2}{3}\sqrt{2a}\sqrt{a} + \frac{1}{\sqrt{2a}}\frac{2}{3}a\sqrt{a}\right]$$

$$= 2\pi\gamma\rho M_1 \left[a - \frac{4a}{3} + \frac{a\sqrt{2}}{3}\right]$$

$$= \frac{2\pi\gamma\rho M_1}{3}a\left(\sqrt{2}-1\right)$$

$$= \frac{\gamma M_1 M_1}{a^2}\left(\sqrt{2}-1\right) \text{ since } M_2 = \frac{2}{3}\pi a^3\rho$$

14. The mass of a unit length of an infinite homogeneous cylinder of radius a is M. It is divided into two parts by a plane through its axis. Show that the pressure due to their mutual attraction is $\dfrac{4\gamma M^2}{3\pi a}$ per unit length of the cylinder.

Solution: Let us first find the attraction of the finite cylinder at any internal point P at a distance C from the centre O.

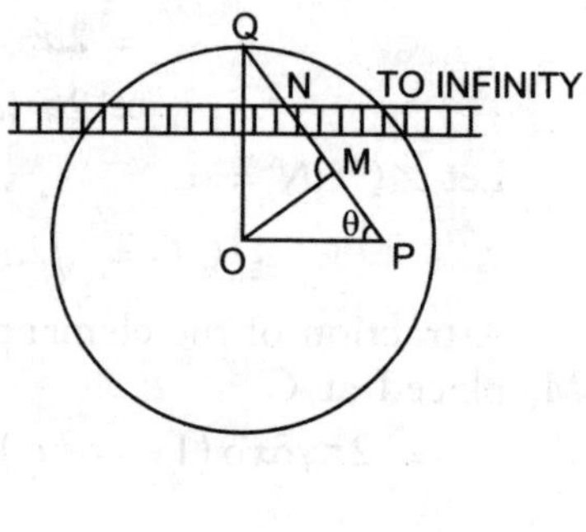

We divide the cylinder into large number of rods of infinite length and let there be one such rod standing on $r\delta\theta\delta r$.

The attraction of this infinite rod at the point P

$$= \frac{2\gamma r\delta\theta\delta r\,\rho}{r} \text{ along } PQ$$

Its resolved part along PO

$$= \frac{2\gamma r\delta\theta\delta r\,\rho}{r}\cos\theta = 2\gamma\rho\cos\theta\,\delta\theta\,\delta r$$

In ΔOPM

$$\cos\theta = \frac{PM}{OP} = \frac{PM}{c}$$

$$PM = c\cos\theta$$

Also $$\sin\theta = \frac{OM}{OP} = \frac{OM}{c}$$

$$OM = c\sin\theta$$

In ΔOMQ

$$OQ^2 = OM^2 + MQ^2$$

$$a^2 = c^2\sin^2\theta + MQ^2$$

$$MQ = \sqrt{a^2 - c^2\sin^2\theta}$$

Now $$PQ = \text{PM} + \text{MQ} = c\cos\theta + \sqrt{a^2 - c^2\sin^2\theta}$$

Hence attraction of the whole cylinder at P in the direction PO

$$= 2\int_{-\pi}^{\pi}\int_{0}^{PQ} 2\gamma\rho\cos\theta\,d\theta\,dr$$

$$= 2\int_{0}^{\pi} 2\gamma\rho\cos\theta\,PQ\,d\theta$$

$$= 4\gamma\rho\int_{0}^{\pi}\cos\theta\left[c\cos\theta + \sqrt{a^2 - c^2\sin^2\theta}\right]d\theta$$

$$= 4\gamma\rho\int_{0}^{\pi}\left[c\cos^2\theta + \sqrt{a^2 - c^2\sin^2\theta}\right]d\theta\cos\theta$$

$$= 4\gamma\rho\int_{0}^{\pi}\left[c\cos^2\theta\right]d\theta$$

The second integral vanishes

$$= 4\gamma\rho c \int_0^{\pi} \frac{1+\cos 2\theta}{2}\, d\theta$$

$$= 2\gamma\rho c \left[\theta + \frac{\sin 2\theta}{2}\right]_0^{\pi}$$

$$= 2\gamma\rho c\pi$$

It follows that attraction of the whole infinite cylinder at any point Q distant r from the centre $= 2\pi\gamma\rho r$.

Mutual attraction between the two halves is the same as attraction of the whole on one half.

Now attraction of the whole cylinder at any point Q in thehalf $= 2\pi\gamma\rho r$. Where $OQ = r$.

We consider an element $r\delta\theta\delta r$ at P at a distance r from centre O.

Hence mass of the element $= \rho r\delta\theta\delta r$

Therefore attraction of the whole cylinder on the one half per unit length of it, resolved perpendicular to the dividing plane

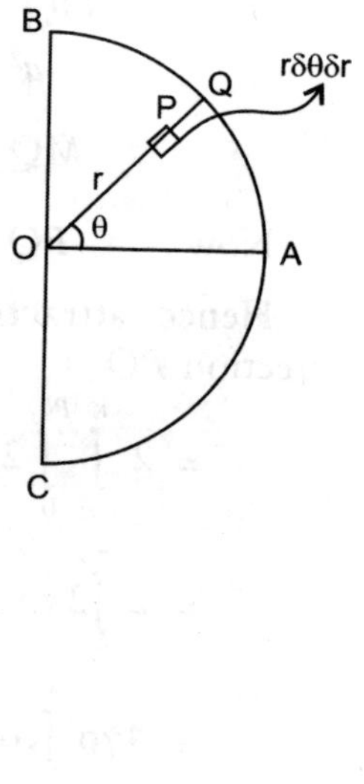

$$= \int_{-\frac{\pi}{2}}^{\frac{\pi}{2}} \int_0^a 2\pi\gamma\rho r\,(r d\theta dr)\,\rho\cos\theta$$

$$= 2\int_0^{\frac{\pi}{2}} \int_0^a 2\pi\gamma\rho^2 r^2 \cos\theta\, d\theta\, dr$$

$$= 4\pi\gamma\rho^2 \int_0^{\frac{\pi}{2}} \frac{a^3}{3} \cos\theta\, d\theta$$

$$= \frac{4\pi\gamma\rho^2 a^3}{3}$$

$$= \frac{4\gamma}{3}\frac{M^2}{\pi a} \qquad \text{since } M = \pi a^2\rho$$

$$= \frac{4\gamma M^2}{3\pi a}$$

15. A solid homoegneous sphere is laid on a thin uniform plate so as to touch it at its centre and the sphere and the plate have their radii and masses equal. Show that the reaction between them due to their mutual gravitation is $4\lambda\mu \sin^2 \frac{\pi}{8}$ of the weight of either, where λ is the radius of either to the radius of earth and μ is the ratio of the density of the sphere to the mean density of the earth.

Solution: Let O be the centre of the sphere which touches the plate BNC at its centre N.

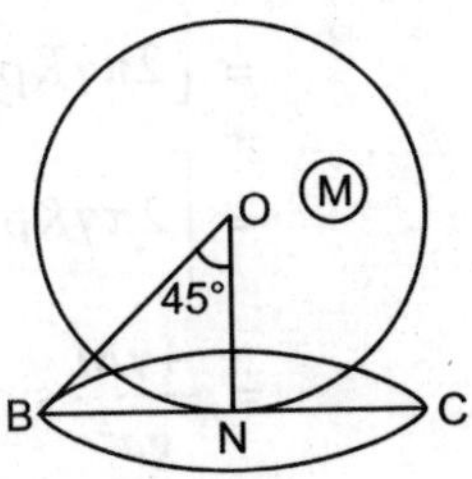

Let a be the radius of the sphere and the plate and M the mass of either.

Let r be the radius of the earth and σ its mean density, then by given conditions

$$\lambda = \frac{a}{r}$$

and $$\mu = \frac{M\Big/\frac{4}{3}\pi a^3}{\sigma} \qquad \text{... (1)}$$

$$\left(\because M = \frac{4}{3}\pi a^3 \rho\right)$$

Again attraction at a point on the surface is $\frac{4}{3}\pi\gamma\sigma r = g$

$$\therefore \qquad \sigma = \frac{3g}{4\pi\gamma r}$$

Hence from (1)

$$\mu = \frac{3M}{4\pi a^3} \times \frac{4\pi\gamma r}{3g}$$

$$= \frac{\gamma M r}{g a^3}$$

Hence $$\lambda\mu = \frac{a}{r}\frac{\gamma M r}{g a^3} = \frac{\gamma M}{g a^2}$$

Since attraction of sphere at an external point is the same as that of a mass M equal to mass of the sphere taken to be concentrated on its centre O, it follows that attraction of this plate upon the sphere is the same as attraction of the plate at a particle of mass M placed at O.

Since radii of the sphere and the plate are equal, therefore $\angle BON = 45°$.

Now, attraction of the plate at the mass M placed at O

$$= \left[2\pi\gamma K\rho\,(1-\cos 45°)\right] M$$

$$= \left[2\pi\gamma K\rho\, 2\sin^2\frac{\pi}{8}\right] M$$

$$= \frac{4\gamma M}{ga^2}\sin^2\frac{\pi}{8}\, Mg \quad \text{since } M = \pi a^2 K\rho$$

$$= 4\lambda\mu\sin^2\frac{\pi}{8} \text{ of the weight of either.}$$

16. Determine at external and internal points the attractions of a solid sphere of radius a, given that its density at a distance r from the centre is $K\left(\frac{r}{a}\right)^n$.

Solution:

Case I: When P is an internal point.

Let O be the centre of the sphere and $OP = c$.

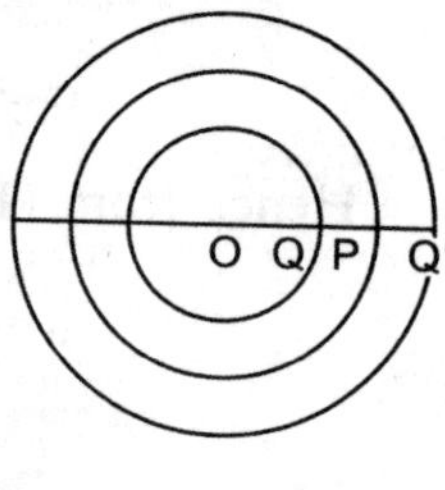

We divide the sphere into a large number of thin concentric shells of radii greater than OP and less than OP.

Then for all the shells of a radius greater than OP, P is an internal point and hence the attraction of all such shell is zero. Hence we are to find attraction at P due to elementary shells of radii less than OP for which P is an external point.

We consider an elementary shell of radius $r < OP$ and thickness δr. Since every point on its surface is at a distance r

from the centre O, therefore the surface density of this elementary shell is uniform and equal to $K\left(\frac{r}{a}\right)^n$.

Hence the mass of this shell $= 4\pi r^2 \delta r\, K\left(\frac{r}{a}\right)^n$

Now attraction of this shell at P

$$= \frac{\gamma \cdot \text{Mass of the shell}}{OP^2}$$

$$= \frac{\gamma 4\pi r^2 \delta r K}{c^2}\left(\frac{r}{a}\right)^n$$

Hence total attraction at P

$$= \frac{4\pi\gamma}{c^2}\int_0^c r^2 K\left(\frac{r}{a}\right)^n dr$$

$$= \frac{4\pi\gamma K}{a^n c^2}\int_0^c r^{n+2} dr$$

$$= \frac{4\pi\gamma K}{a^n c^2}\left[\frac{r^{r+3}}{n+3}\right]_0^c = \frac{4\pi\gamma K c^{n+3}}{a^n c^2 (n+3)}$$

$$= \frac{4\pi\gamma K c^{n+1}}{a^n (n+3)}$$

Case II: When P is an external point.

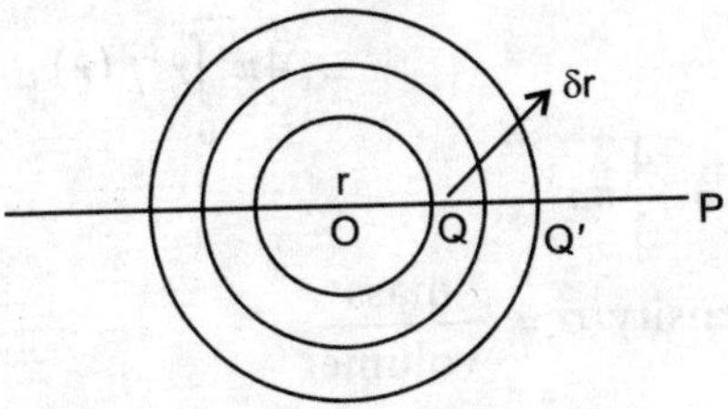

Since P is outside the sphere, therefore it is outside each of these shell and hence the attraction of each shell on a unit mass at P

$$= \frac{\gamma \cdot \text{Mass of the shell}}{OP^2}$$

$$= \frac{\gamma \cdot 4\pi r^2 \delta r \rho}{c^2}$$

$$= \frac{\gamma \cdot 4\pi r^2 \delta r\, K\left(\frac{r}{a}\right)^n}{c^2}$$

Hence the total attraction at P

$$= \frac{4\pi K\gamma}{c^2 a^n} \int_0^a r^{n+2}\, dr$$

$$= \frac{4\pi \gamma K}{c^2 a^n} \cdot \frac{a^{n+3}}{n+3}$$

$$= \frac{4\pi \gamma K}{c^2} \frac{a^3}{n+3}$$

17. If the density of a solid sphere is a function of the distance from the centre, show that its attraction begins to increase as we penetrate into the sphere, if the density at the surface is less than two-thirds of the mean density of the sphere.

Solution: Let us consider a point of the sphere at a distance r from its centre.

Then given $\rho = f(r)$

The mass M of the sphere $= \int_0^a 4\pi r^2 f(r)\, dr$

$$= 4\pi \int_0^a r^2 f(r)\, dr$$

Its volume $= \frac{4}{3}\pi a^3$

Its mean density $\rho = \frac{\text{mass}}{\text{volume}}$

$$= \frac{4\pi \int_0^a r^2 f(r)\, dr}{\frac{4}{3}\pi a^3}$$

$$= \frac{3}{a^3} \int_0^a r^2 f(r)\, dr \quad \text{... (1)}$$

Let F be the force of attraction at any point on its surface, then

$$F = \gamma \int_0^a \frac{f(r)\, 4\pi r^2 dr}{a^2}$$

$$F = \frac{4\pi\gamma}{a^2} \int_0^a r^2 f(r)\, dr$$

$$\therefore \quad \frac{dF}{da} = 4\pi\gamma \left[-\frac{2}{a^3} \int_0^a r^2 f(r)\, dr + \frac{1}{a^2} a^2 f(a) \right]$$

$$= 4\pi\gamma \left[-\frac{2}{3}\rho + f(a) \right] \quad \text{From (1)}$$

which is negative if $f(a) < \frac{2}{3}\rho$.

Hence the density of the sphere on its surface is less than two-thirds of the mean density of the sphere.

Since $\frac{dF}{da}$ is negative, hence F is maximum on the surface.

From above we can say that the value of F on the surface decreases if a increases or F increases if a decreases.

Hence the attraction on its surface shall begin to increase as we penetrate into the sphere.

18. The density of a sphere varies as the depth below the surface. Show that the resultant attraction is greatest at a depth equal to one-third of the radius and that its value is $\frac{4}{3}$ of the value at the surface.

Solution: Let us take a point P at a distance from the centre O of the sphere.

To determine the attraction at P, we divide the sphere into a large number of concentric shells, so that for every elementary shell density is uniform.

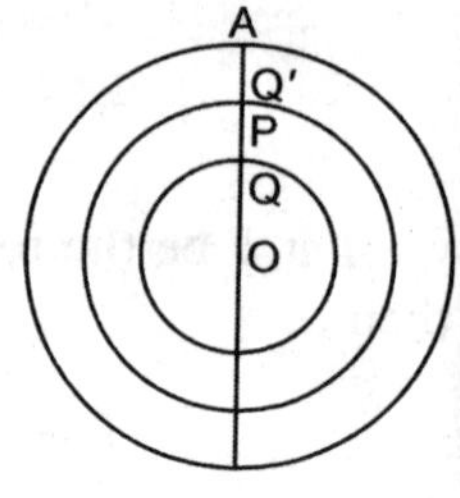

Now for all the shells of radius greater than c; P is an internal point and hence the attraction of all such shells at P is zero. Hence we consider only all such shells whose radii are less than c for which P is an external point.

Its density according to the given condition is $\lambda\,(a - r)$ where λ is a constant.

Hence mass of this shell $= 4\pi r^2 \delta r \lambda\,(a - r)$

Where δr is the thickness of the shell.

Attraction of this shell at $P = \gamma \dfrac{4\pi r^2 \delta r \lambda\,(a - r)}{c^2}$

Therefore, the resultant attraction of the whole sphere at P

$$= \frac{4\pi\gamma\lambda}{c^2} \int_0^c r^2 (a - r)\, dr$$

$$= \frac{4\pi\gamma\lambda}{c^2} \left[\frac{ar^3}{3} - \frac{r^4}{4} \right]_0^c$$

$$= \frac{4\pi\gamma\lambda}{c^2} \left[\frac{ac^3}{3} - \frac{c^4}{4} \right]$$

$$F = 4\pi\gamma\lambda c \left(\frac{a}{3} - \frac{c}{4} \right) \qquad \dots (1)$$

For maximum or minimum F $\dfrac{dF}{dc} = 0$

$$\Rightarrow \quad 4\pi\gamma\lambda \left[\left(\frac{a}{3} - \frac{c}{4} \right) - \frac{c}{4} \right] = 0$$

$$\Rightarrow \quad \frac{a}{3} - \frac{c}{2} = 0$$

$$c = \frac{2}{3} a$$

Also $\dfrac{d^2F}{dc^2} = -\dfrac{1}{2} 4\pi\gamma\lambda < 0$

Hence resultant attraction is greatest at a distance $\frac{2}{3}$ of the radius from the centre or $\frac{1}{3}$ of the radius from the surface.

Also maximum attraction F from (1)

$$= 4\pi\gamma\lambda \frac{2a}{3}\left(\frac{a}{3}-\frac{a}{6}\right)$$

$$= \frac{8\pi\gamma\lambda a^2}{18} = \frac{4}{9}\pi\gamma\lambda a^2 \quad \text{... (2)}$$

Also the attraction at the surface from (1)

$$= 4\pi\gamma\lambda a\left(\frac{a}{3}-\frac{a}{4}\right) \quad \text{by putting } c = a$$

$$= \frac{4\pi\gamma\lambda a^2}{12}$$

$$= \frac{\pi\gamma\lambda a^2}{3} \quad \text{... (3)}$$

From (2) maximum attraction

$$= \frac{4}{9}\pi\gamma\lambda a^2$$

$$= \frac{4}{3}\left(\frac{1}{3}\pi\gamma\lambda a^2\right)$$

$$= \frac{4}{3} \text{ attraction at the surface by (3).}$$

19. If the earth supposed spherical were covered by an ocean of uniform depth h, prove that the value of gravity at the bottom of ocean would exceed that at the top by $3\pi\gamma h\left(\frac{2}{3}\rho - \sigma\right)$ approximately where σ is the density of the ocean and ρ is the mean density of the earth.

Solution: Let a be the radius of the earth.

Let A and B be the bottom and top of the ocean. Let $AB = h$.

Attraction at A due to earth of radius a

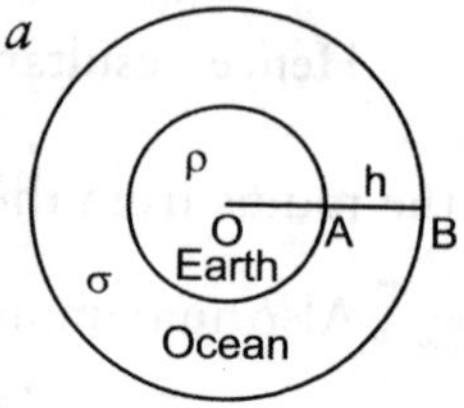

$$= \frac{\gamma}{a^2} \frac{4}{3} \pi a^3 \rho$$

$$= \frac{4}{3} \pi \gamma \rho a \qquad \dots (1)$$

Attraction at A due to ocean for which A is an internal point is zero, since attraction of a spherical shell at an internal point is zero.

Thus total attraction at the bottom A

$$= \frac{4}{3} \pi \gamma \rho a$$

$$= F_1 \text{ (say)}$$

Again the attraction of the earth at B

$$= \gamma \cdot \frac{4}{3} \pi \rho a^3 \frac{1}{(a+h)^2}$$

$$= \frac{4}{3} \pi \gamma \rho a \left(1 + \frac{h}{a}\right)^{-2}$$

$$= \frac{4}{3} \pi \gamma \rho a \left(1 - \frac{2h}{a}\right)$$

Neglecting higher power than $\left(\frac{h}{a}\right)$ as $\frac{h}{a}$ is very small.

Also the attraction of the ocean at B

$$= \gamma \cdot \frac{\frac{4}{3} \pi \left[(a+h)^3 - a^3\right] \sigma}{(a+h)^2}$$

$$= \frac{4}{3} \frac{\pi \gamma \sigma a^3}{(a+h)^2} \left[\left(a + \frac{h}{a}\right)^3 - 1\right]$$

$$= \frac{4}{3} \frac{\pi \gamma \sigma a}{\left(1 + \frac{h}{a}\right)^2} \left[1 + \frac{3h}{a} + \dots - 1\right]$$

$$= \frac{4}{3}\pi\gamma\sigma a\left(1+\frac{h}{a}\right)^{-2}\left(\frac{3h}{a}+.....\right)$$

$$= \frac{4}{3}\pi\gamma\sigma a\left(1-\frac{2h}{a}+.....\right)\left(\frac{3h}{a}+.....\right)$$

$$= \frac{4}{3}\pi\gamma\sigma a\,\frac{3h}{a}$$

$$= \frac{4}{3}\pi\gamma\sigma h$$

Hence the total attraction at B

$$= a\,\frac{4}{3}\,\pi\gamma\rho\left(1-\frac{2h}{a}\right)+\frac{4}{3}\,\pi\gamma\sigma h$$

Therefore the difference between attractions at the bottom and top

$$= \frac{4}{3}\,\pi\gamma\rho a-\left[\frac{4}{3}\,\pi\gamma\sigma h+\frac{4}{3}a\pi\gamma\rho\left(1-\frac{2h}{a}\right)\right]$$

$$= -\frac{4}{3}\pi\gamma\sigma h+\frac{8h}{3}\pi\gamma\rho$$

$$= 4\pi\gamma h\left[\frac{2}{3}\rho-\sigma\right]$$

20. Find the attraction of a solid homogeneous hemisphere of a point O on the edge of its plane base. [M.U. 96H]

Solution: We take O as origin of coordinates, the diameter OA as the x-axis, the tangent to the circular rim in the plane of the base as the y-axis is and the normal to the plane base at O in the direction shown in the figure as z-axis.

Let a be the radius of the base, then the equation of the surface of the sphere is

$$(x-a)^2+y^2+z^2=a^2$$

or $\quad x^2+y^2+z^2-2ax=0 \qquad \text{... (1)}$

Changing to polar coordinates by putting $x = r\sin\theta\cos\phi$, $y = r\sin\theta\sin\phi$, $z = r\cos\theta$.

or $\quad x^2+y^2+z^2=r^2 \qquad$ (1) becomes

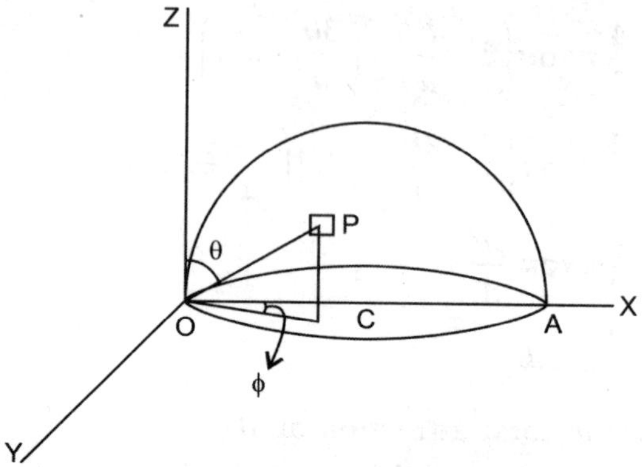

$$r^2 = 2ar \sin\theta \cos\phi$$

or $$r = 2a \sin\theta \cos\phi$$

Let $P\ (r, \theta, \phi)$ be a point inside the hemisphere.

An element of volume at $P = r\ \delta\theta\delta\ rr \sin\theta\delta\phi$

Mass of this element $= \rho r\ \delta\theta\delta rr \sin\theta\ \delta\phi$

$$= \rho r^2 \sin\theta\ \delta r\ \delta\theta\ \delta\phi$$

Its attraction at $O = \dfrac{\gamma\rho r^2 \sin\theta\ \delta r\ \delta\theta\ \delta\phi}{r^2}$ along OP

$$= \gamma\rho \sin\theta\ \delta r\ \delta\theta\ \delta\phi$$

Component of this attraction along z-axis

$$= \gamma\rho \sin\theta\ \delta r\ \delta\theta\ \delta\phi \cos\theta$$

Hence total component of attraction along z-axis

$$= \gamma\rho \int_{\theta=0}^{\frac{\pi}{2}} \int_{\phi=-\frac{\pi}{2}}^{\frac{\pi}{2}} \int_{r=0}^{2a\sin\theta\cos\phi} \cos\theta \sin\theta\ d\theta\ d\phi\ dr$$

$$= \gamma\rho \int_{\theta=0}^{\frac{\pi}{2}} \int_{\phi=-\frac{\pi}{2}}^{\frac{\pi}{2}} \cos\theta \sin\theta\ d\theta\ d\phi\ 2a \sin\theta \cos\phi$$

$$= 2\gamma\rho a \int_{\theta=0}^{\frac{\pi}{2}} \int_{\phi=-\frac{\pi}{2}}^{\frac{\pi}{2}} \cos\theta \sin^2\theta \cos\phi\ d\phi\ d\theta$$

$$= 4\gamma\rho a \int_{\theta=0}^{\frac{\pi}{2}} \int_{\phi=0}^{\frac{\pi}{2}} \cos\theta \sin^2\theta \cos\phi \, d\theta \, d\phi$$

$$= 4\gamma\rho a \left[\frac{\sin^3\theta}{3}\right]_0^{\frac{\pi}{2}} [\sin\phi]_0^{\frac{\pi}{2}}$$

$$= \frac{4}{3}\gamma\rho a$$

$$\therefore \quad Z = \frac{4}{3}\gamma\rho a$$

Again total component of attraction along x-axis

$$X = \gamma\rho \int_{\theta=0}^{\frac{\pi}{2}} \int_{\phi=-\frac{\pi}{2}}^{\frac{\pi}{2}} \int_{r=0}^{2a\sin\theta\cos\phi} \sin\theta \, dr \, d\theta \, d\phi \sin\theta \cos\phi$$

$$= \gamma\rho \int_{\theta=0}^{\frac{\pi}{2}} \int_{\phi=-\frac{\pi}{2}}^{\frac{\pi}{2}} \sin^2\theta \cos\phi \, 2a \sin\theta \cos\theta \cos\phi \, d\theta \, d\phi$$

$$= 2a\gamma\rho \int_{\theta=0}^{\frac{\pi}{2}} \int_{\phi=-\frac{\pi}{2}}^{\frac{\pi}{2}} \sin^3\theta \cos^2\phi \, d\theta \, d\phi$$

$$= 4a\gamma\rho \int_{\theta=0}^{\frac{\pi}{2}} \int_{\phi=0}^{\frac{\pi}{2}} \sin^3\theta \cos^2\phi \, d\theta \, d\phi$$

$$= 4a\gamma\rho \int_{\theta=0}^{\frac{\pi}{2}} \sin^3\theta \, \frac{2-1}{2} \frac{\pi}{2} \, d\theta$$

$$= 4a\gamma\rho \frac{3-1}{3} \frac{\pi}{4}$$

$$= \frac{2}{3}\pi\gamma\rho a$$

By symmetry the component of attraction along OY vanishes i.e. $Y = 0$.

Hence the resultant attraction

$$= \sqrt{X^2 + Y^2 + Z^2}$$

$$= \sqrt{\frac{4}{9}\pi^2\gamma^2\rho^2a^2 + 0 + \frac{16}{9}\gamma^2\rho^2a^2}$$

$$= \frac{2}{3}\gamma\rho a\sqrt{\pi^2 + 4}$$

Its direction with x-axis

$$= \tan^{-1}\left(\frac{Z}{X}\right)$$

$$= \tan^{-1}\frac{\frac{4}{3}\gamma\rho a}{\frac{2}{3}\pi\gamma\rho a}$$

$$= \tan^{-1}\left(\frac{2}{\pi}\right)$$

21. If the northern and southern hemispheres of the earth had been of uniform density ρ and σ respectively the mean density being as at present, prove that the gravity at the equator would be greater than it is now in the ratio

$$\sqrt{1 + \frac{4}{\pi^2}\left(\frac{\rho - \sigma}{\rho + \sigma}\right)^2} : 1$$

and that the deviation of the plumb line from the zenith at any point of the equator would be $\tan^{-1}\left(\frac{2}{\pi}\frac{\rho - \sigma}{\rho + \sigma}\right)$

Solution: Let O be a point on the equator and OCA the equatorial diameter through O. The northern hemisphere is above the equatorial plane and the southern hemisphere is below the equatorial plane.

Let us take O as origin and OCA as x-axis. Let axis of y be taken along the tangent to the circular rim and OZ perpendicular to the base.

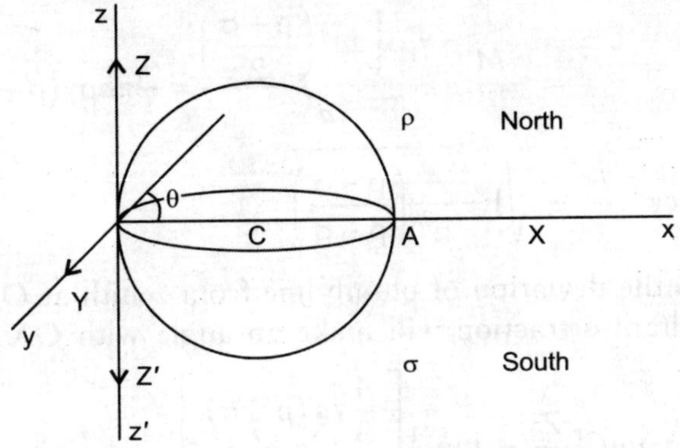

Then by example 20 the components X_1, Y_1, Z_1 of attraction at O along x, y, z axes are

$$X_1 = \frac{2}{3}\pi\gamma\rho a,\ Y_1 = 0 \text{ and } Z_1 = \frac{4}{3}\gamma\rho a$$

Similarly the components of attraction at O due to southern hemisphere will be

$$X_2 = \frac{2}{3}\pi\gamma\sigma a,\ Y_2 = 0 \text{ and } Z_2 = -\frac{4}{3}\gamma\sigma a$$

Hence the components of attraction at O along axes are

$$X = \frac{2}{3}\pi\gamma a\,(\rho+\sigma), Y = 0 \text{ and } Z = \frac{4}{3}\gamma a\,(\rho-\sigma)$$

Hence the resultant attraction F at O

$$= \sqrt{X^2 + Y^2 + Z^2}$$

$$= \sqrt{\frac{4}{9}\pi^2\gamma^2 a^2(\rho+\sigma)^2 + \frac{16}{9}\gamma^2 a^2(\rho-\sigma)^2}$$

$$= \frac{2}{3}\pi\gamma a\,(\rho+\sigma)\sqrt{1 + \frac{4}{\pi^2}\left(\frac{\rho-\sigma}{\rho+\sigma}\right)^2}$$

The mean density of the earth $= \dfrac{\rho+\sigma}{2}$

Then $\quad g$ = the attraction due to gravity at the surface of the earth

$$= \frac{\gamma M}{a^2} = \frac{\gamma \cdot \frac{4}{3}\pi a^3\left(\frac{\rho+\sigma}{2}\right)}{a^2} = \frac{4}{3}\pi a \rho \gamma(\rho+\sigma)$$

Hence $\quad \frac{F}{g} = \sqrt{1+\frac{4}{\pi^2}\left(\frac{\rho-\sigma}{\rho+\sigma}\right)^2} : 1$

Also the deviation of plumb line from zenith at O, that is, the resultant attraction will make an angle with OX

$$= \tan^{-1}\frac{Z}{X} = \tan^{-1}\left[\frac{\frac{4}{3}\gamma a(\rho-\sigma)}{\frac{2}{3}\pi\gamma a(\rho+\sigma)}\right]$$

$$= \tan^{-1}\left[\frac{2}{\pi}\frac{\rho-\sigma}{\rho+\sigma}\right]$$

22. A lune is divided off from a thin spherical shell by two great circles whose plane cuts an angle 2α. Show that the attraction of the rest of the shell on the lune is $\frac{\gamma M^2}{8a^2}\sin\alpha$, where M is the mass of the shell and a is its radius.

Solution: The lined area is the lune which is the surface area of the sphere between the two great circles whose planes are inclined at an angle 2α to each other.

The attraction on the lune due to the rest of the surface of the shell is the same as attraction of the whole surface of the shell on the surface area of the lune.

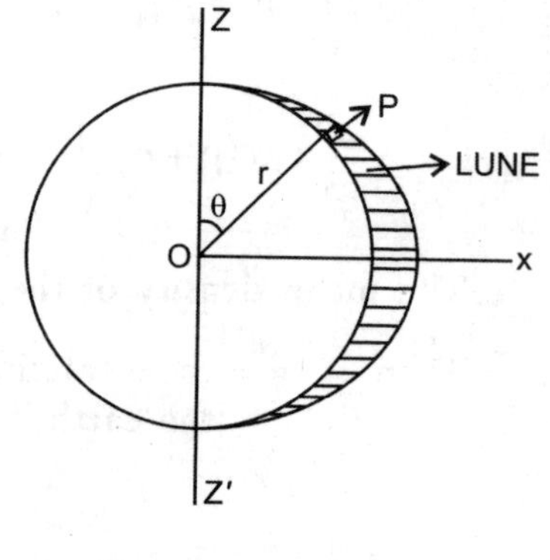

Let us take a point P (a, θ, ϕ) on the lune, then element of the surface area at P is $a\delta\theta\, a \sin\theta\, \delta\phi$.

Attraction of the whole shell at $P = \frac{1}{2}\gamma\frac{M}{a^2}$.

The element of the area having this attraction

$$= a\delta\theta\, a \sin\theta\, \delta\phi$$

$$= a^2 \sin\theta\, \delta\theta\, \delta\phi$$

Hence attraction of the whole shell on the lune, resolved along OX

$$= \int_{\theta=0}^{\pi} \int_{\phi=-\alpha}^{\alpha} \left(\frac{1}{2}\gamma \frac{M}{a^2}\right) \sin\theta \cos\phi\, \rho\, a^2 \sin\theta\, d\delta\, d\phi$$

$$= \frac{1}{2}\gamma M\rho \int_{\theta=0}^{\pi} \int_{\phi=-\alpha}^{\alpha} \sin^2\theta \cos\phi\, d\theta\, d\phi$$

$$= \gamma M\rho \int_{\theta=0}^{\frac{\pi}{2}} \sin^2\theta\, d\theta \int_{\phi=-\alpha}^{\alpha} \cos\phi\, d\phi$$

$$= \gamma M\rho \frac{2-1}{2}\frac{\pi}{2}[\sin\phi]_{-\alpha}^{\alpha}$$

$$= \frac{1}{4}\gamma M\rho\, \pi\, 2 \sin\alpha$$

$$= \frac{1}{2}\gamma M\rho\, \pi \sin\alpha$$

$$= \frac{1}{2}\gamma M \frac{M}{4a^2} \sin\alpha \left(\because M = 4\pi a^2 \rho\right)$$

$$= \frac{\gamma M^2}{8a^2} \sin\alpha$$

EXERCISES

1. If the attraction between two elements of matter of masses m and m' is $mm' f(R)$ where R is the distance between them, show that inward acceleration due to uniform thin spherical shell of mass M and internal radius a at an internal point distant c from centre is F, where

$$F = \frac{M}{4ac^2} \int_{a-c}^{a+c} \left(R^2 + c^2 - a^2\right) f(R)\, dR$$

If F is zero for all values of a and c subject to the condition $c < a$, show that only possible form of $f(R)$ is A/R^2 where A is some constant.

2. Show that the attraction at any internal point of a homogeneous sphere of radius a every element of which attracts a force proportional to its mass and inversely proportional to the cube of the distance is

$$\frac{\pi\mu a}{c} - \pi\mu\,\frac{a^2 + c^2}{2c^2}\log\frac{a + c}{a - c}$$

where c is the distance of the point from the centre of the sphere and μ is the attraction of the unit mass at a unit distance.

3. If ρ be the density of a homogeneous solid sphere and a the radius, prove that the force in astronomical units exerted by the rest of the sphere on a conical portion of itself bounded by a right circular cone of angle 2α with its vertex at the centre is $\frac{1}{3}\pi^2\rho^2 a^4 \sin^2\alpha$.

4. A solid homogeneous sphere of radius R and mass M is divided into two portions by a plane at a perpendicular distance $\frac{R}{2}$ from the centre. Show that the mutual attraction between the two portions of the sphere is $\frac{27\gamma M^2}{256R^2}$.

5. A sphere is described on a radius of another sphere as diameter. If the latter be a homogeneous sphere of mass M and radius a, show that resultant attraction on the portion included in the smaller sphere is $\frac{\gamma M^2}{16a^2}$.

6. A uniform solid sphere of mass M is placed near an infinite plane whose surface density is uniform and equal to σ. Prove that the sphere attracts the plate with a force $2\pi\gamma M\sigma$.

7. From an infinite plate of thickness $2a$ of uniform homogeneous matter a spherical portion touching the two plane faces is cut away. Prove that the attraction of the

plate at a point where the sphere touches either of its face is $\frac{2}{3}$ of its former value.

8. If a sphere consists of concentric layers of uniform density, show that its attraction is the same at any point of its volume if the density at each point varies inversely the distance from the centre.

9. If half the mass of the earth were concentrated in an extremely thin uniform external crust, show that at the centre of a circular gap in the crust the intensity of gravity would be less than its normal value by one forth. [M.U. 94H]

10. Show that the attraction of a uniform cube of density ρ at a point distance r from its centre is $\frac{4}{3}\pi\gamma\rho r$ towards the centre, if r is small.

11. Show that at the southern base of a hemispherical hill of radius a and density ρ, the apparent latitude is diminished by $\frac{1}{2}\frac{\rho a}{\sigma r}$ where σ is the mean density and r is the radius of the earth.

12. Show that attraction of the focus of a small elliptical hole of eccentricity e in a thin spherical shell makes an angle $\tan^{-1}\frac{1-\sqrt{1-e^2}}{e}$ with the radius of the shell.

13. A uniform circular plate, of mass M, rests in contact with a fixed rough gravitating sphere of the same radius. A small mass m is then fastened to the rim of the plate. Show that the plate will turn through an angle whose circular measure is $\frac{m}{M}$, when the squares and higher power of this ratio are neglected.

14. Show that to bring any mass, from the centre of the earth to the surface, requires half as much work as the required to remove it from surface to infinity.

4 THE POTENTIAL OF A ROD AND CIRCULAR DISC

4.1. Definition of the Potential [M.U. 2004H]

The potential of an attracting mass M, at a point P is equal to the work done by the attraction of the mass M on a unit mass as it moves from infinite distance, by any path, curved or straight line, to the point P.

4.2. Derivation of the expression for the potential from infinity

Let M be the attracting mass and m be an element of M placed at the point O. Let P_1 and P_2 be the positions of a unit mass on its path as it moves from infinity to the point P under the attraction of the system.

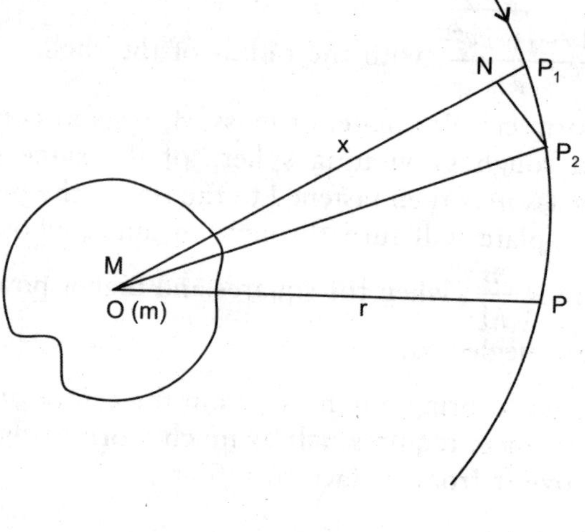

Let $OP_1 = x$, $OP_2 = x + \delta x$

From P_2 we draw P_2N perpendicular to OP_1.

In $\Delta\ OP_2N$

$$\cos P_1OP_2 = \frac{ON}{OP_2}$$

$$ON = (x + \delta x) \cos P_1OP_2$$

Since the points P_1 and P_2 are very near to each other; hence $\angle P_1OP_2$ is very small.

$$\therefore \quad P_1N = OP_1 - ON$$
$$= x - (x + \delta x) = -\delta x$$

This gives us the displacement of the particle in the direction OP_1 as the particle moves from P_1 to P_2.

Now the attraction of the mass m at O, at the point P_1 along $P_1O = \dfrac{\gamma m}{OP_1^2} = \dfrac{\gamma m}{x^2}$.

Hence the work done by the attraction of the mass m at O on the unit particle is displacing it from P_1 to $P_2 = \dfrac{\gamma m}{x^2}(-\delta x)$.

Therefore the work done by the attraction of the mass m at O on the unit particle in displacing it from infinity to P, where $OP = r$

$$= \int_{\infty}^{r} \frac{-\gamma m}{x^2} dx = \left[\frac{\gamma m}{x}\right]_{\infty}^{r}$$

$$= \gamma m \left[\frac{1}{r} - \frac{1}{\infty}\right] = \frac{\gamma m}{r}$$

Similarly the potentials at the point P, due to the elements m_1, m_2, m_3 ..... of the attracting mass M at distances r_1, r_2, r_3 ..... respectively from P are equal to $\dfrac{\gamma m_1}{r_1}, \dfrac{\gamma m_2}{r_2}, \dfrac{\gamma m_3}{r_3}$.

Hence the potential of the attracting mass M at the point P

= the total work done by the whole attracting mass in displacing the unit mass from infinity to the point P

$$= \frac{\gamma m_1}{r_1} + \frac{\gamma m_2}{r_2} + \ldots.. + \ldots..$$

$$= \sum \frac{\gamma m}{r} = \gamma \int \frac{dm}{r}$$

Hence if dm be any element of M whose distance from P is r, then the potential V at P given by $V = \gamma \int \frac{dm}{r}$, where the integral is taken throughout the whole attracting mass.

Corollary: Potential for the law of attraction $\frac{\gamma}{(\text{Distance})^n}$

Here the work done by the attraction of m as the unit mass moves from P_1 to $P_2 = \frac{\gamma m}{x^n}(-\delta x)$.

Hence the whole work done by the attraction of element m as the unit mass moves from infinity to the point P, where $OP = r$ is

$$\int_{\infty}^{r} \frac{-\gamma m}{x^n}\, dx = \frac{\gamma m}{n-1}\left[\frac{1}{x^{n-1}}\right]_{\infty}^{r}$$

$$= \frac{\gamma m}{n-1} \frac{1}{r^{n-1}}$$

Similarly, we can write the potential for other elements m_1, m_2, ...

Hence the potential due to whole mass M

$$= \frac{\gamma}{n-1} \int \frac{dm}{r^{n-1}}$$

where the integral is taken throughout the whole attracting mass.

4.3. Relation between attraction and potential

[M.U. 95H, 2001H]

Let V be the potential of an attracting mass at any point $P\ (x, y, z)$.

We consider an elementary mass dm of the attracting mass M, at the point $Q\ (x_1, y_1, z_1)$.

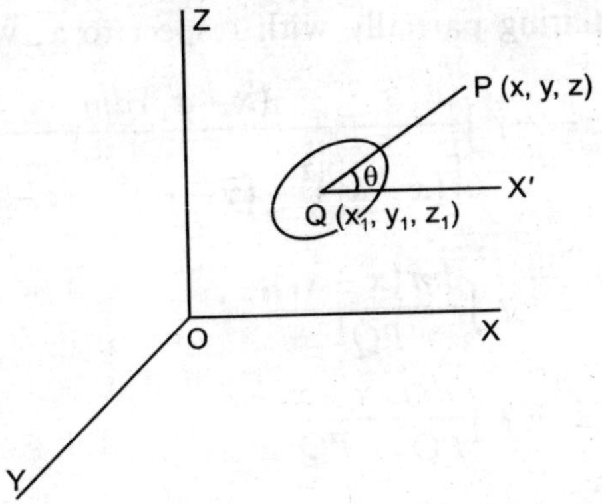

Now attraction of this elementary mass dm at the point P along $PQ = \dfrac{\gamma dm}{PQ^2}$

Its resolved part parallel to x-axis in the sense of x decreasing

$$= \frac{\gamma dm}{PQ^2} \cos \theta$$

$$= \frac{-\gamma dm}{PQ^2} \cos \theta \text{ in the sense of } x \text{ increasing.}$$

Hence attraction at P parallel to x-axis due to the whole attracting mass M

$$= -\gamma \int \frac{dm}{PQ^2} \cos \theta \quad \text{... (1)}$$

Also the potential at P, of the elementary mass dm of Q

$$= \frac{\gamma dm}{PQ} = \gamma \frac{dm}{\sqrt{(x - x_1)^2 + (y - y_1)^2 + (z - z_1)^2}}$$

Therefore potential V at P due to whole attracting mass

$$V = \gamma \int \frac{dm}{\sqrt{(x - x_1)^2 + (y - y_1)^2 + (z - z_1)^2}}$$

Differentiating partially with respect to x, we get

$$\frac{\partial V}{\partial x} = -\gamma \int \frac{(x - x_1)\, dm}{\left[(x-x_1)^2 + (y-y_1)^2 + (z-z_1)^2\right]^{\frac{3}{2}}}$$

$$= -\gamma \int \frac{dm\,(x - x_1)}{PQ^3}$$

$$= -\gamma \int \frac{dm}{PQ^2} \frac{x - x_1}{PQ}$$

$$= -\gamma \int \frac{dm}{PQ^2} \cos\theta \qquad \text{... (2)}$$

From (1) and (2), we have

$\frac{\partial V}{\partial x}$ = component of the attraction of the attracting mass M at the point P (x, y, z) parallel to x-axis.

Similarly

$\frac{\partial V}{\partial y}$ = component of the attraction of the attracting mass M at the point P (x, y, z) parallel to y-axis

and $\frac{\partial V}{\partial z}$ = component of the attraction of the attracting mass M at the point P (x, y, z) parallel to z-axis.

In general the rate of increase in the potential in any direction gives the component of attraction in that direction.

4.4. Attraction along any line

If V is the potential at a point P (x, y, z), then to determine attraction at P along any line drawn through P.

Let V be the potential at any point (x, y, z). We draw a line through P and take on this line a point Q $(x + \delta x, y + \delta y, z + \delta z)$. Let $PQ = \delta s$. Since the point Q is very close to P, therefore potential at Q is $V + \delta V$.

The direction cosine of PQ are $\frac{dx}{ds}, \frac{dy}{ds}, \frac{dz}{ds}$.

Hence the resultant force at P along the line PQ

$$= \text{sum of resolved parts of its three components of attraction along } PQ$$

$$= \frac{\partial V}{\partial x}\frac{dx}{ds} + \frac{\partial V}{\partial y}\frac{dy}{ds} + \frac{\partial V}{\partial z}\frac{dz}{ds}$$

$$= \frac{dV}{ds} \quad \dots (1)$$

$$= \underset{\delta s \to 0}{Lt} \frac{V + \delta V - V}{\delta s}$$

$$= Lt \frac{\text{Potential at } Q - \text{Potential at } P}{\delta s} \quad \dots (2)$$

(1) and (2) gives the formulae to express the force of attraction at any point P in a certain direction.

Thus (1) shows that if V is the potential at a point P (x, y, z) and δs is the small length of a line drawn through P in a certain direction, then force of attraction at P along that line is equal to $Lt\left[\dfrac{\delta V}{\text{Small length in that direction}}\right]$.

Now we apply the above principle when coordinates of P are (r, θ, ϕ).

We consider any line through P, one line in the direction of r, the second one perpendicular to r in the plane of θ, and the third one perpendicular to the plane of θ. The small lengths are respectively dr, $rd\theta$ and $r \sin\theta \, d\phi$ in the above three directions. Hence

attraction at P is $\dfrac{dV}{dr}$ in the direction of r

attraction of P is $\dfrac{dV}{rd\theta}$ perpendicular to r in the plane of θ

and

attraction at P is $\dfrac{dV}{r\sin\theta\, d\phi}$ perpendicular to the plane of θ.

4.5. Potential of a finite rod

To find the potential of a thin uniform straight rod at an external point. [L.N.M.U. 93H; M.U. 94H, 2000H, 2002H; T.M.B.U. 2003H; B.B.A.B.U. 2002H]

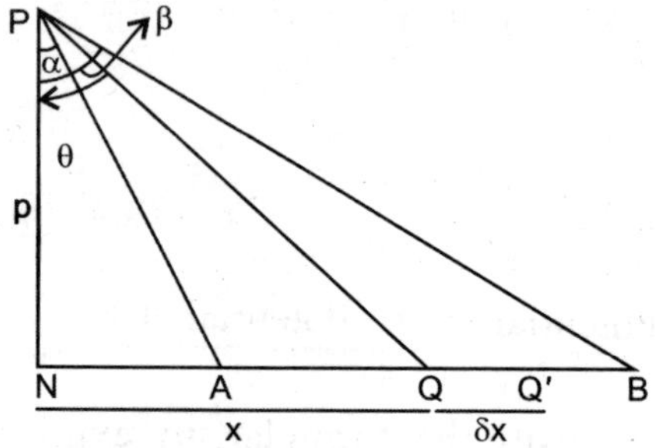

Let AB be the thin uniform straight rod of length a, small cross-section K and uniform density ρ.

Let P be the point where the potential is to be determined.

From P we draw PN perpendicular to BA produced. Let $\angle NPA = \alpha$, $\angle NPB = \beta$, $PN = p$, $\angle NPQ = \theta$.

We consider an element QQ' of the rod such that $NQ = x$, $NQ' = x + \delta x$.

[Mass of this element = $K\rho\delta x$]

Hence potential V of the rod AB at P is given by

$$V = \int \frac{\gamma dm}{PQ} = \gamma \int \frac{K\rho\, dx}{PQ} \qquad \text{... (1)}$$

In ΔPQN

$$\tan\theta = \frac{QN}{PN} = \frac{x}{p}$$

$$x = p\tan\theta$$

$$\therefore \quad dx = p\sec^2\theta\, d\theta$$

Also $$\cos\theta = \frac{PN}{PQ} = \frac{p}{PQ}$$

$$PQ = p\sec\theta$$

When $x = NA$; then $\theta = \alpha$ and when $x = NB$, then $\theta = \beta$.

Hence from (1)

$$V = \gamma \int_{\alpha}^{\beta} \frac{K\rho\, p \sec^2 \theta\, d\theta}{p \sec \theta}$$

$$= \gamma K\rho \int_{\alpha}^{\beta} \sec \theta\, d\theta$$

$$= \gamma K\rho \left[\log \tan \left(\frac{\pi}{4} + \frac{\theta}{2} \right) \right]_{\alpha}^{\beta}$$

$$= \gamma K\rho \log \frac{\tan \left(\frac{\pi}{4} + \frac{\beta}{2} \right)}{\tan \left(\frac{\pi}{4} + \frac{\alpha}{2} \right)}$$

$$= \gamma K\rho \log \tan \left(\frac{\pi}{4} + \frac{\beta}{2} \right) \cot \left(\frac{\pi}{4} + \frac{\alpha}{2} \right)$$

$$= \gamma K\rho \log \tan \left(\frac{\pi}{4} + \frac{\beta}{2} \right) \tan \left\{ \frac{\pi}{2} - \left(\frac{\pi}{4} + \frac{\alpha}{2} \right) \right\}$$

$$V = \gamma K\rho \log \tan \left(\frac{\pi}{4} + \frac{\beta}{2} \right) \tan \left(\frac{\pi}{4} - \frac{\alpha}{2} \right) \qquad \dots (2)$$

Now we have from the figure

$$\frac{\pi}{4} - \frac{\alpha}{2} = \frac{\pi}{4} - \frac{1}{2} \angle APN$$

$$= \frac{\pi}{4} - \frac{1}{2} \left(\frac{\pi}{2} - \angle PAN \right)$$

$$= \frac{1}{2} \angle PAN$$

$$= \frac{1}{2} [\pi - \angle PAB]$$

$$= \frac{\pi}{2} - \frac{\angle PAB}{2}$$

Also

$$\frac{\pi}{4} + \frac{\beta}{2} = \frac{\pi}{4} + \frac{1}{2} \angle BPN$$

$$= \frac{\pi}{4} + \frac{1}{2}\left[\frac{\pi}{2} - \angle PBA\right]$$

$$= \frac{\pi}{2} - \frac{\angle PBA}{2}$$

With these substitutions (2) becomes

$$V = \gamma K \rho \log \tan\left(\frac{\pi}{2} - \frac{\angle PAB}{2}\right) + \log \tan\left(\frac{\pi}{2} - \frac{\angle PBA}{2}\right)$$

$$V = \gamma K \rho \log\left[\cot\frac{PAB}{2}\cot\frac{PBA}{2}\right] \qquad \ldots (3)$$

Another form. In ΔPAB let $PA = r_1$, $PB = r_2$, $AB = a$.

$$\therefore \qquad 2S = r_1 + r_2 + a$$

$$\therefore \quad \cot\frac{PAB}{2}\cot\frac{PBA}{2}$$

$$= \sqrt{\frac{S(S-r_2)}{(S-r_1)(S-a)}} \times \sqrt{\frac{S(S-r_1)}{(S-r_2)(S-a)}}$$

$$= \frac{S}{S-a} = \frac{2S}{2S-2a} = \frac{r_1 + r_2 + a}{r_1 + r_2 - a}$$

Hence from (3)

$$V = \gamma K \rho \log \frac{r_1 + r_2 + a}{r_1 + r_2 - a} \qquad \ldots (4)$$

Corollary. If $r_1 + r_2 = PA + PB =$ constant, then V is constant i.e. the potential at the point P due to the rod AB is constant if the sum of distances of P from A and B is constant.

Hence if A and B are the two foci of the ellipse, then the potential at any point P on the ellipse is constant as the sum of any point of the ellipse from the foci is constant. This ellipse is called the *equipotential* of the rod AB.

4.6. Potential of an infinite rod

To find the potential of a uniform rod of infinite length in both the directions, at any external point P.

Let AB be a rod of infinite length. Let P be the point at which potential is to be determined.

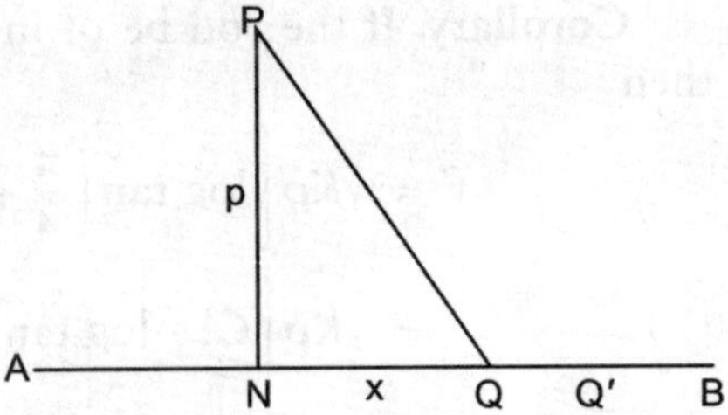

From P we draw PN perpendicular to AB. Let ρ be the density and K the thickness of the rod. Let $PN = p$.

We consider an element $QQ' = \delta x$ at the point Q at a distance from Q.

Mass of the element $QQ' = K\rho\delta x$

Thus the potential of the element QQ' at the point P

$$= \frac{\gamma K\rho\delta x}{PQ} = \frac{\gamma K\rho\delta x}{\sqrt{p^2 + x^2}}$$

Hence the potential V at P, due to the rod of infinite length in both the directions is given by

$$V = \int_{-\infty}^{\infty} \frac{\gamma K\rho dx}{\sqrt{p^2 + x^2}}$$

$$= 2\gamma K\rho \int_0^{\infty} \frac{dx}{\sqrt{p^2 + x^2}}$$

$$= 2\gamma K\rho \left[\log \left(x + \sqrt{p^2 + x^2} \right) \right]_0^{\infty}$$

$$= C - 2\gamma K\rho \log p$$

where C is an infinite constant.

Another method. We know that the attraction of an infinite rod is $\frac{2\gamma K\rho}{p}$ along the perpendicular from P to the rod.

If V be the potential, then we know that $\frac{dV}{dp} = -$ force of attraction $= -\frac{2\gamma K\rho}{p}$.

Integrating, we get $V = C - 2\gamma K\rho \log p$

Corollary. If the rod be of infinite length in one direction, then

$$V = \gamma K\rho\left[\log\tan\left(\frac{\pi}{4}+\frac{\theta}{2}\right)\right]_{\alpha}^{\frac{\pi}{2}}$$

$$= \gamma K\rho\left[C' - \log\tan\left(\frac{\pi}{4}+\frac{\alpha}{2}\right)\right]$$

where C' is an infinite constant

$$= \gamma K\rho\left[C' - \log\frac{1+\tan\frac{\alpha}{2}}{1-\tan\frac{\alpha}{2}}\right]$$

$$= \gamma K\rho\left[C' - \log\frac{\cos\frac{\alpha}{2}+\sin\frac{\alpha}{2}}{\cos\frac{\alpha}{2}-\sin\frac{\alpha}{2}}\right]$$

$$= \gamma K\rho\left[C' - \log\frac{1+\sin\alpha}{\cos\alpha}\right]$$

4.7. Potential of a circular disc

To determine the potential of a thin uniform circular disc of radius *a*, small thickness *K* and density ρ at an external point *P* distant *p* from the centre.

[M.U. 2003H; T.M.B.U. 94H, 96H, 98H, 2004H; B.B.A.B.U. 99H]

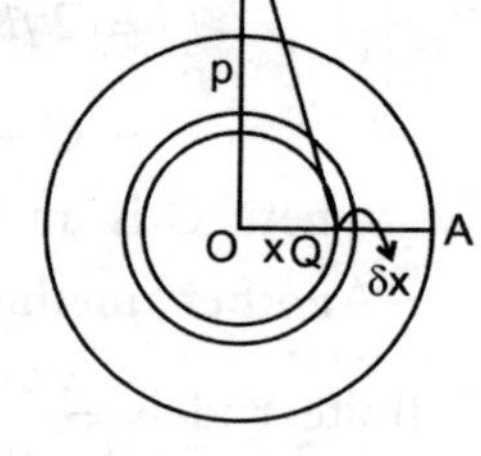

Let O be the centre of the circular disc of radius a, small thickness K and density ρ. Let P be a point on the axis of the disc at a distance p from O i.e. $OP = p$.

We consider an element of the disc included between two concentric circles of radii x and $x + \delta x$.

The area between these two concentric circles

$$= \pi\,(x + \delta x)^2 - \pi x^2$$

$$= 2\pi x\delta x \qquad \text{Since } \delta x \text{ is very small.}$$

Mass of this elementary ring $= K\rho 2\pi x\delta x$

Since the distance of every element of the ring from the point P is equal to PQ.

Hence the potential of the elementary ring at P

$$= \gamma \frac{2\pi K\rho x\delta x}{PQ}$$

$$= \gamma \frac{2\pi K\rho x\delta x}{\sqrt{p^2 + x^2}}$$

Hence the potential at P due to the whole of disc

$$= \int_0^a \frac{\gamma 2\pi K\rho x\delta x}{\sqrt{p^2 + x^2}}$$

$$= 2\pi\gamma K\rho \left[\sqrt{p^2 + x^2}\right]_0^a$$

$$= 2\pi\gamma K\rho \left[\sqrt{p^2 + a^2} - p\right]$$

Another Form $= 2\pi\gamma K\rho\,[PA - PO]$

where P is the point at which potential is to be determined, O is the centre of the circular disc and A is extremity of the radius perpendicular to axes.

WORKED OUT EXAMPLES

1. Prove that the potential of a circle of uniform surface density ρ and radius a at a point on its circumference $4\gamma\rho a$.

[L.N.M.U. 94H; T.M.B.U. 200H, 2002H; B.B.A.B.U. 97H, 2001H, 2004H; M.U. 2004H]

Solution: Let C be the centre and P the point on the circumference of the circle of radius a, where the potential of the circle is to be determined.

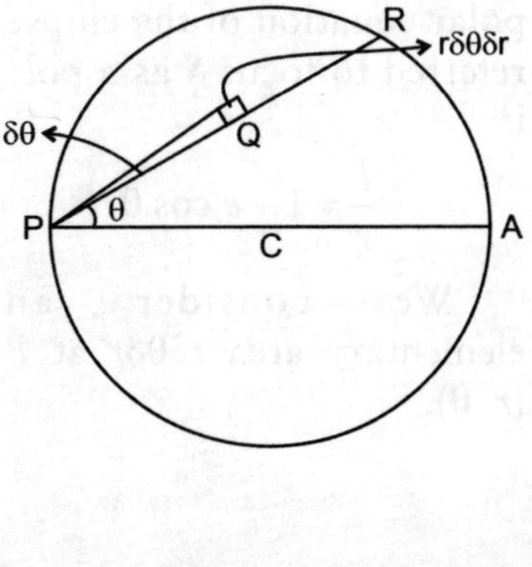

Let PA be the diameter of the circle through P. Then the equation of the circle with P as pole and PA as the initial line is

$$r = 2a\cos\theta \qquad \text{... (1)}$$

We consider an elementary area $r\delta\theta\delta r$ at the point $Q\ (r, \theta)$.

Mass of the el mentary area = $\rho r\delta\theta\delta r$.

The potential at P of this elementary area at P

$$= \gamma \frac{r\delta\theta\delta r\rho}{PQ} = \frac{\gamma r\delta\theta\delta r\rho}{r} = \gamma\rho\delta\theta\delta r$$

Therefore the potential at P, of the circle

$$= \gamma\rho \int_{\theta=-\frac{\pi}{2}}^{\frac{\pi}{2}} \int_{r=0}^{2a\cos\theta} d\theta\, dr$$

$$= \gamma\rho \int_{-\frac{\pi}{2}}^{\frac{\pi}{2}} [r]_0^{2a\cos\theta}\, d\theta$$

$$= \gamma\rho 2a \int_{-\frac{\pi}{2}}^{\frac{\pi}{2}} \cos\theta\, d\theta$$

$$= \gamma\rho 2a\,[\sin\theta]_{-\frac{\pi}{2}}^{\frac{\pi}{2}}$$

$$= 4\gamma\rho a$$

2. The density of an elliptic lamina varies as the distance from the major axis, the mass of a unit element of area at a unit distance being μ. Show that the potential due to the lamina at the focus is $2\gamma\mu h^2$.

Solution: Let S be the focus and AA' be the major axis. The polar equation of the ellipse referred to focus S as a pole is

$$\frac{l}{r} = 1 - e\cos\theta$$

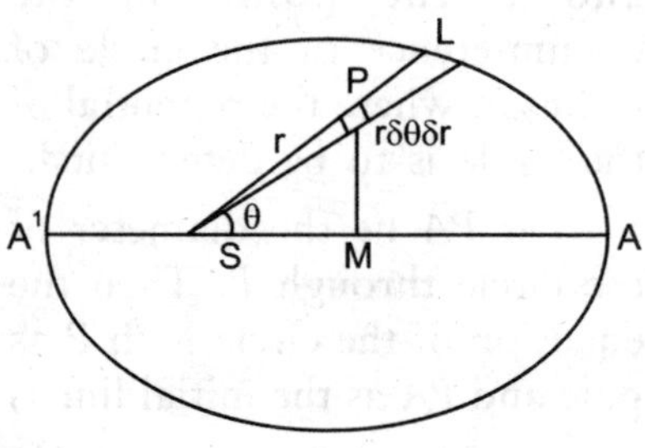

We consider an elementary area $r\delta\theta\delta r$ at P (r, θ).

By given condition density at P is $= \mu PM$

$$= \mu r \sin\theta$$

So mass of the elementary area

$$= \mu r \sin\theta \; r\delta\theta\delta r$$

Potential at the focus S, due to the elementary mass

$$= \gamma \frac{\mu r \sin\theta \; r\delta\theta\delta r}{r} = \gamma\mu r \sin\theta \; \delta\theta\delta r$$

Hence potential at the focus S, due to the elliptic lamina

$$= \int_{\theta=-\pi}^{\pi} \int_{r=0}^{l/1-e\cos\theta} \gamma\mu r \sin\theta \; d\theta dr$$

$$= 2\gamma\mu \int_{\theta=0}^{\pi} \int_{r=0}^{l/1-e\cos\theta} r \sin\theta \; d\theta \; dr$$

$$= 2\gamma\mu \int_{\theta=0}^{\pi} \left[\frac{r^2}{2}\right]_{r=0}^{l/1-e\cos\theta} \sin\theta \, d\theta$$

$$= \gamma\mu \int_{\theta=0}^{\pi} \frac{l^2 \sin\theta \; d\theta}{(1-e\cos\theta)^2}$$

$$= \frac{\gamma\mu l^2}{e}\left[\frac{-1}{1-e\cos\theta}\right]_0^{\pi}$$

$$= \frac{-\gamma\mu l^2}{e}\left[\frac{1}{1+e} - \frac{1}{1-e}\right]$$

$$= \frac{-\mu\gamma l^2}{e} \frac{-2e}{1-e^2}$$

$$= \frac{2\mu\gamma l^2}{1-e^2}$$

$$= \frac{2\mu\gamma b^4}{a^2\left(1-e^2\right)} = \frac{2\mu\gamma b^4}{b^2} = 2\mu\gamma b^2$$

3. Show that the potential of a uniform circular disc of mass M and radius a, at a point in its plane distant c from its centre is

$$\frac{4\gamma M}{\pi a^2}\int_0^{\frac{\pi}{2}}\sqrt{a^2-c^2\sin^2\theta\,d\theta}$$

$$\text{or}\quad \frac{4\gamma M}{\pi a^2}\int_0^{\sin^{-1}\frac{a}{c}}\sqrt{a^2-c^2\sin^2\theta\,d\theta}$$

according as c is less or greater than a.

Solution: Let O be the centre of the disc and P be the point at which potential is to be determined. Given $OP = c$.

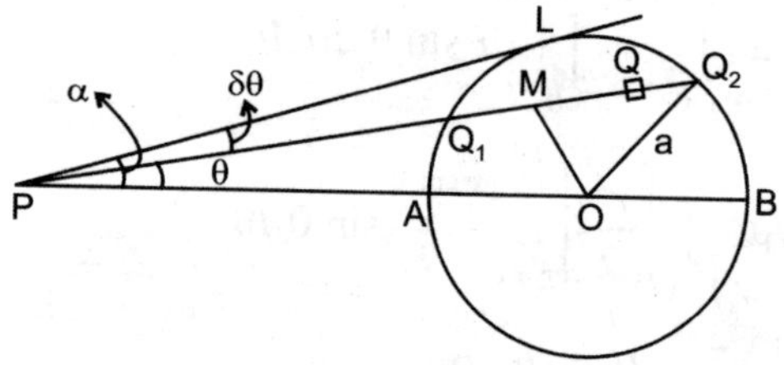

Taking P as pole and the diameter through P as the initial line.

Through P we draw a secant PQ_1Q_2. From O we draw OM perpendicular, so that $Q_1M = Q_2M$.

In ΔOPM
$$\sin\theta = \frac{OM}{OP} = \frac{OM}{c}$$
$$OM = c\sin\theta$$
$$\cos\theta = \frac{PM}{OP} = \frac{PM}{c}$$
$$PM = c\cos\theta$$

In ΔOQ_2M
$$OQ_2^2 = OM^2 + MQ_2^2$$
$$a^2 = c^2\sin^2\theta + MQ_2^2$$
$$MQ_1 = MQ_2 = \sqrt{a^2 - c^2\sin^2\theta}$$

Now $PQ_1 = PM - Q_1M = c\cos\theta - \sqrt{a^2 - c^2\sin^2\theta}$

$PQ_2 = PM + Q_2M = c\cos\theta + \sqrt{a^2 - c^2\sin^2\theta}$

If PL be the tangent at P to the circle then

$$\sin\alpha = \frac{OL}{OP} = \frac{a}{c} \text{ or } \alpha = \sin^{-1}\frac{a}{c}$$

Let us take an elementary area $r\delta\theta\delta r$ at Q (r, θ). Where $PQ = r$ and $\angle OPB = \theta$.

The mass of the elementary area at $Q = \rho r\delta\theta\delta r$.

The potential at P of the element at Q

$$= \frac{\gamma\rho r\delta\theta\delta r}{PQ}$$

$$= \frac{\gamma\rho r\delta\theta\delta r}{r}$$

$$= \gamma\rho\delta\theta\delta r$$

Case I. When $c > a$, P is an external point.

In this case, potential at P due to the whole disc

$$= 2\gamma\rho \int_{\theta=0}^{\alpha}\int_{r=PQ_1}^{PQ_2} d\theta\, dr$$

$$= 2\gamma\rho \int_{\theta=0}^{\alpha} d\theta\,(PQ_2 - PQ_1)$$

$$= 2\gamma\rho \int_{\theta=0}^{\alpha} 2\sqrt{a^2 - c^2\sin^2\theta}\, d\theta$$

$$= 4\gamma\rho \int_{\theta=0}^{\sin^{-1}\frac{a}{c}} \sqrt{a^2 - c^2\sin^2\theta}\, d\theta \qquad \left(\because \sin\alpha = \frac{a}{c}\right)$$

$$= \frac{4\gamma M}{\pi a^2} \int_{0}^{\sin^{-1}\frac{a}{c}} \sqrt{a^2 - c^2\sin^2\theta}\, d\theta \qquad (\because M = \pi a^2\rho)$$

Case II. $c < a$. i.e. P is a internal point.

In this case potential at P due to the whole disc

$$= \gamma\rho \int_{\theta=-\pi}^{\pi} \int_{r=0}^{PQ_2} d\theta\, dr$$

$$= 2\gamma\rho \int_{\theta=0}^{\pi} d\theta\, PQ_2$$

$$= 2\gamma\rho \int_{\theta=0}^{\pi} d\theta \left[c\cos\theta + \sqrt{a^2 - c^2\sin^2\theta}\right]$$

$$= 2\gamma\rho \left[c\{\sin\theta\}_0^{\pi} + \int_0^{\pi} \sqrt{a^2 - c^2\sin^2\theta}\, d\theta\right]$$

$$= 2\gamma\rho \int_0^{\pi} \sqrt{a^2 - c^2\sin^2\theta}\, d\theta$$

$$= \frac{4\gamma M}{\pi a^2} \int_0^{\frac{\pi}{2}} \sqrt{a^2 - c^2\sin^2\theta} \qquad (\because M = \pi a^2\rho)$$

4. Show that the potential of a uniform circular disc at a point of itself is

$$\int_0^{\frac{\pi}{2}} \frac{\gamma\rho a\,(a - c\cos\theta)\, d\theta}{\sqrt{a^2 - 2ac\cos\theta + c^2}}$$

where c is the distance of the point from the centre and ρ is the mass per unit area. [M.U. 95H]

Solution: Let O be the centre of the disc and P be a point on the disc at a distance c from O, i.e. $OP = c$.

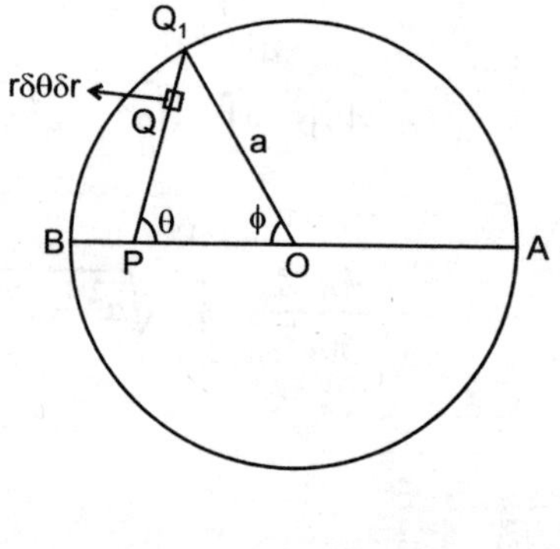

Referred to P as pole and the diameter AP as initial line, let the coordinates of a point Q of the disc be (r, θ).

We consider an element $r\delta\theta\delta r$ at Q.

Mass of the element at $Q = \rho r\delta\theta\delta r$.

$$\text{Its potential at } P = \gamma \frac{\rho r\delta\theta\delta r}{PQ} = \frac{\gamma\rho r\delta\theta\delta r}{r}$$

$$= \gamma\rho\delta\theta\delta r$$

Hence potential at P, due to the whole disc

= twice the potential at P due to the area above the diameter AB

$$= 2\gamma\rho \int_{\theta=0}^{\pi} \int_{r=0}^{PQ_1} d\theta\, dr$$

$$= 2\gamma\rho \int_0^{\pi} PQ_1 d\theta \qquad \text{... (1)}$$

Now in ΔOPQ_1 $OQ_1 = a$, $OP = c$, $PQ_1 = r_1$

$$\cos\theta = \frac{c^2 + r_1^2 - a^2}{2cr_1}$$

$$\therefore \quad r_1^2 = a^2 - c^2 + 2cr_1 \cos\theta$$

$$\therefore \quad 2r_1 dr_1 = 2c\,(dr_1 \cos\theta - r_1 \sin\theta\, d\theta)$$

$$\text{or} \quad (c\cos\theta - r_1)\, dr_1 = cr_1 \sin\theta\, d\theta \qquad \text{... (2)}$$

$$\text{Again} \quad r_1^2 = a^2 + c^2 - 2ac\cos\phi$$

$$\therefore \quad 2r_1 dr_1 = 2ac\sin\phi\, d\phi$$

$$r_1 dr_1 = ac\sin\phi\, d\phi \qquad \text{... (3)}$$

Dividing (2) by (3), we get

$$\frac{c\cos\theta - r_1}{r_1} = \frac{r_1 \sin\theta\, d\theta}{a\sin\phi\, d\phi} \qquad \text{... (4)}$$

Also in ΔOPQ_1

$$\frac{PQ_1}{\sin\phi} = \frac{OQ_1}{\sin\theta}$$

$$\frac{r_1}{\sin\phi} = \frac{a}{\sin\theta}$$

$$\frac{r_1 \sin \theta}{a \sin \phi} = 1$$

Hence from (4)

$$\frac{c \cos \theta - r_1}{r_1} = \frac{d\theta}{d\phi}$$

$\therefore$
$$r_1 d\theta = (\cos \theta - r_1)\, d\phi = \frac{c r_1 \cos\theta - r_1^2}{r_1}\, d\phi$$

But
$$c = r_1 \cos \theta + a \cos \phi$$

$$r_1 \cos \theta = c - a \cos \phi$$

Hence
$$r_1 d\theta = \frac{c\,(c - a \cos \phi) - \left(a^2 + c^2 - 2ac \cos \phi\right)}{\sqrt{a^2 + c^2 - 2ac \cos \phi}}\, d\phi$$

$$= \frac{ac \cos \phi - a^2}{\sqrt{a^2 + c^2 - 2ac \cos \phi}}\, d\phi$$

$$= \frac{a\,(c \cos \phi - a)}{\sqrt{a^2 + c^2 - 2ac \cos \phi}}\, d\phi$$

Also from figure it is clear that when $\theta = 0°$, $\phi = \pi$ and when $\theta = \pi$, $\phi = 0°$.

Hence from (1), we get potential of P due to the disc

$$= 2\gamma\rho \int_{\pi}^{0} \frac{a\,(c \cos \phi - a)}{\sqrt{a^2 + c^2 - 2ac \cos \phi}}\, d\phi$$

$$= 2\gamma\rho \int_{0}^{\pi} \frac{a\,(a - c \cos \phi)}{\sqrt{a^2 + c^2 - 2ac \cos \phi}}\, d\phi$$

$$= \gamma\rho \int_{0}^{2\pi} \frac{a\,(a - c \cos \phi)}{\sqrt{a^2 + c^2 - 2ac \cos \phi}}$$

$$= \gamma\rho \int_{0}^{2\pi} \frac{a\,(a - c \cos \theta)}{\sqrt{a^2 + c^2 - 2ac \cos \theta}}$$

[By using properties of definite integrals]

5. Find the potential of a uniform lamina bounded by two concentric circles whose radii are a and b, at a point in its plane distant c from the common centre, the law of attraction be $\dfrac{\mu}{(\text{distance})^5}$.

Solution: Let us first find the attraction of a circular disc of radius a at an external and internal point.

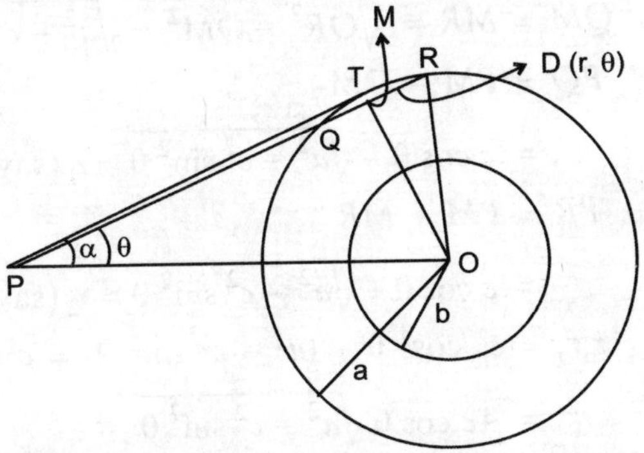

We consider an element $r\delta\theta\delta r$ at $D\ (r, \theta)$.

Mass of the element $= \rho r\delta\theta\delta r$

Its attraction at P according to the given law

$$= \frac{\mu r\delta\theta\delta r\rho}{r^5} = \frac{\mu\delta m}{r^5}$$

If V be the potential at P due to this element, then

$$\frac{dV}{dr} = \frac{-\mu\rho r\delta\theta\delta r}{r^5} = \frac{-\mu\delta m}{r^5}$$

$$V = \frac{\mu\delta m}{4r^4},\ = \frac{\mu r\delta\theta\delta r\rho}{4r^4}$$

$$= \frac{\mu\delta\theta\delta r\rho}{4r^3}$$

Through P we draw a secant through $D\ (r, \theta)$ which meets the circle of radius a at Q and R.

Let $OP = c$.

In ΔOPM

$$\sin\theta = \frac{OM}{OP} = \frac{OM}{c}$$
$$OM = c\sin\theta$$
$$\cos\theta = \frac{OM}{OP} = \frac{PM}{c}$$
$$PM = c\cos\theta$$
$$QM = MR = \sqrt{OR^2 - OM^2} = \sqrt{a^2 - c^2\sin^2\theta}$$
$$PQ = PM - QM$$
$$= c\cos\theta - \sqrt{a^2 - c^2\sin^2\theta} = r_1 \text{ (say)}$$
$$PR = PM + MR$$
$$= c\cos\theta + \sqrt{a^2 - c^2\sin^2\theta} = r_2 \text{ (say)}$$
$$r_1 r_2 = c^2\cos^2\theta - (a^2 - c^2\sin^2\theta) = c^2 - a^2$$

and $r_2^2 - r_1^2 = 4c\cos\theta\sqrt{a^2 - c^2\sin^2\theta}$

Let PT be the tangent at P to the circle of radius a. Let $\angle TPO = \alpha$. Then

$$\sin\alpha = \frac{a}{c}$$

or $$\alpha = \sin^{-1}\frac{a}{c}$$

Case I. When P is an external point, then potential at P, due to the whole disc

$$= \frac{\mu\rho}{4}\int_{\theta=-\alpha}^{\alpha}\int_{r=PQ}^{PR}\frac{1}{r^3}\,d\theta\,dr$$
$$= \frac{2\mu\rho}{4}\int_{0}^{\alpha}\int_{PQ}^{PR}\frac{1}{r^3}\,d\theta\,dr$$
$$= \frac{\mu\rho}{2}\int_{0}^{\alpha}\left[-\frac{1}{2r^2}\right]_{PQ}^{PR}d\theta$$

$$= \frac{\mu\rho}{4}\int_0^{\alpha}\left[-\frac{1}{r^2}\right]_{r_1}^{r_2} d\theta$$

$$= \frac{\mu\rho}{4}\int_0^{\alpha}\left[\frac{1}{r_1^2}-\frac{1}{r_2^2}\right] d\theta$$

$$= \frac{\mu\rho}{4}\int_0^{\alpha}\frac{r_2^2-r_1^2}{r_1^2\,r_2^2}\, d\theta$$

$$= \frac{\mu\rho}{4}\int_0^{\alpha}\frac{4c\cos\theta\sqrt{a^2-c^2\sin^2\theta}}{\left(c^2-a^2\right)^2}\, d\theta$$

$$= \frac{\mu\rho}{\left(c^2-a^2\right)^2}\int_0^{\alpha=\sin^{-1}\frac{a}{c}} c\cos\theta\sqrt{a^2-c^2\sin^2\theta}\, d\theta \quad \ldots (1)$$

Putting $c \sin \theta = a \sin \phi$

$c \cos \theta d\theta = a \cos \phi \, d\phi$

When $\theta = 0, \phi = 0$

$\theta = \alpha, a \sin \phi = a, \theta = \frac{\pi}{2}$

Hence from (1) potential becomes

$$= \frac{\mu\rho}{\left(c^2-a^2\right)^2}\int_0^{\frac{\pi}{2}} a\cos\phi\, d\phi\, a\cos\phi$$

$$= \frac{\mu\rho a^2}{\left(c^2-a^2\right)^2}\,\frac{1}{2}\,\frac{\pi}{2} = \frac{\mu\rho\pi a^2}{4\left(c^2-a^2\right)^2}$$

Case II. When P is an internal point, then the potential at P due to whole disc

$$= \frac{\mu\rho}{4}\int_{\alpha=-\pi}^{\pi}\int_{-r_1}^{r_2}\frac{d\theta\, dr}{r^3}$$

$$= \frac{2\mu\rho}{4}\int_0^{\pi}\int_{-r_1}^{r_2}\frac{d\theta\, dr}{r^3}$$

$$= \frac{\mu\rho}{2}\int_0^{\pi}\left[-\frac{1}{2r^2}\right]_{-r_1}^{r_2} d\theta$$

$$= \frac{\mu\rho}{4}\int_0^{\pi}\left(\frac{1}{r_1^2}-\frac{1}{r_2^2}\right) d\theta$$

$$= \frac{\mu\rho}{4}\int_0^{\pi}\frac{r_2^2-r_1^2}{r_1^2\, r_2^2}\, d\theta$$

$$= \frac{\mu\rho}{4}\int_0^{\pi}\frac{4\, c\cos\theta\sqrt{a^2-c^2\sin^2\theta}}{\left(c^2-a^2\right)^2}\, d\theta$$

$$= \frac{\mu\rho c}{\left(c^2-a^2\right)^2}\int_0^{\pi}\cos\theta\sqrt{a^2-c^2\sin^2\theta}\, d\theta$$

$= 0$ by property of definite integral.

Hence the potential at a point P external to both the concentric circles of radii a and b, $(a > b)$

$$= \frac{\mu\rho\pi}{4}\left[\frac{a^2}{\left(c^2-a^2\right)^2}-\frac{b^2}{\left(c^2-b^2\right)^2}\right]$$

Again when the point P is within the substance of concentric circles of radii a and b, $(a > b)$ then the potential $= \dfrac{\mu\rho\pi b^2}{4\left(c^2-b^2\right)^2}$.

Lastly when the point P be within both the concentric circles of radii a and b, then the potential $= 0$.

6. The surface density of a circular disc of radius a is $\rho\left(1-\dfrac{r^2}{a^2}\right)^{\frac{1}{2}}$ at a distance r from the centre of the disc. Prove that the potential at a point on the axis of the disc at a distance $a\cot\phi$ from its centre is

$$\pi\gamma\rho a\left(\phi\,\mathrm{cosec}^2\phi-\cot\phi\right)$$

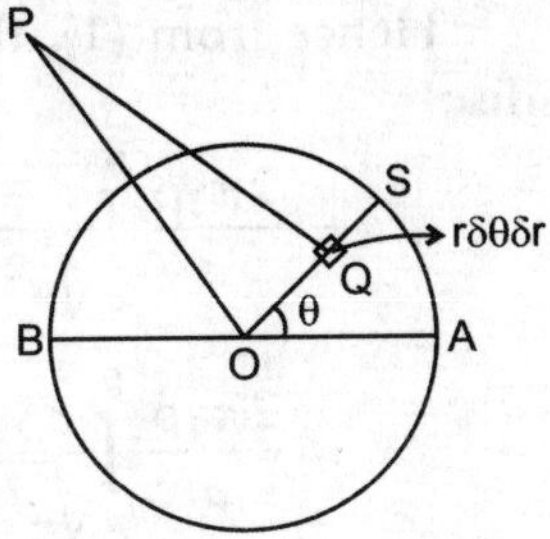

Solution: Let O be the centre of the disc and P a point on the axis through O, such that $OP = a \cot \phi$.

Taking O as pole and OA as initial line.

We consider an element $r\delta\theta\delta r$ at $Q\ (r, \theta)$

Mass of the elementary area

$$= r\delta\theta\delta r\rho\left(1 - \frac{r^2}{a^2}\right)^{\frac{1}{2}}$$

Its potential at P

$$= \frac{\gamma r\delta\theta\delta r\rho\left(a^2 - r^2\right)^{\frac{1}{2}}}{a\,PQ}$$

$$= \frac{\gamma r\rho\sqrt{a^2 - r^2}\ \delta\theta\ \delta r}{a\sqrt{r^2 + a^2\cot^2\phi}}$$

Hence the potential at P, due to the whole of the disc

$$= \frac{\gamma\rho}{a}\int_{\theta=0}^{2\pi}\int_{r=0}^{a}\frac{rd\theta dr\sqrt{a^2 - r^2}}{\sqrt{r^2 + a^2\cot^2\phi}}$$

$$= \frac{\gamma\rho}{a}\int_0^a\frac{2\pi r\sqrt{a^2 - r^2}}{\sqrt{r^2 + a^2\cot^2\phi}}dr$$

$$= \frac{2\pi\gamma\rho}{a}\int_0^a\frac{r\sqrt{a^2 - r^2}}{\sqrt{r^2 + a^2\cot^2\phi}}dr \qquad \text{... (1)}$$

Putting $a^2 - r^2 = y^2$

$-2rdr = 2ydy$

When $r = a,\ y = 0$

$r = 0,\ y = a$

Hence from (1), the potential at P due to the whole of the disc

$$= \frac{2\pi\gamma\rho}{a}\int_a^0 \frac{-y\,dy\,y}{\sqrt{a^2 + a^2\cot^2\phi - y^2}}$$

$$= \frac{2\pi\gamma\rho}{a}\int_a^0 \frac{-y^2 dy}{\sqrt{a^2\operatorname{cosec}^2\phi - y^2}}$$

$$= \frac{2\pi\gamma\rho}{a}\int_a^0 \frac{a^2\operatorname{cosec}^2\phi - y^2 - a^2\operatorname{cosec}^2\phi}{\sqrt{a^2\operatorname{cosec}^2\phi - y^2}}\,dy$$

$$= \frac{2\pi\gamma\rho}{a}\left[\int_a^0 \sqrt{a^2\operatorname{cosec}^2\phi - y^2}\,dy - a^2\operatorname{cosec}^2\phi\int_a^0 \frac{dy}{\sqrt{a^2\operatorname{cosec}^2\phi - y^2}}\right]$$

$$= \frac{2\pi\gamma\rho}{a}\left[\frac{y}{2}\sqrt{a^2\operatorname{cosec}^2\phi - y^2} + \frac{a^2}{2}\operatorname{cosec}^2\phi\sin^{-1}\left(\frac{y}{a\operatorname{cosec}\phi}\right) - a^2\operatorname{cosec}^2\phi\sin^{-1}\left(\frac{y}{a\operatorname{cosec}\phi}\right)\right]_a^0$$

$$= \frac{2\pi\gamma\rho}{a}\left[0 - \frac{a}{2}a\cot\phi - \frac{a^2}{2}\operatorname{cosec}^2\phi\sin^{-1}(\sin\phi) + a^2\operatorname{cosec}^2\phi\sin^{-1}(\sin\phi)\right]$$

$$= \frac{2\pi\gamma\rho}{a}\left[-\frac{a^2}{2}\cot^2\phi + \frac{a^2}{2}(\operatorname{cosec}^2\phi)\,\phi\right]$$

$$= \frac{\pi\gamma\rho a^2}{a}\left[\phi\operatorname{cosec}^2\phi - \cot\phi\right]$$

$$= \pi\gamma\rho a\left[\phi\operatorname{cosec}^2\phi - \cot\phi\right]$$

7. Show that the potential of a surface of a cube at the centre of the cube is

$$\frac{\gamma M}{Q}\left[\sigma \log\left(2+\sqrt{3}\right)-\pi\right]$$

where $2a$ is the length of a side and M is the mass of a face supposed indefinitely thin.

Deduce that the potential of the cube at its centre is

$$\frac{\gamma M}{4a}\left[\sigma \log\left(2+\sqrt{3}\right)-\pi\right]$$

where M is the mass and $2a$ the length of one of the edges of the cube.

Deduce also that the value of the potential of the cube at one of its corners is one half the value at its centre.

Solution: Let P be the centre of the cube and $ABCD$ its one face of small thickness K and edge $2a$.

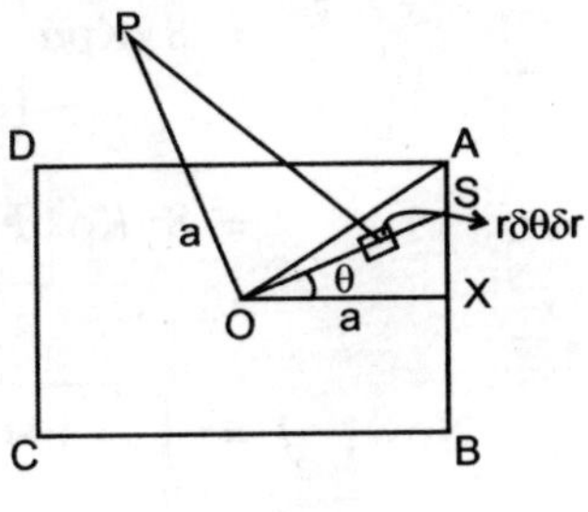

Hence P lies on the normal to the face through O. Where $OP = a$. The required potential at P due to ΔOXA.

We consider an elementary area $r\delta\theta\delta r$ of mass $K\rho r\delta\theta\delta r$ at $Q\ (r, \theta)$.

Its potential at P

$$= \frac{\gamma K\rho r\delta\theta\delta r}{PQ}$$

$$= \frac{\gamma K\rho r\delta\theta\delta r}{\sqrt{a^2+r^2}}$$

Therefore the potential at P due to triangle OXA

$$= \gamma K\rho \int_{\theta=0}^{\frac{\pi}{4}} \int_{r=0}^{OS} \frac{r\, d\theta\, dr}{\sqrt{a^2+r^2}}$$

Hence the potential due to face $ABCD$

$$= 8\gamma K\rho \int_{\theta=0}^{\frac{\pi}{4}} \int_{r=0}^{a\sec\theta} \frac{r\, d\theta\, dr}{\sqrt{a^2+r^2}}$$

Since $OS = a \sec \theta$

$$= 8\gamma K\rho \int_{\theta=0}^{\frac{\pi}{4}} \left[\sqrt{a^2+r^2}\right]_0^{a\sec\theta} d\theta$$

$$= 8\gamma K\rho a \int_0^{\frac{\pi}{4}} \left[\sqrt{\sec^2\theta+1}-1\right] d\theta$$

$$= 8\gamma K\rho a \left[-\frac{\pi}{4} + \int_0^{\frac{\pi}{4}} \sqrt{\sec^2\theta+1}\, d\theta\right]$$

$$= 8\gamma K\rho \left[I - \frac{\pi}{4}\right] \qquad \text{... (1)}$$

Now $\quad I = \int_0^{\frac{\pi}{4}} \sqrt{1+\sec^2\theta}\, d\theta$

$$= \int_0^{\frac{\pi}{4}} \frac{\sqrt{1+\cos^2\theta}}{\cos\theta} d\theta$$

$$= \int_0^{\frac{\pi}{4}} \frac{\sqrt{2-\sin^2\theta}}{\cos\theta} d\theta$$

Putting $\sin\theta = \sqrt{2}\sin\phi$

$$\cos\theta\, d\theta = \sqrt{2}\cos\phi\, d\phi$$

When $\theta = 0, \phi = 0$

$$\theta = \frac{\pi}{4}, \phi = \frac{\pi}{6}$$

$$I = \int_0^{\frac{\pi}{6}} \frac{\sqrt{2}\cos\phi}{1-2\sin^2\phi}\sqrt{2}\cos\phi\, d\phi$$

$$= 2\int_0^{\frac{\pi}{6}} \frac{\cos^2\phi}{1-2\sin^2\phi}\, d\phi$$

$$= 2\int_0^{\frac{\pi}{6}} \frac{1}{\sec^2\phi - 2\tan^2\phi}\, d\phi$$

$$= \int_0^{\frac{\pi}{6}} \frac{2\sec^2\phi}{\left(1-\tan^2\phi\right)\left(1+\tan^2\phi\right)}\, d\phi$$

Let $y = \tan\phi$

$\therefore \quad dy = \sec^2\phi\, d\phi$

$$I = 2\int_0^{\frac{1}{\sqrt{3}}} \frac{dy}{\left(1+y^2\right)\left(1-y^2\right)}$$

$$= \int_0^{\frac{1}{\sqrt{3}}} \left(\frac{1}{1+y^2} + \frac{1}{1-y^2}\right) dy$$

$$= \left[\tan^{-1} y + \frac{1}{2}\log\frac{1+y}{1-y}\right]_0^{\frac{1}{\sqrt{3}}}$$

$$= \frac{\pi}{6} + \frac{1}{2}\log\frac{\sqrt{3}+1}{\sqrt{3}-1}$$

$$= \frac{\pi}{6} + \frac{1}{2}\log\frac{\left(\sqrt{3}+1\right)^2}{2}$$

$$= \frac{\pi}{6} + \frac{1}{2}\log\frac{4+2\sqrt{3}}{2}$$

$$= \frac{\pi}{6} + \frac{1}{2}\log\left(2+\sqrt{3}\right)$$

Hence from (1) the required potential becomes

$$= 8\gamma K\rho a\left[\frac{\pi}{6}+\frac{1}{2}\log\left(2+\sqrt{3}\right)-\frac{\pi}{4}\right]$$

$$= 8\gamma K\rho a\left[\frac{1}{2}\log\left(2+\sqrt{3}\right)-\frac{\pi}{12}\right]$$

$$= \frac{2\gamma M}{a}\left[\frac{1}{2}\log\left(2+\sqrt{3}\right)-\frac{\pi}{12}\right] \because M = 4a^2K\rho$$

$$= \frac{\gamma M}{a}\left[\log\left(2+\sqrt{3}\right)-\frac{\pi}{6}\right]$$

This gives us the potential due to face $ABCD$. Hence the potential due to all six faces is

$$= 6\frac{\gamma M}{a}\left[\log\left(2+\sqrt{3}\right)-\frac{\pi}{6}\right]$$

$$= \frac{\gamma M}{a}\left[6\log\left(2+\sqrt{3}\right)-\pi\right] \qquad \text{... (2)}$$

$$= 4\gamma K\rho a\left[6\log\left(2+\sqrt{3}\right)-\pi\right] \because M = 4a^2K\rho$$

Second Part. Potential of a cube at its centre.

Let us consider a concentric cubical shell of edge $2x$ and thickness δx.

Potential at P due to all the six faces is obtained from (2) by writing x for a and δx for K.

$$= 4\gamma\rho\left[6\log\left(2+\sqrt{3}\right)-\pi\right]\int_0^a x\,dx$$

$$= 2\gamma\rho\left[6\log\left(2+\sqrt{3}\right)-\pi\right]a^2$$

$$= \gamma 2\rho a^2\left[6\log\left(2+\sqrt{3}\right)-\pi\right]$$

$$= \gamma\frac{M}{4a}\left[6\log\left(2+\sqrt{3}\right)-\pi\right] \qquad \text{... (3)}$$

$$\left(\because M = 8a^3\rho\right)$$

Third Part. The whole solid cube of edge $2a$ is made up of eight sub-cubes each of edge a and having one common corner at the centre P. These eight sub-cubes are similarly placed about the centre P; hence each of them must have same potential at P and each of these potentials must be $\frac{1}{8}$th of the total potential.

Hence from (3), potential at P; a corner of the sub-cube of edge a

$$= \frac{1}{8} 2\gamma\rho a^2 \left[6 \log\left(2+\sqrt{3}\right) - \pi\right]$$

Therefore potential at P, a corner of a cube of edge $2a$

$$= \frac{1}{8} 2\gamma\rho\left(2a^2\right)\left[6 \log\left(2+\sqrt{3}\right) - \pi\right]$$

$$= \gamma\rho a^2 \left[6 \log\left(2+\sqrt{3}\right) - \pi\right]$$

= one half of the potential at the centre from (3).

8. In the plane of a thin uniform circular ring of radius a centimetre and mass M grammes a point P is taken at a distance c from the centre ($c > a$). Show that the potential at P due to gravitation of ring is

$$\frac{\gamma M}{c+a}\left[1+\left(\frac{1}{2}K\right)^2+\left(\frac{1.3}{2.4}\right)^2 K^4+\left(\frac{1.3.5}{2.4.6}\right)^2 K^6+.....\right]$$

where $K = \dfrac{2\sqrt{ac}}{a+c}$.

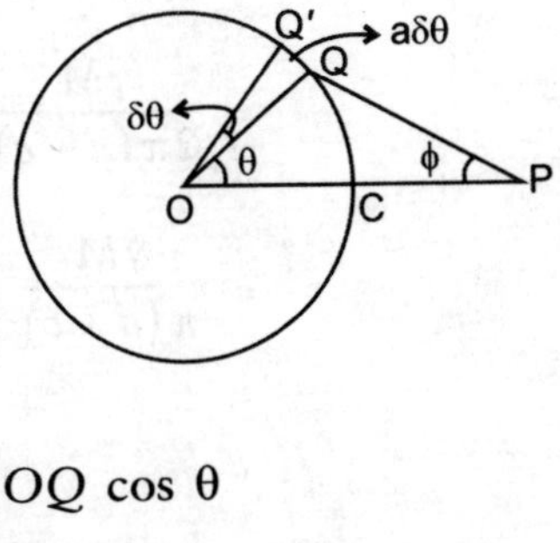

Solution: Let O be the centre of the ring and Q a point on it such that $\angle POQ = \theta$, then the element $QQ' = a\delta\theta$.

Join PQ and let $PQ = R$

Now

$$R^2 = PQ^2$$
$$= OP^2 + OQ^2 - 2OP\ OQ\cos\theta$$
$$R^2 = c^2 + a^2 - 2ac\cos\theta$$
$$= (a+c)^2 - 2ac\,(1+\cos\theta)$$

$$= (a+c)^2 - 4ac\cos^2\frac{\theta}{2}$$

$$= (a+c)^2\left[1 - \frac{4ac}{(a+c)^2}\cos^2\frac{\theta}{2}\right]$$

$$R^2 = (a+c)^2\left[1 - K^2\cos^2\frac{\theta}{2}\right]$$

Hence

$$R = (a+c)\left(1 - K^2\cos^2\frac{\theta}{2}\right)^{\frac{1}{2}} \qquad \dots (1)$$

Mass of the element $QQ' = a\delta\theta\rho$, where ρ is the line density.

Hence potential at P, due to this elementary mass

$$= \frac{\gamma a\delta\theta\rho}{R}$$

$$= \frac{\gamma a\delta\theta M}{R2\pi a} \quad (\because M = 2\pi a\rho)$$

$$= \frac{\gamma M}{2\pi}\frac{\delta\theta}{R}$$

$$= \frac{\gamma M}{2\pi(a+c)}\left(1 - K^2\cos^2\frac{\theta}{2}\right)^{-\frac{1}{2}}\delta\theta$$

Hence potential at P, due to the whole ring

$$= \frac{\gamma M}{2\pi(a+c)}\int_0^{2\pi}\left[1 - K^2\cos^2\frac{\theta}{2}\right]^{-\frac{1}{2}}d\theta$$

$$= \frac{\gamma M}{\pi(a+c)}\int_0^{\pi}\left[1 - K^2\cos^2\phi\right]^{-\frac{1}{2}}d\phi$$

where $\frac{\theta}{2} = \phi$

$$= \frac{2\gamma M}{\pi(a+c)}\int_0^{\frac{\pi}{2}}\left[1 - K^2\cos^2\phi\right]^{-\frac{1}{2}}d\phi$$

$$= \frac{2\gamma M}{\pi(a+c)} \int_0^{\frac{\pi}{2}} \left[1 + \frac{1}{2} K^2 \cos^2 \phi + \frac{1.3}{2.4} K^4 \cos^4 \phi + \ldots\right] d\phi$$

$$= \frac{2\gamma M}{\pi(a+c)} \left[\frac{1}{2}\pi + \frac{1}{2} K^2 \frac{1}{2}\frac{1}{2}\pi + \frac{1.3}{2.4} K^4 \frac{3.1}{4.2}\frac{\pi}{2} + \ldots\right]$$

$$= \frac{\gamma M}{c+a}\left[1 + \left(\frac{1}{2}\right)^2 K^2 + \left(\frac{1.3}{2.4}\right)^2 K^4 + \ldots\right]$$

9. Show that the potential of an infinite uniform thin cylinderical shell at a point P is $c - 4\pi\gamma a M \log a$ or $c - 4\pi\gamma a M \log r$ according as P is inside or outside the cylinder, the mass per unit area being M, the radius of the shell a and r being the distance of P from its axis.

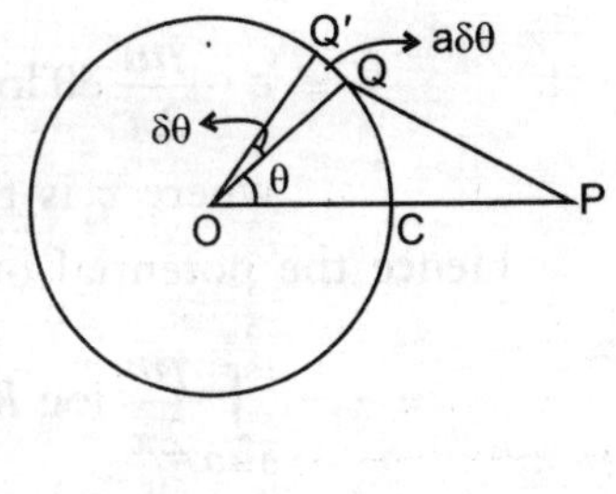

Solution: Let us consider the normal section of the cylinder through P and the centre O.

Let the hollow cylinder be made up of an infinite number of successive filaments each of infinite length. Let us consider the infinite rod standing on the element $QQ' = a\delta\theta$ of the circle.

Then its potential at P

$= c - 2\gamma a\delta\theta M \log PQ$ by the formula

$$V = c - 2\gamma p \log p$$

$= c - \gamma a\delta\theta M \log PQ^2$

$= c - \gamma a\delta\theta M \log (a^2 + r^2 - 2ar \cos \theta)$

Let O be the centre of a thin homogeneous ring of mass m, radius a and line density ρ.

$\therefore\ m = 2\pi a\rho$

We consider an element $a\delta\theta$ of the ring at Q such that $\angle QOP = \theta$.

Mass of the element at $Q = \rho a\delta\theta$.

Let $PQ = R$. Since the law of attraction is inversely as the distance, therefore the attraction of the elementary mass $\rho a\delta\theta$ at P along PQ

$$= \frac{\gamma\rho\, a\delta\theta}{QP} = \frac{\gamma m\delta\theta}{2\pi R} \quad (\because m = 2\pi a\rho)$$

If V is the potential at P, due to the elementary mass at Q, then

$$\frac{\partial V}{\partial R} = -\frac{\gamma m}{2\pi R}\,\delta\theta \qquad \text{... (1)}$$

Here negative sign is taken in R.H.S. as $\frac{\gamma m}{2\pi R}\,\delta\theta$ acts in the direction of R decreasing while $\frac{\partial V}{\partial R}$ acts in the direction of R increasing.

Integrating (1) with respect to R, we get

$$V = c - \frac{\gamma m}{2\pi}\,\delta\theta \log R$$

where c is the constant of integration.

Hence the potential of the whole ring at P

$$= c - \int_{\theta=0}^{2\pi} \frac{\gamma m}{2\pi} \log R\, d\theta$$

$$= c - \frac{\gamma m}{4\pi} \int_0^{2\pi} \log\left(a^2 + c^2 - 2ac\cos\theta\right) d\theta \qquad \text{... (2)}$$

Case I. When $c > a$

Then from (2), the potential of this ring at P

$$= c - \frac{\gamma m}{4\pi} \int_0^{2\pi} \log\left[c^2\left(1 - \frac{2a}{c}\cos\theta + \frac{a^2}{c^2}\right)\right] d\theta$$

$$= c - \frac{\gamma m}{4\pi} \int_0^{2\pi} d\theta \left[2\log c + \log\left\{1 - \frac{a}{c}\left(e^{i\theta} + e^{-i\theta}\right) + \frac{a^2}{c^2}\, e^{i\theta} e^{-i\theta}\right\}\right]$$

$$= c - \frac{\gamma m}{4\pi} \int_0^{2\pi} \left[2 \log c + \log \left(1 - \frac{a}{c} e^{i\theta} \right) - \frac{a}{c} e^{-i\theta} \left(1 - \frac{a}{c} e^{i\theta} \right) \right] d\theta$$

$$= c - \frac{\gamma m}{4\pi} \int_0^{2\pi} \left[2 \log c - \frac{a}{c} e^{i\theta} - \frac{1}{2} \frac{a^2}{c^2} e^{2i\theta} \ldots\ldots - \frac{a}{c} e^{-i\theta} - \frac{1}{2} \frac{a^2}{c^2} e^{-2i\theta} \ldots\ldots \right]$$

$$= c - \frac{\gamma m}{4\pi} \int_0^{2\pi} \left[2 \log c - \frac{2a}{c} \cos\theta - \frac{a^2}{c^2} \cos 2\theta \ldots\ldots \right] d\theta$$

$$= c - \frac{\gamma m}{4\pi} 4\pi \log c$$

$$= c - \gamma m \log c$$

Case II. Let $c < a$

Then from (2) the potential of the ring at P

$$= c - \frac{\gamma m}{4\pi} \int_0^{2\pi} \log \left(a^2 + c^2 - 2ac \cos\theta \right) d\theta$$

$$= c - \frac{\gamma m}{4\pi} \int_0^{2\pi} \log \left[a^2 \left(1 - \frac{2c}{a} \cos\theta + \frac{c^2}{a^2} \right) \right] d\theta$$

$$= c - \frac{\gamma m}{4\pi} \int_0^{2\pi} \left[2 \log a + \log \left\{ 1 - \frac{c}{a} \left(e^{i\theta} + e^{-i\theta} \right) + \frac{c^2}{a^2} e^{i\theta} e^{-i\theta} \right\} \right] d\theta$$

$$= c - \frac{\gamma m}{4\pi} \int_0^{2\pi} \left[2 \log a + \log \left\{ \left(1 - \frac{c}{a} e^{i\theta} \right) - \frac{c}{a} e^{-i\theta} \left(1 - \frac{C}{a} e^{i\theta} \right) \right\} \right] d\theta$$

$$= c - \frac{\gamma m}{4\pi}\int_0^{2\pi}\left[2\log a + \log\left(1-\frac{c}{a}e^{i\theta}\right) + \log\left(1-\frac{c}{a}e^{-i\theta}\right)\right]d\theta$$

$$= c - \frac{\gamma m}{4\pi}\int_0^{2\pi}\left[2\log a - \frac{c}{a}e^{i\theta} - \frac{1}{2}\frac{c^2}{a^2}e^{2i\theta}\ldots\ldots - \frac{c}{a}e^{-i\theta} - \frac{1}{2}\frac{c^2}{a^2}e^{-2i\theta}\ldots\ldots\right]d\theta$$

$$= c - \frac{\gamma m}{4\pi}\int_0^{2\pi}\left[2\log a - \frac{2c}{a}\cos\theta - \frac{c^2}{a^2}\cos 2\theta\right]d\theta$$

$$= c - \frac{\gamma m}{4\pi}4\pi\log a$$

$$= c - \gamma m \log a$$

10. A number of n equal infinitely long, homogeneous straight filaments lie on a cylinder of radius a and are at equal distance from one another. Show that the potential of any point P can be put in the form $c - \gamma m \log (r^{2n} - 2a^n r^n \cos n\theta + a^{2n})$.

Solution: The figure is a normal section of the cylinder through the point P and the centre O, A_1, A_2 are the points where the filaments touch the section. Join PA_1, PA_2, PA_3..... It can be easily seen that PA_1, PA_2 ..... are perpendicular respectively to the filaments which touch the section at A_1, A_2, ...

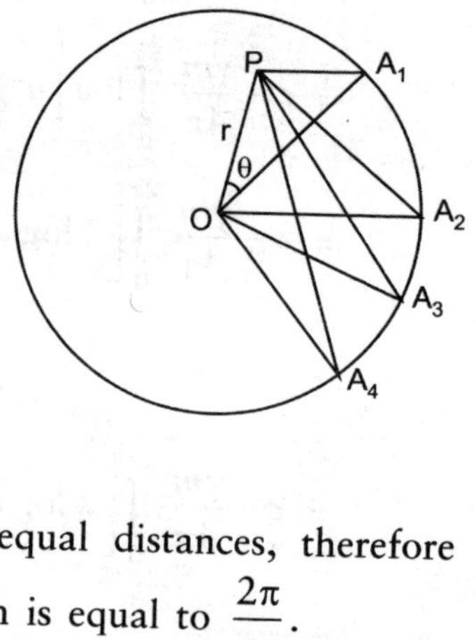

Let $OP = r$ and $\angle POA_1 = \theta$

Since A_1, A_2, A_3 ..... are at equal distances, therefore $\angle A_1OA_2 = \angle A_2OA_3 = \ldots\ldots$ and each is equal to $\frac{2\pi}{n}$.

Now $\angle POA_2 = \theta + \frac{2\pi}{2n}$, $\angle POA_3 = \theta + \frac{4\pi}{n}$ and so on.

$$PA_1^2 = r^2 + a^2 - 2ar\cos\theta$$

$$PA_2^2 = r^2 + a^2 - 2ar\cos\theta\left(\theta + \frac{2\pi}{n}\right)$$

$$PA_3^2 = r^2 + a^2 - 2ar\cos\theta\left(\theta + \frac{4\pi}{n}\right)$$

$$PA_1^2 \cdot PA_2^2 \cdot PA_3^2 \ldots\ldots PA_n^2$$

$$= \left(r^2 + a^2 - 2ar\cos\theta\right)\left\{r^2 + a^2 - 2ar\cos\left(\theta + \frac{2\pi}{n}\right)\right\}$$

to n factors

$$= r^{2n} + a^{2n} - 2r^n a^n \cos n\theta \qquad \ldots (1)$$

[By DeMoiver's property of a circle]

Using the formula $C - 2\gamma K\rho \log P$ for the potential of an infinite rod at an external point, we have potentials at P of given n filaments as

$$C_1 - 2\gamma m \log PA_1,\ C_2 - 2\gamma m \log PA_2,\ \ldots\ldots$$

where C_1, C_2, C_3 ..... are constants.

Hence potential of all the n filaments

$$= (C_1 + C_2 + \ldots. + C_n) - 2\gamma m \log (PA_1\ PA_2 \ldots PA_n)$$

$$= C - \gamma m \log\left(PA_1^2 - PA_2^2 - \ldots\ldots PA_n^2\right)$$

$$= C - \gamma m \log (r^{2n} + a^{2n} - 2r^n a^n \cos n\theta) \qquad \text{from (1)}$$

where $C = C_1 + C_2 + \ldots\ldots + C_n$ is a constant.

11. Prove that the potential due to a thin rod AB of uniform line density ρ at any point P in the line AB produced is $\gamma\rho \log \dfrac{PA}{PB}$.

Two such rods each of length $2a$ are placed so that they lie in the same straight line with their nearer ends at a distance $2a$ apart. Prove that a particle released from rest at a point in the line of the rods at a small distance x from the point midway between them begins to move with acceleration $\dfrac{16\gamma\rho x}{9a^2}$ approximately.

Solution: We consider an element δx of mass $\rho\delta x$ at Q where $PQ = x$.

Its potential at $P = \dfrac{\gamma\rho\delta x}{PQ} = \dfrac{\gamma\rho\delta x}{x}$

Hence potential of the rod AB at P

$$= \gamma\rho \int_{PB}^{PA} \frac{dx}{x}$$

$$= \gamma\rho \left[\log x\right]_{PB}^{PA}$$

$$= \gamma\rho \log \frac{PA}{PB}$$

Second Part

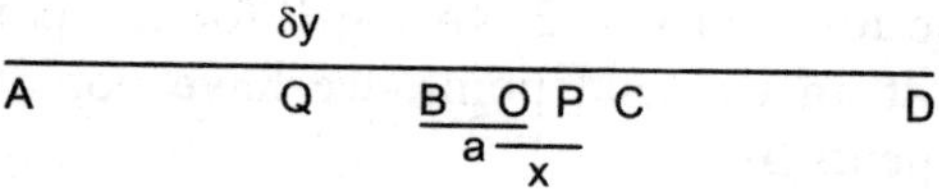

Let the two rods be AB and CD, such that $AB = CD = 2a$. Also $BC = 2a$.

Let O be the middle point of BC.

Let $OP = x$

Let us take a point Q on AB such that $PQ = y$.

Mass of an element of $AB = \rho\delta y$.

Attraction at P, due to this elementary mass $= \dfrac{\gamma\rho\delta y}{y^2}$

Hence attraction at P, due to the rod AB

$$= \gamma\rho \int_{PB}^{PA} \frac{dy}{y^2} = \gamma\rho \int_{a+x}^{3a+x} \frac{dy}{y^2}$$

$$= -\gamma\rho \left[\frac{1}{y}\right]_{a+x}^{3a+x}$$

$$= \gamma\rho \left[\frac{1}{a+x} - \frac{1}{3a+x}\right] \text{along } PB$$

Similarly attraction at P due to the rod CD

$$= \gamma\rho\left[\frac{1}{a-x} - \frac{1}{3a-x}\right] \text{ along } PC$$

$$= -\gamma\rho\left[\frac{1}{a-x} - \frac{1}{3a-x}\right] \text{ along } PB$$

Hence attraction at P due to both the rods AB and CD

$$= \gamma\rho\left[\left(\frac{1}{a+x} - \frac{1}{a-x}\right) - \left(\frac{1}{3a+x} + \frac{1}{3a-x}\right)\right]$$

$$= \gamma\rho\left[\frac{-2x}{a^2-x^2} + \frac{2x}{9a^2-x^2}\right]$$

$$= -2\gamma\rho x\left[\frac{1}{a^2}\left(1-\frac{x^2}{a^2}\right)^{-1} - \frac{1}{9a^2}\left(1-\frac{x^2}{9a^2}\right)^{-1}\right]$$

$$= -2\gamma\rho x\left[\frac{1}{a^2}\left(1+\frac{x^2}{a^2}+\ldots..\right) - \frac{1}{9a^2}\left(1+\frac{x^2}{9a^2}+\ldots..\right)\right]$$

$$= -2\gamma\rho x\left[\frac{1}{a^2} - \frac{1}{9a^2}\right] \text{ approximately as } \frac{x}{a} \text{ is small}$$

$$= -\frac{16\gamma\rho x}{9a^2} \text{ nearly.}$$

12. A solid right circular cylinder is of density ρ and length l and the radius of each end is a. Prove that the potential due to it, at the centre of each end is

$$\pi\gamma\rho\left[l\sqrt{a^2+l^2} - l^2 + a^2 \sin h^{-1}\left(\frac{l}{a}\right)\right]$$

where Y is the constant of gravitation.

If in the above cylinder $l = \dfrac{8a}{3}$, show that potential at the centre of the cylinder is $2\pi\gamma\rho a^2\left(\dfrac{4}{9} + \log 3\right)$.

Solution: Let $ABCD$ be a right circular cylinder of density ρ and length l. The radius of each end is a. Let P be the centre of one end where the potential is to be determined.

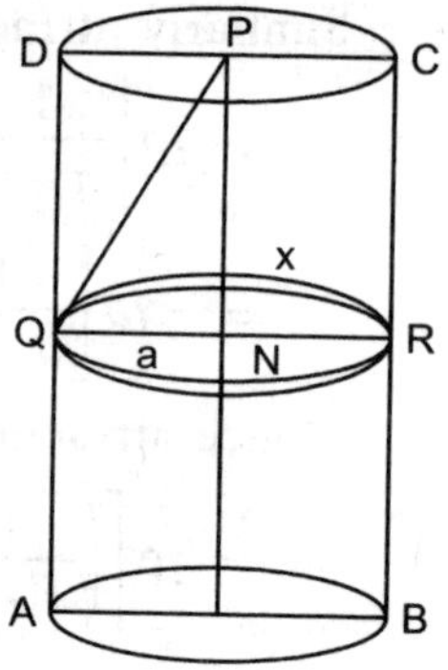

We consider an elementary circular disc QR of thickness δx at a distance x from P i.e. $PN = x$.

Potential of this disc at P

$$= 2\pi\gamma\delta x\rho\ (PQ - PN)$$

$$= 2\pi\gamma\rho\left[\sqrt{a^2 + x^2} - x\right]\delta x$$

Hence potential at P, due to the cylinder

$$= 2\pi\gamma\rho\int_0^l\left[\sqrt{a^2 + x^2} - x\right]dx$$

$$= 2\gamma\pi\rho\left[\frac{x\sqrt{a^2 + x^2}}{2} + \frac{a^2}{2}\sin h^{-1}\frac{x}{a} - \frac{x^2}{a}\right]_0^l$$

$$= 2\pi\gamma\rho\left[\frac{l}{2}\sqrt{a^2 + l^2} + \frac{a^2}{2}\sin h^{-1}\frac{l}{a} - \frac{l^2}{2} - 0\right]$$

$$= \pi\gamma\rho\left[l\sqrt{a^2 + l^2} + a^2\sin h^{-1}\frac{l}{a} - l^2\right]$$

$$= \pi\gamma\rho\left[l\sqrt{a^2 + l^2} - l^2 + a^2\sin h^{-1}\frac{l}{a}\right]$$

Second Part. Here we are required to determine the potential of the cylinder at the middle point of the axis. It can be easily obtained by putting $\frac{l}{2}$ for l and multiplying the result by 2.

Thus required potential

$$= 2\pi\gamma\rho\left[\frac{l}{2}\sqrt{a^2 + \frac{l^2}{4}} + a^2\sin h^{-1}\frac{l}{2a} - \frac{l^2}{4}\right]$$

Given $l = \frac{8a}{3}$

Hence the potential at the centre of the ellipse

$$= 2\pi\gamma\rho\left[\frac{4a}{3}\sqrt{a^2 + \frac{16a^2}{9}} + a^2\sin h^{-1}\frac{4}{3} - \frac{16a^2}{9}\right]$$

$$= 2\pi\gamma\rho a^2\left[\frac{4}{3}\frac{5}{3}+\sin h^{-1}\frac{4}{3}-\frac{16}{9}\right]$$

$$= 2\pi\gamma\rho a^2\left[\frac{4}{9}+\log\frac{4+\sqrt{4^2+3^2}}{3}\right]$$

$$= 2\pi\gamma\rho a^2\left[\frac{4}{9}+\log 3\right]$$

13. Show that the potential of a solid hemisphere of radius a and density ρ, at an external point P situated on the axis at a distance d from the centre is

$$\frac{2\pi\gamma\rho}{3d}\left[a^3 \pm \left(a^2+d^2\right)^{\frac{3}{2}} - d^3 - \frac{3}{2} - a^2 d\right]$$

The upper or lower sign being taken according as P is on the convex or plane side of the body.

Solution: Let O be the centre of the base. Given $OP = d$. If $ON = x$, then,

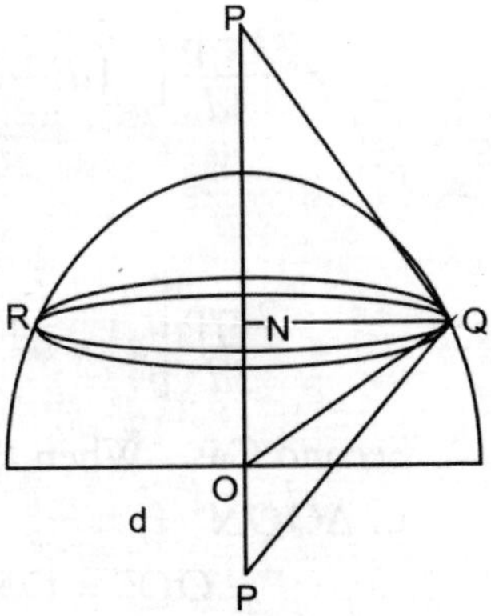

$$PN = OP - ON = d - x$$

$$OQ = a$$

In ΔOQN

$$OQ^2 = ON^2 + NQ^2$$

$$a^2 = x^2 + NQ^2$$

$$a^2 - x^2 = NQ^2$$

In ΔPQN

$$PQ^2 = PN^2 + QN^2$$

$$= (d-x)^2 + a^2 - x^2$$

Ist Case. When P is on the convex side.

We consider an elementary disc QR of width δx at a distance x from the centre O.

Potential at P due to this elementary disc

$$= 2\pi\gamma\delta x\rho\,(PQ - PN)$$

$$= 2\pi\gamma\delta x\rho\left[\sqrt{(d-x)^2+\left(a^2-x^2\right)}-(d-x)\right]$$

$$= 2\pi\gamma\rho\left[\sqrt{d^2 + a^2 - 2dx} - (d - x)\right]\delta x \qquad \dots (1)$$

Hence potential at P, due to the hemisphere

$$= 2\pi\gamma\rho\int_0^a\left[\sqrt{d^2 + a^2 - 2dx} - (d - x)\right]dx$$

$$= 2\pi\gamma\rho\left[-\frac{2}{3.2d}\left(d^2 + a^2 - 2dx\right)^{\frac{3}{2}} - dx + \frac{x^2}{2}\right]_0^a$$

$$= 2\pi\gamma\rho\left[-\frac{1}{3d}\left(d^2 + a^2 - 2da\right)^{\frac{3}{2}}\right.$$

$$\left. - da + \frac{a^2}{2} + \frac{1}{3d}\left(a^2 + d^2\right)^{\frac{3}{2}}\right]$$

$$= 2\pi\gamma\rho\left[-\frac{1}{3d}(d - a)^3 - da + \frac{a^2}{2} + \frac{1}{3d}\left(a^2 + d^2\right)^{\frac{3}{2}}\right]$$

$$= \frac{2\pi\gamma\rho}{3d}\left[-\left(d^3 - 3d^2a + 3da^2 - a^3\right)\right.$$

$$\left. + \left(d^2 + a^2\right)^{\frac{3}{2}} - 3d^2a + \frac{3da^2}{2}\right]$$

$$= \frac{2\pi\gamma\rho}{3d}\left[a^3 - d^3 + \left(d^2 + a^2\right)^{\frac{3}{2}} - \frac{3da^2}{2}\right]$$

Second Case. When P is on the plane side of the hemisphere.

In ΔOQN

$$OQ^2 = ON^2 + QN^2$$

$$a^2 = x^2 + QN^2$$

$$a^2 - x^2 = QN^2$$

In ΔPQN

$$PQ^2 = PN^2 + QN^2$$

$$= (PO + ON)^2 + a^2 - x^2$$

$$= (d + x)^2 + a^2 - x^2$$

$$= d^2 + 2dx + a^2$$

Hence potential at P, due to the elementary disc QR

$$= 2\pi\gamma\rho\,(PQ - PN)\,\delta x$$

$$= 2\pi\gamma\rho\left[\sqrt{d^2 + a^2 + 2dx} - (d + x)\right]\delta x \qquad \dots (2)$$

Hence potential at P, due to the hemisphere

$$= 2\pi\gamma\rho\int_0^a\left[\sqrt{d^2 + a^2 + 2dx} - (d + x)\right]dx$$

$$= 2\pi\gamma\rho\left[\frac{2}{3.2d}\left(a^2 + d^2 + 2dx\right)^{\frac{3}{2}} - dx - \frac{x^2}{2}\right]_0^a$$

$$= 2\pi\gamma\rho\left[\frac{1}{3d}\left(a^2 + d^2 + 2ad\right)^{\frac{3}{2}} - da - \frac{a^2}{2} - \frac{1}{3d}\left(a^2 + d^2\right)^{\frac{3}{2}}\right]$$

$$= \frac{2\pi\gamma\rho}{3d}\left[(a + d)^3 - 3d^2a - \frac{3da^2}{2} - \left(a^2 + d^2\right)^{\frac{3}{2}}\right]$$

$$= \frac{2\pi\gamma\rho}{3d}\left[a^3 + 3a^2d + 3ad^2 + d^3 - 3ad^2 - \frac{3a^2d}{2} - \left(a^2 + d^2\right)^{\frac{3}{2}}\right]$$

$$= \frac{2\pi\gamma\rho}{3d}\left[a^3 + 3a^2d + d^3 - \frac{3a^2d}{2} - \left(a^2 + d^2\right)^{\frac{3}{2}}\right]$$

$$= \frac{2\pi\gamma\rho}{3d}\left[a^3 - \frac{3}{2}a^2d + d^3 - \left(a^2 + d^2\right)^{\frac{3}{2}}\right].$$

14. If the radius of a sphere be a, its density ρ and the distance of an internal point from the centre O be b. Show that the difference of the potentials at P due to the two portions into which the sphere is divided by a plane through P perpendicular to OP is $\dfrac{4\pi\gamma\rho}{3b}\left[a^3 - \left(a^2 - b^2\right)^{\frac{3}{2}}\right]$.

Solution: Let O be the centre of the sphere of radius a and density ρ. Let CD be a plane through P perpendicular to the diameter AB through P. Now we shall find potentials V_1 and V_2 at P due to the two portions $CDAC$ and $CDBC$ of the sphere respectively.

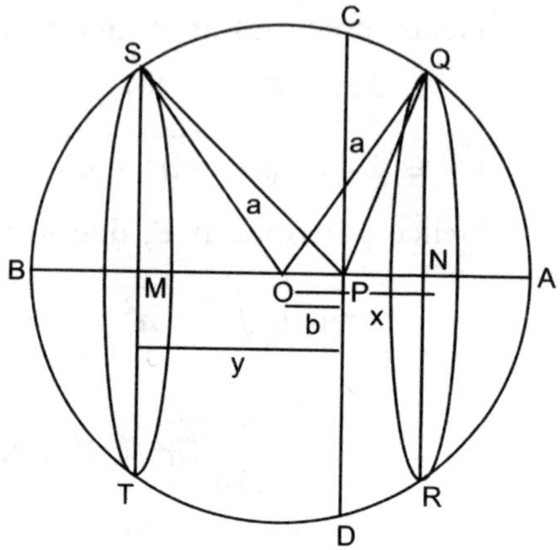

Case I. To find potential V_1 at P due to the portion $CDAC$.

We consider an elementary disc QR perpendicular to PA of thickness δx at a distance $PN = x$ from P.

Then the potential at P, due to the elementary disc QR

$$= 2\pi\gamma\rho\delta x\ (PQ - PN) \quad \dots (1)$$

Now $PN = x$,

$$\begin{aligned} PQ^2 &= PN^2 + QN^2 \\ &= PN^2 + OQ^2 - ON^2 \\ &= x^2 + a^2 - (b + x)^2 \\ &= a^2 - b^2 - 2bx \end{aligned}$$

Hence from (1) the potential at P due to the elementary disc QR

$$= 2\pi\gamma\rho\left[\sqrt{a^2 - b^2 - 2bx} - x\right]\delta x$$

Hence the potential V_1 at P, due to the portion $CDAC$ is given by

$$= 2\pi\gamma\rho \int_0^{a-b} \left[\sqrt{a^2 - b^2 - 2bx} - x\right] dx$$

$$= 2\pi\gamma\rho\left[-\frac{2}{3.2b}\left(a^2 - b^2 - 2bx\right)^{\frac{3}{2}} - \frac{x^2}{2}\right]_0^{a-b}$$

$$= 2\pi\gamma\rho\left[-\frac{1}{3b}\left\{a^2 - b^2 - 2b(a-b)\right\}^{\frac{3}{2}} - \frac{(a-b)^2}{2} + \frac{1}{3b}\left(a^2 - b^2\right)^{\frac{3}{2}}\right]$$

$$= 2\pi\gamma\rho\left[-\frac{1}{3b}(a-b)^3 + \frac{1}{3b}\left(a^2 - b^2\right)^{\frac{3}{2}} - \frac{1}{2}(a-b)^2\right] \quad \ldots (2)$$

Case III. To find the potential V_2 at P due to the portion *CBDC*.

We consider an elementary circular disc *ST* of thickness δy at a distance y from P.

Then the potential at P, due to the elementary disc *ST*

$$= 2\pi\gamma\rho\ (PS - PM)\ \delta y \quad \ldots (3)$$

Now $PM = OP + OM = b + y$

and
$$PS^2 = PM^2 + MS^2$$
$$= PM^2 + (OS - OM)^2$$
$$= y^2 + a^2 - (y - b)^2$$
$$= a^2 - b^2 + 2by$$

$\therefore$
$$PS = \sqrt{a^2 - b^2 + 2by}$$

Therefore, the potential at P, due to the elementary disc *ST* from (3)

$$= 2\pi\gamma\rho\left[\sqrt{a^2 - b^2 + 2by} - y\right] dy$$

Hence the potential V_2 at P, due to the portion *CBDC* is given by

$$V_2 = 2\pi\gamma\rho\int_0^{a+b}\left[\sqrt{a^2 - b^2 + 2by} - y\right] dy$$

$$= 2\pi\gamma\rho\left[\frac{2}{3.2b}\left(a^2 - b^2 + 2by\right)^{\frac{3}{2}} - \frac{y^2}{2}\right]_0^{a+b}$$

$$= 2\pi\gamma\rho\left[\frac{1}{3b}\left\{a^2 - b^2 + 2b(a+b)\right\}^{\frac{3}{2}} - \frac{(a+b)^2}{2} - \frac{1}{3b}\left(a^2 - b^2\right)^{\frac{3}{2}}\right]$$

$$= 2\pi\gamma\rho\left[\frac{1}{3b}(a+b)^3 - \frac{1}{2}(a+b)^2 - \frac{1}{3b}\left(a^2 - b^2\right)^{\frac{3}{2}}\right] \quad \ldots (4)$$

Subtracting (2) from (4) we get the difference of two potentials as

$$V_2 - V_1 = 2\pi\gamma\rho\left[\frac{1}{3b}\left\{(a+b)^3 + (a-b)^3\right\} - \frac{1}{2}\left\{(a+b)^2 - (a-b)^2\right\} - \frac{2}{3b}\left(a^2 - b^2\right)^{\frac{3}{2}}\right]$$

$$= 2\pi\gamma\rho\left[\frac{2}{3b}\left(a^3 + 3ab^2\right) - \frac{1}{2}\,4ab - \frac{2}{3b}\left(a^2 - b^2\right)^{\frac{3}{2}}\right]$$

$$= \frac{4\pi\gamma\rho}{3b}\left[a^3 + 3ab^2 - 3ab^2 - \left(a^2 - b^2\right)^{\frac{3}{2}}\right]$$

$$= \frac{4\pi\gamma\rho}{3b}\left[a^3 - \left(a^2 - b^2\right)^{\frac{3}{2}}\right].$$

15. Show that the quantity of work necessary to move one condensed unit of mass along any path from the middle point of the base of a homogeneous solid cone to the vertex is

$$\pi\gamma\rho h^2 \sin^2\alpha\cos\alpha\left[\log\frac{\cos\alpha\,(1+\cos\alpha)}{\sin\alpha\,(1-\sin\alpha)} + \frac{\cos^3\alpha + \sin^3\alpha - 1}{\sin^2\alpha\cos^2\alpha}\right]$$

where h is the height and 2α the vertical angle of the cone and ρ is the density.

Solution: Let V be the vertex and O be the centre of the base of the cone.

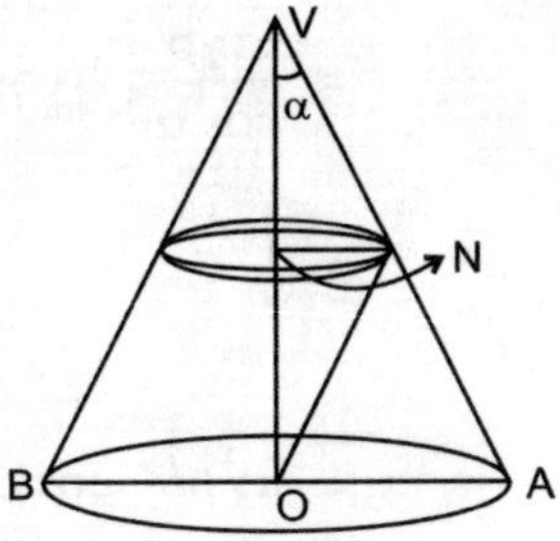

The work done in moving the particle from O to V

= Potential at O – Potential at V

Let us first find potential at O.

We consider the plane section of width δx and at a height x above the base.

Then potential at O by the formula

$$= 2\pi\gamma\rho\left[\sqrt{p^2+a^2}-p\right]\delta x \quad \text{is}$$

$$= 2\pi\gamma\rho\left[\sqrt{x^2+(h-x)^2\tan^2\alpha}-x\right]\delta x$$

since $p = AN = x$

and $\sqrt{p^2+a^2} = \sqrt{x^2+(h-x)^2\tan^2\alpha}$

Hence the potential of the cone at O

$$= 2\pi\gamma\rho\int_0^h\left[\frac{1}{\cos\alpha}\sqrt{x^2\left(\sin^2\alpha+\cos^2\alpha\right)-2hx\sin^2\alpha+h^2\sin^2\alpha}-x\cos\alpha\right]dx$$

$$= \frac{2\pi\gamma\rho}{\cos\alpha}\int_0^h\left[\sqrt{\left(x-h\sin^2\alpha\right)^2+h^2\sin^2\alpha\cos^2\alpha}-x\cos\alpha\right]dx$$

$$= \frac{2\pi\gamma\rho}{\cos\alpha}\left[\frac{1}{2}\left(x-h\sin^2\alpha\right)^2\sqrt{\left(x-h\sin^2\alpha\right)^2+h^2\sin^2\alpha\cos^2\alpha}+\frac{1}{2}h^2\sin^2\alpha\cos^2\alpha\log\left\{\frac{\left(x-h\sin^2\alpha\right)+\sqrt{\left(x-h\sin^2\alpha\right)^2+h^2\sin^2\alpha\cos^2\alpha}}{h\sin\alpha\cos\alpha}\right\}-\cos\alpha\frac{x^2}{2}\right]_0^h$$

$$= \frac{\pi\gamma\rho}{\cos\alpha}\Big[h\cos^2\alpha\, h\cos\alpha + h\sin^2\alpha\, h\sin\alpha + h^2\sin^2\alpha\cos^2\alpha\log\frac{h\cos^2\alpha + h\cos\alpha}{-h\sin^2\alpha + h\sin\alpha} - h^2\cos\alpha\Big]$$

$$= \pi\gamma\rho h^2\cos\alpha\sin^2\alpha\left[\frac{\cos^3\alpha + \sin^3\alpha - \cos\alpha}{\sin^2\alpha\cos^2\alpha} + \log\frac{\cos\alpha\,(1+\cos\alpha)}{\sin\alpha\,(1-\sin\alpha)}\right] \quad \ldots (1)$$

To find the potential at V

We consider an elementary disc QR parallel to the base at a distance x from the vertex and having small thickness δx.

Its potential at the vertex V

$$= 2\pi\gamma\rho\delta x\ (VQ - NN)$$

$$= 2\pi\gamma\rho\delta x\ (x\sec\alpha - x)$$

$$= 2\pi\gamma\rho\ (\sec\alpha - 1)\ x\delta x$$

Hence potential at the vertex V, due to the whole cone

$$= 2\pi\gamma\rho\,(\sec\alpha - a)\int_0^h x\,dx$$

$$= 2\pi\gamma\rho\,(\sec\alpha - 1)\frac{h^2}{2}$$

$$= \frac{\pi\gamma\rho\,(1-\cos\alpha)}{\cos\alpha}h^2$$

$$= \frac{\pi\gamma\rho\sin^2 h\cos\alpha\,(1-\cos\alpha)\,h^2}{\sin^2\alpha\cos^2\alpha} \quad \ldots (2)$$

Hence the required work done is obtained by subtracting (2) from (1)

$$= \pi\gamma\rho h^2\sin^2\alpha\cos\alpha\left[\frac{\cos^3\alpha + \sin^3\alpha - 1}{\sin^2\alpha\cos^2\alpha} + \log\frac{\cos\alpha\,(1+\cos\alpha)}{\sin\alpha\,(1-\sin\alpha)}\right].$$

EXERCISES

1. Find the attraction and potential of a long (infinite) thin uniform cylindrical shell at any point P.
[**Ans.** When P is an external point, attraction $= \dfrac{4\pi\gamma Ma}{r}$ along PO, potential $= C - 4\pi\gamma Ma \log r$ where $OP = r$, when P is an internal point, Potential $V = C - 4\pi\gamma Ma \log a$, attraction = zero, where a is the radius of the base of the cylinder.]

2. The density of an infinite circular cylinder of radius r at a distance r from its axis is proportional to $\sqrt{a^2 - r^2}$. Show that the attraction at an internal point distant r from the axis is $\dfrac{2\gamma m}{a^3 r}\left[a^3 - (a^2 - r^2)^{\frac{3}{2}}\right]$ where m is the mass per unit length of this cylinder and γ is the gravitational constant.

3. A quantity of matter attracting according to law of nature is uniformly distributed on the circumference of a circle. Prove that the chord of contact of tangents drawn from an external point divides the mass into two parts having equal potentials at that point.

4. Four uniform rods each of same mass per unit length from a square $ABCD$. Any point P is taken inside the square and E, F, G, H are the feet of the perpendiculars from P upon AB, BC, CD and DA respectively. Prove that the potential at P due to the square $ABCD$ is the same as that due to four rods EF, FG, GH, HE each of the same mass per unit length as that of rods forming the square.

5. O is the centre of a homogeneous hemisphere and A is the other end of the radius perpendicular to its base. If the radius be a centimetres, the density ρ grammes per cubic centimetre and Y be the constant of gravitation, show that the work done against the attraction of the hemisphere in carrying one gramme from O to A is $2\pi\gamma\rho a^2\left[1 - \dfrac{2\sqrt{2}}{3}\right]$ ergs.

6. Find out the potential of a solid uniform right circular cone at the centre of its base.

[**Ans.** $\pi\gamma\rho h^2 \sin^2\alpha\cos\alpha\left[\dfrac{\cos^3\alpha+\sin^3\alpha-\cos\alpha}{\sin^2\alpha\cos^2\alpha}\right.$

$$\left.+\log\frac{\cos\alpha\,(1+\cos\alpha)}{\sin\alpha\,(1-\sin\alpha)}\right]$$

where h is the height and α is the semi vertical angle of the cone.]

7. Show that the potential of a uniform thin equilateral triangle ABC at a point P, situated on a perpendicular to its plane drawn through its centre O is

$$\frac{2\gamma M\cot\alpha}{a}\left[\tan\alpha\log\left(\frac{2+\sqrt{3}\sin\alpha}{2-\sqrt{3}\sin\alpha}\right)\right.$$

$$\left.-\frac{4\pi}{3}+4\tan^{-1}\left(\sqrt{3}\cos\alpha\right)\right]$$

where M is the mass of the triangle, a is its side and $\angle OPA=\alpha$.

8. Prove that the potential of a uniform circular cylinder of length $2a$, radius of base a, and mass M at the middle point of its axis is $\dfrac{\gamma M}{a}\left[\left(\sqrt{2}-a\right)+\log\left(\sqrt{2}+1\right)\right]$.

9. If V_n be the potential of any point due to a distribution of matter attracting according to the nth power of distance. V_{n-2} the potential when attracting according to $(n-2)$th power of the distance, prove that

$$\nabla^2 V_n=(n-1)(n+2)\,V_{n-2}$$

10. Matter is distributed between two infinite cylinder $r=\dfrac{1}{2}a$ and $r=a$ in such a way that the density is equal to $\lambda\left(\dfrac{a}{r}-\dfrac{r}{a}\right)$ and mass per unit length parallel to the axis is M. Prove that the law of potential within the matter is

$$V = \frac{11}{6}\pi\gamma\lambda a^2 \log r - 4\pi\gamma\lambda\left(ar - \frac{r^2}{9a}\right) + B$$

where B is a constant.

11. Determine the potential of a solid uniform right circular cone at the centre of its base. [T.M.B.U. 92H]

[**Ans.** $\pi\gamma\rho\lambda^2 \sin^2\alpha\cos\alpha\left[\log\left(\frac{\cos\alpha}{\sin\alpha} - \frac{1+\cos\alpha}{1-\sin\alpha}\right) + \frac{\sin^3\alpha + \cos^3\alpha - \cos\alpha}{\sin^2\alpha\cos^2\alpha}\right]$

where λ is the height and α, the semivertical angle of the arc.]

12. Show that the potential of a thin homogeneous ring of mass m and radius a at any point in its plane at a distance c from its centre is $c - \gamma m \log c$ or $c - \gamma m \log a$ according as c is greater or less than a, the law of force being inversely as the distance.

5 POTENTIAL OF SPHERICAL SHELLS AND SOLID SPHERES

5.1. Potential of a Spherical Shell

[M.U. 2000H, 2005H; T.M.B.U. 2003H; B.B.A.B.U. 2000H, 2003H]

Let O be the centre of the spherical shell, a, K and ρ be its radius, thickness and density. Let P be the point at which the potential of the shell is to be derived. Let $OP = c$.

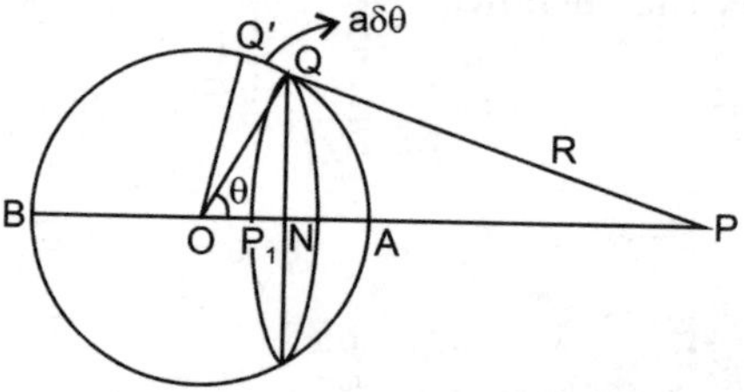

If M is the mass of the shell then $M = 4\pi^2 K\rho$

From any point Q of the shell we draw QN perpendicular to OP

Let $\angle POQ = \theta$, $PQ = R$

In ΔONQ $\quad \sin\theta = \dfrac{QN}{OQ} = \dfrac{QN}{a}$

$$QN = a \sin\theta$$

This shell is generated by the revolution of semi-circumference AQB about AB.

We consider an elementary arc $a\delta\theta$ at Q which when revolved about the diameter AB will generate a circular strip of radius $a \sin\theta$.

Area of this strip = $(2\pi\ a \sin\theta)\ a\delta\theta$

Mass of this circular strip = $(2\pi\ a \sin\theta)\ a\delta\theta K\rho$

Its potential at $P = \dfrac{\gamma(2\pi a \sin\theta)\ a\delta\theta K\rho}{PQ}$

$$= \frac{\gamma(2\pi\ a \sin\theta)\ a\delta\theta K\rho}{R} \quad \text{... (1)}$$

In ΔOPQ

$$\cos\theta = \frac{OP^2 + OQ^2 - PQ^2}{2OPOQ}$$

$$\cos\theta = \frac{c^2 + a^2 - R^2}{2ac}$$

$$\therefore \quad 2ac \sin\theta\delta\theta = 2R\delta R$$

$$\frac{a \sin\theta\delta\theta}{R} = \frac{\delta R}{c}$$

Hence from (1), the potential due to element at Q

$$= \frac{2\pi\gamma K\rho a\delta R}{c}$$

Case I. Let P be an external part i.e. $c > a$.

Hence potential at P due to the shell

$$= \frac{2\pi\gamma K\rho a}{c}\int_{PA}^{PB} dR$$

$$= \frac{2\pi\gamma K\rho a}{c}[PB - PA]$$

$$= \frac{2\pi\gamma K\rho a}{c}[a + c - (c - a)]$$

$$= \frac{2\pi\gamma K\rho a}{c}\,2a$$

$$= \gamma\,\frac{4\pi a^2 K\rho}{c} = \frac{\gamma M}{c}$$

$$= \gamma\cdot\frac{\text{Mass of the shell}}{OP}.$$

This shows that potential of a spherical shell at an external point is the same as that of a mass of the spherical shell concentrated at its centre.

Case II. Let P be an internal point i.e. $c < a$.

In this case P is P_1

Hence the potential at P, due to the spherical shell

$$= \frac{2\pi\gamma K\rho a}{c} \int_{P_1A}^{P_1B} dR$$

$$= \frac{2\pi\gamma K\rho a}{c} [R]_{P_1A}^{P_1B}$$

$$= \frac{2\pi\gamma K\rho a}{c} [P_1B - P_1A]$$

$$= \frac{2\pi\gamma K\rho a}{c} [c + a - (a - c)]$$

$$= \frac{2\pi\gamma K\rho a}{c} 2c$$

$$= 4\pi\gamma K\rho a$$

$$= \gamma \cdot \frac{4\pi a^2 K\rho}{a}$$

$$= \gamma \cdot \frac{\text{Mass of the shell}}{\text{Radius of the shell}}$$

$$= \text{Constant.}$$

Case III. In this case point P is on the surface.

Hence $OP = c = a$

Putting $c = a$ in Case I or II we get required potential at P

$$= \frac{\gamma M}{a}.$$

5.2. Potential of a uniform solid sphere at any point

[L.N.M.U. 94H]

Let O be the centre of a solid sphere of mass M, radius a and density ρ.

$$M = \frac{4}{3} \pi a^3 \rho \qquad \text{... (1)}$$

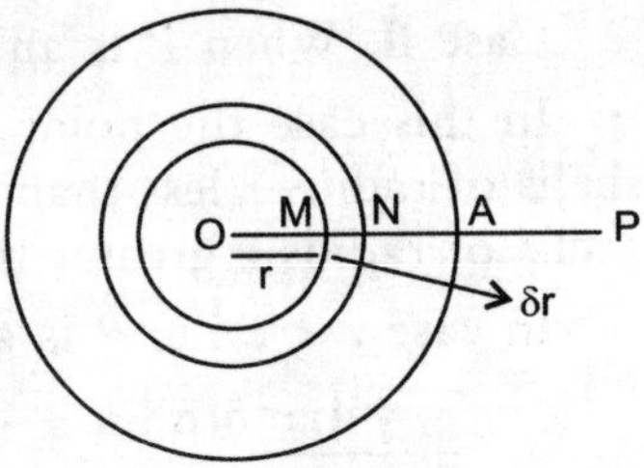

Let P be the point at a distance c from O where the potential is to be determined.

We divide the sphere into a large number of concentric shells. Let two such concentric shells be of radii r and $r + \delta r$.

Then volume of this shell

$$= \frac{4}{3}\pi\left[(r+\delta r)^3 - r^3\right]$$

$$= \frac{4}{3}\pi\left[3r^2\delta r\right] \text{ Neglecting higher power than } \delta r$$

$$= 4\pi r^2 \delta r$$

Thus its mass $= 4\pi r^2 \delta r \rho$.

Case I. When P is an external point i.e. $c > a$.

In this case P is external to all the concentric shells into which the sphere is divided and therefore each of these concentric shells produces a potential at P.

Now potential at P due to this elementary shell

$$= \gamma \cdot \frac{\text{mass of the shell}}{OP}$$

$$= \gamma \cdot \frac{4\pi r^2 \delta r \rho}{c} = \frac{4\pi\gamma\rho}{c} r^2 \delta r$$

Hence the potential at P, due to the solid sphere

$$= \frac{4\pi\gamma\rho}{c}\int_0^a r^2 dr$$

$$= \frac{4\pi\gamma\rho}{c}\frac{a^3}{3}$$

$$= \frac{\gamma M}{c} \qquad \text{... (2) from (1)}$$

This shows that the potential of a solid sphere of mass M at an external point P is the same as that of a mass M concentrated at the centre of the sphere.

Case II. When P is an internal point i.e. $c < a$.

In this case the point P is external to all the concentric shells of radius r less than c and internal to all the concentric shells of radius r greater than c.

In case $r < c$ i.e. P is an external point then its potential

$$= \frac{\gamma\, 4\pi r^2 \delta r \rho}{OP}$$

$$= \frac{4\gamma\, \pi \rho r^2 \delta r}{c}$$

In case $r > c$ i.e. P is an internal point then its potential

$$= \frac{\gamma \cdot \text{Mass of the shell}}{\text{radius of the shell}}$$

$$= \frac{\gamma \cdot 4\pi r^2 \delta r \rho}{r}$$

$$= 4\pi\rho\gamma r \delta \rho$$

Hence the potential at P due to the solid sphere

$$= \int_{r=0}^{c} \frac{4\pi\gamma\rho r^2 dr}{c} + \int_{r=c}^{a} 4\pi\rho\gamma r dr$$

$$= \frac{4\pi\gamma\rho}{c} \frac{a^3 c^3}{3} + \frac{4\pi\rho\gamma}{2}\left(a^2 - c^2\right)$$

$$= 2\pi\gamma\rho\left[a^2 - c^2 + \frac{2c}{3}\right]$$

$$= 2\pi\gamma\rho\left[a^2 - \frac{c^2}{3}\right] \quad \text{... (3)}$$

Case III. When P is a point on the surface of the shpere i.e. $c = a$.

Putting $c = a$ in (2) or (3), the potential at P

$$= \frac{2\pi\gamma\rho 2a^2}{3}$$

$$= \gamma \cdot \frac{4}{3}\pi a^3 \frac{\rho}{a}$$

$$= \gamma \cdot \frac{\text{Mass of the sphere}}{\text{Radius of the sphere}}.$$

5.3. To find the potential of a spherical shell of finite thickness bounded by spheres of radii *a* and *b*

Let O be the centre and ρ the density of the attracting matter which is enclosed between the two spheres.

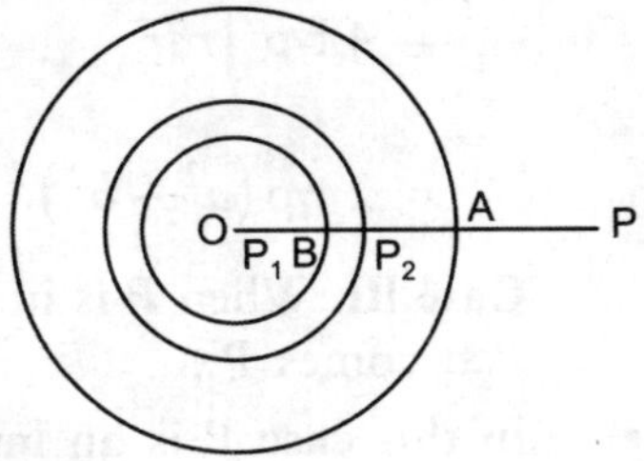

We divide the shell into an infinite number of concentric shells. Let two of such shells be of radii r and $r + \delta r$.

Hence volume of this shell

$$= \frac{4}{3}\pi\left[(r+\delta r)^3 - r^3\right]$$

$$= \frac{4}{3}\pi\left[3r^2\delta r\right] \text{ (since } \delta r \text{ is very small)}$$

$$= 4\pi r^2 \delta r$$

Hence its mass $= 4\pi r^2 \delta r \rho$.

Case I. When the point P is external to both the spheres.

Here P is a point external to the whole matter and let $OP = c$.

Then potential at P due to elementary shell $= \dfrac{\gamma 4\pi r^2 \delta r \rho}{c}$

$$\text{Hence the total potential} = \frac{4\pi\gamma\rho}{c}\int_b^a r^2\,dr$$

$$= \frac{4}{3}\frac{\pi\gamma\rho}{c}\left(a^3 - b^3\right).$$

Case II. When P is inside the inner surface.

In this case P is internal to the whole matter i.e. P becomes P_1.

Hence potential at P due to an elementary shell

$$= \frac{\gamma \cdot 4\pi r^2 \delta r \rho}{r} = 4\pi\gamma\rho r\delta r$$

Hence total potential

$$= 4\pi\gamma\rho \int_b^a r dr$$

$$= 2\pi\gamma\rho\left(a^2 - b^2\right).$$

Case III. When P is in between the inner and outer surface i.e. P becomes P_2.

In this case P is an internal point for all such elementary shells whose radii are greater than c and P is an external point for all such elementary shells whose radii are less than r.

Thus potential at P, due to the elementary shells

$$= \frac{\gamma 4\pi r^2 \delta r \rho}{c} \qquad \text{when } r < c$$

and $$= \frac{\gamma 4\pi r^2 \delta r \rho}{r} \qquad \text{when } r > c$$

Hence the potential at P due to the annulus

$$= \frac{4\pi\gamma\rho}{c} \int_b^c r^2 dr + 4\pi\gamma\rho \int_c^a r dr$$

$$= \frac{4\pi\gamma\rho}{c} \frac{c^3 - b^3}{3} + \frac{4\pi\gamma\rho\left(a^2 - c^2\right)}{2}$$

$$= 2\pi\gamma\rho\left[a^2 - c^2 + \frac{2\left(c^3 - b^3\right)}{3c}\right]$$

$$= 2\pi\gamma\rho\left[a^2 - c^2 + \frac{2c^2}{3} - \frac{2b^3}{3c}\right]$$

$$= 2\pi\gamma\rho\left[a^2 - \frac{c^2}{3} - \frac{2b^3}{3c}\right].$$

WORKED OUT EXAMPLES

1. Show that half of the potential of uniform spherical shell at an external point O is due to that portion of the sphere which is nearer to O than the centre is. [L.N.M.U. 94H]

Solution: Let C be the centre and a the radius of a uniform spherical shell. Let O be an external point at a distance c from the centre C of the shell. i.e. $CO = c$.

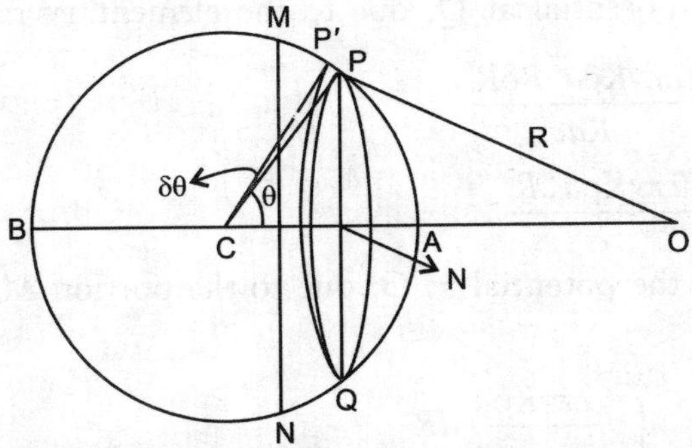

The spherical shell of radius a is generated by the revolution of the semi circular arc of radius a about its diameter. Let M be a point on this semi circular arc such that $OM = c$. Let AB be the diameter through O. Then the arc AM when revolved about AB will generate that portion of the shell every point of which is nearer to O than the centre c is.

We consider an elementary arc $a\delta\theta$ of arc AM at P such that $\angle PCO = \theta$. This arc $a\delta\theta$ when revolved about AB will generate a circular ring of radius $PN = a \sin\theta$.

Now mass of the elementary ring generated

$$= 2\pi (a \sin\theta) K\rho a\delta\theta$$

The potential at O, due to this elementary ring

$$= \gamma \cdot \frac{2\pi\, a \sin\theta\, K\rho a\delta\theta}{OP}$$

$$= \frac{2\pi\gamma K\rho a^2 \sin\theta\, \delta\theta}{R} \qquad \text{where } OP = R$$

In ΔOPC,

$$\cos\theta = \frac{a^2 + c^2 - R^2}{2ac}$$

$$\therefore \quad \sin\theta\,\delta\theta = \frac{-2R\delta R}{2ac}$$

$$\Rightarrow \quad \sin\theta\,\delta\theta = \frac{R\delta R}{ac}$$

Hence potential at Q, due to the elementary ring PQ

$$= \frac{2\pi\gamma K\rho a^2 R\delta R}{Rac}$$

$$= \frac{2\pi\gamma K\rho a\,\delta R}{c}$$

Hence the potential at O, due to the portion MAN of the shell

$$= \int_{R=CA}^{CM} \frac{2\pi\gamma K\rho a}{c}\, dR$$

$$= \frac{2\pi\gamma K\rho a}{c}[CM - CA]$$

$$= \frac{2\pi\gamma K\rho a}{c}\left[c - (OC - OA)\right]$$

$$= \frac{2\pi\gamma K\rho a}{c}\left[c(c-a)\right]$$

$$= \frac{2\pi\gamma K\rho a^2}{c} = \frac{1}{2}\frac{\gamma M}{c} \quad \left[\because M = 4\pi K\rho a^2\right]$$

$$= \frac{1}{2} \text{ of the potential at O, due to the whole shell.}$$

2. Prove that if the law of potential be $\frac{A}{r}e^{-\frac{r}{\lambda}}$ the potential of a uniform, thin spherical shell of radius a at an external point is the same as that of a particle of mass $\frac{\lambda}{a}\sin h\frac{a}{\lambda}$ times that of the shell placed at the centre. [T.M.B.U. 91H]

Solution: Let O be the centre of the spherical shell and P is the point at which potential is to be determined. Let $OP = c$, $PQ = R$.

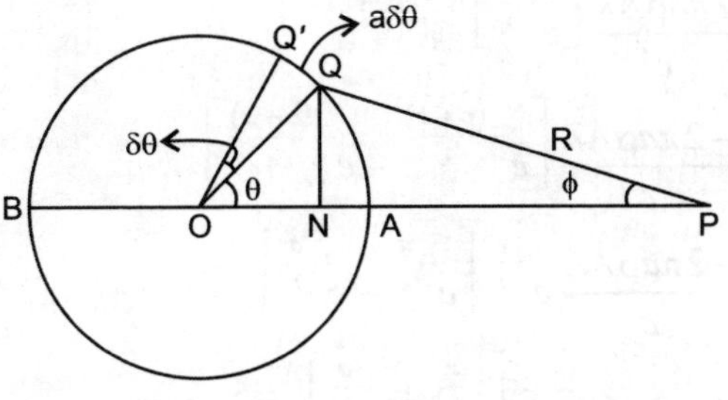

Let Q be a point on the shell such that $PQ = R$.

We consider an elementary area $a\delta\theta$. This area when rotated about the diameter AB will generate a circular strip of radius $QN = a \sin \theta$.

Mass of the elementary circular strip $= \rho a\delta\theta 2\pi a \sin \theta$

Its potential at P according to given law

$$= \frac{A}{R} e^{-\frac{R}{\lambda}} (2\pi a \sin \theta)\, a\delta\theta\rho \qquad \text{... (1)}$$

In ΔOPQ

$$\cos O = \frac{OP^2 + OQ^2 - PQ^2}{2\, OP\, OQ}$$

$$\cos \theta = \frac{c^2 + a^2 - R^2}{2ca}$$

$$\therefore \quad a \sin \theta \delta\theta = \frac{R}{c} \delta R$$

Hence from (1) the potential at P due to the element

$$= \frac{A}{R} e^{-\frac{R}{\lambda}} 2\pi a\rho \frac{R}{c} \delta R$$

Hence potential at P due to the shell

$$= \frac{2\pi a\rho A}{c} \int_{PA}^{PB} e^{-\frac{R}{\lambda}} dR$$

$$= \frac{2\pi a\rho A}{c}\left[-\lambda e^{-\frac{R}{\lambda}}\right]_{PA}^{PB}$$

$$= \frac{2\pi a\rho A\lambda}{c}\left[e^{-\frac{R}{\lambda}}\right]_{PB}^{PA}$$

$$= \frac{-2\pi a\rho A\lambda}{c}\left[e^{-\frac{(c+a)}{\lambda}} - e^{-\frac{(c-a)}{\lambda}}\right]$$

$$= \frac{-2\pi a\rho A\lambda}{c} e^{-\frac{c}{\lambda}}\left[e^{-\frac{a}{\lambda}} - e^{-\frac{a}{\lambda}}\right]$$

$$= \frac{4\pi a\rho A\lambda}{c} e^{-\frac{c}{\lambda}}\left[\frac{e^{\frac{a}{\lambda}} - e^{-\frac{a}{\lambda}}}{2}\right]$$

$$= \frac{4\pi a\rho A\lambda}{c} e^{-\frac{c}{\lambda}} \sin h\left(\frac{a}{\lambda}\right)$$

$$= \frac{\lambda}{a}\sin h\left(\frac{a}{\lambda}\right)\frac{4\pi a^2\rho\, Ae^{-\frac{c}{\lambda}}}{c}$$

$$= KmA\,\frac{e^{-\frac{c}{\lambda}}}{c} \text{ where } K = \frac{\lambda}{a}\sin h\left(\frac{a}{\lambda}\right)$$

This shows that the potential is same as that of mass which is K times the mass of the shell placed at the centre whose distance from P is c.

3. If AB is a diameter of a spherical shell of uniform surface density. Find the position of a plane perpendicular to AB which divides the shell into two portions such that their potentials at A are equal.

If the surface density of the shell is σ, find the attraction of its centre due to each portion of the shell.

Solution: Let LMN be a plane at right angles to AB which divides the spherical shell into two portions, whose potentials at A are equal.

Let O be the centre of the shell and a its radius. Let Q be a point on the semicircumference ALB, such that $AQ = R$, $\angle AOQ = \theta$

$\therefore\ QQ' = a\delta\theta$

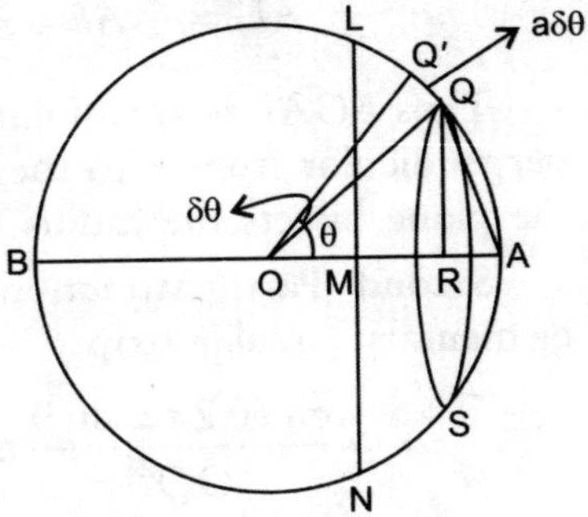

If the arc $a\delta\theta$ revolves about AB, then it will generate a circular strip of radius $QR = a \sin \theta$.

Mass of the circular strip $= 2\pi a \sin \theta a\delta\theta\rho$

Its potential at A

$$= \frac{\gamma\, \rho a\, \delta\theta\, 2\pi\, a \sin \theta}{AQ}$$

$$= \frac{\gamma\, \rho a\, \delta\theta\, 2\pi\, a \sin \theta}{R}$$

In ΔOAQ

$$\cos \theta = \frac{a^2 + a^2 - R^2}{2a^2}$$

$$\therefore \quad \sin \theta\delta\theta = \frac{R\delta R}{a^2}$$

Hence potential at A due to circular strip

$$= 2\pi\gamma\rho \frac{a^2 R\delta R}{a^2 R}$$

$$= 2\pi\gamma\rho\delta R$$

Therefore, potential at A due to the portion LAN

$$= 2\pi\gamma\rho \int_O^{AL} dR$$

$$= 2\pi\gamma\rho AL \qquad \text{... (1)}$$

Again potential at A due to the portion LBN

$$= 2\pi\gamma\rho \int_{AL}^{AB} dR = 2\pi\gamma\rho\,(AB - AL) \qquad \text{... (2)}$$

If the two portions have the same potential, then

$$2\pi\gamma\rho AL = 2\pi\gamma\rho\ (AB - AL)$$

or $\quad 2AL = AB$

$$AL = \frac{1}{2} AB = AO = OL = \text{radius of the shell}.$$

Thus ΔOAL is an equilateral triangle and as such LM, the perpendicular from L to the base OA must bisect OA. Hence the plane bisects the radius OA.

Second Part. Attraction at the centre O, due to the elementary circular strip

$$= \gamma \frac{\sigma a \, \delta\theta \, 2\pi \, a \sin\theta}{OQ^2} \text{ along } OQ$$

$$= \frac{2\pi\gamma\sigma a^2 \sin\theta\delta\theta}{a^2}$$

$$= 2\pi\gamma\sigma \sin\theta\delta\theta \text{ along } OQ$$

Its resolved part along $OA = 2\pi\gamma\sigma \sin\theta\delta\theta \cos\theta$

Hence attraction at the centre O due to the portion LAN

$$= 2\pi\gamma\sigma \int_0^{\frac{\pi}{3}} \sin\theta \cos\theta \, d\theta$$

$$= 2\pi\gamma\sigma \left[\frac{\sin^2\theta}{2}\right]_0^{\frac{\pi}{3}}$$

$$= \frac{\pi\gamma\sigma \, 3}{4} = \frac{3\pi\gamma\sigma}{4}$$

Also attraction at the centre O, due to the portion LBN

$$= 2\pi\gamma\sigma \int_{\frac{\pi}{3}}^{\pi} \sin\theta \cos\theta \, d\theta$$

$$= 2\pi\gamma\sigma \left[\frac{\sin^2\theta}{2}\right]_{\frac{\pi}{3}}^{\pi}$$

$$= -\frac{\pi\gamma\sigma 3}{4} = \frac{-3}{4}\pi\gamma\sigma$$

Hence attractions at the centre are same for both the parts, but are opposite in the directions.

4. Show that the potential of a uniform spherical shell, of small thickness K and density ρ and radius a, at an external point distant c from the centre is

$$-\frac{2\pi\gamma K\rho a}{(n+1)(n+3)c}\left[(c+a)^{n+3}-(c-a)^{n+3}\right]$$

If the law of force be that of the nth power of the distance.

Solution: Let O be the centre of the sphere and P be a point at a distance C from the centre O, i.e. $OP = c$.

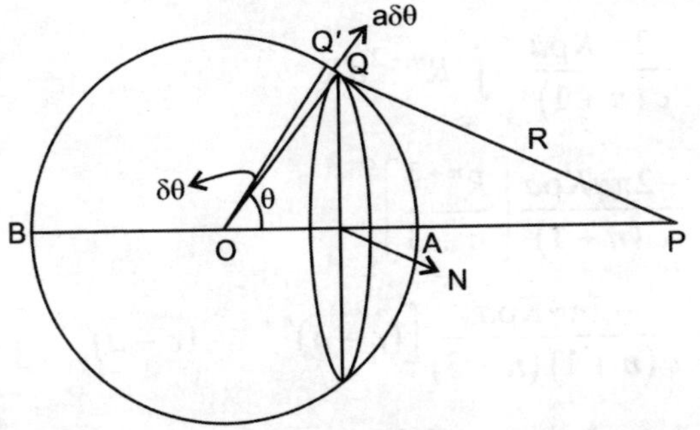

Let us take a point Q on the shell. From Q we draw QN perpendicular to AB. Let $\angle POQ = \theta$. Hence $QQ' = a\delta\theta$.

This arc when revolved about AB will generate a circular ring of radius $QN = a \sin\theta$.

Mass of the ring $= 2\pi\ (a\sin\theta)\ a\ \delta\theta K\rho$ ... (1)

Here the law of force is that of nth power of the distance.

Force on a unit mass placed at a distance R from a mass m is $-\gamma m R^n$

$$\text{Hence potential of } m = \int_{\infty}^{r}\left(-\gamma m\, R^n dR\right)$$

$$= \frac{-\gamma m r^{n+1}}{n+1}$$

Hence from (1), its potential at P

$$= \frac{-\gamma\ a\delta\theta\ 2\pi a\sin\theta\ K\rho}{n+1}R^{n+1} \qquad \text{... (2)}$$

In ΔOPQ $\cos\theta = \dfrac{a^2+c^2-R^2}{2ac}$

$$\sin\theta\delta\theta = \frac{R\delta R}{ac}$$

Hence from (2) potential at P

$$= \frac{-2\pi\gamma K\rho a}{c(n+1)} R^{n+2}\delta R$$

Therefore, potential at P, due to the whole spherical shell

$$= \frac{-2\pi\gamma K\rho a}{c(n+1)} \int_{c-a}^{c+a} R^{n+2} dR$$

$$= \frac{-2\pi\gamma K\rho a}{c(n+1)} \left[\frac{R^{n+3}}{n+3}\right]_{c-a}^{c+a}$$

$$= \frac{-2\pi\gamma K\rho a}{c(n+1)(n+3)} \left[(c+a)^{n+3} - (c-a)^{n+3}\right]$$

5. Show that the potential of a zone of thin homogeneous spherical shell at any point P on the axis of the zone is $\dfrac{2\gamma M}{r_1 + r_2}$ where M is the mass of the zone and r_1, r_2 are the distances of the point P from the bounding edges of the zone.

Solution: The zone of the spherical shell is $ABDC$. It is the surface of the frustum of the shell between the two planes AC and BD. One element of the surface is the circular strip QS.

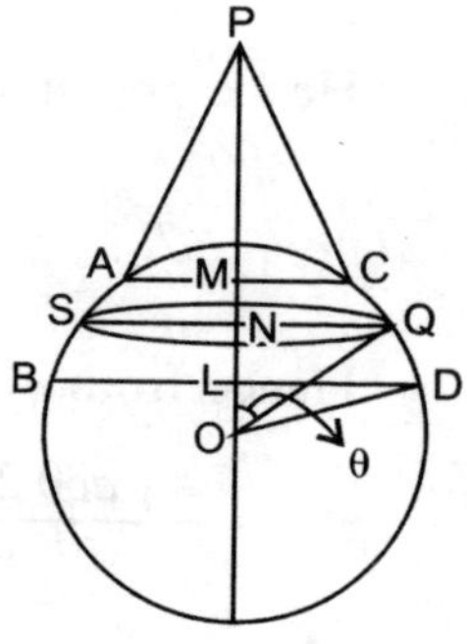

If a is the radius of the shell, K its thickness and ρ the density, then mass of this strip $= 2\pi\ (a\sin\theta)\ a\delta\theta K\rho$ where $\angle QOP = \theta$.

Potential at P, due to the circular strip

$$= \gamma\,\frac{a\delta\theta\ 2\pi a\sin\theta\ K\rho}{PQ}$$

Let $PQ = R$ and $OP = c$

In ΔOPQ

$$\cos\theta = \frac{OP^2 + OQ^2 - PQ^2}{2\,OP\,OQ}$$

$$\Rightarrow \quad \cos\theta = \frac{c^2 + a^2 - R^2}{2ca}$$

$$\therefore \quad \sin\theta\delta\theta = \frac{-2R\delta R}{2ac}$$

$$\Rightarrow \quad \sin\theta\delta\theta = \frac{R\delta R}{ac}$$

Hence the potential at P, due to the elementary strip becomes

$$= \frac{2\pi\gamma K\rho a\delta R}{c}$$

Hence potential at P, due to the zone $ABDC$

$$= \frac{2\pi\gamma K\rho a}{c}\int_{r_1}^{r_2} dR \qquad \text{where } r_1 = PC, r_2 = PD$$

$$= \frac{2\pi\gamma K\rho a}{c}(r_2 - r_1) \qquad \ldots (1)$$

In ΔOLD

$$OD^2 = OL^2 + LD^2$$

In ΔPLD

$$PD^2 = PL^2 + LD^2$$

Hence

$$OD^2 - OL^2 = PD^2 - PL^2$$

or $\quad a^2 - OL^2 = r_2^2 - (PO - OL)^2$

or $\quad a^2 - OL^2 = r_2^2 - (c - OL)^2$

or $\quad a^2 = r_2^2 - c^2 + 2c\,OL$

or $\quad OL = \dfrac{a^2 + c^2 - r_2^2}{2c}$

Similarly $\quad OM = \dfrac{a^2 + c^2 - r_1^2}{2c}$

Also from figure

$$LM = OM - OL = \frac{r_2^2 - r_1^2}{2c}$$

This gives distance between the two ends of the zone.

Area of the surface of the zone

$$= 2\pi a \times \text{distance between the ends}$$

$$= \frac{2\pi a\left(r_2^2 - r_1^2\right)}{2c}$$

Hence mass of the zone $= M = \dfrac{2\pi a\left(r_2^2 - r_1^2\right)}{2c}$

Thus from (1), required potential

$$= \frac{\gamma}{c}\frac{2cM}{r_2^2 - r_1^2}(r_2 - r_1)$$

$$= \frac{2\gamma M}{r_1 + r_2}$$

6. If the density of a sphere at a point distant x from its centre is $\dfrac{K}{c}\sin\dfrac{K}{c}$ where K and c and given constants. Prove that the attraction at an internal point distant x from the centre is $4\pi\gamma Kc\left(\dfrac{c}{x^2}\sin\dfrac{x}{c} - \dfrac{1}{x}\cos\dfrac{x}{c}\right)$ and find its potential.

Solution: Let P be an internal point at a distance x from the centre O of the sphere.

We divide the sphere into a large number of concentric shells, each of indefinitely small thickness.

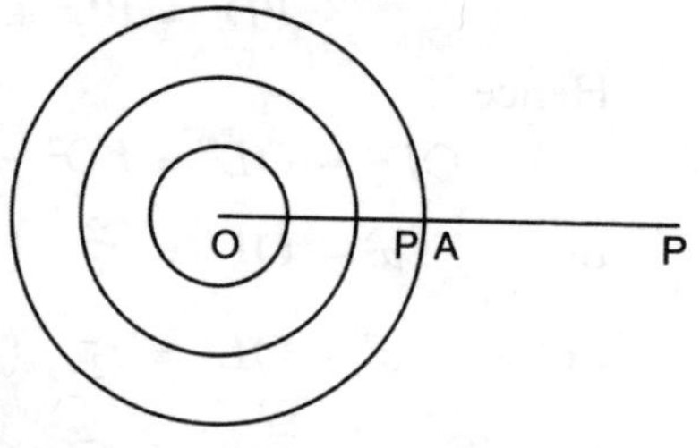

Therefore, we get some shells whose radii are greater than OP, and P is, therefore an internal point for such shells. Hence the attraction of all such shells is zero.

Hence we need to consider only such shells whose radius is less than x.

Let y be the radius of an elementary shell. Hence $y < x$.

By the given density law, its surface density $= \dfrac{K}{y} \sin \dfrac{y}{c}$

Mass of the elementary shell $= 4\pi y^2 \delta y \dfrac{K}{y} \sin \dfrac{y}{c}$

The attraction at the point P, due to this elementary shell

$$= \gamma \frac{4\pi y^2 \delta y \dfrac{K}{y} \sin \dfrac{y}{c}}{OP^2}$$

$$= \frac{\gamma\, 4\pi y^2 \delta y \dfrac{K}{y} \sin \dfrac{y}{c}}{x^2} \quad (\because OP = n)$$

$$= \frac{4\pi\gamma K}{x^2} y \sin \frac{y}{c}\, \delta y$$

Hence attraction at P, due to the sphere

$$= \frac{4\pi\gamma K}{x^2} \int_0^x y \sin \frac{y}{c}\, dy$$

$$= \frac{4\pi\gamma K}{x^2} \left[-yc \cos \frac{y}{c} + c^2 \sin \frac{y}{c} \right]_0^x$$

$$= \frac{4\pi\gamma K}{x^2} \left[-cx \cos \frac{x}{c} + c^2 \sin \frac{x}{c} \right]$$

This proves the first part.

Now we shall find out the potential at P.

The total potential at P for all shells for which P is an external point

$$= \int_O^x \frac{\gamma\, 4\pi y^2 dy \rho}{OP}$$

$$= \int_O^x \gamma \frac{4\pi y^2 dy \dfrac{K}{y} \sin \dfrac{y}{c}}{x}$$

$$= \frac{4\pi\gamma K}{x} \int_O^x y \sin \frac{y}{c}\, dy$$

$$= \frac{4\pi\gamma K}{x} \left[y\left(-c \cos \frac{y}{c}\right) + c \int \cos \frac{y}{c}\, dy \right]_O^x$$

$$= \frac{4\pi\gamma K}{x} \left[-cy \cos \frac{y}{c} + c^2 \sin \frac{y}{c} \right]_O^x$$

$$= 4\pi\gamma Kc \left[\frac{c}{x} \sin \frac{x}{c} - \cos \frac{x}{c} \right]$$

Again the total potential at P for all shells for which P is an internal point

$$= \int \gamma \frac{\text{mass of the shell}}{\text{radius of the shell}}$$

$$= \int_x^a \frac{\gamma\, 4\pi y^2 dy \rho}{y}$$

$$= \int_x^a 4\pi\gamma y dy \frac{K}{y} \sin \frac{y}{c}$$

$$= 4\pi K\gamma \int_x^a \sin \frac{y}{c}\, dy$$

$$= 4\pi K\gamma \left[-c \cos \frac{y}{c} \right]_x^a$$

$$= 4\pi cK\gamma \left[\cos \frac{x}{c} - \cos \frac{a}{c} \right]$$

Hence the total potential at P

$$= 4\pi\gamma Kc \left[\frac{c}{x} \sin \frac{x}{c} - \cos \frac{a}{c} \right]$$

7. A solid sphere of radius a is such that its density at any point is proportional to the nth power of the distance of the point from the centre of the sphere. Find the potential at any external point and show that its potential at an internal point

at a distance r from the centre is $\frac{\gamma M}{n+2}\left(\frac{n+3}{a}-\frac{r^{n+2}}{a^{n+3}}\right)$

where M is the total mass of the sphere. [I.A.S. 75]

Solution: Let P be an external point at a distance r from the centre O of the solid sphere.

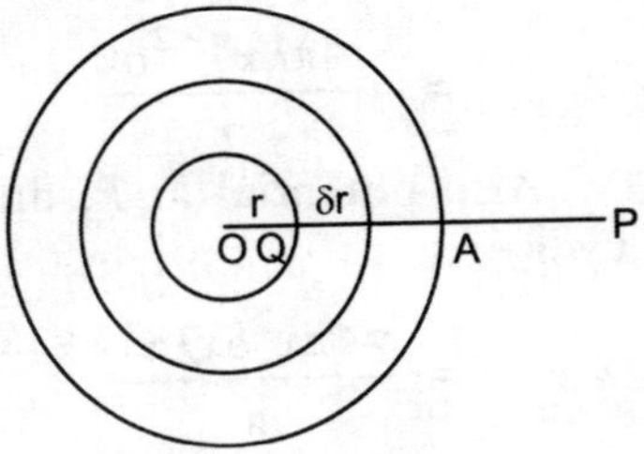

Density at a distance x from the centre $= \lambda x^n$

We divide the sphere into a large number of concentric shells and one of them be of radius x and width δx.

Its mass $= 4\pi x^2 \delta x \lambda x^n$

$= 4\pi\lambda x^{n+2}\,\delta x$

Hence mass of the solid sphere

$$= M = 4\pi\lambda \int_0^a x^{n+2}dx$$

$$= \frac{4\pi\lambda a^{n+3}}{n+3} \quad \text{... (1)}$$

Now if P is an external point, then potential at P due to the elementary shell

$$= \frac{\gamma 4\pi\lambda x^{n+2}\delta x}{c} \quad \text{where } OP = c$$

Hence potential at P, due to the given solid sphere

$$= \frac{\gamma 4\pi\lambda}{r}\int_0^a x^{n+2}dx$$

$$= \frac{\gamma 4\pi\lambda}{r}\frac{a^{n+3}}{n+3}$$

$$= \frac{\gamma M}{c} \quad \text{From (1)}$$

If P is an internal point such that $OP = r$ then potential at P due to an elementary shell of radius $x < r$.

$$= \gamma \frac{4\pi x^2 \delta x \lambda x^n}{r}$$

$$= \gamma \frac{4\pi\lambda x^{n+2}\delta x}{r}$$

Also potential at P, due to an elementary shell of radius $x > r$

$$= \frac{\gamma 4\pi x^2 \delta x \lambda x^n}{x}$$

$$= \gamma 4\pi\lambda x^{n+1}\delta x$$

Therefore, when P is an internal point, the potential of the sphere on it

$$= \frac{\gamma 4\pi\lambda}{r}\int_0^r x^{n+2}dx + \gamma 4\pi x \int x^{n+1}dx$$

$$= \frac{\gamma 4\pi\lambda}{r}\frac{x^{n+3}}{n+3} + \frac{\gamma 4\pi\lambda}{n+2}\left(a^{n+2} - r^{n+2}\right)$$

$$= \gamma 4\pi\lambda\left[r^{n+2}\left(\frac{1}{n+3} - \frac{1}{n+2}\right) + \frac{a^{n+2}}{n+2}\right]$$

$$= \gamma 4\pi\lambda\left[-\frac{r^{n+2}}{(n+3)(n+2)} + \frac{a^{n+2}}{n+2}\right]$$

$$= \frac{\gamma}{n+2}\frac{4\pi\lambda a^{n+3}}{n+3}\left[-\frac{r^{n+2}}{a^{n+3}} + \frac{n+3}{a}\right]$$

$$= \frac{\gamma}{n+2}M\left[\frac{n+3}{a} - \frac{r^{n+2}}{a^{n+3}}\right] \qquad \text{From (1).}$$

8. The density at a distance r from the centre in a sphere of attracting matter is $\rho_0 - \lambda r$, where ρ_0 is the density at the centre and λ is constant. Find the potential at any internal point and prove that the potential at the centre is $4\pi\gamma a^2\left(\frac{\rho_0}{\sigma} + \frac{\rho_1}{3}\right)$

where a is the radius of the sphere, ρ_1 the density at the surface of the sphere and γ is the constant of gravitation. [I.A.S. 73]

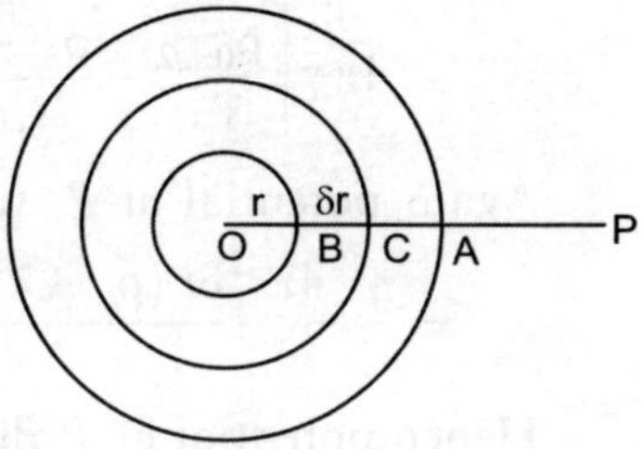

Solution: Given the density at a distance $r = \rho_0 - \lambda r$.

Also given that ρ_1 is the density at the surface of the sphere

$$\rho_1 = \rho_0 - \lambda a$$

(At the surface $r = a$)

$$\lambda = \frac{\rho_0 - \rho_1}{a} \qquad \ldots (1)$$

Let P be an internal point and O the centre of the sphere. Let $OP = c$. We are to find potential of the sphere at P.

We divide the sphere into a large number of concentric shells. Let two such shells be of radii r and $r + \delta r$.

Hence volume of this shell

$$= \frac{4}{3}\pi\left[(r+\delta r)^3 - r^3\right]$$

$$= 4\pi r^2 \delta r \quad (\because \delta r \text{ is very small})$$

Hence its mass $= 4\pi r^2 \delta r\,(\rho_0 - \lambda r)$

Potential at P, which is an external point $r < c$ to the elementary shell

$$= \frac{\gamma \cdot 4\pi r^2 \delta r\,(\rho_0 - \lambda r)}{c} \text{ when } r < c$$

Hence potential at P due to all such shells for which $r < c$

$$= \int_0^c \frac{\gamma\, 4\pi r^2 (\rho_0 - \lambda r)}{c}\, dr$$

$$= \frac{4\pi\gamma}{c}\int_0^c (\rho_0 r^2 - \lambda r^3)\, dr$$

$$= \frac{4\pi\gamma}{c}\left[\rho_0 \frac{r^3}{3} - \frac{\lambda r^4}{4}\right]_0^c$$

$$= \frac{4\pi\gamma}{c}\left[\frac{\rho_0 c^3}{3} - \frac{\lambda c^4}{4}\right]$$

$$= 4\pi\gamma\left[\frac{\rho_0}{3}c^2 - \frac{\rho_0 - \rho_1}{a}\frac{c^3}{4}\right] \quad \text{... (2) From (1)}$$

Again potential at P, which is an internal point i.e. $r > c$

$$= \frac{\gamma \cdot 4\pi r^2 \delta r\,(\rho_0 - \lambda r)}{r}$$

Hence potential at P due to all such shells for which P is an internal point

$$= 4\pi\gamma \int_c^a \left(\rho_0 r - \lambda r^2\right) dr$$

$$= 4\pi\gamma\left[\frac{\rho_0}{2}\left(a^2 - c^2\right) - \frac{\rho_0 - \rho_1}{3a}\left(a^3 - c^3\right)\right]$$

$$\text{... (3) From (1)}$$

Adding (2) and (3), we get the required potential

$$= 4\pi\gamma\left[\rho_0\left\{\frac{c^2}{3} + \frac{a^2 - c^2}{2}\right\} - \frac{\rho_0 - \rho_1}{a}\left\{\frac{c^3}{4} + \frac{a^3 - c^3}{3}\right\}\right]$$

$$= 4\pi\gamma\left[\frac{\rho_0}{\sigma}\left(3a^2 - c^2\right) - \frac{\rho_0 - \rho_1}{12a}\left(4a^3 - c^3\right)\right] \quad \text{... (4)}$$

This gives the potential of the sphere at any internal point at a distance c from the centre.

Putting $c = 0$ in (4), we get

Potential at the centre

$$= 4\pi\gamma\left[\frac{\rho_0}{\sigma}3a^2 - \frac{\rho_0 - \rho_1 a^2}{3}\right]$$

$$= 4\pi\gamma a^2\left[\frac{\rho_0}{2} - \frac{\rho_0 - \rho_1}{3}\right]$$

$$= 4\pi\gamma a^2\left[\frac{3\rho_0 - 2\rho_0 + 2\rho_1}{\sigma}\right]$$

$$= 4\pi\gamma a^2 \left(\frac{2\rho_1 + \rho_0}{\sigma}\right)$$

$$= 4\pi\gamma a^2 \left[\frac{\rho_0}{\sigma} + \frac{\rho_1}{3}\right]$$

9. The internal and external radii of a thin spherical shell of density ρ are $a - t$ and a. Prove that the difference of the potentials at the two points one inside and the other outside both close to the surface is $2\pi\gamma\rho t^2$.

Solution: Let OB and OA be the internal and external radii of the thin spherical shell such that

$OB = a - t$ and $OA = a$.

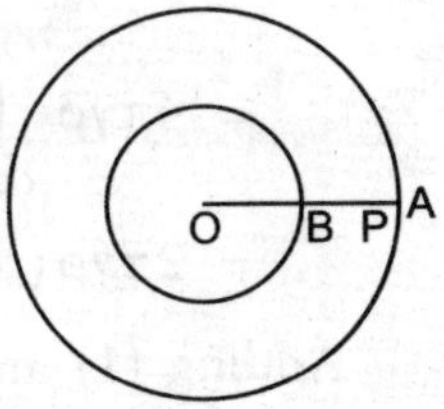

The point B is inside the sphere close to the inner surface and the point A is outside the sphere close to the outer surface.

We take a point P in the substance of the shell at a distance c from the centre, so that $OP = c$.

We divide the sphere into a large number of concentric shells. Let two such shells be of radius r and $r + \delta r$.

$$\text{Volume of the shell} = \frac{4}{3}\pi\left[(r + \delta r)^3 - r^3\right]$$

$$= \frac{4}{3}\pi 3r^2 \delta r \ (\because \delta r \text{ is very small})$$

$$= 4\pi r^2 \delta r$$

Mass of the shell $= 4\pi r^2 \delta r \rho$

$$\text{Potential at } P \text{ due to elementary shell} = \gamma \frac{4\pi r^2 \delta r \rho}{c}$$

When $r < c$ i.e. P is an external point.

Hence, the potential at P due to all such shells for which P is an external point

$$= \frac{4\pi\gamma\rho}{c} \int_{OB}^{OP} r^2 dr$$

$$= \frac{4\pi\gamma\rho}{3c}\left[r^3\right]_{a-t}^{c}$$

$$= \frac{4\pi\gamma\rho}{3c}\left[c^3-(a-t)^3\right] \qquad \dots (1)$$

Again potential at P where $r > c$ i.e. P is an internal point

$$= \frac{\gamma\, 4\pi r^2\delta r\rho}{r} = 4\pi\gamma\rho r\delta r$$

Hence potential at P due to all such shells

$$= 4\pi\gamma\rho\int_{OP}^{OA} r\,dr = 2\pi\gamma\rho\left[r^2\right]_c^a$$

$$= 2\pi\gamma\rho\left(a^2-c^2\right) \qquad \dots (2)$$

Adding (1) and (2) we get potential at P

$$= \frac{4\pi\gamma\rho}{3c}\left[c^3-(a-t)^3\right]+4\pi\gamma\rho\frac{\left(a^2-c^2\right)}{2} \qquad \dots (3)$$

In order to get potential at B, we put $c = a - t$ in (3).
Hence potential at B

$$= 2\pi\,\gamma\rho\left[a^2-(a-t)^2\right]$$

$$= 2\pi\,\gamma\rho\left[2at-t^2\right] \qquad \dots (4)$$

In order to get the potential at A we put $c = a$ in (3).
Hence potential at A

$$= \frac{4\pi\,\gamma\rho}{3a}\left[a^3\,(a-t)^3\right]$$

$$= \frac{4\pi\,\gamma\rho}{3a}\left[a^3-\left(a^3-3a^2t+3at^2-t^3\right)\right]$$

$$= \frac{4\pi\,\gamma\rho}{3a}\left[3a^2t-3at^2\right] \text{ Neglecting } t^3$$

$$= 4\pi\,\gamma\rho\left(at-t^2\right) \qquad \dots (5)$$

Subtracting (5) from (4), we get

Potential at B – Potential at A

$$= 2\pi\gamma\rho\left[2at - t^2 - 2at + 2t^2\right]$$

$$= 2\pi\gamma\rho t^2$$

10. Find the potential at any point in the interior of a sphere of radius a, the density of the sphere at a distance r from the centre being $\rho_0\,(1 - Kr^n)$.

Show that if the sphere be divided into two parts by a plane through the centre, the mutual pressure between the parts is

$$\frac{1}{3}\pi^2\rho_0^2a^4\left[1 - \frac{4(n+6)}{(n+3)(n+4)}Ka^n + \frac{6}{(n+2)(n+3)}K^2a^{2n}\right]$$

Solution: Let P be an internal point of a sphere whose centre is O. Let $OP = c$. We divide the sphere into a infinite number of spherical shells. Let two of such shells be of radii $r + \delta r$ and r.

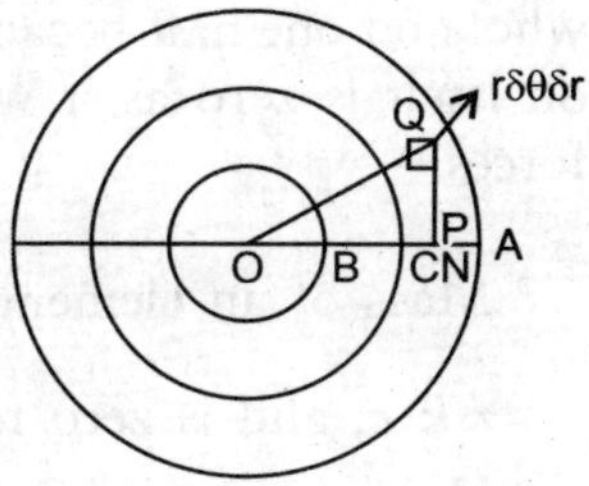

Volume of the shell

$$= \frac{4}{3}\pi\left[(r+\delta r)^3 - r^3\right]$$

$$= 4\pi r^2\delta r \;(\because \delta r \text{ is very small})$$

At a distance r from the centre the density $= \rho_0\,(1 - Kr^n)$

So mass of the elementary shell $= 4\pi r^2\delta r\rho_0\,(1 - Kr^n)$

Potential at P, due to the elementary shell

$$= \frac{\gamma 4\pi r^2\delta r\,\rho_0\left(1 - Kr^n\right)}{c} \quad \text{for } r < c$$

and potential at P, due to the elementary shell

$$= \frac{\gamma 4\pi r^2\delta r\,\rho_0\left(1 - Kr^n\right)}{r} \quad \text{for } r > c.$$

Hence potential at P due to the whole sphere

$$= \frac{4\pi\gamma\rho_0}{c}\int_0^c r^2\left(1 - Kr^n\right)dr + 4\pi\gamma\rho_0\int_c^a r\left(1 - Kr^n\right)dr$$

$$= \frac{4\pi\gamma\rho_0}{c}\left[\frac{c^3}{3} - \frac{Kc^{n+3}}{n+3}\right]$$

$$+ 4\pi\gamma\rho_0\left[\frac{a^2 - c^2}{2} - \frac{K\left(a^{n+2} - c^{n+2}\right)}{n+2}\right]$$

$$= 4\pi\gamma\rho_0\left[\frac{c^2}{3} - \frac{Kc^{n+2}}{n+3} + \frac{a^2 - c^2}{2} - \frac{K\left(a^{n+2} - c^{n+2}\right)}{n+2}\right]$$

$$= 4\pi\gamma\rho_0\left[\frac{a^2}{2} - \frac{Ka^{n+2}}{n+2} - \frac{c^2}{\sigma} + \frac{Kc^{n+2}}{(n+2)(n+3)}\right]$$

This gives the potential of the sphere at an external point.

Second Part. Here we have to find the attraction of one half on the other which would be same as the attraction of the whole on one half because we know that attraction of one half on itself is zero as it will form a pair of equal and opposite forces.

Mass of an elementary shell $= \gamma \dfrac{4\pi r^2 \delta r \rho_0 \left(1 - Kr^n\right)}{c^2}$

$r < c$, and is zero for values of r greater than c.

Hence attraction at an internal point due to the sphere

$$= \gamma \int_0^c \frac{4\pi r^2 \rho_0 \left(1 - Kr^n\right)}{c^2}\, dr$$

$$= \frac{\gamma 4\pi\rho_0}{c^2}\left[\frac{c^3}{3} - \frac{Kc^{n+3}}{n+3}\right]$$

$$= 4\pi\gamma\rho_0\left[\frac{c}{3} - \frac{Kc^{n+1}}{n+3}\right]$$

From above we can say that the attraction of a sphere at an internal point P at a distance r from the centre

$$= 4\pi\gamma\rho_0\left[\frac{r}{3} - \frac{Kr^{n+1}}{n+3}\right]$$

Now we consider an elementary area $r\delta\theta\delta r$ at Q, which when revolved about diameter will generate a circular ring of radius $r \sin \theta$.

Its mass $= (2\pi\, r \sin \theta)\, \rho_0\, (1 - Kr^n)\, r\delta\theta\delta r$

Hence attraction of the sphere, on its one half, resolved perpendicular to the base

$$= \int_{\theta=0}^{\frac{\pi}{2}} \int_{r=0}^{a} 4\pi\gamma\rho_0 \left(\frac{r}{3} - \frac{Kr^{n+1}}{n+3}\right) \times \rho_0 \left(1 - Kr^n\right) 2\pi r^2 \sin\theta \cos\theta \, d\theta \, dr$$

$$= 8\pi^2\gamma\rho_0^2 \int_0^a \left(\frac{r^3}{3} - \frac{Kr^{n+3}}{n+3}\right)\left(1 - Kr^n\right)\left[\frac{\sin^2\theta}{2}\right]_0^{\frac{\pi}{2}} dr$$

$$= 4\pi^2\gamma\rho_0^2 \int_0^a \left[\frac{r^3}{3} - \frac{Kr^{n+3}}{n+3} - \frac{Kr^{n+3}}{3} + \frac{K^2 r^{2n+3}}{n+3}\right] dr$$

$$= 4\pi^2\gamma\rho_0^2 \left[\frac{a^4}{12} - \frac{K(n+6)}{3(n+3)}\frac{a^{n+4}}{n+4} + \frac{K^2}{n+3}\frac{a^{2n+4}}{2n+4}\right]$$

$$= 4\pi^2\gamma\rho_0^2 \frac{a^4}{12}\left[1 - \frac{4(n+6)}{(n+3)(n+4)} Ka^n + \frac{6K^2 a^{2n}}{(n+3)(n+2)}\right]$$

EXERCISES

1. P is a point outside a thin uniform spherical shell at a distance c from the centre. Prove that the sphere of centre P and radius c cuts the shell into two portions whose potentials at P are equal.
2. Show that the potential of a closed hemispherical shell, made of uniform, thin material of surface density σ, at a point on the axis of symmetry at a distance a from its plane face remote from its curved surface is $2\pi\gamma\sigma a$, where a is the radius of the hemisphere.
3. The density of a solid sphere varies as the distance from the centre. Show that potential at an external point is

$V = \frac{\pi\gamma\rho}{3a}\left(4a^3 - c^3\right)$ where ρ is the density at the surface, a the radius of the sphere and c the distance of the point from the centre. [B.B.A.B.U. 92H]

4. Find the potential of a solid homogeneous attracting sphere of radius a and density $\frac{3\mu}{2\pi}$ together with a uniform distribution on the surface of the sphere of repelling matter of surface density $\frac{\mu a}{2\pi}$ at any point inside the sphere and also at any point outside the sphere.

   [**Ans.** At external point P potential $= 0$

   At internal point P potential $= \gamma\mu\ (a^2 - c^2)$

   where $OP = c$]

6 THE WORK DONE BY MUTUAL ATTRACTIVE FORCES

6.1. To find the work done by the mutual attraction of the particles of a self-attracting system; when particles are brought from an infinite distance from one another to the position they occupy in the given system.

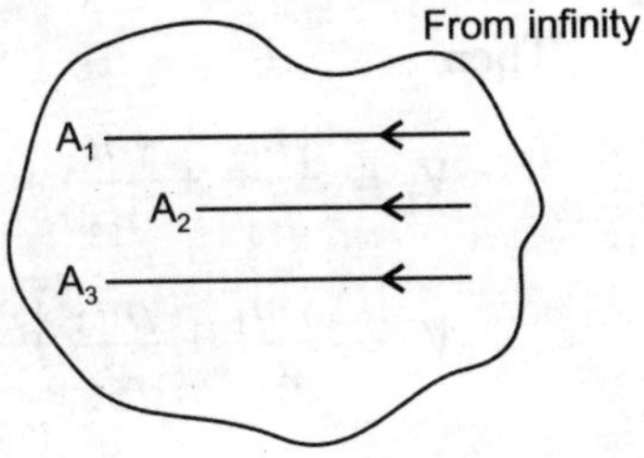

Let A_1, A_2, A_3..... be the positions of the particles m_1, m_2, m_3..... of a self-attracting system A. Let the distance between m_1 and m_2 be denoted by r_{12} and that between m_2 and m_3 by r_{23} and so on.

First of all, we bring m_1 from an infinite distance to its assigned position A_1. In this process no work is done, as there are no particles of the system near enough to exert attraction on it.

When m_1 has occupied its proper place A_1, then we bring m_2 from infinity. The work done by the attraction of m_1 in bringing m_2 from infinity to its proper place A_2 = the potential of m_1 on m_2

$$= \gamma \frac{m_1 m_2}{r_{12}}$$

When m_1 and m_2 have occupied their assigned positions, then we bring m_3 from infinity to A_3. The work done by the attraction of m_1 and m_2 in bringing m_3 from infinity to its proper place A_3

= potential of m_1 on m_3 + potential of m_2 on m_3

$$= \frac{\gamma m_1 m_3}{r_{13}} + \frac{\gamma m_2 m_3}{r_{23}}$$

This process will continue for all particles of the system. Hence the total work done

$$= \frac{\gamma m_1 m_2}{r_{12}} + \gamma m_3 \left(\frac{m_1}{r_{13}} + \frac{m_2}{r_{23}} \right) + \gamma m_4 \left(\frac{m_1}{r_{14}} + \frac{m_2}{r_{24}} + \frac{m_3}{r_{34}} \right) + \ldots\ldots$$

$$= \gamma \sum \frac{m_1 m_2}{r_{12}} \qquad \ldots (1)$$

Let V_1, V_2, V_3..... be the potentials of the system at A_1, A_2, A_3..... when all the particles have been brought to their positions.

Then

$$V_1 = \frac{\gamma m_2}{r_{12}} + \frac{\gamma m_3}{r_{13}} + \frac{\gamma m_4}{r_{14}} + \ldots\ldots$$

$$V_2 = \frac{\gamma m_1}{r_{21}} + \frac{\gamma m_3}{r_{23}} + \frac{\gamma m_4}{r_{24}} + \ldots\ldots$$

$$V_3 = \frac{\gamma m_1}{r_{31}} + \frac{\gamma m_2}{r_{32}} + \frac{\gamma m_4}{r_{34}} + \ldots\ldots$$

Multiplying these equations by m_1, m_2, m_3..... respectively and adding columnwise, we get

$$V_1 m_1 + V_2 m_2 + V_3 m_3 + \ldots\ldots = 2 \sum \gamma \frac{m_1 m_2}{r_1 r_2}$$

as $\dfrac{\gamma m_1 m_2}{r_{12}}$ comes twice.

Hence $V_1 m_1 + V_2 m_2 + \ldots\ldots = 2 \sum \dfrac{\gamma m_1 m_2}{r_{12}}$

or

$$\frac{1}{2} \sum V_1 m_1 = \sum \frac{\gamma m_1 m_2}{r_{12}} \qquad \ldots (2)$$

Hence from (1) and (2), the total work done in collecting the system is

$$\frac{1}{2}\sum V_1 m_1 = \frac{1}{2}\int V dm$$

Where V is the potential of the body at a point of the element dm of the body and the integration is to be taken so as to cover the entire mass of the body.

The expression $\frac{1}{2}\int V dm$ is called the work done by the mutual attraction of the particles.

Conversely. The work done by the mutual attraction of the particles as its particles are scattered to an infinite distance from one another is $-\frac{1}{2}\int V dm$.

6.2. Work done in changing the configuration

To find the total work done by the mutual attraction of the particles when they move from a body A to form another body B.

The required work done in changing the particles of the body A to form another body B

= The work done in scattering particles from the body A to infinity + the work done in bringing them from infinity to form the body B

$$= -\frac{1}{2}\int V dm + \frac{1}{2}\int V^1 dm^1$$

where the first intergal is taken to cover the first body A and the second integral is taken to cover the second body B.

WORKED OUT EXAMPLES

1. Show that if M be the mass of a sphere of radius a, the loss of gravitational potential energy in assembling the particles from a state of diffusion at an infinite distance is $\frac{3}{5}\gamma\frac{M^2}{a}$.

Solution: We know that the potential of a sphere of radius a at an internal point at a distance r from the centre is

$$V = \pi\gamma\rho\left(2a^2 - \frac{2r^2}{3}\right)$$

Also $$M = \frac{4}{3}\pi a^3\rho \qquad \dots (1)$$

Mass dm of the element having this potential

$= 4\pi r^2 \delta r \rho$

Hence the required work done

$$= \frac{1}{2}\int V dm$$

$$= \frac{1}{2}\int_0^a \pi\gamma\rho\left(2a^2 - \frac{2r^2}{3}\right) 4\pi r^2 \rho\, dr$$

$$= 2\pi^2\gamma\rho^2 \int_0^a \left(2a^2 r^2 - \frac{2r^4}{3}\right) dr$$

$$= 2\pi^2\gamma\rho^2 \left[\frac{2a^2 a^3}{3} - \frac{2a^5}{15}\right]$$

$$= \frac{16}{15}\gamma\pi^2\rho^2 a^6 = \frac{3}{5}\gamma\frac{M^2}{a} \text{ From (1).}$$

2. The radius of the sphere is a and its mass is M. If the density at any point of it varies inversely as the distance from the centre, show that the work done in bringing the particles of the sphere from infinity under their attraction is $\frac{2}{3}\gamma\frac{M^2}{a}$.

Solution: We divide the sphere into an infinite number of concentric shells, each of indefinitely small thickness. Let one of the shells be of radius x. Then the density at any point P of it is $\frac{K}{x}$ where K is a constant.

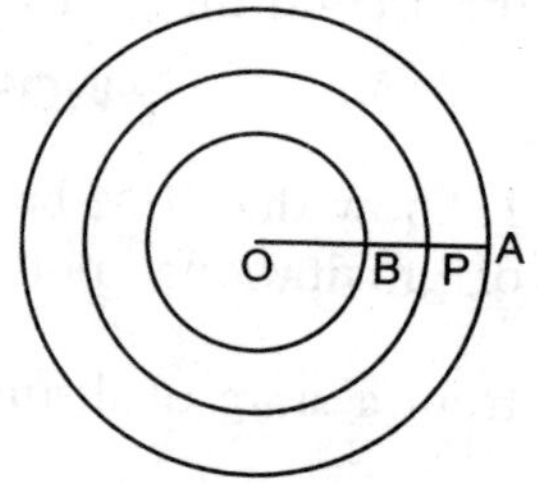

Let M be the mass of the sphere

Then $$M = \int_0^a 4\pi x^2 \frac{K}{x}\, dx$$

$$= 4\pi \frac{Ka^2}{2} = 2\pi K a^2 \qquad \text{... (1)}$$

Since the point P is inside the sphere, then for all the shell of radius y less than OP, P is an external point and hence the potential for such shell

$$= \gamma \frac{4\pi\rho y^2 \delta y}{OP}$$

$$= \gamma \frac{4\pi \frac{K}{y} y^2 \delta y}{x}$$

$$= 4\pi\gamma K \frac{y\delta y}{x}$$

For all the shells of radius z greater than OP, P is an internal point and hence the potential for such a shell

$$= \frac{\gamma 4\pi\rho z^2 \delta z}{z} = \frac{\gamma 4\pi \frac{K}{z} z^2 \delta z}{z}$$

$$= 4\pi\gamma K \delta z$$

Hence finally the potential of the sphere of radius a at an internal point distant x from the centre is

$$= \int_0^x 4\pi\gamma K \frac{ydy}{x} + \int_x^a 4\pi K\gamma dz$$

$$= \frac{4\pi\gamma K}{x} \frac{x^2}{2} + 4\pi K\gamma (a - x)$$

$$= 2\pi\gamma K (x + 2a - 2x)$$

$$= 2\pi\gamma K (2a - x)$$

The element dm of the mass having this potential

$$= 4\pi x^2 \frac{K}{x} \delta x = 4\pi K x \delta x$$

Hence the required work done

$$= \frac{1}{2}\int_0^a V dm$$

$$= \frac{1}{2}\int_0^a 2\pi\gamma K(2a - x)\, 4\pi K x dx$$

$$= 4\pi^2 K^2 \gamma \int_0^a (2ax - x^2)\, dx$$

$$= 4\pi^2 K^2 \gamma \left[ax^2 - \frac{x^3}{3} \right]_0^a$$

$$= 4\pi^2 K^2 \gamma \left[a^3 - \frac{a^3}{3} \right]$$

$$= 4\pi^2 K^2 \gamma \frac{2}{3} a^3$$

$$= \frac{2}{3}\gamma\, 4\pi^2 K^2 a^3$$

$$= \frac{2}{3}\gamma \frac{M^2}{a} \qquad \text{From (1).}$$

3. Show that the work done in collecting the particles of a thin circular disc attracting according to Newtonian Law form an infinite distance is $\frac{8}{3}\gamma\frac{M^2}{\pi a}$, where M is the mass of the disc and a its radius.

Solution: Let O be the centre of the disc and P be the internal point at which potential is to be determined.

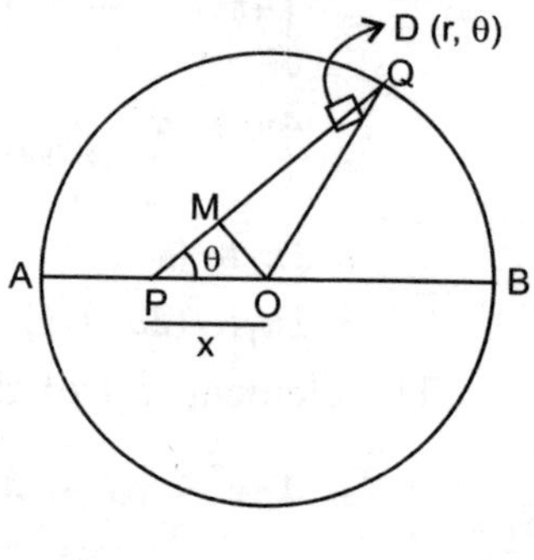

Taking P as pole and PO as initial line. Let coordinates of D be (r, θ).

Join PD and produce it to meet the sphere at Q. From O we draw OM perpendicular to PQ.

Let $\angle OPD = \theta$, $PD = r$. Join OQ.

In ΔOPM $\quad \cos\theta = \dfrac{PM}{OP} = \dfrac{PM}{x}$

$$PM = x\cos\theta$$

$$\sin\theta = \frac{OM}{OP} = \frac{OM}{x}$$

$$OM = x\sin\theta$$

In ΔOQM, $\quad OQ^2 = OM^2 + MQ^2$

$$MQ^2 = OQ^2 - OM^2 = a^2 - x^2\sin^2\theta$$

Now we consider an elementary area $r\delta\theta\delta r$ at D.

Mass of the elementary area $= \rho r\delta\theta\delta r$.

Then its potential at $P = \gamma\dfrac{4\delta\theta\delta r\rho}{PD}$

$$= \frac{\gamma r\delta\theta\delta r\rho}{r}$$

$$= \gamma\delta\theta\delta r\rho$$

Therefore, the potential at P due to the whole of the disc

$$= \gamma\rho\int_{\theta=-\pi}^{\pi}\int_{r=0}^{PQ} d\theta\, dr$$

$$= \gamma\rho\int_{\theta=-\pi}^{\pi} PQ\, d\theta$$

$$= \gamma\rho\int_{\theta=-\pi}^{\pi} (PM + MQ)\, d\theta$$

$$= \gamma\rho\int_{\theta=-\pi}^{\pi}\left(x\cos\theta + \sqrt{a^2 - x^2\sin^2\theta}\right) d\theta$$

$$= \gamma\rho\left[\{x\sin\theta\}_{-\pi}^{\pi} + \int_{-\pi}^{\pi}\sqrt{a^2 - x^2\sin^2\theta}\, d\theta\right]$$

$$= 2\gamma\rho\int_{0}^{\pi}\sqrt{a^2 - x^2\sin^2\theta}\, d\theta$$

$$= 4\rho\gamma \int_0^{\frac{\pi}{2}} \sqrt{a^2 - x^2 \sin^2\theta}\, d\theta$$

Again the element dm having this potential $= 2\pi x \delta x \rho$

Hence the required work done

$$= \frac{1}{2}\int V dm$$

$$= \frac{1}{2}\int_0^{\frac{\pi}{2}}\int_0^{a} 4\rho\gamma \sqrt{a^2 - x^2\sin^2\theta}\, d\theta\, 2\pi x\, \rho dx$$

$$= 4\pi\gamma\rho^2 \int_0^{\frac{\pi}{2}} \left\{\frac{\left(a^2 - x^2\sin^2\theta\right)}{-3\sin^2\theta}\right\}_0^{\frac{3}{2}} d\theta$$

$$= \frac{4\pi\gamma\rho^2}{3}\int_0^{\frac{\pi}{2}} \frac{a^3 - a^3\cos^3\theta}{\sin^2\theta}\, d\theta$$

$$= \frac{4}{3}\pi\gamma\rho^2 a^3 \int_0^{\frac{\pi}{2}} \frac{(1-\cos\theta)\left(1+\cos^2\theta+\cos\theta\right)}{(1-\cos\theta)(1+\cos\theta)}\, d\theta$$

$$= \frac{4}{3}\pi\gamma\rho^2 a^3 \int_0^{\frac{\pi}{2}} \left(\frac{1}{1+\cos\theta} + \cos\theta\right) d\theta$$

$$= \frac{4}{3}\pi\gamma\rho^2 a^3 \left[\{\sin\theta\}_0^{\frac{\pi}{2}} + \frac{1}{2}\int_0^{\frac{\pi}{2}} \sec^2\frac{\theta}{2}\, d\theta\right]$$

$$= \frac{4}{3}\pi\gamma\rho^2 a^3 \left[1 + \left\{\tan\frac{\theta}{2}\right\}_0^{\frac{\pi}{2}}\right]$$

$$= \frac{4}{3}\pi\gamma\rho^2 a^3\, [1 + 1 - 0]$$

$$= \frac{8}{3}\pi\gamma\rho^2 a^3$$

$$= \frac{8}{3}\frac{\gamma M^2}{\pi a} \text{ since } M = \pi a^2 \rho.$$

4. A sphere of radius a, mass M and density varying directly as the distance from the centre, is built up of matter brought in small amount from a state of complete dispersion at infinity. Show that the work W made available during the process is given by $W = \frac{4}{7}\gamma\frac{M^2}{a}$, where γ is the constant of gravitaton.

Show that if the matter is now redistributed so as to form a sphere of the same radius but of uniform density, a further amount of work $\frac{.1}{20}W$ is made available.

Solution: Here density $\rho = \lambda r$ at a distance r from the centre, λ being constant.

$$\text{The mass of the sphere} = M = \int_0^a 4\pi r^2 \lambda r dr$$

$$= 4\pi\lambda\frac{a^4}{4} = \pi\lambda a^4 \quad \text{... (1)}$$

Potential of the sphere of radius a at a distance r from the centre is

$$V = \int_0^r \gamma\frac{4\pi x^2\lambda x dx}{r} + \int_r^a \gamma\frac{4\pi x^2 \lambda x dx}{x}$$

$$= \frac{\gamma 4\pi\lambda}{r}\int_0^r x^3 dx + 4\pi\lambda\gamma\int_r^a x^2 dx$$

$$= \frac{\gamma 4\pi\lambda}{r}\frac{r^4}{4} + \frac{4\pi\lambda\gamma}{3}\left(a^3 - r^3\right)$$

$$= \gamma\frac{\pi\lambda}{3}\left[3r^3 + 4a^3 - 4r^3\right]$$

$$= \frac{\gamma\pi\lambda}{3}\left(4a^3 - r^3\right)$$

The element of mass dm having this potential $= 4\pi r^2 \delta r \lambda r$

Hence, if W be the amount of work done then

$$W = \frac{1}{2}\int V dm$$

$$= \frac{1}{2}\int_0^a \gamma \frac{\pi\lambda}{3}\left(4a^3 - r^3\right) 4\pi r^2 r\lambda dr$$

$$= \frac{2}{3}\gamma\pi^2\lambda^2 \int_0^a \left(4a^3 r^3 - r^6\right) dr$$

$$= \frac{2}{3}\gamma\pi^2\lambda^2 \left[a^7 - \frac{a^7}{7}\right]$$

$$= \frac{2}{3}\gamma\pi^2\lambda^2 \frac{6a^7}{7}$$

$$= \frac{4}{7}\gamma\,\pi^2\lambda^2 6a^7$$

$$= \frac{4}{7}\gamma\frac{M^2}{a} \qquad \text{... (2) From (1)}$$

Second Part. The work done in taking particles of the sphere of the variable density λr to infinity.

$$= -\frac{1}{2}\int V dm$$

$$= -\frac{4}{7}\frac{\gamma M^2}{a}$$

$$= -W \qquad \text{From (2)}$$

The matter from infinity is brought from infinity so as to form a sphere of uniform density but radius a.

Here $M = \frac{4}{3}\pi a^3 \rho$ ... (3)

If V^1 be the potential of the sphere at a distance r from centre (at an internal point) then its potential is

$$V^1 = \gamma\int_0^r \frac{4\pi x^2 \rho dx}{r} + \gamma\int_r^a \frac{4\pi x^2 \rho dx}{x}$$

$$= \frac{4\pi\gamma\rho}{r}\frac{r^3}{3} + 4\pi\gamma\rho\frac{(a^2 - r^2)}{2}$$

$$= \pi\gamma\rho\left[\frac{4}{3}r^2 + 2a^2 - 2r^2\right]$$

$$= \pi\gamma\rho\left[2a^2 - \frac{2r^2}{3}\right]$$

Also the element dm^1 having this potential = $4\pi r^2 \delta r \rho$

Hence the work done in bringing the particles from infinity to form the sphere of uniform density

$$= \frac{1}{2}\int V^1 dm$$

$$= \frac{1}{2}\int_0^a 2\pi\gamma\rho\left(a^2 - \frac{r^2}{3}\right)4\pi r^2 dr\rho$$

$$= 4\pi^2\gamma\rho^2 \int_0^a \left(a^2 r^2 - \frac{r^4}{3}\right) dr$$

$$= 4\gamma\pi^2\rho^2\left[\frac{a^5}{3} - \frac{a^5}{15}\right]$$

$$= 16\gamma\pi^2\rho^2\frac{a^5}{15}$$

$$= \frac{3}{5}\gamma\frac{M^2}{a} \qquad \text{From (3)}$$

But $W = \frac{4}{7}\gamma\frac{M^2}{a}$

Hence this amount of work is $\frac{3}{5}\cdot\frac{7}{4}W = \frac{21}{20}W$

Therefore the work acquired for redistribution

$$= -\frac{1}{2}\int V dm + \frac{1}{2}\int V^1 dm^1$$

$$= -W + \frac{21}{20}W = \frac{1}{20}W$$

Thus a further work of amount $\frac{1}{20}W$ is made available.

5. Prove that the work done by the gravitation of the forces when a uniform spherical shell of mass M of the external and internal radii a and b respectively is changed to a solid sphere of the same density is

$$\frac{3\gamma M^2}{10c^4}\left(2c^5 - 2a^5 - 3b^5 + 5a^2b^3\right)$$

where $c^2 = a^3 - b^3$

Solution: We know that the potential V of the shell of external and internal radii a and b at any point P at a distance r from the centre is

$$V = 2\pi\gamma\rho\left[a^2 - \frac{r^2}{3} - \frac{2}{3}\frac{b^3}{r}\right]$$

Also the element of the mass having this potential

$$= 4\pi r^2 \delta r \rho$$

Hence the work done in taking the particles from the shell to infinity

$$= -\frac{1}{2}\int V dm$$

$$= -\frac{1}{2}\int_b^a 2\pi\gamma\rho\left[a^2 - \frac{r^2}{3} - \frac{2}{3}\frac{b^3}{r}\right]4\pi^2\rho dr$$

$$= -4\pi^2\rho^2\gamma\int_b^a\left[a^2 - \frac{r^2}{3} - \frac{2}{3}\frac{b^3}{r}\right]r^2 dr$$

$$= -4\pi^2\rho^2\gamma\int_b^a\left[a^2r^2 - \frac{r^4}{3} - \frac{2}{3}b^3r\right]dr$$

$$= -4\pi^2\rho^2\gamma\left[a^2\frac{r^3}{3} - \frac{r^5}{15} - \frac{b^3}{3}r^2\right]_b^a$$

$$= -4\pi^2\rho^2\gamma\left[\frac{a^2\left(a^3 - b^3\right)}{3} - \frac{a^5 - b^5}{15} - \frac{b^3}{3}\left(a^2 - b^2\right)\right]$$

$$= -4\pi^2\rho^2\gamma\left[\frac{4a^5}{15} + \frac{6b^5}{15} - \frac{2}{3}a^2b^3\right]$$

Let c be the radius of the solid sphere of the same density and the same mass, then

$$M = \frac{4}{3}\pi c^3\rho$$

$$= \frac{4}{3}\pi\left(a^3 - b^3\right)\rho$$

i.e. $\quad c^3 = a^3 - b^3$ and $\pi\rho = \dfrac{3M}{4c^3}$

Hence the work done

$$= -4\gamma\frac{9M^2}{16c^6}\left[\frac{4}{15}a^5 - \frac{2}{3}a^2b^3 + \frac{6}{15}b^5\right] \qquad \ldots (1)$$

Again the work done on bringing the particles from infinity to form a solid sphere of radius c

$$= \frac{3}{5}\gamma\frac{M^2}{c} \qquad \ldots (2)$$

Hence the required work done from (1) and (2)

$$= \frac{3}{5}\gamma\frac{M^2}{c} - \frac{9\gamma M^2}{4c^6}\left(\frac{4}{15}a^5 - \frac{2}{3}a^2b^3 + \frac{6}{15}b^5\right)$$

$$= \frac{3}{5}\gamma\frac{M^2}{c} - \frac{3\gamma M^2}{2c^6}\left[\frac{2a^5}{5} + \frac{3b^5}{5} - a^2b^3\right]$$

$$= \frac{3\gamma M^2}{10c^6}\left[2c^5 - 2a^5 - 3b^5 + 5a^2b^3\right]$$

6. Find the negative potential energy W for a spherical distribution of mass M and radius a in which the density varies uniformely from ρ_1 at the surface to ρ_0 at the centre, and deduce that of $\rho_0 = 0$.

$$W = \frac{26GM^2}{35a} \text{ while if } \rho_0 = 0;\ \rho_1 \neq 0$$

the value W is reduced to the ratio $\dfrac{10}{13}$. G denotes the gravitational constant.

Solution: Let ρ_r denote the density at a distance r from the centre, then $\rho_r = \rho_0 - \lambda r$.

But when $r = a$ $\rho = \rho_1$

$$\therefore \quad \rho_1 = \rho_0 - \lambda a$$

$$\lambda = \frac{\rho_0 - \rho_1}{a}$$

Hence the density at a distance r from the centre

$$= \rho_0 - \frac{\rho_0 - \rho_1}{a} r$$

If M be the mass of the sphere then

$$M = \int_0^a 4\pi r^2 \left(\rho_0 - \frac{\rho_0 - \rho_1}{a} r \right) dr$$

$$= 4\pi \left[\rho_0 \frac{a^3}{3} - \frac{\rho_0 - \rho_1}{a} \frac{a^4}{4} \right]$$

$$= 4\pi a^3 \left[\frac{1}{12} \rho_0 + \frac{\rho_1}{4} \right]$$

$$= \pi a^3 \left(\frac{1}{3} \rho_0 + \rho_1 \right)$$

$$\left. \begin{aligned} &\text{When } \rho_1 = 0, M = \frac{1}{3} \pi \rho_0 a^3 \\ &\text{When } \rho_0 = 0, M = \pi \rho_1 a^3 \end{aligned} \right\} \quad \ldots (1)$$

Now potential of the sphere at a point at a distance r from the centre is

$$V = \gamma \int_0^r \frac{4\pi x^2}{r} \left(\rho_0 - \frac{\rho_0 - \rho_1}{a} x \right) dx + \gamma \int_r^a \frac{4\pi x^2}{x} \left(\rho_0 - \frac{\rho_0 - \rho_1}{a} x \right) dx$$

$$= \frac{4\pi\gamma}{4} \left\{ \rho_0 \frac{r^3}{3} - \frac{\rho_0 - \rho_1}{a} \frac{r^4}{4} \right\} + 4\pi\gamma \left\{ \rho_0 \frac{a^2 - r^2}{2} - \frac{\rho_0 - \rho_1}{a} \frac{(a^3 - r^3)}{3} \right\}$$

$$= 4\pi\gamma\left[\rho_0 r^2\left(\frac{1}{3}-\frac{1}{2}\right)-\frac{\rho_0-\rho_1}{a}r^3\left(\frac{1}{4}-\frac{1}{3}\right)\right.$$

$$\left.+\rho_0 a^2\left(\frac{1}{2}-\frac{1}{3}\right)+\frac{\rho_1 a^2}{3}\right]$$

$$= 4\pi\gamma\left[\rho_0\frac{a^2}{6}+\frac{\rho_1 a^2}{3}-\rho_0\frac{r^2}{6}+\frac{\rho_0-\rho_1}{a}\frac{r^3}{12}\right] \quad \dots (2)$$

The element of mass dm having this potential

$$= 4\pi r^2\left[\rho_0-\frac{\rho_0-\rho_1}{a}r\right]\delta r$$

Hence the work done in collecting the particles from infinity

$$= \frac{1}{2}\int V dm$$

$$= \frac{1}{2}\int_0^a 4\pi\gamma\left[\rho_0\frac{a^2}{6}+\frac{\rho_1 a^2}{3}-\frac{\rho_0 r^2}{6}+\frac{\rho_0-\rho_1}{a}\frac{r^3}{12}\right]$$

$$\times 4\pi r^2\left(\rho_0-\frac{\rho_0-\rho_1}{a}r\right)dr$$

$$= 8\pi^2\gamma\int_0^a\left[\left(\rho_0\frac{a^2}{6}+\frac{\rho_1 a^2}{3}\right)\rho_0 r^2\right.$$

$$-\left(\rho_0\frac{a^2}{6}+\frac{\rho_1 a^2}{3}\right)\frac{\rho_0-\rho_1}{a}r^3-\frac{\rho_0^2}{6}r^4$$

$$\left.+\frac{\rho_1(\rho_0-\rho_1)}{4a}r^5-\frac{(\rho_0-\rho_1)^2}{12a^2}r^6\right]dr$$

$$= 8\pi^2\gamma\left[\left(\rho_0\frac{a^2}{6}+\rho_1\frac{a^2}{3}\right)\rho_0\frac{a^3}{3}\right.$$

$$-\left(\rho_0\frac{a^2}{6}+\rho_1\frac{a^2}{3}\right)\frac{\rho_0-\rho_1 a^4}{a4}-\frac{\rho_0^2}{6}\frac{a^5}{5}$$

$$\left.+\frac{\rho_0(\rho_0-\rho_1)}{4a}\frac{a^6}{6}-\frac{(\rho_0-\rho_1)^2}{12a^2}\frac{a^7}{7}\right]$$

$$= 8\pi^2\gamma a^5\left[\left(\frac{1}{18}-\frac{1}{24}-\frac{1}{30}+\frac{1}{24}-\frac{1}{84}\right)\rho_0^2\right.$$

$$\left.+\left(\frac{1}{9}-\frac{1}{12}+\frac{1}{24}-\frac{1}{24}+\frac{1}{42}\right)\rho_0\rho_1+\left(\frac{1}{12}-\frac{1}{84}\right)\rho_1^2\right]$$

$$= 8\pi^2\gamma a^5\left[\frac{13}{90\times 7\times 2}\rho_0{}^2+\frac{13\,\rho_0\rho_1}{3\times 2\times 42}+\frac{1}{14}\rho_1{}^2\right] \quad \ldots (3)$$

When $\rho_1 = 0$, then from (3)

$$W_1 = 8\pi^2\gamma a^5\,\frac{13}{90\times 7\times 2} = \frac{26\gamma M^2}{35a} \quad \ldots (4)$$

When $\rho_1 = 0$, then $M = \frac{\pi}{3}\rho_0 a^3$ from (1) ... (5)

When $\rho_0 = 0$, then from (3)

$$W_2 = 8\pi^2\gamma a^5\,\frac{1}{14}\rho_1{}^2 = \frac{4}{7}\frac{\gamma M^2}{a} \quad \text{From (1)}$$

Dividing (5) by (4), we get ratio as $\frac{10}{13}$.

7. A uniform shell of gravitating matter in which the volume of the matter is equal to the hollow it encloss contracts under its own gravitation into a uniform solid sphere of the same density. Prove that the work done by the gravitating forces is

$$3\left(2^{2/3}-1\right)\frac{\gamma M^2}{10a}$$

where M is the mass and a the radius of the solid sphere.

Solution: Let b be the outer radius of the shell a is given to be the radius of the hollow.

Thus volume of the shell $= \frac{4}{3}\pi\left(b^3-a^3\right)$

Given that

Volume of the shell = volume of the hollow it encloses

$$\therefore \quad \frac{4}{3}\pi a^3 = \frac{4}{3}\pi\left(b^3-a^3\right)$$

or $\quad b^3 = 2a^3$

$\therefore \quad b = 2^{\frac{1}{3}} a$

Now potential of the shell at any point at a distance r from the centre of the sphere

$$V = \gamma \int_a^r \frac{4\pi x^2 dx \rho}{r} + \gamma \int_r^b \frac{4\pi x^2 dx \rho}{x}$$

$$= 4\pi\gamma\rho \left[\frac{r^3 - a^3}{3r} + \frac{b^2 - r^2}{2} \right]$$

$$= 4\pi\gamma\rho \left[\frac{r^2}{3} - \frac{r^2}{2} + \frac{b^2}{2} - \frac{a^3}{3r} \right]$$

$$= 4\pi\gamma\rho \left[-\frac{1}{6} r^2 - \frac{a^3}{3r} + \frac{1}{2} b^2 \right]$$

Also element of the mass having this potential = $4\pi r^2 \delta r \rho$

Therefore, the work done in taking the particles to infinity

$$= -\frac{1}{2} \int V dm$$

$$= -\frac{1}{2} \int_a^b 4\pi\gamma\rho \left(\frac{-r^2}{6} - \frac{a^3}{3r} + \frac{b^2}{2} \right) 4\pi r^2 \rho dr$$

$$= -8\pi^2 \rho^2 \gamma \int_a^b \left(\frac{-r^4}{6} - \frac{a^3 r}{3} + \frac{b^2 r^2}{2} \right) dr$$

$$= -8\pi^2 \rho^2 \gamma \left[-\frac{r^5}{30} - \frac{a^3 r^2}{6} + \frac{b^2 r^3}{6} \right]_a^b$$

$$= -8\pi^2 \rho^2 \gamma \left[-\frac{1}{30} (b^5 - a^5) - \frac{a^3}{6} (b^2 - a^2) + \frac{b^2}{6} (b^3 - a^3) \right]$$

$$= -8\pi^2 \rho^2 \gamma \left[\frac{4}{30} b^5 + \frac{6}{30} a^5 - \frac{2}{6} a^3 b^2 \right]$$

$$= -8\pi^2\rho^2\gamma\left[\frac{4}{30}a^5 \cdot 2^{\frac{5}{3}} + \frac{6}{30}a^5 - \frac{2}{6}a^3a^2 2^{\frac{2}{3}}\right]$$

$$= -8\pi^2\rho^2\gamma\left[\frac{8a^5}{30}2^{\frac{2}{3}} + \frac{6}{30}a^5 - \frac{2}{6}a^5 2^{\frac{2}{3}}\right]$$

$$= -8\pi^2\rho^2\gamma a^5\left[\frac{8}{30}2^{\frac{2}{3}} - \frac{2}{6}2^{\frac{2}{3}} + \frac{6}{30}\right]$$

$$= -8\gamma\frac{a^5 9M^2}{16a^6}\left[-\frac{2}{30}2^{\frac{2}{3}} + \frac{6}{30}\right]$$

$$= -\frac{3\gamma M^2}{a}\left[-\frac{2^{\frac{2}{3}}}{10} + \frac{3}{10}\right]$$

$$= \frac{3\gamma M^2}{10a}\left(2^{\frac{2}{3}} - 3\right)$$

Now work done in bringing the particles from infinity to form the sphere of radius a is $\frac{1}{2}\int V^1 dm^1 = \frac{3}{5}\gamma\frac{M^2}{a}$.

Hence the required work done

$$= -\frac{1}{2}\int V dm + \frac{1}{2}\int V^1 dm^1$$

$$= \frac{3\gamma M^2}{10a}\left(2^{\frac{2}{3}} - 3\right) + \frac{3}{5}\gamma\frac{M^2}{a}$$

$$= \frac{3\gamma M^2}{10a}\left[2^{\frac{2}{3}} - 3 + 2\right]$$

$$= \frac{3\gamma M^2}{10a}\left(2^{\frac{2}{3}} - 1\right)$$

EXERCISES

1. A self-attracting sphere of uniform density and radius a, changes to one of uniform density and radius b, show that

the work done by its mutual attractive forces is $\frac{3}{5}\gamma M^2\left(\frac{1}{b}-\frac{1}{a}\right)$ where M is the mass of the sphere.

2. The density of a sphere of mass M and radius a at a distance r from the centre is proportional to $(a - r)$. Prove that the potential at this distance is $\frac{\gamma M}{a^4}\left(2a^3 - 2ar^2 + r^3\right)$ and the potential energy exhausted in collecting the elements of the sphere is $\frac{26\gamma M^2}{35a}$ where γ is the gravitational constant.

3. Inside a sphere of radius a the density at a distance r from the centre is $\rho\left(1-\frac{Kr^2}{a^2}\right)$ where ρ and K are constants. Prove that the work done in collecting the elements of the sphere from a state of infinite scatter is $\frac{16\pi^2\gamma\rho^2 a^5}{15}\left(1-\frac{8K}{7}+\frac{K^2}{3}\right)$.

4. Prove that the work done in moving the particles of a homogeneous oblate spheroid of eccentricity $\sin\beta$ and semi major axis a to infinity is $\frac{3}{5}\frac{\gamma M^2}{a}\frac{\sin\beta}{\beta}$ where M is its mass.

7 GENERAL THEOREMS

7.1. Some Definitions

1. Solid Angle. The solid angle dw of a cone is measured by the area intercepted by the cone on the surface of a sphere of unit radius, having its centre at the vertex of the cone.

The solid angle subtended at a point by a surface of any form is measured by the solid angle of the cone whose vertex is at the given point and whose base is the given surface.

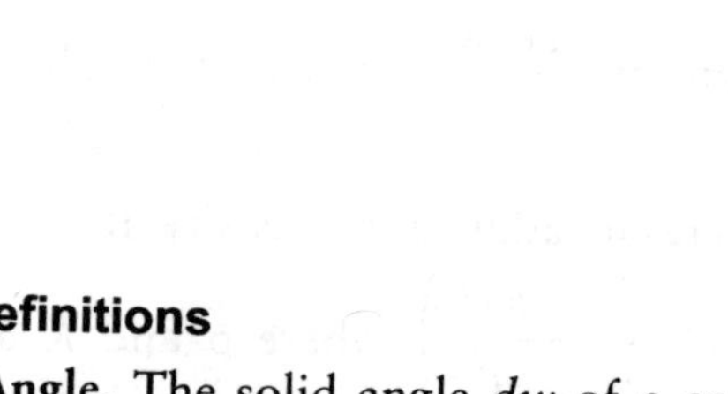

Let PP' be a small element of area ds which subtends a solid angle dw at O. Let the normal to ds make an acute angle Y with OP, and let $OP = r$. Then the cross-section at P of the cone which ds subtends at O is $ds \cos \gamma$, and this cross-section and the small area dw intercepted on the unit sphere are similar figures so that $ds \cos \gamma : dw = r^2 : 1$.

Hence $dw = \dfrac{ds \cos \gamma}{r^2}$

or $\quad ds = r^2 \sec^2/dw$

2. Solid angle in polar coordinates. Let the solid angle dw be an element of the surface of a unit sphere. Let the element be $PQRS$ bounded by meridians and small circles, where the angular coordinates of P are θ and ϕ.

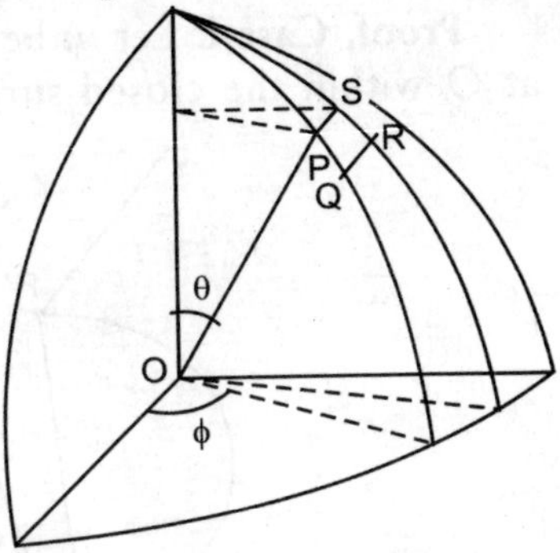

Then since the arc PS subtends an angle $d\phi$ at the centre of a circle of radius $\sin\theta$, therefore

$PS = \sin\theta\, d\phi$, and $PQ = d\theta$, so that

$$dw = PQ \cdot PS = \sin\theta\, d\theta\, d\phi$$

7.2. Volume in terms of solid angles

Let us consider a cone of small solid angle dw and length R. Let PP' and QQ' be cross-sections at distances r and $r + dr$ from the vertex O. Then the area $PP' = r^2 dw$

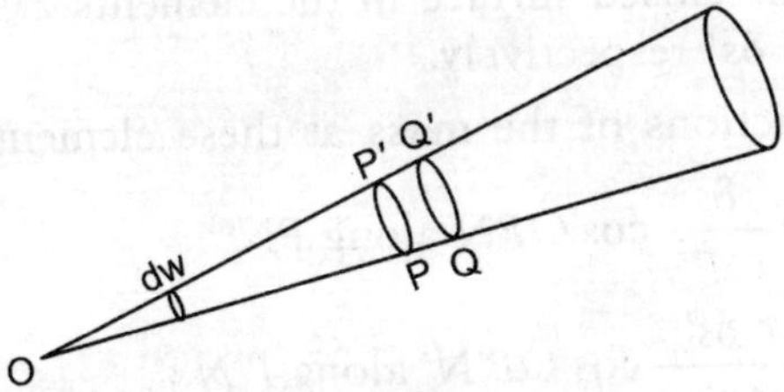

The volume of the frustum $PQ\,Q'P' = r^2 dw dr$ neglecting an infinitesimal of higher order.

$$\text{Hence the volume of the cone} = dw \int_0^R r^2 dr$$

$$= \frac{1}{3} R^3 dw$$

7.3. Gauss Theorem [L.N.M.U. 93H]

Statement. If N be the normal attraction at any point of the element δs of any closed surface, measured positively along the normal outwards, due to any attracting mass, then

$$\int N ds = -4\pi\gamma M$$

where M is the amount of the attraction mass within the surface, the integral being taken over the whole surface.

Proof. Case I. Let m be any element of the attracting mass at O within the closed surface.

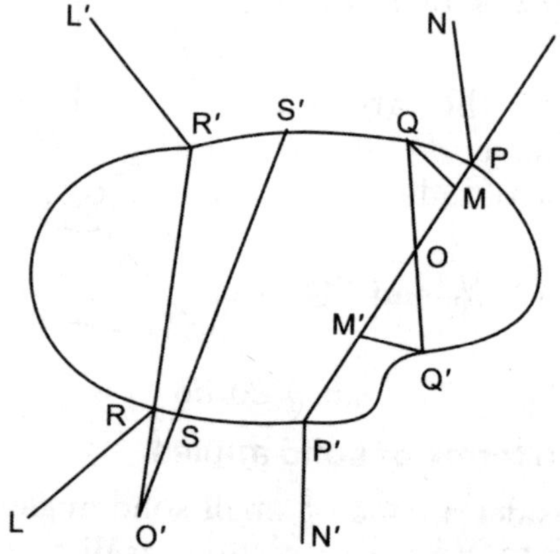

Through O we draw cone of very small vertical angle, which cuts the closed surface in the elements PQ and $P'Q'$ of areas δs and $\delta s'$ respectively.

The attractions of the mass at these element are

$$\gamma m \frac{\delta s}{OP^2} \cos OPN \text{ along } PN \qquad \dots (1)$$

and $$\gamma m \frac{\delta s'}{OP'^2} \cos OP'N' \text{ along } P'N' \qquad \dots (2)$$

where PN and $P'N'$ are outward drawn normals at P and P' respectively.

Through Q and Q' we draw normal sections QM and $Q'M'$ of this slender cone. Lt δw be the solid angle of the cone and let θ be the angle between the element QM and QP, so that

$$\theta = \text{the supplement of the angle between the normals } OM \text{ and } PN$$
$$= \pi - OPN$$

Then $\quad \delta w = \dfrac{\text{area } QM}{OQ^2} = \dfrac{\delta s \cos\theta}{OQ^2} = \dfrac{-\delta s \cos OPN}{OP^2}$

in the limit when PQ is very small.

Similarly $\quad \delta w = -\dfrac{\delta s' \cos OP'N'}{OP'^2}$

From (1) and (2), the normal attractions for the element δS and $\delta s'$ at P and P' are each $-\gamma m \delta w$.

Therefore, the total normal attraction for the whole surface

$$= -\gamma m \sum \delta w = -\gamma m\, 4\pi$$

This result is true for the single particle of mass m at O i.e. $\int N ds = -4\pi\gamma m$.

Similarly for all other particles of attracting mass inside the surface.

Hence for the whole mass $\int N ds = -4\pi\gamma M$

Case II. Let m_1 be any element of the attracting mass at O_1 outside the closed surface. Through O we draw a cone of very small vertical angle, which cuts the closed surface in the elements RS and $R'S'$ of areas δs_1 and $\delta s_1'$ respectively. Then proceeding as, Case I, the normal attractions of RS and $R'S'$ are $\gamma m_1 \delta w_1$ in magnitude, but opposite in sign, because at R the attraction is positive measured along the outward drawn normal RL and at R' is negative. Hence the elements of the normal attraction for the surface RS and $R'S'$ are $\gamma m_1 \delta w_1$ and $-\gamma m_1 \delta w_1$, so that their sum is zero.

The same is applicable for all such slender cones drawn through O_1. Hence the surface integral of normal attraction is zero for any such elementary mass as m_1 outside the closed surface, and so it is zero for the total mass M_1, lying outside the closed surface.

7.4. Poisson's Equation for the Potential

[M.U. 92H, 95H, 98H, 01H, 03H; T.M.B.U. 91H, 93H, 96H, 98H, 2000H, 2003H; B.B.A.B.U. 97H, 99H, 2001H, 2003H]

Statement. If V be the potential of an attracting matter at any point p (x, y, z) where the density is ρ, then

$$\frac{\partial^2 V}{\partial x^2}+\frac{\partial^2 V}{\partial y^2}+\frac{\partial^2 V}{\partial z^2}=-4\pi\gamma\rho$$

Proof. We know from Gauss's theorem that if N be the normal attraction at any point of a closed surface measured outwards, then

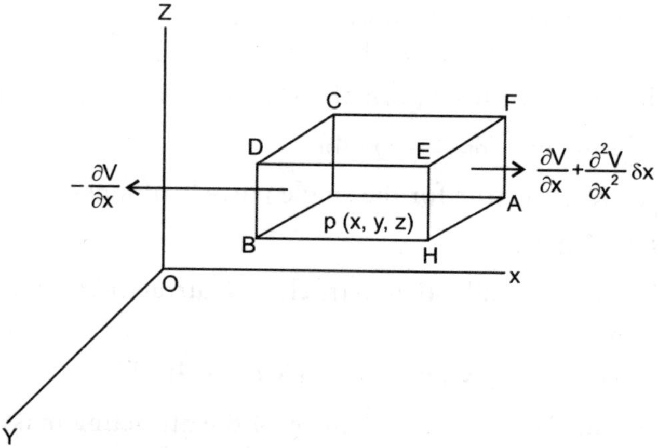

$$\int N ds = 4\pi\gamma M \qquad \text{... (1)}$$

where M is the amount of the attraction matter contained by the closed surface.

Let the closed surface be taken as the small rectangular parallelopiped; whose one of the angular points be $p\ (x, y, z)$ and whose edges PA, PB, PC are parallel to the axes and of lengths δx, δy, δz respectively.

Since V is the potential at P, $\frac{\partial V}{\partial x}$ is the attraction at P along the direction of x increasing it along PA. The face $PBDC$ being very small, the attraction at each point of it is ultimately the same and equal to $-\frac{\partial V}{\partial x}$ towards the negative direction of Ox.

Thus for the whole face $PBDC$ of area $\delta y \delta z$, the component of $\int N ds = -\frac{\partial V}{\partial x}\,\delta y\,\delta z$

Let $\dfrac{\partial V}{\partial x} = f(x)$

Then the component attraction parallel to the positive direction of Ox at each point of $AHEF$

$$= \delta(x + \delta x) = \delta(x) + \delta x f(x) + ...$$

$$= \frac{\partial V}{\partial x} + \frac{\partial^2 V}{\partial x^2}\,\delta x + ...$$

Hence the component of $\int N ds$ due to this face of area $\delta y \cdot \delta z$

$$= \left(\frac{\partial V}{\partial x} + \frac{\partial^2 V}{\partial x^2}\,\delta x + ...\right)\delta y\,\delta z$$

Hence the sum of the components of $\int N ds$ due to the faces $PBDC$ and $AHEF$

$$= \left[\frac{\partial^2 V}{\partial x^2} + ...\right]\delta x\,\delta y\,\delta z$$

Similarly the components for the faces perpendicular to y and z axes are

$$\left[\frac{\partial^2 V}{\partial y^2} + ...\right]\delta x\,\delta y\,\delta z \text{ and } \left[\frac{\partial^2 V}{\partial z^2} + ...\right]\delta x\,\delta y\,\delta z$$

If the small parallelopiped be inside the attracting mass, then

$$M = \text{mass of the parallelopiped}$$
$$= \rho\ \delta x \cdot \delta y \cdot \delta z$$

Hence, from equation (1), we have

$$\delta x \cdot \delta y \cdot \delta z \left[\frac{\partial^2 V}{\partial x^2} + \frac{\partial^2 V}{\partial y^2} + \frac{\partial^2 V}{\partial z^2} + ...\right] = -4\pi\gamma \cdot \delta x \cdot \delta y \cdot \delta z\ \rho$$

Taking limit and cancelling $\delta x\ \delta y\ \delta z$ on both the sides, we get

$$\frac{\partial^2 V}{\partial x^2} + \frac{\partial^2 V}{\partial y^2} + \frac{\partial^2 V}{\partial z^2} = -\,4\pi\gamma\rho$$

7.5. Poisson's Theorem (Polar Coordinates) [T.M.B.U. 2001H]

Statement. If V is the potential of an attracting matter at any point $p\ (r, \theta, \phi)$ where the density is ρ, then

$$\frac{\partial^2 V}{\partial r^2} + \frac{2}{r}\frac{\partial^2 V}{\partial r^2} + \frac{1}{r^2}\frac{\partial^2 V}{\partial \theta^2} + \frac{\cot\theta}{r^2}\frac{\partial V}{\partial \theta} + \frac{1}{r^2 \sin^2\theta}\frac{\partial^2 V}{\partial \phi^2} = -4\pi\gamma\rho.$$

Proof. Let us take the closed surface of a small parallelopiped whose one corner is the point $p\ (r, \theta, \phi)$ and the three concurrent edges PA, PB, PC are δr, $r\delta\theta$ and $r \sin \theta\delta\phi$ respectively.

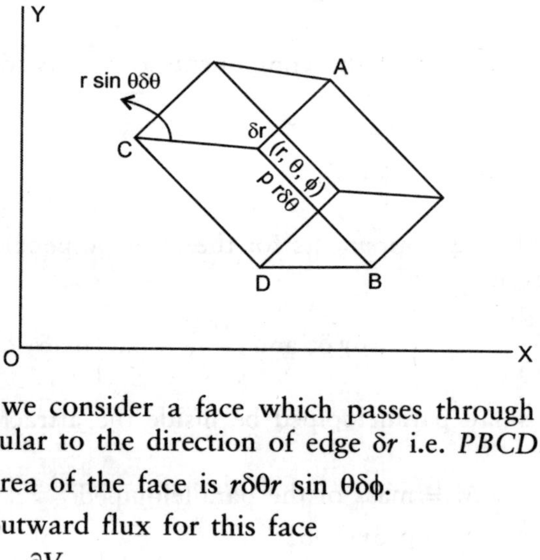

Now we consider a face which passes through P and is perpendicular to the direction of edge δr i.e. $PBCD$.

The area of the face is $r\delta\theta r \sin \theta\delta\phi$.

The outward flux for this face

$$= \frac{-\partial V}{\partial r} r\delta\theta\, r \sin \theta\delta\phi \qquad \dots (1)$$

Let $\dfrac{\partial V}{\partial r} r\, \delta\theta\, r \sin \theta\delta\phi = f(r)$

The outward flux for the opposite face is

$$= f(r + \delta r)$$

$$= f(r) + \delta r\, f(r) + \dots..$$

$$= f(r) + \delta r \frac{\partial}{\partial r} f(r)$$

$$= \frac{\partial V}{\partial r} r\delta\theta\, r \sin\theta\delta\phi + \frac{\partial}{\partial r}\left[\frac{\partial V}{\partial r} r\delta\theta\, r\sin\theta\delta\phi\right]\delta r \qquad \ldots (2)$$

Adding (1) and (2) the total outward flux for the pair of opposite faces is

$$\frac{\partial}{\partial r}\left[\frac{\partial V}{\partial r} r\delta\theta\, r\sin\theta\delta\phi\right]\delta r \qquad \ldots (3)$$

Now we consider the face whose area is $\delta r\, r\sin\theta\delta\phi$ and the length of edge normal to the face is $r\delta\theta$. Hence the total outward flux due to the pair of opposite faces is

$$\frac{\partial}{r\,\partial\theta}\left[\frac{\partial V}{r\,\partial\theta}\delta r\, r\sin\theta\delta\phi\right] r\delta\theta \qquad \ldots (4)$$

Again we consider the face whose area is $\delta r\, r\delta\theta$ and the length of the edge normal to it is $r\sin\theta\delta\phi$. Hence the total outward flux for the pair of opposite faces.

$$\frac{\partial}{r\sin\theta\,\partial\phi}\left[\frac{\partial V}{r\sin\theta\,\partial\phi}\delta r\, r\delta\theta\right](r\sin\theta\delta\phi) \qquad \ldots (5)$$

Also the attracting mass inside the surfaces

$$= \delta r\; r\;\delta\theta\; r\;\sin\;\theta\;\delta\phi\rho \qquad \ldots (6)$$

Hence by Gauss's theorem we have

$$\frac{\partial}{\partial r}\left(\frac{\partial V}{\partial r} r\delta\theta\, r\sin\theta\delta\phi\right)\delta r + \frac{\partial}{r\,\partial\theta}\left(\frac{\partial V}{r\partial\theta}\delta r\, r\sin\theta\delta\phi\right) r\delta\theta$$

$$+ \frac{\partial}{r\sin\theta\partial\phi}\left(\frac{\partial V}{r\sin\theta\partial\phi}\delta r\, r\delta\theta\right) r\sin\theta\delta\phi$$

$$= -4\pi\gamma\left[\delta r\, r\delta\theta\, r\sin\theta\delta\phi\rho\right]$$

$$\Rightarrow \frac{1}{r^2}\frac{\partial}{\partial r}\left(r^2\frac{\partial V}{\partial r}\right)\delta r\, r\delta\theta\, r\sin\theta\delta\phi$$

$$+ \frac{1}{r^2\sin\theta}\frac{\partial}{\partial\theta}\left(\sin\theta\frac{\partial V}{\partial\theta}\right)\delta r\, r\delta\theta\, r\sin\theta\delta\phi$$

$$+ \frac{1}{r^2\sin^2\theta}\frac{\partial}{\partial\phi}\left(\frac{\partial V}{\partial\phi}\right)\delta r\, r\delta\theta r\sin\theta\delta\phi$$

$$= -4\pi\gamma\left[\delta r\, r\delta\theta\, r\sin\theta\delta\phi\right]\rho$$

$$\Rightarrow \frac{1}{r^2}\left[2r\cdot\frac{\partial V}{\partial r}+r^2\frac{\partial^2 V}{\partial r^2}\right]$$
$$+\frac{1}{r^2\sin\theta}\left[\cos\theta\frac{\partial V}{\partial\theta}+\sin\theta\frac{\partial^2 V}{\partial\theta^2}\right]$$
$$+\frac{1}{r^2\sin^2\theta}\frac{\partial^2 V}{\partial\phi^2}=-4\pi\gamma\rho$$

$$\Rightarrow \frac{\partial^2 V}{\partial r^2}+\frac{2}{r}\frac{\partial V}{\partial r}+\frac{\cot\theta}{r^2}\frac{\partial V}{\partial\theta}+\frac{1}{r^2}\frac{\partial^2 V}{\partial\theta^2}$$
$$+\frac{1}{r^2\sin^2\theta}\frac{\partial^2 V}{\partial\phi^2}=-4\pi\gamma\rho$$

7.6. Laplace's Theorem

[M.U. 93H, 97H, 99H, 2002H, 2004H; T.M.B.U. 94H, 97H, 99H, 2002H; B.B.A.B.U. 2002H]

Statement. If V be the potential of an attracting mass at any point $P(x, y, z)$ which does not coincide with any of the attracting particles, then

$$\frac{\partial^2 V}{\partial x^2}+\frac{\partial^2 V}{\partial y^2}+\frac{\partial^2 V}{\partial z^2}=0$$

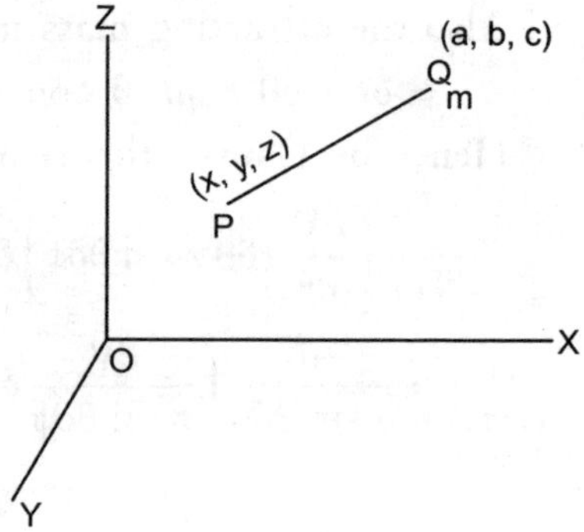

Proof. Let m be the mass of a particle of an attracting system.

Let $Q(a, b, c)$ be the point where m is situated and $P(x, y, z)$ is any point which is not in contact with any of the attracting particles.

Potential at P due to attracting particle m is $\dfrac{\gamma m}{PQ}=\dfrac{\gamma m}{r}$.

Where $r^2 = (x-a)^2 + (y-b)^2 + (z-c)^2$

$$\therefore \quad r\frac{\partial r}{\partial x} = x - a$$

If V be the potential at P due to the whole attracting matter then

$$V = \sum \frac{\gamma m}{r}$$

$$\therefore \quad \frac{\partial V}{\partial x} = \sum \left(\frac{-\gamma m}{r^2} \frac{\partial r}{\partial x} \right)$$

$$= -\gamma \sum \frac{m}{r^2} \frac{x-a}{r}$$

$$= -\gamma \sum \frac{m}{r^3}(x-a)$$

$$\therefore \quad \frac{\partial^2 V}{\partial x^2} = -\gamma \sum \left[\frac{m}{r^3} - \frac{3m}{r^4} \frac{\partial r}{\partial x}(x-a) \right]$$

$$= -\gamma \sum \left[\frac{m}{r^3} - \frac{3m}{r^4} \frac{(x-a)^2}{r} \right]$$

$$= -\gamma \sum \left[\frac{m}{r^3} - \frac{3m}{r^5}(x-a)^2 \right]$$

Similarly $$\frac{\partial^2 V}{\partial y^2} = -\gamma \sum \left[\frac{m}{r^3} - \frac{3m}{r^5}(y-b)^2 \right]$$

and $$\frac{\partial^2 V}{\partial z^2} = -\gamma \sum \left[\frac{m}{r^3} - \frac{3m}{r^5}(z-c)^2 \right]$$

Hence $$\frac{\partial^2 V}{\partial x^2} + \frac{\partial^2 V}{\partial y^2} + \frac{\partial^2 V}{\partial z^2}$$

$$= -\gamma \sum \left[\frac{3m}{r^3} - \frac{3m}{r^5} \sum (x-a)^2 \right]$$

$$= -\gamma \sum \left[\frac{3m}{r^3} - \frac{3m}{r^3} \right]$$

$$= 0$$

7.7. Independent Proof of Poisson's Theorem

Statement. If V be the potential of a body at any point $P(x, y, z)$ which is inside the mass of the body where the density is ρ, then

$$\frac{\partial^2 V}{\partial x^2}+\frac{\partial^2 V}{\partial y^2}+\frac{\partial^2 V}{\partial z^2}=-4\pi\gamma\rho$$

Proof. Let (x, y, z) be the coordinates of a point P, which is inside the attracting matter. Now draw a sphere of small radius t enclosing the point P and let (a, b, c) be the coordinates of the centre of this sphere. Take the radius t so small that the matter in this sphere may be regarded as of uniform density ρ.

The whole matter which is attracting may be taken as made up of two parts first by the matter within the sphere whose potential is say V_2 and the matter without the sphere whose potential is say V_1.

$\therefore \quad V = V_1 + V_2$ or $\nabla^2 V = \nabla^2 V_1 + \nabla^2 V_2$

Since P is external to the attracting matter which produces the potential V_1, therefore by Laplace's theorem $\nabla^2 V_1 = 0$.

Hence $\nabla^2 V = \nabla^2 V_2$

The point $P(x, y, z)$ is inside the sphere whose centre is (a, b, c) and radius t. If r be the distance of P from the centre then $r^2 = (x - a)^2 + (y - b)^2 + (z - c)^2$

$$\therefore \quad r\frac{\partial r}{\partial x}=x-a$$

Since V_2 is the potential of this sphere at the internal point P, therefore

$$V_2 = \frac{2}{3}\pi\gamma\rho\left(3t^2-r^2\right)$$

$$\therefore \quad \frac{\partial V_2}{\partial x} = \frac{2}{3}\pi\gamma\rho\left(-2r\frac{\partial r}{\partial x}\right)=-\frac{4}{3}\pi\gamma\rho\,(x-a)$$

$$\therefore \quad \frac{\partial^2 V_2}{\partial x^2} = -\frac{4}{3}\pi\gamma\rho$$

Similarly,

$$\frac{\partial^2 V}{\partial y^2} = -\frac{4}{3}\pi\gamma\rho \text{ and } \frac{\partial^2 V}{\partial z^2}=-\frac{4}{3}\pi\gamma\rho$$

$$\therefore \quad \nabla^2 V = \nabla^2 V_2 = \frac{\partial^2 V}{\partial x^2}+\frac{\partial^2 V}{\partial y^2}+\frac{\partial^2 V}{\partial z^2}$$

$$= -4\pi\gamma\rho.$$

7.8. Green's Theorem

Statement. If ϕ and ψ be the scalar point functions which together with their derivatives in any direction are continuous within the region V bounded by a closed surface S, show that

(i) $$\iiint_V \left(\vec{\nabla}\phi \cdot \vec{\nabla}\psi\right) dv = \iint_S \left(\phi\, \vec{\nabla}\psi\right) \cdot \vec{n} ds - \iiint_V \phi \overrightarrow{\nabla^2} \psi dv$$

$$= \iint_S (\psi \nabla \phi) \cdot \vec{n} ds - \iiint_V \psi \nabla^2 \phi dv$$

(ii) $$\iiint_V \left(\phi \nabla^2 \psi - \psi \nabla^2 \phi\right) dv = \iint_S \left(\phi \vec{\nabla}\psi - \psi \vec{\nabla}\phi\right) \cdot \vec{n} ds$$

$$= \iint_S \left(\phi \frac{d\psi}{dn} - \psi \frac{d\phi}{dn}\right) ds$$

Proof. According to Gauss's Divergence theorem

$$\iint_S \vec{F} \cdot \vec{n} ds = \iiint_V div\, \vec{F} dv \quad \dots (1)$$

Replacing $\vec{F}$ by $\phi \vec{\nabla} \psi$ in (1), we get

$$\iint_S \left(\phi \vec{\nabla}\psi\right) \cdot \vec{n} ds = \iiint_V div\left(\phi \vec{\nabla}\psi\right) dv$$

$$= \iiint_V \left[\phi\, div\left(\vec{\nabla}\psi\right) + \vec{\nabla}\psi \cdot \vec{\nabla}\phi\right] dv$$

$$\left[\because div\left(\phi \vec{a}\right) = \phi\, div\, \vec{a} + \vec{a}\, \vec{\nabla}\, \phi\right]$$

$$= \iiint_V \left[\phi\, \vec{\nabla} \cdot \left(\vec{\nabla}\psi\right) + \left(\vec{\nabla}\psi\right) \cdot \left(\vec{\nabla}\phi\right)\right] dv$$

$$= \iiint_V \phi \overrightarrow{\nabla^2} \psi dv + \iiint_V \left(\vec{\nabla}\phi\right)\left(\vec{\nabla}\psi\right) dv$$

$$\iiint_V \left(\vec{\nabla}\phi\right) \cdot \left(\vec{\nabla}\psi\right) dv = \iint_S \left(\phi \vec{\nabla}\psi\right) \cdot \vec{n}\, ds - \iiint_V \phi \overrightarrow{\nabla^2} \psi\, dv \quad \dots (2)$$

Interchanging the roles of ϕ and ψ in (2), we have

$$\iiint_V \left(\vec{\nabla}\psi\right) \cdot \left(\vec{\nabla}\phi\right) dv = \iint_S \left(\psi \vec{\nabla}\phi\right) \vec{n}\, ds - \iiint_V \psi \overrightarrow{\nabla^2} \phi dv \quad \dots (3)$$

From (2) and (3), the result (1) follows.

For (ii), we subtract (2) from (3)

$$\iint_S (\phi\vec{\nabla}\psi - \psi\vec{\nabla}\phi)\cdot\vec{n}\,ds = \iiint_V (\phi\nabla^2\psi - \psi\nabla^2\phi)\,dv \quad \ldots (4)$$

Also since $\frac{d\phi}{dn}, \frac{d\psi}{dn}$ are directional derivatives in the directions of $\vec{n}$, we have

$$\phi\vec{\nabla}\psi - \psi\vec{\nabla}\phi = \left(\phi\frac{d\psi}{dn} - \psi\frac{d\phi}{dn}\right)\vec{n} \quad \ldots (5)$$

Using (5) in (4), we get

$$\iint_S \left(\phi\overrightarrow{\nabla^2}\psi - \psi\nabla^2\phi\right) dv = \iint_S \left(\phi\frac{d\psi}{dn} - \psi\frac{d\phi}{dn}\right)\vec{n}$$

7.9. Stoke's Theorem

Statement. Let S be a piecewise smooth open surface bounded by a piecewise smooth simple closed curve C. Let $F(x, y, z)$ be a continuous vector function which has continuous first partial derivatives in a region of space which contains S in its interior.

Then $\iint_S \left(\text{curl}\,\vec{F}\right)\cdot\vec{n}\,ds = \int_C \vec{F}\cdot d\vec{r}$

Proof. Let R be the projection of S on the xy plane which is bounded by a simple closed curve K.

Again let S be represented by $z = f(x, y)$ where f is a single valued continuous and differentiable function. Similarly we may have projections of S on other planes and S be represented by $x = g(y, z)$ and $y = h(x, z)$ etc.

Let $\vec{F} = F_1\vec{I} + F_2\vec{J} + F_3\vec{K}$

Curl $\vec{F} = \vec{\nabla}\times\vec{F} = \vec{\nabla}\times\left(F_1\vec{I} + F_2\vec{J} + F_3\vec{K}\right)$

$$\text{Curl } F_1\vec{I} = \begin{vmatrix} \vec{I} & \vec{J} & \vec{K} \\ \frac{\partial}{\partial x} & \frac{\partial}{\partial y} & \frac{\partial}{\partial z} \\ F_1 & 0 & 0 \end{vmatrix} = \frac{\partial F_1}{\partial z}\vec{J} - \frac{\partial F_1}{\partial y}\vec{K}$$

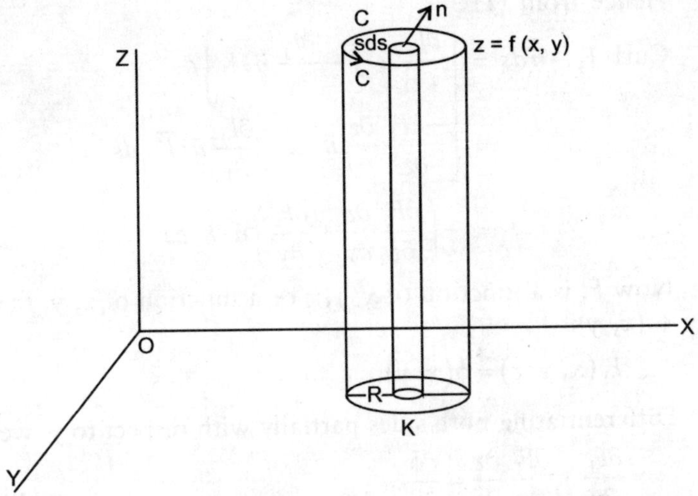

$$\therefore \text{Curl } F_1\vec{I}\cdot\vec{n}\,ds = \left(\frac{\partial F_1}{\partial z}\,\vec{n}\cdot\vec{J} - \frac{\partial F_1}{\partial y}\,\vec{n}\cdot\vec{K}\right)ds \qquad \text{... (1)}$$

Now if $\vec{r}$ is the position vector of any point on S, then

$$\vec{r} = x\vec{I} + y\vec{J} + z\vec{K}$$
$$= x\vec{I} + y\vec{J} + f(x, y)\vec{K}$$

$$\therefore \quad \frac{\partial \vec{r}}{\partial y} = \vec{J} + \frac{\partial f}{\partial y}\vec{K} = \vec{J} + \frac{\partial z}{\partial y}\vec{K}$$

$$\therefore \quad \vec{n}\cdot\frac{\partial \vec{r}}{\partial y} = \vec{n}\cdot\vec{J} + \frac{\partial z}{\partial y}\,\vec{n}\cdot\vec{K}$$

But $\frac{\partial \vec{r}}{\partial y}$ is a vector which is tangent to S and $\vec{n}$ is normal so that

$$\vec{n}\,\frac{\partial \vec{r}}{\partial y} = 0$$

$$\vec{n}\cdot\vec{J} + \frac{\partial z}{\partial y}\,\vec{n}\cdot\vec{K} = 0$$

$$\vec{n}\cdot\vec{J} = -\frac{\partial z}{\partial y}\,\vec{n}\cdot\vec{K}$$

Hence from (1)

$$\text{Curl } F_1\vec{I}\cdot\vec{n}\,ds = \left[\frac{\partial F_1}{\partial z}\,\vec{n}\cdot\vec{J} - \frac{\partial F_1}{\partial y}\,\vec{n}\cdot\vec{K}\right]ds$$

$$= \left[\frac{-\partial F_1}{\partial z}\frac{\partial z}{\partial y}\,\vec{n}\cdot\vec{K} - \frac{\partial F_1}{\partial y}\,\vec{n}\cdot\vec{K}\right]ds$$

$$= -\left(\frac{\partial F_1}{\partial z}\frac{\partial z}{\partial y} + \frac{\partial F_1}{\partial y}\right)\vec{n}\cdot\vec{K}\,ds \qquad \dots (2)$$

Now F_1 is a function of x, y, z or a function of $x, y, f(x, y)$ say $\phi(x, y)$

$$F_1(x, y, z) = \phi(x, y)$$

Differentiating both sides partially with respect to y, we get

$$\frac{\partial F_1}{\partial y} + \frac{\partial F_1}{\partial z}\frac{\partial z}{\partial y} = \frac{\partial \phi}{\partial y} \qquad \dots (3)$$

Hence from (2), we get

$$\text{Curl } F_1\vec{I}\cdot\vec{n}\,ds = -\frac{\partial \phi}{\partial y}\,dx\,dy$$

$$\therefore \quad \int_S \text{Curl } F_1\vec{I}\cdot\vec{n}\,ds = \iint_R -\frac{\partial \phi}{\partial y}\,dx\,dy \qquad \dots (4)$$

By Green's Theorem

$$\int_C (M\,dx + N\,dy) = \iint_S \left(\frac{\partial N}{\partial x} - \frac{\partial M}{\partial y}\right)dx\,dy$$

where S is a plane surface i.e. R

Choosing $M = \phi$ and $N = 0$, we get

$$\int_K \phi\,dx = \iint_R \left(0 - \frac{\partial \phi}{\partial y}\right)dx\,dy = \iint_R -\frac{\partial \phi}{\partial y}\,dx\,dy$$

where K is the boundary of R

Now at each point (x, y) of boundary K, the value of ϕ is the same as the value of F_1 at each point (x, y, z) of C.

$$\therefore \quad F_1(x, y, z) = \phi(x, y)$$

$$\int_K \phi\,dx = \int_C F_1\,dx$$

$$\int_C F_1 dx = \int_K \phi\, dx = \iint_R -\frac{\partial \phi}{\partial y}\, dx\, dy \qquad \ldots (5)$$

Hence (4) by the help of (5) becomes

$$\iint_S \text{Curl } F_1 \vec{I} \cdot \vec{n}\, ds = \int_C F_1 dx$$

Similarly considering the projection on other coordinate planes we have

$$\int \text{Curl } F_2 \vec{J} \cdot \vec{n}\, ds = \int_C F_2 dy$$

$$\int \text{Curl } F_3 \vec{K} \cdot \vec{n}\, ds = \int_C F_3 dz$$

Adding all these, we get

$$\int_S \text{Curl}\left(F_1 \vec{I} + F_2 \vec{J} + F_3 \vec{K}\right) \cdot \vec{n}\, ds = \int_C \left(F_1 dx + F_2 dy + F_3 dz\right)$$

or $$\int_S \text{Curl } \vec{F} \cdot \vec{n}\, ds = \int_C \vec{F} \cdot d\vec{r}$$

Cartesian Form of Stokes Theorem

Let F_1, F_2, F_3 be the components of vector point function $\vec{F}$ so that $\vec{F} = F_1 \vec{I} + F_2 \vec{J} + F_3 \vec{K}$ and a unit outward drawn normal.

$$\vec{n} = l\vec{I} + m\vec{J} + n\vec{K}$$

where l, m, n are direction cosines.

Again $\vec{r} = x\vec{I} + y\vec{J} + z\vec{K}$

or $d\vec{r} = dx\vec{I} + dy\vec{J} + dz\vec{K}$

$$\therefore \quad \int_C \vec{F} \cdot d\vec{r} = \int_C \left(F_1 dx + F_2 dy + F_3 dz\right)$$

$$\text{Curl } \vec{F} = \begin{vmatrix} \vec{I} & \vec{J} & \vec{K} \\ \dfrac{\partial}{\partial x} & \dfrac{\partial}{\partial y} & \dfrac{\partial}{\partial z} \\ F_1 & F_2 & F_3 \end{vmatrix}$$

$$= \vec{I}\left(\frac{\partial F_3}{\partial y} - \frac{\partial F_2}{\partial z}\right) + \vec{J}\left(\frac{\partial F_1}{\partial z} - \frac{\partial F_3}{\partial x}\right) + \vec{K}\left(\frac{\partial F_2}{\partial x} - \frac{\partial F_1}{\partial y}\right)$$

$$\therefore \ \vec{n}\cdot\text{Curl}\,\vec{F} = l\left(\frac{\partial F_3}{\partial y} - \frac{\partial F_2}{\partial z}\right) + m\left(\frac{\partial F_1}{\partial z} - \frac{\partial F_3}{\partial x}\right) + n\left(\frac{\partial F_2}{\partial x} - \frac{\partial F_1}{\partial y}\right)$$

Hence $\vec{n}\cdot\text{Curl}\,\vec{F}\,ds = \sum\left(\frac{\partial F_3}{\partial y} - \frac{\partial F_2}{\partial z}\right) l\,ds$

$$= \sum\left(\frac{\partial F_3}{\partial y} - \frac{\partial F_2}{\partial z}\right) dy\,dz$$

Since $l ds = \cos\alpha\, ds = dy\, dz$

Now by Stokes Theorem

$$\int_C \vec{F}\cdot d\vec{r} = \int_S \vec{n}\cdot\text{curl}\,\vec{F}ds$$

or $\int_S (F_1 dx + F_2 dy + F_3 dz)$

$$= \int_C \left[\left(\frac{\partial F_3}{\partial y} - \frac{\partial F_2}{\partial z}\right) dy\,dz + \left(\frac{\partial F_1}{\partial z} - \frac{\partial F_3}{\partial x}\right) dz\,dx + \left(\frac{\partial F_2}{\partial x} - \frac{\partial F_1}{\partial y}\right) dx\,dy\right]$$

7.10. To find the distribution for a given potential

If the potential of a distribution is given throughout all space we can determine the corresponding distribution. If V be known we can find $\overrightarrow{\nabla^2} V$ for every point of the space and when $\overrightarrow{\nabla^2} V = 0$ the corresponding density of the distribution is zero by Poisson's equation which in other words mean that there is no attracting mass at all such points. But when $\overrightarrow{\nabla^2} V$ is not zero then we know by Gauss's Theorem that

$$\overrightarrow{\nabla^2} V = -4\pi\gamma \text{ density}$$

density is $-\dfrac{1}{4\pi\gamma}\overrightarrow{\nabla^2}V$

If the form of the potential function inside any surface S is different from its form outside and if there be an abrupt charge in the value of $\dfrac{\partial V}{\partial n}$ as we pass across the surface, then the surface distribution σ on S is given by

$$\frac{\partial V_1}{\partial n_1}\delta s+\frac{\partial V_2}{\partial n_2}\delta s=-4\pi\gamma\left(\delta s\cdot\sigma\right)$$

$$\frac{\partial V_1}{\partial n_1}+\frac{\partial V_2}{\partial n_2}=-4\pi\gamma\sigma$$

Where δn_1 and δn_2 are the small lengths of the normals drawn outward from each of the two faces δs, δs.

Thus δn_2 is in the direction of the outward normal to the given surface S and δn_1 in the opposite direction.

Hence we have $-\dfrac{\partial V_1}{\partial n_1}+\dfrac{\partial V_2}{\partial n_2}=-4\pi\gamma\sigma$

If δn be an element of outward normal at any point of the given surface S, then above equation becmes in limit

$$-\frac{\partial V_1}{\partial n}+\frac{\partial V_2}{\partial n}=-4\pi\gamma\sigma$$

$$\Rightarrow\quad \sigma=\frac{1}{4\pi\gamma}\left(\frac{\partial V_1}{\partial n}-\frac{\partial V_2}{\partial n}\right)$$

This gives the formula for surface density of attracting matter.

WORKED OUT EXAMPLES

1. Find what distribution of matter will give rise to the follwing potentials:

$$V=\frac{4\gamma Aaz}{r^3},\ \text{when } r>a$$

$$V=\gamma A\,\frac{3a^2+4az-3r^2}{a^3}\quad \text{when } r<a$$

where $r^2 = x^2 + y^2 + z^2$

Solution: We know that

$x = r \sin\theta \cos\phi,\ y = r \sin\theta \sin\phi,\ z = r\cos\theta$

So that $x^2 + y^2 = r^2 \sin^2\theta$ and $x^2 + y^2 + z^2 = r^2$

Also Poisson's equation in polar form is

$$\frac{\partial^2 V}{\partial r^2} + \frac{2}{r}\frac{\partial V}{\partial r} + \frac{1}{\partial^2}\frac{\partial^2 V}{\partial \theta^2} + \frac{\cot\theta}{\partial^2}\frac{\partial V}{\partial \theta} + \frac{1}{r^2 \sin^2\theta}\frac{\partial^2 V}{\partial \phi^2} = -4\pi\gamma\rho \qquad \ldots (1)$$

Case I. When $r < a$, let the potential be denoted by V_1

$$V_1 = \gamma A \frac{3a^2 + 4az - 3r^2}{a^3}$$

$$V_1 = \frac{\gamma A}{a^3}\left(3a^2 + 4ar\cos\theta - 3r^2\right)$$

$$\therefore \quad \frac{\partial V_1}{\partial r} = \frac{\gamma A}{a^3}(4a\cos\theta - 6r)$$

$$\frac{\partial^2 V_1}{\partial r^2} = \frac{\gamma A}{a^3}(-6)$$

$$\frac{\partial V_1}{\partial \theta} = \frac{\gamma A}{a^3}(-4ar\sin\theta)$$

$$\frac{\partial^2 V_1}{\partial \theta^2} = \frac{\gamma A}{a^3}(-4ar\cos\theta)$$

$$\frac{\partial V_1}{\partial \phi} = 0,\ \frac{\partial^2 V_1}{\partial \phi^2} = 0$$

If ρ_1 be the density at any point when $r < a$, then from (1), on substituting the values of various derivatives, we get

$$\frac{\gamma A}{a^3}\left[-6 + \frac{2}{r}(4a\cos\theta - 6r) + \frac{1}{r^2}(-4ar\cos\theta) + \frac{\cot\theta}{r^2}(-4ar\sin\theta)\right] = -4\pi\gamma\rho_1$$

$$\rho_1 = -\frac{1}{4\pi\gamma}\frac{\gamma A}{a^3}\left[-6 + \frac{8a}{r}\cos\theta - 12 - \frac{4a}{r}\cos\theta - \frac{4a}{r}\cos\theta\right]$$

$$= \frac{A \times 18}{4\pi a^3} = \frac{9A}{2\pi a^3}$$

Case II. When $r > a$ i.e. for external points

$$V_2 = \frac{4\gamma Aaz}{r^3} = \frac{4\gamma Aar\cos\theta}{r^3} = \frac{4\gamma Aa\cos\theta}{r^2}$$

$$\frac{\partial V_2}{\partial r} = 4\gamma Aa\left(-\frac{2\cos\theta}{r^3}\right)$$

$$\frac{\partial^2 V_2}{\partial r^2} = 4\gamma Aa\left(\frac{6}{r^4}\cos\theta\right)$$

$$\frac{\partial V_2}{\partial \theta} = 4\gamma Aa\left(-\frac{\sin\theta}{r^2}\right)$$

$$\frac{\partial^2 V_2}{\partial \theta^2} = 4\gamma Aa\left(-\frac{\cos\theta}{r^2}\right)$$

$$\frac{\partial V_2}{\partial \phi} = 0, \frac{\partial^2 V_2}{\partial \phi^2} = 0$$

Now if ρ_2 be the density of the matter at any point where $r > a$, then on substituting the values of various derivates in (1), we get

$$4\gamma Aa\left[\frac{6\cos\theta}{r^4} - \frac{4\cos\theta}{r^4} - \frac{\cos\theta}{r^4} - \frac{\cos\theta}{r^4}\right] = -4\pi\gamma\rho_2$$

$$-4\pi\gamma\rho_2 = 0$$

Above gives that $\rho_2 = 0$ show that there is no attracting matter when $r > a$.

Surface density. Let σ be the surface density when $r = a$, then

$$\sigma = \frac{1}{4\pi\gamma}\left[\frac{\partial V_1}{\partial r} - \frac{\partial V_2}{\partial r}\right]_{r=a}$$

$$= \frac{1}{4\pi\gamma}\left[\frac{\gamma A}{a^3}(4a\cos\theta - 6r) - 4\gamma Aa\left(-\frac{2}{r^3}\cos\theta\right)\right]_{r=a}$$

$$= \frac{1}{4\pi\gamma}\left[\frac{\gamma A}{a^2}(4\cos\theta - 6) + \frac{8\gamma A}{a^2}\cos\theta\right]$$

$$= \frac{\gamma A}{a^2 4\pi\gamma}[12\cos\theta - 6]$$

$$= \frac{3A}{2\pi a^2}(2\cos\theta - 1)$$

$$= \frac{3A}{2\pi a^2}\left(\frac{2z}{a} - 1\right)$$

as on the surface $r = a$, $z = a\cos\theta$.

Thus the distribution is a solid sphere of radius a and density $\frac{9A}{2\pi a^2}$ together with a surface density $\frac{3A}{2\pi a^2}\left(\frac{2r}{a} - 1\right)$.

2. The potential of a certain distribution of matter at a point (x, y, z) is

$$\frac{4\gamma\mu\pi}{3}\frac{a^4}{r} + \frac{4\gamma\mu\pi}{15}a^6\frac{(2x^2 - y^2 - z^2)}{r^5}$$

$$\text{or} \quad \frac{4\gamma\mu\pi}{3}a^2 + \frac{4\gamma\mu\pi}{15}a(2x^2 - y^2 - z^2)$$

according as $r = \sqrt{x^2 + y^2 + z^2}$ is greater or less than a. Find the distribution.

Solution: We have $x = r\sin\theta\cos\phi$, $y = r\sin\theta\sin\phi$, $z = r\cos\theta$

$$2x^2 - (y^2 + z^2) = 3x^2 - (x^2 + y^2 + z^2)$$
$$= 3r^2\sin^2\theta\cos^2\phi - r^2$$

Case I. When $r < a$, then potential

$$V_1 = \frac{4\gamma\mu\pi}{3}a^3 + \frac{4\gamma\mu\pi}{15}a(3r^2\sin^2\theta\cos^2\phi - r^2)$$

$$\frac{\partial V_1}{\partial r} = \frac{4\pi\gamma\mu a}{15}(3\sin^2\theta\cos^2\phi - 1)\,2r$$

$$\frac{\partial^2 V_1}{\partial r^2} = \frac{4\pi\gamma\mu a}{15}(6r^2\sin\theta\cos\theta\cos^2\phi)$$

$$\frac{\partial^2 V_1}{\partial \theta^2} = \frac{4\pi\gamma\mu a}{15}\left[6r^2\left(\cos^2\theta - \sin^2\theta\right)\cos^2\phi\right]$$

$$\frac{\partial V_1}{\partial \phi} = -\frac{4\pi\gamma\mu}{15}a\left(6r^2\sin^2\theta\sin\phi\cos\phi\right)$$

$$\frac{\partial^2 V_1}{\partial \phi^2} = \frac{4\pi\gamma\mu}{15}\left[6r^2\left(\sin^2\phi - \cos^2\phi\right)\sin^2\theta\right]$$

Poisson's equation in polar coordinates is

$$\frac{\partial^2 V}{\partial r^2} + \frac{2}{r}\frac{\partial V}{\partial r} + \frac{1}{r^2}\frac{\partial^2 V}{\partial \theta^2} + \frac{\cot\theta}{r^2}\frac{\partial V}{\partial \theta} + \frac{1}{r^2\sin^2\theta}\frac{\partial^2 V}{\partial \phi^2} = -4\pi\gamma\rho$$

On putting the values of various derivatives, we get

$$\frac{4\gamma\mu\pi a}{15}\Big[\left(6\sin^2\theta\cos^2\phi - 2\right) + \left(12\sin^2\theta\cos^2\phi - 4\right) + \left(6\cos^2\theta\cos^2\phi - 6\sin^2\theta\cos^2\phi\right) + \left(6\cos^2\theta\cos^2\phi\right) + \left(-6\cos^2\phi + 6\sin^2\phi\right)\Big] = -4\pi\gamma\rho_1$$

where ρ_1 is the density of the matter at any point where $r < a$,

or $$\frac{4\gamma\mu\pi a}{15}\left[12\cos^2\phi - 6 - 6\cos^2\phi\right] = -4\pi\gamma\rho_1$$

or $$\frac{4\gamma\mu\pi a}{15}\left[12\cos^2\phi - 6.2\cos^2\phi\right] = -4\pi\gamma\rho_1$$

$\therefore \quad \rho_1 = 0$

This shows that there is no attracting matter when $r < a$.

Case II. When $r > a$, then the potential V_2

$$V_2 = \frac{4\pi\gamma\mu}{3}\frac{a^4}{r} + \frac{4\pi\gamma\mu a^6 r^2}{15\, r^5}\left(3\sin^2\theta\cos^2\phi - 1\right)$$

$$= \frac{4\pi\gamma\mu}{3}\frac{a^4}{r} + \frac{4\pi\gamma\mu a^6}{15}\frac{\left(3\sin^2\theta\cos^2\phi - 1\right)}{r^3}$$

$$\frac{\partial V_2}{\partial r} = 4\pi\gamma\mu a^4\left[-\frac{1}{3r^2} - \frac{3a^2}{15^5}\frac{\left(3\sin^2\theta\cos^2\phi - 1\right)}{r^4}\right]$$

$$\frac{\partial^2 V_2}{\partial r^2} = 4\pi\gamma\mu a^4\left[\frac{2}{3r^3} + \frac{12a^2\left(3\sin^2\theta\cos^2\phi - 1\right)}{15r^5}\right]$$

$$\frac{\partial V_2}{\partial \theta} = \frac{4\pi\gamma\mu a^6}{15}\frac{\left(3.2\sin\theta\cos\theta\cos^2\phi\right)}{r^3}$$

$$\frac{\partial^2 V_2}{\partial \theta^2} = \frac{4\pi\gamma\mu a^6}{15}\frac{\left[6\cos^2\phi\left(\cos^2\theta - \sin^2\theta\right)\right]}{r^3}$$

$$\frac{\partial V_2}{\partial \phi} = 4\pi\gamma\mu a^4\left[\frac{a^2}{15}\times\frac{-6\sin^2\theta\cos\phi\sin\phi}{r^3}\right]$$

$$\frac{\partial^2 V_2}{\partial \phi^2} = 4\pi\gamma\mu a^4\left[\frac{a^2}{15}\times\frac{-6\sin^2\theta\left(\cos^2\phi - \sin^2\phi\right)}{r^3}\right]$$

If ρ_2 be the density at any point when $r > a$, then substituting values of derivatives in Poisson's equation, we get

$$4\pi\gamma\mu a^4 0 = -4\pi\gamma\rho_2$$

$$\therefore \qquad \rho_2 = 0$$

This shows that there is no attracting matter, when $r > a$.

Surface Density. Let σ be the surface density i.e. density when $r = a$, then

$$\sigma = \frac{1}{4\pi\gamma}\left[\left(\frac{\partial V_1}{\partial r}\right) - \left(\frac{\partial V_2}{\partial r}\right)\right]_{r=a}$$

$$= \frac{1}{4\pi\gamma}\left[\frac{8\pi\gamma\rho a^2}{15}\left(3\sin^2\theta\cos^2\phi - 1\right)\right.$$

$$\left. + 4\pi\gamma\mu a^4\left\{\frac{1}{3a^2} + \frac{3a^2}{15}\left(\frac{3\sin^2\theta\cos^2\phi - 1}{a^4}\right)\right\}\right]$$

$$= \frac{1}{4\pi\gamma}4\pi\gamma\mu a^2\sin^2\theta\cos^2\phi$$

$$= \mu a^2\sin^2\theta\cos^2\phi$$

$$= \mu x^2$$

Thus the distribution is a thin spherical shell of radius a and density μx^2.

3. What distribution of matter will produce a potential

$$\frac{\gamma M}{a}\left(1-\frac{x}{3a}\right) \text{ or } \frac{\gamma M}{r}\left(1-\frac{ax}{3r^2}\right)$$

according as $r=\sqrt{x^2+y^2+z^2}$ is less or greater than a.

[M.U. 2001H; B.B.A.B.U. 99H]

Solution: Poisson's equation in polar coordinates is

$$\frac{\partial^2 V}{\partial r^2}+\frac{2}{r}\frac{\partial V}{\partial r}+\frac{1}{r^2}\frac{\partial^2 V}{\partial \theta^2}+\frac{\cot\theta}{r^2}\frac{\partial V}{\partial \theta}+\frac{1}{r^2\sin^2\theta}\frac{\partial^2 V}{\partial \phi^2}=-4\pi\gamma\rho \qquad \text{... (1)}$$

Case I. When $r < a$

Given

$$V_1 = \frac{\gamma M}{a}\left(1-\frac{x}{3a}\right) = \frac{\gamma M}{a}\left(1-\frac{r\sin\theta\cos\phi}{3a}\right)$$

$$\therefore \frac{\partial V_1}{\partial r} = \frac{\gamma M}{a}\left(-\frac{\sin\theta\cos\phi}{3a}\right), \frac{\partial^2 V_1}{\partial r^2}=0$$

$$\frac{\partial V_1}{\partial \theta} = \frac{\gamma M}{a}\left(\frac{-r\cos\theta\cos\phi}{3a}\right), \frac{\partial^2 V_1}{\partial \theta^2}=\frac{\gamma M}{a}\left(\frac{r\sin\theta\cos\phi}{3a}\right)$$

$$\frac{\partial V_1}{\partial \phi} = \frac{\gamma M}{a}\left(\frac{r\sin\theta\sin\phi}{3a}\right), \frac{\partial^2 V_1}{\partial \phi^2}=\frac{\gamma M}{a}\left(\frac{r\sin\theta\cos\phi}{3a}\right)$$

Let ρ_1 be the density at any point of the matter where $r < a$, then on putting the values of various derivatives in (1), we get

$$\frac{\gamma M}{a}\left[0-\frac{2\sin\theta\cos\phi}{r3a}+\frac{1}{r}\frac{\sin\theta\cos\phi}{3a}-\frac{\cot\theta}{r}\frac{\cos\theta\cos\phi}{3a}+\frac{1}{r\sin\theta}\frac{\cos\phi}{3a}\right]=-4\pi\gamma\rho_1$$

$$\frac{\gamma M}{3a^2}\left[\frac{\cos\phi}{r}\left\{-2\sin\theta+\sin\theta-\frac{\cos^2\theta}{\sin\theta}+\frac{1}{\sin\theta}\right\}\right]=-4\pi\gamma\rho_1$$

or $$\frac{\gamma M\cos\phi}{3a^2 r}\left[\frac{-\sin^2\theta-\cos^2\theta+1}{\sin\theta}\right]=-4\pi\gamma\rho_1$$

or $$0=-4\pi\gamma\rho_1$$

$$\rho_1=0$$

This shows that there exists no matter inside the sphere.

Case II. When $r > a$, then

$$V_2=\gamma M\left(\frac{1}{r}-\frac{a\sin\theta\cos\phi}{3r^2}\right)$$

$$\frac{\partial V_2}{\partial r}=\gamma M\left(-\frac{1}{r^2}+\frac{2a}{3r^3}\sin\theta\cos\phi\right)$$

$$\frac{\partial^2 V_2}{\partial r^2}=\gamma M\left(\frac{-2}{r^3}-\frac{2a\sin\theta\cos\phi}{r^4}\right)$$

$$\frac{\partial V_2}{\partial\theta}=\gamma M\left(\frac{-a\cos\theta\cos\phi}{3r^2}\right)$$

$$\frac{\partial^2 V_2}{\partial\theta^2}=\gamma M\left(\frac{a\sin\theta\sin\phi}{3r^2}\right)$$

$$\frac{\partial V_2}{\partial\phi}=\gamma M\left(\frac{a\sin\theta\sin\phi}{3r^2}\right)$$

$$\frac{\partial^2 V_2}{\partial\phi^2}=\gamma M\left(\frac{a\sin\theta\cos\phi}{3r^2}\right)$$

If ρ_2 be the density outside the sphere, we have by equation (1)

$$\gamma M\left[\left(\frac{2}{r^3}-\frac{2a\sin\theta\cos\phi}{r^4}\right)+\frac{2}{r}\left(-\frac{1}{r^2}+\frac{2a\sin\theta\cos\phi}{3r^3}\right)\right.$$
$$+\frac{1}{r^2}\left(\frac{a\sin\theta\cos\phi}{3r^2}\right)+\frac{\cot\theta}{r^2}\left(-\frac{a\cos\theta\cos\phi}{3r^2}\right)$$
$$\left.+\frac{1}{r^2\sin^2\theta}\left(\frac{a\sin\theta\cos\phi}{3r^2}\right)\right]=-4\pi\gamma\rho_2$$

$$\Rightarrow \frac{\gamma M}{r^4}\left[-\frac{a}{3}\sin\theta\cos\phi+\frac{a\sin\theta\cos\phi}{3\sin^2\theta}\right.$$
$$\left.-\frac{a\cot\theta\cos\theta\cos\phi}{3}\right]=-4\pi\gamma\rho_2$$

$$\Rightarrow \frac{\gamma Ma}{r^4}\left[-\frac{1}{3}\sin\theta\cos\phi+\frac{\sin\theta\cos\phi}{3\sin^2\theta}\left(1-\cos^2\theta\right)\right]$$
$$=-4\pi\gamma\rho_2$$

$$\Rightarrow \frac{\gamma Ma}{r^4}\left[-\frac{1}{3}\sin\theta\cos\phi+\frac{1}{3}\sin\theta\cos\phi\right]=-4\pi\gamma\rho_2$$

$$\rho_2 = 0$$

Hence no matter exists outside the sphere.

If σ be the surface density of the sphere, then

$$4\pi\gamma\sigma = \left[\frac{\partial V_1}{\partial r}-\frac{\partial V_2}{\partial r}\right]_{r=a}$$

$$= \frac{\gamma M}{a}\left(\frac{-\sin\theta\cos\phi}{3a}\right)-\gamma M\left(-\frac{1}{a^2}+\frac{2\sin\theta\cos\phi}{3a^2}\right)$$

$$= \frac{\gamma M}{a^2}(1-\sin\theta\cos\phi)$$

$$= \frac{\gamma M}{a^2}\left(1-\frac{x}{a}\right)$$

$$(\because x = r\sin\theta\cos\phi = a\sin\theta\cos\phi \text{ at } r=a)$$

So that $\sigma = \dfrac{M}{4\pi a^2}\left(1-\dfrac{x}{a}\right)$

Thus the distribution is a spherical surface of density $\dfrac{M}{4\pi a^2}\left(1-\dfrac{x}{a}\right)$.

4. In the interior of a spherical distribution of matter of radius a the gravitational potential at a distance r from the centre is

$$\frac{A\sin\dfrac{\pi r}{a}}{\dfrac{\pi r}{a}}+C$$

Prove that the density at any point is

$$\frac{\pi A}{4Ga^2}\frac{\sin\frac{\pi r}{a}}{\frac{\pi r}{a}}$$

and the mass of the whole distribution is $\frac{Aa}{G}$, where G is the constant of gravitation. Prove also that the negative potential energy is $\frac{3A^2a}{4G}$.

Solution: When G is the constant of gravitation, the Poisson's equation in polar coordinates is

$$\frac{\partial^2 V}{\partial r^2}+\frac{2}{r}\frac{\partial V}{\partial r}+\frac{1}{\partial^2}\frac{\partial^2 V}{\partial \theta^2}+\frac{\cot\theta}{r^2}\frac{\partial V}{\partial \theta}$$
$$+\frac{1}{\partial^2\sin^2\theta}\frac{\partial^2 V}{\partial \phi^2}=-4\pi G\rho \quad \text{... (1)}$$

Here $$V=\frac{A\sin\frac{\pi r}{a}}{\frac{\pi r}{a}}+C$$

$$=\frac{Aa}{\pi}\left[\frac{1}{r}\sin\frac{\pi r}{a}\right]+C$$

$$\therefore \quad \frac{\partial V}{\partial r}=\frac{Aa}{\pi}\left[-\frac{1}{r^2}\sin\frac{\pi r}{a}+\frac{1}{r}\frac{\pi}{a}\cos\frac{\pi r}{a}\right]$$

$$\frac{\partial^2 V}{\partial r^2}=\frac{Aa}{\pi}\left[\frac{2}{r^3}\sin\frac{\pi r}{a}-\frac{\pi}{ar^2}\cos\frac{\pi r}{a}\right.$$
$$\left.-\frac{\pi}{ar^2}\cos\frac{\pi r}{a}-\frac{\pi^2}{a^2r}\sin\frac{\pi r}{a}\right]$$

$$=\frac{Aa}{\pi}\left[\frac{2}{r^3}\sin\frac{\pi r}{a}-\frac{2\pi}{ar^2}\cos\frac{\pi r}{a}-\frac{\pi^2}{a^2r}\sin\frac{\pi r}{a}\right]$$

$$\frac{\partial V}{\partial \theta}=0,\ \frac{\partial^2 V}{\partial \theta^2}=0,\ \frac{\partial V}{\partial \phi}=0,\ \frac{\partial^2 V}{\partial \phi^2}=0$$

Putting these values in equation (1), we get

$$\frac{Aa}{\pi}\left[\frac{2}{r^3}\sin\frac{\pi r}{a}-\frac{2\pi}{ar^2}\cos\frac{\pi r}{a}-\frac{\pi^2}{a^2 r}\sin\frac{\pi r}{a}\right.$$

$$\left.+\frac{2}{r}\left(-\frac{1}{r^2}\sin\frac{\pi r}{a}+\frac{\pi}{ar}\cos\frac{\pi r}{a}\right)\right]=-4\pi G\rho$$

$$\Rightarrow \quad \frac{Aa}{\pi}\left[-\frac{\pi^2}{a^2 r}\sin\frac{\pi r}{a}\right]=-4\pi G\rho$$

$$\therefore \quad \rho = \frac{A}{4Ga}\frac{\sin\frac{\pi r}{a}}{r}$$

$$= \frac{\pi A}{4Ga^2}\frac{\sin\frac{\pi r}{a}}{\frac{\pi r}{a}} \qquad \ldots (2)$$

Thus the matter is a solid sphere of radius a and density ρ given by (2).

Mass of the distribution

Mass of an elementary shell

$$= 4\pi r^2\delta r\,\rho = 4\pi r^2\delta r\,\frac{\pi A}{4Ga^2}\frac{\sin\frac{\pi r}{a}}{\frac{\pi r}{a}}$$

Thus if M be the mass of the whole sphere then

$$M = \int_0^a 4\pi r^2 dr\,\frac{\pi A}{4Ga^2}\frac{\sin\frac{\pi r}{a}}{\frac{\pi r}{a}}$$

$$= \frac{\pi A}{Ga}\int_0^a r\sin\frac{\pi r}{a}\,dr$$

$$= \frac{\pi A}{Ga}\left[-r\frac{a}{\pi}\cos\frac{\pi r}{a}+\frac{a^2}{\pi^2}\sin\frac{\pi r}{a}\right]_0^a$$

$$= \frac{\pi A}{Ga}\left[\frac{a^2}{\pi}\right]=\frac{Aa}{G}$$

Negative Potential Energy

$$= \frac{1}{2}\int V dm$$

$$= \frac{1}{2}\int_0^a \left(\frac{A \sin \frac{\pi r}{a}}{\frac{\pi r}{a}} + c \right) \frac{4\pi r^2 dr \pi}{4Ga^2} \frac{A \sin \frac{\pi r}{a}}{\frac{\pi r}{a}}$$

Putting $\frac{\pi r}{a} = y$

$$\frac{\pi}{a} dr = dy$$

Hence

$$\frac{1}{2}\int V dm = \frac{1}{2}\int_0^\pi \left(\frac{A \sin y}{y} + c \right) \frac{4\pi a^2 y^2}{\pi^2} \frac{\pi A}{4Ga^2} \frac{\sin y}{y} dy$$

$$= \frac{1}{2}\frac{a}{\pi}\frac{A}{G}\int_0^\pi \left(\frac{A \sin y}{y} + c \right) y \sin y \, dy$$

$$= \frac{1}{2}\frac{a}{\pi}\frac{A}{G}\int_0^\pi \left(A \sin^2 y + Ay \sin y \right) dy$$

$$= \frac{1}{2}\frac{aA}{\pi G}\left[A\, 2 \cdot \frac{1}{2}\frac{\pi}{2} + c \left\{ -y \cos y + \sin y \right\}_0^\pi \right]$$

$$= \frac{1}{2}\frac{aA}{G\pi}\left[\frac{A\pi}{2} + c\pi \right]$$

$$= \frac{1}{2}\frac{aA}{G}\left(\frac{A}{2} + c \right) \qquad \ldots (3)$$

Now to determine C, let us determine potential at the centre of the sphere.

Potential at the centre

$$= G\int_0^a \frac{4\pi r^2 dr}{r} \frac{\pi A \sin \frac{\pi r}{a}}{4Ga^2 \left(\frac{\pi r}{a} \right)}$$

$$= G\frac{\pi A}{Ga}\int_0^a \sin\frac{\pi r}{a}\,dr$$

$$= \frac{\pi A}{a}\left[-\frac{a}{\pi}\cos\frac{\pi r}{a}\right]_0^a$$

$$= 2A$$

Also putting $r = 0$ in the given result, we get

$$V = A\frac{\sin\frac{\pi r}{a}}{\frac{\pi r}{a}} + C = A + C$$

Equating the values of the potential at the centre, we get

$$2A = A + C$$

Hence putting $C = A$ in (3) we get

$$\frac{1}{2}\int V dm = \frac{1}{2}\frac{aA}{G}\frac{3A}{2}$$

$$= \frac{3A^2 a}{4G}$$

5. The values of the potential V at any point at a distance r from a fixed point O are

$$V = 2\pi\gamma\rho\left(a^2 - b^2\right) \text{ if } r < b < a$$

$$V = 2\pi\gamma\rho\left(a^2 - \frac{r^2}{3} - \frac{2b^3}{3r}\right) \text{ if } b < r < a$$

$$V = \frac{4\pi\gamma\rho}{3}\left(\frac{a^3 - b^3}{r}\right) \text{ if } b < a < r$$

Show that the attracting system is a spherical shell of density ρ whose boundaries are spheres of centre O and radii a and b.

Solution: Since $a > b$, the outer boundary is a surface of radius a and the inner boundary is the surface of radius b.

Since in each case value of V is a function of r alone and hence the Poisson's equation becomes

$$\frac{\partial^2 V}{\partial r^2} + \frac{2}{r}\frac{\partial V}{\partial r} = -4\pi\gamma\rho \qquad \text{... (1)}$$

Case I. Let V_1 be the potential at any point inside the sphere of radius b and ρ_1 be the density there

$$V_1 = 2\pi\gamma\rho\ (a^2 - b^2)$$

$$\frac{\partial V_1}{\partial r} = 0, \frac{\partial^2 V_1}{\partial r^2} = 0$$

Hence (1) becomes $-\ 4\pi\gamma\rho_1 = 0$

$$\rho_1 = 0$$

Hence no attracting matter exists inside the sphere of radius b.

Case II. Let V_2 be the potential at any point on the space between the two spheres of radii a and b i.e. $b < r < a$ and ρ_2 be the density there

$$V_2 = 2\pi\gamma\rho\left(a^2 - \frac{r^2}{3} - \frac{2b^2}{3r}\right)$$

$$\frac{\partial V_2}{\partial r} = 2\pi\gamma\rho\left(\frac{-2r}{3} + \frac{2b^2}{3r^2}\right)$$

$$\frac{\partial^2 V_2}{\partial r^2} = 2\pi\gamma\rho\left(\frac{-2}{3} - \frac{4b^3}{3r^3}\right)$$

Hence putting these values in (1), we get

$$2\pi\gamma\rho\left[-\frac{2}{3} - \frac{4b^3}{3r^3} - \frac{4}{3} + \frac{4b^3}{3r^3}\right] = -\pi\gamma\rho_2$$

$$\Rightarrow\ -\ 4\pi\gamma\rho = -\ 4\pi\gamma\rho_2$$

$$\Rightarrow\ \rho = \rho_2$$

This shows that attracting matter exists within the space enlcosed by the two spheres and is of density ρ.

Let V_3 be the potential outside the sphere of radius a and ρ_3 be the density there.

$$V_3 = \frac{4\pi\gamma\rho}{3}\left(\frac{a^3 - b^3}{r}\right)$$

$$\frac{\partial V_3}{\partial r} = \frac{-4\pi\gamma\rho}{3}\frac{a^3-b^3}{r^2}$$

$$\frac{\partial^2 V_3}{\partial r^2} = \frac{8\pi\gamma\rho}{3}\frac{a^3-b^3}{r^3}$$

Hence from (1), we get

$$\frac{8\pi\gamma\rho}{3}\left(a^3-b^3\right)\left[\frac{1}{r^3}-\frac{1}{r^3}\right] = -4\pi\gamma\rho_3$$

$\Rightarrow \rho_3 = 0$

This shows that there is no attracting matter outside the sphere of radius a.

Hence the attracting matter is a spherical shell of density ρ bounded by the spheres of radii a and b.

6. The potential inside the finite elliptic cylinder $\frac{x^2}{a^2}+\frac{y^2}{b^2}=1$ is $V=\frac{x^2}{a^2}+\frac{y^2}{b^2}-1$ and outside it is zero. Find the distribution of matter.

Solution: Poisson's equation in Cartesian coordinates is

$$\frac{\partial^2 V}{\partial x^2}+\frac{\partial^2 V}{\partial y^2}+\frac{\partial^2 V}{\partial z^2} = -4\pi\gamma\rho \qquad \ldots (1)$$

Let V_1 be the potential for points inside the cylinder and ρ_1 be the density

$$V_1 = \frac{x^2}{a^2}+\frac{y^2}{b^2}-1$$

$$\frac{\partial V_1}{\partial x} = \frac{2x}{a^2}, \frac{\partial^2 V_1}{\partial x^2} = \frac{2}{a^2}, \frac{\partial^2 V_1}{\partial y^2} = \frac{2}{b^2}$$

$$\frac{\partial^2 V_1}{\partial z^2} = 0$$

Hence from (1), we get

$$\frac{2}{a^2}+\frac{2}{b^2} = -4\pi\gamma\rho_1$$

$$\rho_1 = -\frac{1}{2\pi\gamma}\left(\frac{1}{a^2}+\frac{1}{b^2}\right)$$

Also we are given that $V_2 = 0$ outside the cylinder and ρ_2 be the density.

So from (1), we get $\rho_2 = 0$.

Surface density. Let σ be the surface density, then

$$\frac{\partial V_1}{\partial n} - \frac{\partial V_2}{\partial n} = 4\pi\gamma\sigma \qquad \dots (2)$$

Let λ, μ, ν be the direction cosine of the normal at any point (x, y, z) of the cylinder $\frac{x^2}{a^2}+\frac{y^2}{b^2}=1$, Tangent to the cylinder $\frac{X^2}{a^2}+\frac{Y^2}{b^2}-1=0$ is

$$\frac{Xx}{a}+\frac{Yy}{b^2}-1=0$$

Hence $$\frac{\lambda}{\frac{x}{a^2}} = \frac{\mu}{\frac{y}{b^2}} = \frac{\nu}{0}$$

$$= \frac{\sqrt{\lambda^2+\mu^2+\nu^2}}{\sqrt{\frac{x^2}{a^4}+\frac{y^2}{b^4}}}$$

$$= \frac{1}{\sqrt{\frac{x^2}{a^4}+\frac{y^2}{b^4}}}$$

$$= p$$

where p is the length of perpendicular from origin on the tangent.

$$\therefore \quad \lambda = \frac{px}{a^2}, \mu = \frac{py}{b^2}, \nu = 0$$

Now $$\frac{\partial V_1}{\partial n} = \frac{\partial V_1}{\partial x}\lambda + \frac{\partial V_1}{\partial y}\mu + \frac{\partial V_1}{\partial z}\nu$$

$$= \frac{2x}{a^2} + \frac{px}{a^2} + \frac{2y}{b^2} \cdot \frac{py}{b^2}$$

$$= 2p\left(\frac{x^2}{a^4} + \frac{y^2}{b^4}\right) = 2p\,\frac{1}{p^2} = \frac{2}{p}$$

Also $V_2 = 0$

$$\therefore \quad \frac{\partial V_2}{\partial n} = 0$$

Hence from (2), we get

$$\frac{2}{p} - 0 = 4\pi\gamma\sigma$$

$$\sigma = \frac{1}{2\pi\gamma\rho}$$

Hence distribution is a uniform solid cylinder of density $-\frac{1}{2\pi\gamma}\left(\frac{1}{a^2} - \frac{1}{b^2}\right)$ for points inside it and whose surface density is $\frac{1}{2\pi\gamma\rho}$.

7. Find the distribution of matter which will produce the following potentials:

$V = 1$ within the ellipsoid $\frac{x^2}{\mu^2 a^2} + \frac{y^2}{\mu^2 b^2} + \frac{z^2}{\mu^2 c^2} = 1$

$$V = \frac{1}{1-\mu^2}\left[1 - \frac{x^2}{a^2} - \frac{y^2}{b^2} - \frac{z^2}{c^2}\right] \quad (\mu < 1)$$

between the above ellipsoid and

$$\frac{x^2}{a^2} + \frac{y^2}{b^2} + \frac{z^2}{c^2} = 1$$

Solution: $V = 0$ outside the ellipsoid

$$\frac{x^2}{a^2} + \frac{y^2}{b^2} + \frac{z^2}{c^2} = 1$$

Let V_1 be the potential within the ellipsoid.

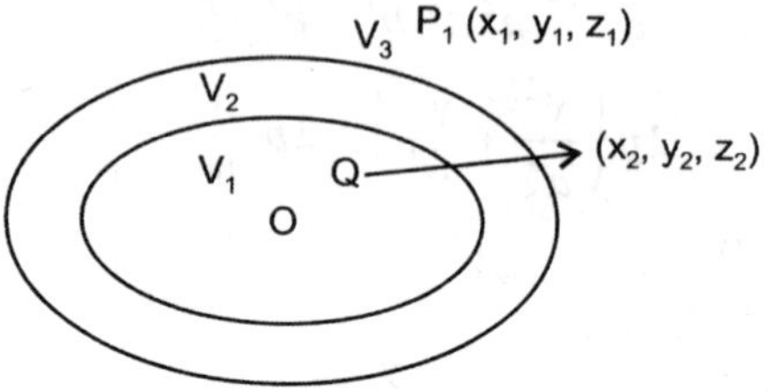

Poisson's equation in Cartesian coordinates is

$$\frac{\partial^2 V}{\partial x^2} + \frac{\partial^2 V}{\partial y^2} + \frac{\partial^2 V}{\partial z^2} = -4\pi\gamma\rho \qquad \dots (1)$$

$$V_1 = 1$$

$$\therefore \quad \frac{\partial V_1}{\partial x} = 0, \frac{\partial^2 V_1}{\partial x^2} = 0, \frac{\partial^2 V_1}{\partial y^2} = 0, \frac{\partial^2 V_1}{\partial z^2} = 0$$

Hence if ρ_1 be the density of the matter within the ellipsoid, then from (1)

$$\rho_1 = 0$$

This shows that there is no attracting matter within the ellipsoid.

Let V_2 denotes the potential between the ellipsoids

$$\frac{x^2}{\mu^2 a^2} + \frac{y^2}{\mu^2 b^2} + \frac{z^2}{\mu^2 c^2} = 1$$

and $$\frac{x^2}{a^2} + \frac{y^2}{b^2} + \frac{z^2}{c^2} = 1$$

then $$V_2 = \frac{1}{1-\mu^2}\left[1 - \frac{x^2}{a^2} - \frac{y^2}{b^2} - \frac{z^2}{c^2}\right]$$

$$\frac{\partial V_2}{\partial x} = \frac{-2x}{a^2\left(1-\mu^2\right)}, \frac{\partial^2 V_2}{\partial x^2} = \frac{-2}{a^2\left(1-\mu^2\right)}$$

Similarly $$\frac{\partial^2 V_2}{\partial y^2} = \frac{-2}{b^2\left(1-\mu^2\right)}, \frac{\partial^2 V_2}{\partial z^2} = \frac{-2}{c^2\left(1-\mu^2\right)}$$

If ρ_2 be the density of the matter at any point within this region then from (1), we get

$$\frac{-2}{(1-\mu^2)}\left(\frac{1}{a^2}+\frac{1}{b^2}+\frac{1}{c^2}\right)=-4\pi\gamma\rho_2$$

$$\therefore \quad \rho_2=\frac{1}{2\pi\gamma(1-\mu^2)}\left(\frac{1}{a^2}+\frac{1}{b^2}+\frac{1}{c^2}\right)$$

If V_3 denotes the potential outside the ellipsoid

$\frac{x^2}{a^2}+\frac{y^2}{b^2}+\frac{z^2}{c^2}=1$ then

$$V_3 = 0$$

Hence (1) gives $\rho_3 = 0$, where ρ_3 is the density outside the ellipsoid $\frac{x^2}{a^2}+\frac{y^2}{b^2}+\frac{z^2}{c^2}=1$

Surface density. If σ_1 is the surface density on the ellipsoid $\frac{x^2}{a^2}+\frac{y^2}{b^2}+\frac{z^2}{c^2}=1$, then

$$\sigma_1 = \frac{1}{4\pi\gamma}\left(\frac{\partial V_2}{\partial n}-\frac{\partial V_3}{\partial n}\right) \text{ on the surface}$$

$$= \frac{1}{4\pi\gamma}\left(\frac{\partial V_2}{\partial x}l_2+\frac{\partial V_2}{\partial y}m_2+\frac{\partial V_2}{\partial z}n_2\right) \text{ as } \frac{\partial V_3}{\partial n}=0$$

$$= \frac{1}{4\pi\gamma}\frac{-2\phi_2}{(1-\mu^2)}\left(\frac{x^2}{a^4}+\frac{y^2}{b^4}+\frac{z^2}{c^4}\right)$$

$$= \frac{-p_2}{2\pi\gamma(1-\mu^2)}\frac{1}{p_2^2}$$

$$= -\frac{1}{2\pi\gamma(1-\mu^2)p_2}$$

Again we take a point Q on the surface

$$\frac{x^2}{\mu^2a^2}+\frac{y^2}{\mu^2b^2}+\frac{z^2}{\mu^2c^2}=1.$$

If (ρ_1, m_1, n_1) be the direction cosine of the normal at Q, then

$$\frac{l_1}{\frac{x}{\mu^2 a^2}} = \frac{m_1}{\frac{y}{\mu^2 b^2}} = \frac{n_1}{\frac{z}{\mu^2 c^2}}$$

$$= \frac{1}{\sqrt{\frac{x^2}{\mu^4 a^4} + \frac{y^2}{\mu^4 b^4} + \frac{z^2}{\mu^4 c^4}}} = p_1$$

If σ_1 be the surface density of the ellipsoid

$$\frac{x^2}{\mu^2 a^2} + \frac{y^2}{\mu^2 b^2} + \frac{z^2}{\mu^2 c^2} = 1.$$

We have

$$\sigma_1 = \frac{1}{4\pi\gamma}\left[\frac{\partial V_2}{\partial n} - \frac{\partial V_1}{\partial n}\right]$$

$$= \frac{1}{4\pi\gamma}\frac{\partial V_2}{\partial n}$$

$$= \frac{1}{4\pi\gamma}\left[\frac{\partial V_2}{\partial x} l_1 + \frac{\partial V_2}{\partial y} m_1 + \frac{\partial V_2}{\partial z} n_1\right]$$

$$= \frac{1}{4\pi\gamma}\frac{-2p_1\mu^2}{(1-\mu^2)}\left(\frac{x^2}{\mu^4 a^4} + \frac{y^2}{\mu^4 b^4} + \frac{z^2}{\mu^4 c^4}\right)$$

$$= \frac{1}{4\pi\gamma}\left[\frac{-2p_1}{1-\mu^2}\frac{\mu^2}{p_1{}^2}\right]$$

$$= -\frac{1}{2\pi\gamma(1-\mu^2)}\frac{\mu^2}{p_1}$$

Similarly $\sigma_2 = -\dfrac{1}{2\pi\gamma(1-p_1^2)}\dfrac{1}{p}$

Thus the matter consists of homoeid of density $\dfrac{1}{1-\mu^2}\dfrac{1}{2\pi\gamma}\left(\dfrac{1}{a^2} + \dfrac{1}{b^2} + \dfrac{1}{c^2}\right)$ together with surface densities on the outer and inner surfaces equal to $-\frac{1}{2\pi\gamma\left(1-\mu^2\right)}\frac{1}{p_2}$ and $-\frac{1}{2\pi\gamma\left(1-\mu^2\right)}\frac{\mu^2}{p_1}$ respectively.

8. The potential outside a certain cylindrical boundary is zero, inside it is

$$V = x^3 - 3xy^2 - ax^2 + 3ay^2$$

Find the distribution of matter. [M.U. 93H, 2004H]

Solution: Let V_1 and V_2 be the potentials inside and outside the boundary, then since on the boundary, we have $V_1 = V_2$

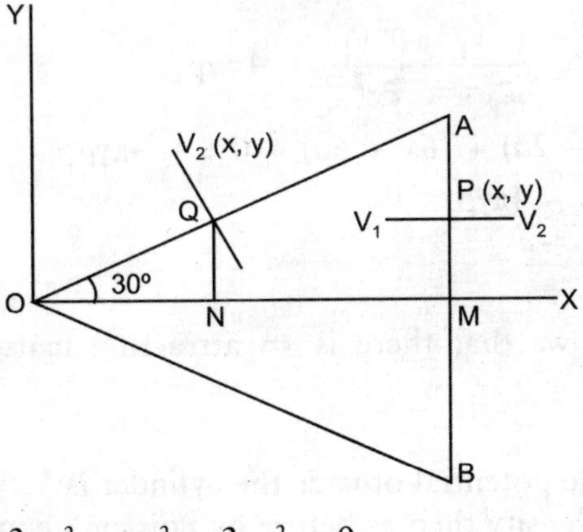

$$\therefore \quad x^3 - 3xy^2 - ax^2 + 3ay^2 = 0$$

$$\text{or} \quad x^3 - ax^2 - 3xy^2 + 3ay^2 = 0$$

$$\text{or} \quad x^2(x-a) - 3y^2(x-a)$$

$$\text{or} \quad (x-a)(x^2 - 3y^2) = 0$$

$$\left(x-a\right)\left(x-\sqrt{3}y\right)\left(x+\sqrt{3}y\right) = 0 \qquad \ldots (1)$$

This gives the equation of the boundary, i.e. equation of the surface of the cylinder.

From (1) we conclude that the section of the cylinder is an equilateral triangle ABO, whose height $OM = a$.

$$V_1 = x^3 - 3xy^2 - ax^2 + 3ay^2$$

$$\frac{\partial V_1}{\partial x} = 3x^2 - 3y^2 - 2ax$$

$$\frac{\partial^2 V_1}{\partial x^2} = 6x - 2a$$

$$\frac{\partial V_1}{\partial y} = -6xy + 6ay, \frac{\partial^2 V_1}{\partial y^2} = -6x + 6a$$

$$\frac{\partial^2 V_1}{\partial z^2} = 0$$

If ρ_1 be the density at any point inside the cylinder, then as the potential V_1 satisfies Poisson's equation

$$\frac{\partial^2 V_1}{\partial x^2} + \frac{\partial^2 V_1}{\partial y^2} + \frac{\partial^2 V_1}{\partial z^2} = -4\pi\gamma\rho_1$$

$$\Rightarrow (6x - 2a) + (6x + 6a) + 0 = -4\pi\gamma\rho_1$$

$$\Rightarrow 4a = -4\pi\gamma\rho_1$$

$$\therefore \rho_1 = \frac{-a}{\pi\gamma}$$

This shows that there is an attracting matter of density $\frac{-a}{\pi\gamma}$.

Again the potential otuside the cylinder is $V_2 = 0$ given and if ρ_2 be the density then as before by Poisson's equation we can show that $\rho_2 = 0$ i.e. there is no attracting matter outside the cylinder.

Surface density. Let σ_1 be the density at any point $P(x, y)$ on AB, whose equation is $x = a$, then

$$\sigma_1 = \left[\frac{\partial V_1}{\partial x} - \frac{\partial V_2}{\partial x}\right]\frac{1}{4\pi\gamma}$$

$$= \frac{1}{4\pi\gamma}\left[3x^2 - 3y^2 - 2x\right]_{x=a}$$

$$= \frac{1}{4\pi\gamma}\left(3a^2 - 3y^2 - 2a^2\right)$$

$$= \frac{1}{4\pi\gamma}\left(a^2 - 3y^2\right)$$

$$= \frac{1}{4\pi\gamma}3\left(\frac{a^2}{3} - y^2\right)$$

$$= \frac{3}{4\pi\gamma}\left(\frac{a}{\sqrt{3}} - y\right)\left(\frac{a}{\sqrt{3}} + y\right)$$

In ΔOAM $\tan 30 = \dfrac{AM}{OM}$

$$AM = \frac{a}{\sqrt{3}} = BM$$

and $PM = y$

$$\frac{a}{\sqrt{3}} - y = AM - PM = AP$$

and $\dfrac{a}{\sqrt{3}} + y = BM + PM = PB$

$$\sigma_1 = \frac{3}{4\pi\gamma}AP \cdot PB$$

Again let σ_2 be the surface density at any point Q on OA, then

$$\sigma_2 = \frac{1}{4\pi\gamma}\left[\frac{\partial V_1}{\partial n} - \frac{\partial V_2}{\partial n}\right]_{x=\sqrt{3}y}$$

$$= \frac{1}{4\pi\gamma}\left[\left(\frac{\partial V_1}{\partial x}\cos 120 + \frac{\partial V_1}{\partial y}\sin 120\right) - 0\right]$$

$$= \frac{1}{4\pi\gamma}\left[\left(3x^2 - 3y^2 - 2ax\right)\left(-\frac{1}{2}\right)\right.$$

$$\left. + (-6xy + 6ay) \times \frac{\sqrt{3}}{2}\right]_{x=\sqrt{3}y}$$

$$= \frac{1}{4\pi\gamma}\left[-\frac{3x^2}{2} + \frac{3}{2}y^2 + ax\right.$$

$$\left. - 3\sqrt{3}xy + 3\sqrt{3}ay\right]_{x=\sqrt{3}y}$$

$$= \frac{1}{4\pi\gamma} 4x(a-x)$$

$$= \frac{3}{4\pi\gamma} \frac{2x}{\sqrt{3}} \left(\frac{2a}{\sqrt{3}} - \frac{2x}{\sqrt{3}} \right)$$

In ΔONQ $\cos 30 = \frac{ON}{OQ}$

$$\Rightarrow \qquad ON = OQ \cos 30$$

$$\Rightarrow \qquad x = OQ \frac{\sqrt{3}}{2}$$

$$\Rightarrow \qquad OQ = \frac{2x}{\sqrt{3}}$$

Also $\qquad AB = OA = \frac{2a}{\sqrt{3}}$

Hence $\qquad \sigma_2 = \frac{3}{4\pi\gamma} OQ\,(OA - OQ)$

$$= \frac{3}{4\pi\gamma} OQ \cdot QA$$

In a similar manner we can find density σ_2 at any point R on AB.

EXERCISES

1. Find the distribution throughout a sphere, of radius a and on its surface which for a point distant r from the centre gives potential $\lambda\,(2a^2 - r^2)$ for internal points and potential $\frac{\lambda a^4}{r}$ for external points.

$$\left[\textbf{Ans. } \rho_1 = \frac{3\lambda r}{\pi\gamma},\ \rho_2 = 0,\ \sigma = \frac{-\lambda a^2}{2\pi\gamma} \right]$$

2. If the potential within an attracting medium having spherical symmetry is given by $V = \left(c^2 + r^2\right)^{-\frac{1}{2}}$ where r is the

distance from the centre and c is constant. Prove that the density is given by $\dfrac{3c^2}{4\pi\left(c^2+r^2\right)^{\frac{3}{2}}}$.

3. If the potential $V = \mu\,(1 - Lx^2 - My^2 - Nz^2)$ at all points within the ellipsoid $Lx^2 + My^2 + Nz^2 = 1$ and is zero at all external points, find the distribution.

$$\left[\textbf{Ans. } \rho_1 = \frac{\mu(L+M+N)}{2\pi\gamma},\ \rho_2 = 0,\ \sigma = \frac{-\mu}{2\pi\gamma}\cdot\frac{1}{p}\right]$$

4. If the potential at a distance r from the origin is e^{-r^2}, show that the density is $\rho = e^{-r^2}\dfrac{\left(3-2r^2\right)}{2\pi}$. [M.U. 82H]

8 EQUIPOTENTIAL SURFACES

8.1. Definition [T.M.B.U. 95H, 2004H]

The locus of a point P at which the potential of an attracting matter is the same is called equipotential surface of that attracting matter.

We know that the potential V at any point $P(x, y, z)$ for any attracting matter M will be some function of (x, y, z),

i.e. $V = \phi(x, y, z)$

If the potential V have a constant value C for all point P whose coordinates are (x, y, z) then $\phi(x, y, z) = C$... (1) is the locus of the point P, which is the equation of a surface at every point of which the attracting mass M has got the same potential. Hence equation (1) is the equation of an equipotential surface of the attracting mass M. The constant C is called the parameter. For different values of C we will have a number of equipotential surface belonging to same family.

8.2. To show that the attracting force at any point *P* is normal to the equipotential surface which passes through *P*.

[M.U. 91H; T.M.B.U. 95H; B.B.A.B.U. 96H]

Let us consider any point P' very close to P on the equipotential surface passing through P.

Then the potential at P = the potential at P' ... (1)

Then the attracting force in the direction PP'

$$= Lt \frac{\text{Potential at } P' - \text{Potential at } P}{PP'}$$

$= 0$ from (1)

This shows that the attracting force for every direction PP' lying in the tangent plane at P is zero.

Hence the resultant attraction at P must be in the direction of the normal to the equipotential surface through P.

8.3. Lines of Force

A line of force of an attracting matter is a curve such that at every point of it the resultant attraction acts along the tangent to this curve.

8.4. The potential of any attracting mass or masses cannot be an absolute maximum or minimum at any point at which there is none of the attracting mass. [I.A.S. 78]

Let the point be P at which there is none of the attracting mass. With centre P, we describe a very small sphere.

Let us suppose that the potential V is an absolute maximum at P.

Then V must be greater than the potential at any point Q of the sphere.

Therefore $\frac{dV}{dn}$ must be negative whatever be the direction in which δn is drawn from P.

Hence the force N of attraction, which equals $\frac{dV}{dn}$ at any point Q of the sphere must be always negative. This is true for all the points of the small sphere whose centre is P. Hence $\int N ds$ taken over the sphere must be a negative quantity.

Since the very small sphere with centre P contains none of the attracting mass, therefore by Gauss's theorem $\int N ds = 0$.

Hence our assumption is wrong.

Thus it is impossible that the potential at P should be maximum.

Similarly if we suppose that the potential V at P is an absolute minimum, then $\int N ds$ taken over the sphere must be a positive quantity, which is a contradiction to $\int N ds = 0$, by Gauss's theorem.

8.5. Earnshaw's Theorem

Statement. If a particle be inequilibrium under the action of forces following the law of the inverse square, the equilibrium cannot be stable for all displacements.

Proof. Let the particle be at rest at P and be displaced through a small displacement δn to Q. If it is to return towards P, then $\frac{dV}{dn}$ must be negative, and if the equilibrium is to be stable this must be true for all such displacements. Hence V must be an absolute maximum which is impossible.

Similarly, if the equilibrium is unstable for all displacements then $\frac{dV}{dn}$ be positive for all directions and therefore V is an absolute minimum at P, which is also not possible.

8.6. If the potential has given constant value *V* for all the points over a closed surface enclosing no attracting matter, then it has the same value *V* at all the points in the interior of the closed surface.

If the potential is not same at all points inside the closed surface S, then there will be some point inside the surface S at which potential is either greater or less than at any other internal point. This implies that there is some point inside the surface where the potential is either a maximum or minimum. But this is impossible. Hence the theorem.

8.7. The mean value of the potential of any attracting system of particles, taken for all points on any spherical surface is equal to the potential at the centre due to that part of the system which lies outside the sphere plus the quotient of the mass inside the sphere by the radius.

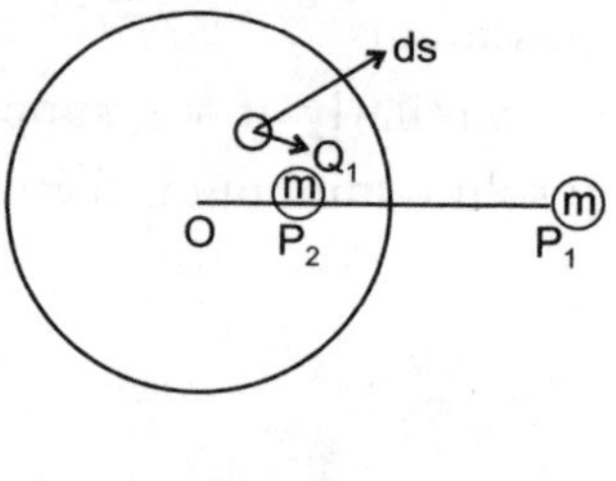

Let a be the radius and O the centre of a spherical surface and let ds be an element of the surface.

Let m be the mass of a particle placed at P_1 external to the sphere and m' the mass of the particle placed at P_2 inside the sphere.

Let Q be a point of the element ds. Let V be the potential at O, due to both the particles m and m' and V_1 the potential at the centre O, due to the mass m which is outside the sphere, so $V_1 = \dfrac{m}{OP_1}$.

By mean value of the potential over sphere is meant the quantity $\int \dfrac{Vds}{4\pi a^2}$.

So we are to prove that $\dfrac{1}{4\pi a^2}\int Vds = V_1 + \dfrac{m'}{a}$

We have $V = \dfrac{m}{P_1Q} + \dfrac{m'}{P_2Q}$

$$\therefore \quad \frac{1}{4\pi a^2}\int Vds = \frac{m}{4\pi a^2}\int \frac{ds}{P_1Q} + \frac{m'}{4\pi a^2}\int \frac{ds}{P_2Q} \quad \text{... (1)}$$

But $\int \dfrac{ds}{P_1Q}$ is the potential at P_1 due to a thin layer placed on the sphere of unit density, and is, therefore, equal to $\dfrac{4\pi a^2}{OP_1}$.

Also $\int \dfrac{ds}{P_2Q}$ is the potential at P_2 due to the same layer, and is, therefore equal to $\dfrac{4\pi a^2}{a}$.

Hence (1) becomes

$$\frac{1}{4\pi a^2}\int Vds = \frac{m}{4\pi a^2}\frac{4\pi a^2}{OP_1} + \frac{m'}{4\pi a^2}\frac{4\pi a^2}{a}$$

$$= \frac{m}{OP_1} + \frac{m'}{a}$$

$$= V_1 + \frac{m'}{a} \text{ since } \frac{m}{OP_1} = V_1$$

8.8. If the potential of a mass distribution is constant throughout any finite space unoccupied by matter it is also constant throughout all external space which can be reached without passing through external matter.

Let R be the finite space, containing no attracting matter at every point of which potential is V. If possible let the potential be something different from V, in the neighbourng space external to R. We take a point O in the space R and draw a sphere such that part of the sphere is inside R and part of it outside R. Then on the part including the centre O of the sphere inside R the potential is V and on the part of the sphere outside R the potential is different from V (either more or less than V). Hence mean value of the potential over the surface of the sphere is either more or less than V, which is impossible, as the potential at the centre O is V and there is no attracting matter inside.

Hence potential must be V throughout all external space if it is V throughout a finite space R.

8.9. If the two finite distributions of matter have the same equipotential surfaces outside both distributions, their attractions at every external point have the same direction and are proportional to the masses of the distribution.

Let M and M_1 be the masses of the two distributions of matter and V, V_1 be their potentials at any external point lying on a surface equipotential to both.

Since V is constant when V_1 is constant, therefore there must be some functional relation between V and V_1 so that

$$V_1 = f(V)$$

$$\therefore \quad \frac{\partial V_1}{\partial x} = f'(V)\frac{\partial V}{\partial x}$$

$$\frac{\partial^2 V_1}{\partial x^2} = f''(V)\left(\frac{\partial V}{\partial x}\right)^2 + f'(V)\frac{\partial^2 V}{\partial x^2}$$

Similarly

$$\frac{\partial^2 V_1}{\partial y^2} = f''(V)\left(\frac{\partial V}{\partial y}\right)^2 + f'(V)\frac{\partial^2 V}{\partial y^2}$$

$$\frac{\partial^2 V_1}{\partial z^2} = f''(V)\left(\frac{\partial V}{\partial z}\right)^2 + f'(V)\frac{\partial^2 V}{\partial z^2}$$

Now

$$\overrightarrow{\nabla^2} V_1 = \sum \frac{\partial^2 V_1}{\partial x^2}$$

$$= f''(V)\left[\left(\frac{\partial V}{\partial x}\right)^2 + \left(\frac{\partial V}{\partial y}\right)^2 + \left(\frac{\partial V}{\partial z}\right)^2\right] + f'(V)\,\overline{\nabla^2} V \quad \dots (1)$$

But V and V_1 are the potential of the two attracting matters at a point external to both the matters. Hence by Laplace's theorem

$$\overrightarrow{\nabla^2} V = 0, \overrightarrow{\nabla^2} V_1 = 0$$

Hence (1) becomes,

$$f''(V)\left[\left(\frac{\partial V}{\partial x}\right)^2 + \left(\frac{\partial V}{\partial y}\right)^2 + \left(\frac{\partial V}{\partial z}\right)^2\right] = 0$$

Hence of the second factor is not equal to zero, i.e. if V is not constant then

$$f''(V) = 0$$

Integrating it, we have $f'(V) = A$.

Again integrating we have $V_1 = f(V) = AV + B \quad \dots (2)$

where A and B are constants.

Now using the fact that V and V_1 vanish at infinity in the ratio of the masses M, M_1 of the distributions, we have

$$B = 0 \text{ and } A = \frac{M_1}{M}, \text{ so from (2)}$$

$$V_1 = \frac{M_1}{M} V$$

$$\text{i.e.} \quad \frac{V}{V_1} = \frac{M}{M_1}$$

Hence the potentials are proportional to the masses of the distributions.

Also since attraction of an attracting matter at any point of an equipotential surface is along the inward normal, hence of both the distributions, attractions at any point of their common equipotential surface, have same directions.

8.10. To find the condition that a family of surfaces be a possible family of equipotential surfaces in free space

[L.N.M.U. 94H; M.U. 94H, 96H, 99H, 2002H, 2005H; T.M.B.U. 95H, 2000H, 2002H, 2004H; B.B.A.B.U. 92H, 95H, 98H, 2000H, 2002H, 2004H]

Let V be the potential and if it is constant at these points where $\phi\ (x, y, z)$ is constant then V should be a function of $\phi\ (x, y, z)$

Let
$$V = F\left[\phi(x, y, z)\right] = F(\phi)$$

$$\therefore \quad \frac{\partial V}{\partial x} = F'(\phi)\frac{\partial \phi}{\partial x}$$

$$\frac{\partial^2 V}{\partial x^2} = F''(\phi)\left(\frac{\partial \phi}{\partial x}\right)^2 + F'(\phi)\frac{\partial^2 \phi}{\partial x^2}$$

Similarly

$$\frac{\partial^2 V}{\partial y^2} = F''(\phi)\left(\frac{\partial \phi}{\partial y}\right)^2 + F'(\phi)\frac{\partial^2 \phi}{\partial y^2}$$

$$\frac{\partial^2 V}{\partial z^2} = F''(\phi)\left(\frac{\partial \phi}{\partial z}\right)^2 + F'(\phi)\frac{\partial^2 \phi}{\partial z^2}$$

$$\therefore \quad \nabla^2 V = \frac{\partial^2 V}{\partial x} + \frac{\partial^2 V}{\partial y^2} + \frac{\partial^2 V}{\partial z^2}$$

$$= F''(\phi)\left[\left(\frac{\partial \phi}{\partial x}\right)^2 + \left(\frac{\partial \phi}{\partial y}\right)^2 + \left(\frac{\partial \phi}{\partial z}\right)^2\right]$$

$$+ F'(\phi)\left[\frac{\partial^2 \phi}{\partial x^2} + \frac{\partial^2 \phi}{\partial y^2} + \frac{\partial^2 \phi}{\partial z^2}\right] = 0 \qquad \dots (1)$$

Since in free space $\nabla^2 V = 0$ by Laplace's equation.

Hence from (1), we get

$$\frac{\dfrac{\partial^2\phi}{\partial x^2}+\dfrac{\partial^2\phi}{\partial y^2}+\dfrac{\partial^2\phi}{\partial z^2}}{\left(\dfrac{\partial\phi}{\partial x}\right)^2+\left(\dfrac{\partial\phi}{\partial y}\right)^2+\left(\dfrac{\partial\phi}{\partial z}\right)^2}=-\frac{F''(\phi)}{F'(\phi)}$$

= a function of ϕ only.

Hence the required condition that ϕ (x, y, z) = constant be a possible family of equipotential in free space is

$$\frac{\dfrac{\partial^2\phi}{\partial x^2}+\dfrac{\partial^2\phi}{\partial y^2}+\dfrac{\partial^2\phi}{\partial z^2}}{\left(\dfrac{\partial\phi}{\partial x}\right)^2+\left(\dfrac{\partial\phi}{\partial y}\right)^2+\left(\dfrac{\partial\phi}{\partial z}\right)^2} = \text{a function of } \phi \text{ only.}$$

WORKED OUT EXAMPLES

1. If the law of attraction of a thin uniform straight rod is that of the inverse cube, show that the equipotential surface are generated by the revolution of a family of curves, whose polar equation is $r^2 - a^2 = \pm\, 2ar \sin\theta \cot(cr \sin\theta)$ about the initial line, $2a$ being the length of the rod and c, a parameter.

Solution: Let O be the mid-point of the thin uniform straight rod. Given $AB = 2a$.

Here the law of attraction is of the inverse cube of the distance.

Then the potential of a mass m at P (r, θ) is

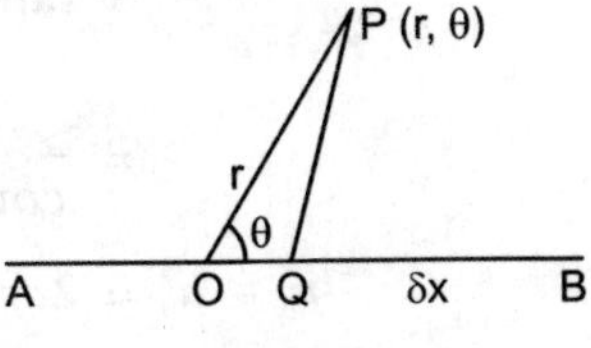

$$= \int_{\infty}^{r} -\frac{\gamma m}{R^3}\,dR$$

$$= \frac{1}{2}\gamma m\left[\frac{1}{R^2}\right]_{\infty}^{r} = \frac{\gamma m}{2r^2}$$

Let $OQ = x$, we consider an element δx at Q. Then the potential at P due to the element at Q

$$= \frac{\gamma K\rho\delta x}{2PQ^2} = \frac{\gamma K\rho\delta r}{2\left(r^2+x^2-2rx\cos\theta\right)}$$

Hence the potential V at P due to the rod AB is given by

$$V = \frac{\gamma K\rho}{2} \int_{-a}^{a} \frac{dx}{(x - r\cos\theta)^2 + r^2\sin^2\theta}$$

$$= \frac{\gamma K\rho}{2r\sin\theta} \left[\tan^{-1} \frac{x - r\cos\theta}{r\sin\theta}\right]_{-a}^{a}$$

$$= \frac{\gamma K\rho}{2r\sin\theta} \left[\tan^{-1} \frac{a - r\cos\theta}{r\sin\theta} + \tan^{-1} \frac{a + r\cos\theta}{r\sin\theta}\right]$$

$$= \frac{\gamma K\rho}{2r\sin\theta} \tan^{-1} \frac{\dfrac{a + r\cos\theta}{r\sin\theta} + \dfrac{a - r\cos\theta}{r\sin\theta}}{1 - \dfrac{a + r\cos\theta}{r\sin\theta}\,\dfrac{a - r\cos\theta}{r\sin\theta}}$$

$$= \frac{\gamma K\rho}{2r\sin\theta} \tan^{-1} \frac{2ar\sin\theta}{r^2 - a^2} \qquad \ldots (1)$$

For the equipotential surface

$$V = \text{constant} = \frac{\gamma K\rho}{2} c \qquad \text{(say)}$$

Hence from (1)

$$\frac{\gamma K\rho}{2r\sin\theta} \tan^{-1} \frac{2ar\sin\theta}{r^2 - a^2} = \frac{\gamma K\rho}{2} c$$

$$\tan^{-1} \frac{2ar\sin\theta}{r^2 - a^2} = cr\sin\theta$$

$$\frac{2ar\sin\theta}{r^2 - a^2} = \tan(cr\sin\theta)$$

$$= \frac{1}{\cot(cr\sin\theta)}$$

$$r^2 - a^2 = 2ar\sin\theta\cot(cr\sin\theta)$$

2. Two infinite straight rods alike in every respect intersect one another at right angles. Show that the equipotential curves in their plane are rectangular hyperbola.

Solution: Let K and ρ be the area of the cross-section and density of two alike rods AB and CD infinite in length and intersecting at O.

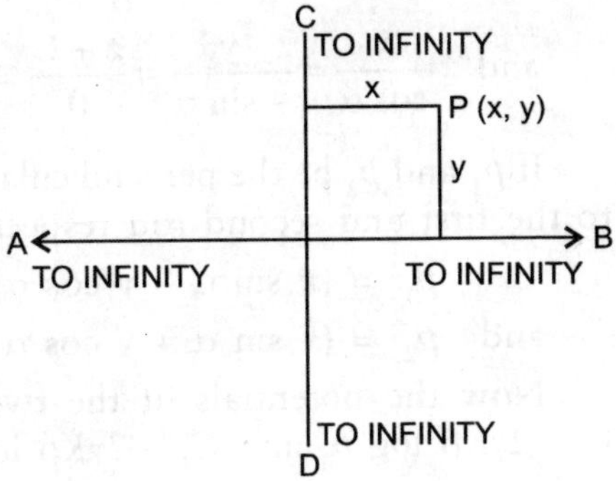

Let us take AB and CD as the axes of x and y respectively. Let P (x, y) be any point in their plane.

Then the potential at P due to $AB = C_1 - 2\gamma K\rho \log y$

The potential at P due to $CD = C_2 - 2\gamma K\rho \log x$

Hence the total potential V at P due to both the rods AB and CD is given by

$$V = C_1 + C_2 - 2\gamma K\rho (\log x + \log y)$$

$$= C_1 + C_2 - 2\gamma K\rho \log xy$$

The equipotential surface is given by V = constant.

$\therefore$ $C_1 + C_2 - 2\gamma K\rho \log xy$ = constant

$\log xy$ = const. = $\log C^2$

$\therefore$ $xy = C^2$

which represents a system of rectangular hyperbola.

3. The equation of two infinite rods of the same density are $y = x \tan \alpha$, $z = C$, $y = -x \tan \alpha$, $z = -C$.

Find the equation to their equipotential surfaces.

Also show that for a particle placed on the x-axis the region in which displacements are stable are separated from those in which they are unstable by the surfaces.

$$(Cy \cos \alpha - xz \sin \alpha) = \pm (xy \sin \alpha \cos \alpha + Cz)$$

Solution: The equation of the two rods are given as $y = x \tan \alpha$, $z = C$, and $y = -x \tan \alpha$, $z = -C$.

These equations can be written in symmetrical form

$$\frac{x}{\cos \alpha} = \frac{y}{\sin \alpha} = \frac{z - C}{0}$$

and $$\frac{x}{\cos\alpha} = \frac{y}{-\sin\alpha} = \frac{z+C}{0}$$

If p_1 and p_2 be the perpendiculars from any point $P(x, y, z)$ to the first and second rod respectively, then

$$p_1^2 = (x \sin\alpha - y\cos\alpha)^2 + (z - C)^2$$

and $$p_2^2 = (x \sin\alpha + y\cos\alpha)^2 + (z + C)^2$$

Now the potentials of the two rods at any point P are $C_1 - 2\gamma K\rho \log p_1$ and $C_2 - 2\gamma K\rho \log p_2$

Total potential due to the two rods are

$$C_1 + C_2 - 2\gamma K\rho \log p_1 - 2\gamma K\rho \log p_2$$
$$= C - \gamma K\rho \log (p_1^2\, p_2^2)$$

Equipotential surfaces are given by V = constant

$$\therefore \quad C - \gamma K\rho \log(p_1^2\, p_2^2) = \text{constant}$$

$$\therefore \quad p_1^2\, p_2^2 = \text{constant}$$

Putting the values of p_1^2 and p_2^2 found above, we get

$$\left[(x\sin\alpha - y\cos\alpha)^2 + (z-C)^2\right]$$
$$\left[(x\sin\alpha + y\cos\alpha)^2 + (z+C)^2\right] = \text{constant}$$

$$\Rightarrow \left[\left(x^2\sin^2\alpha + y^2\cos^2\alpha + z^2 + C^2\right)\right.$$
$$\left. - 2\left(xy\sin\alpha\cos\alpha + Cz\right)\right]$$
$$\times\left[\left(x^2\sin^2\alpha + y^2\cos^2\alpha + z^2 + C^2\right)\right.$$
$$\left. + 2\left(xy\sin\alpha\cos\alpha + Cz\right)\right] = \text{constant}$$

$$\Rightarrow \left(x^2\sin^2\alpha + y^2\cos^2\alpha + z^2 + C^2\right)^2$$
$$- 4\left(xy\sin\alpha\cos\alpha + Cz\right)^2 = \text{constant} \qquad \dots (1)$$

This gives equation of equipotential surface.

Second Part. Let us take any point $(x, 0, 0)$ on the x-axis.

Let $V(x, y, z)$ stand for the left hand expression of equation (1).

Now for a particle placed on x-axis, the separating surface is given by

$$V(x, y, z) = V(x, 0, 0)$$

where y and z are small compared with x.

From (1)

$$V(x, 0, 0) = (x^2 \sin^2 \alpha + C^2)^2$$

Hence equation of the separating surface is

$$V(x, y, z) = V(x, 0, 0)$$

$$\Rightarrow (x^2 \sin^2 \alpha + y^2 \cos^2 \alpha + z^2 + C^2)^2$$
$$- 4(xy \sin \alpha \cos \alpha + Cz^2) = (x^2 \sin^2 \alpha + C^2)^2$$

$$\Rightarrow (x^2 \sin^2 \alpha + y^2 \cos^2 \alpha + z^2 + C^2) - (x^2 \sin^2 \alpha + C^2)^2$$
$$= 4(xy \sin \alpha \cos \alpha + Cz)^2$$

$$\Rightarrow (y^2 \cos^2 \alpha + z^2)^2 + 2(y^2 \cos^2 \alpha + z^2)(x^2 \sin^2 \alpha + C^2)$$
$$= 4(xy \sin \alpha \cos \alpha + Cz)^2$$

Neglecting powers of y and z greater than 2, we get

$$2(x^2 y^2 \sin^2 \alpha \cos^2 \alpha + x^2 z^2 \sin^2 \alpha$$
$$+ C^2 y^2 \cos^2 \alpha + C^2 z^2) = 4(xy \sin \alpha \cos \alpha + Cz)^2$$

$$\Rightarrow x^2 z^2 \sin^2 \alpha + C^2 y^2 \cos^2 \alpha$$
$$= (x^2 y^2 \sin^2 \alpha \cos^2 \alpha + C^2 z^2 + 4xyCz \sin \alpha \cos \alpha)$$

$$\Rightarrow x^2 z^2 \sin^2 \alpha + C^2 y^2 \cos^2 \alpha - 2(xz \sin \alpha)(Cy \cos \alpha)$$
$$= x^2 y^2 \sin^2 \alpha \cos^2 \alpha + C^2 z^2 + 2xyCz \sin \alpha \cos \alpha$$

$$\Rightarrow (Cy \cos \alpha - xz \sin \alpha)^2 = (xy \sin \alpha \cos \alpha + Cz)^2$$

$$\Rightarrow (Cy \cos \alpha - xz \sin \alpha) = \pm (xy \sin \alpha \cos \alpha + Cz)$$

4. Show that a family of right circular cones with a common axis and vertex is a possible family of equipotential surfaces and find the potential function. [M.U. 97H, 2000H; T.M.B.U. 91H, 97H; B.B.A.B.U. 97H, 01H, 04H]

Solution: Let us take the common axis of the family of right circular cones as the z-axis. Then the equation of the family of cones is

$$\frac{x^2 + y^2}{z^2} = \text{constant}$$

Let $\phi\,(x, y, z) = \dfrac{x^2 + y^2}{z^2} = \text{constant}$

Then

$$\frac{\partial \phi}{\partial x} = \frac{2x}{z^2}, \frac{\partial \phi}{\partial y} = \frac{2y}{z^2}, \frac{\partial \phi}{\partial z^2} = \frac{-2}{z^3}\left(x^2 + y^2\right)$$

$$\frac{\partial^2 \phi}{\partial x^2} = \frac{2}{z^2}, \frac{\partial^2 \phi}{\partial y^2} = \frac{2}{z^2}, \frac{\partial^2 \phi}{\partial z^2} = \frac{6}{z^4}\left(x^2 + y^2\right)$$

Now

$$\frac{F''(\phi)}{F'(\phi)} = -\frac{\dfrac{\partial^2 \phi}{\partial x^2} + \dfrac{\partial^2 \phi}{\partial y^2} + \dfrac{\partial^2 \phi}{\partial z^2}}{\left(\dfrac{\partial \phi}{\partial x}\right)^2 + \left(\dfrac{\partial \phi}{\partial y}\right)^2 + \left(\dfrac{\partial \phi}{\partial z}\right)^2}$$

$$= -\frac{\dfrac{2}{z^2} + \dfrac{2}{z^2} + \dfrac{6}{z^4}\left(x^2 + y^2\right)}{\dfrac{4x^2}{z^4} + \dfrac{4y^2}{z^4} + \dfrac{4\left(x^2 + y^2\right)^2}{z^6}}$$

$$= -\frac{2 + \dfrac{3\left(x^2 + y^2\right)}{z^2}}{\dfrac{2\left(x^2 + y^2\right)}{z^2} + 2\left(\dfrac{x^2 + y^2}{z^2}\right)^2}$$

$$= -\frac{2 + 3\phi}{2\phi + 2\phi^2}$$

which is a function of ϕ only.

Hence the set of right circular cones under consideration is a family of equipotential surfaces.

Now let us find the potential function

$$\frac{F''(\phi)}{F'(\phi)} = -\frac{2 + 2\phi + \phi}{2\phi\,(1 + \phi)}$$

$$= -\left[\frac{1}{\phi} + \frac{1}{2\,(1 + \phi)}\right]$$

Integrating, we get

$$\log F'(\phi) = -\left[\log \phi + \frac{1}{2}\log(1+\phi)\right] + \log A$$

$$\log F'(\phi) = \log \frac{A}{\phi\sqrt{1+\phi}}$$

$$F'(\phi) = \frac{A}{\phi\sqrt{1+\phi}}$$

Integrating again w.r.t. ϕ, we get

$$F(\phi) = \int \frac{A\,d\phi}{\phi\sqrt{1+\phi}}$$

Putting $\phi = \tan^2\theta$

$$\therefore \quad d\phi = 2\tan\theta\sec^2\theta\,d\theta$$

$$F(\phi) = A\int \frac{2\tan\theta\sec^2\theta\,d\theta}{\tan^2\theta\sec\theta}$$

$$= 2A\int \operatorname{cosec}\theta\,d\theta$$

$$= 2A\log\tan\frac{\theta}{2} + B$$

$$\therefore \quad V = F(\phi) = 2A\log\tan\frac{\theta}{2} + B$$

This gives the law of potential.

5. Show that the cylinders $x^2 + y^2 = 2\lambda x$ are a possible set of equipotential surfaces in empty space but the spheres $x^2 + y^2 + z^2 = 2\lambda x$ are not. [B.B.A.B.U. 2003H]

In the former case, find the potential as a function of x.

Solution: Here

$$\phi(x, y, z) = \frac{x^2 + y^2}{2x}$$

$$= \frac{x}{2} + \frac{y^2}{2x}$$

$$= \lambda = \text{constant}$$

$$\therefore \qquad \frac{\partial \phi}{\partial x} = \frac{1}{2} - \frac{y^2}{2x^2}, \frac{\partial \phi}{\partial y} = \frac{y}{x}$$

$$\frac{\partial \phi}{\partial z} = 0, \frac{\partial^2 \phi}{\partial x^2} = \frac{y^2}{x^3}, \frac{\partial^2 \phi}{\partial y^2} = \frac{1}{x}$$

$$\frac{\partial^2 \phi}{\partial z^2} = 0$$

Now

$$\frac{F''(\phi)}{F'(\phi)} = -\frac{\dfrac{\partial^2 \phi}{\partial x^2} + \dfrac{\partial^2 \phi}{\partial y^2} + \dfrac{\partial^2 \phi}{\partial z^2}}{\left(\dfrac{\partial \phi}{\partial x}\right)^2 + \left(\dfrac{\partial \phi}{\partial y}\right)^2 + \left(\dfrac{\partial \phi}{\partial z}\right)^2}$$

$$= -\frac{\dfrac{y^2}{x^3} + \dfrac{1}{x}}{\dfrac{1}{4}\left(1 - \dfrac{y^2}{x^2}\right)^2 + \dfrac{y^2}{x^2}}$$

$$= -\frac{4x\left(x^2 + y^2\right)}{\left(x^2 + y^2\right)^2}$$

$$= -\frac{2}{\dfrac{x^2 + y^2}{2x}} = -\frac{2}{\phi} \qquad \text{... (1)}$$

= a function of ϕ only.

Hence the given family of cylinders represents equipotential surfaces.

Again in case of the family of sphere

$$\phi\ (x, y, z) = \frac{x^2 + y^2 + z^2}{2x}$$

$$= \frac{1}{2}x + \frac{1}{2}\frac{y^2}{x} + \frac{1}{2}\frac{z^2}{x}$$

$$= \lambda, \text{ a constant}$$

$$\frac{\partial\phi}{\partial x} = \frac{1}{2} - \frac{1}{2}\frac{y^2}{x^2}, \frac{\partial\phi}{\partial y} = \frac{y}{x}, \frac{\partial\phi}{\partial z} = \frac{z}{x}$$

$$\frac{\partial^2\phi}{\partial x^2} = \frac{y^2}{x^3} + \frac{z^2}{x^3}, \frac{\partial^2\phi}{\partial y^2} = \frac{1}{x}, \frac{\partial^2\phi}{\partial z^2} = \frac{1}{x}$$

Now

$$\frac{F''(\phi)}{F'(\phi)} = -\frac{\frac{\partial^2\phi}{\partial x^2} + \frac{\partial^2\phi}{\partial y^2} + \frac{\partial^2\phi}{\partial z^2}}{\left(\frac{\partial\phi}{\partial x}\right)^2 + \left(\frac{\partial\phi}{\partial y}\right)^2 + \left(\frac{\partial\phi}{\partial z}\right)^2}$$

$$= -\frac{\frac{y^3}{x^3} + \frac{z^2}{x^3} + \frac{1}{x} + \frac{1}{x}}{\left(\frac{1}{2} - \frac{1}{2}\frac{y^2}{x^2} - \frac{1}{2}\frac{z^2}{x^2}\right)^2 + \frac{y^2}{x^2} + \frac{z^2}{x^2}}$$

$$= -\frac{4x\left(2x^2 + y^2 + z^2\right)}{x^4 + y^4 + z^2 - 2x^2y^2 - 2x^2z^2 + 2y^2z^2 + 4x^2y^2 + 4z^2x^2}$$

$$= -\frac{4x\left(2x^2 + y^2 + z^2\right)}{\left(x^2 + y^2 + z^2\right)^2}$$

$$= \frac{-4x\left(x^2 + 2x\lambda\right)}{4x^2\lambda^2}$$

$$= -\frac{1}{\lambda^2}(x + 2\lambda)$$

which is not a function of ϕ.

Hence the family of spheres is not the equipotential surfaces.

In case of system of cylinders, we have from (1)

$$\frac{F''(\phi)}{F'(\phi)} = -\frac{2}{\phi}$$

Integrating, we get

$$\log F'(\phi) = -2\log\phi + \log A = \log\frac{A}{\phi^2}$$

$$F'(\phi) = \frac{A}{\phi^2}$$

Integrating again, we get

$$F(\phi) = -\frac{A}{\phi} + B$$

Also law of potential is $V = F(\phi)$

$$\therefore \qquad V = -\frac{A}{\phi} + B$$

But $\phi = \lambda$

$$\therefore \qquad V = -\frac{A}{\lambda} + B$$

6. Show that the system of coaxial cylinders $x^2 + y^2 + 2\lambda x + C^2 = 0$ can form a system of equipotential surface and find the law of potential. [L.N.M.U. 93H; M.U. 2003H; T.M.B.U. 98H, 2004H]

Solution: Here $x^2 + y^2 + 2\lambda x + C^2 = 0$

$\Rightarrow (x + \lambda)^2 + y^2 = \lambda^2 - C^2$

$\Rightarrow \phi(x, y, z) = (x + \lambda)^2 + y^2 = \lambda^2 - C^2 =$ a constant

$$\frac{\partial\phi}{\partial x} = 2(x+\lambda), \frac{\partial\phi}{\partial y} = 2y, \frac{\partial\phi}{\partial z} = 0$$

$$\frac{\partial^2\phi}{\partial x^2} = 2, \frac{\partial^2\phi}{\partial y^2} = 2, \frac{\partial^2\phi}{\partial z^2} = 0$$

Now

$$\frac{F''(\phi)}{F'(\phi)} = -\frac{\dfrac{\partial^2\phi}{\partial x^2} + \dfrac{\partial^2\phi}{\partial y^2} + \dfrac{\partial^2\phi}{\partial z^2}}{\left(\dfrac{\partial\phi}{\partial x}\right)^2 + \left(\dfrac{\partial\phi}{\partial y}\right)^2 + \left(\dfrac{\partial\phi}{\partial z}\right)^2}$$

$$= -\frac{2+2+0}{4(x+\lambda)^2 + 4y^2 + 0}$$

$$= -\frac{1}{\phi}, \text{ a function of } \phi \text{ only.}$$

Hence the system of coaxial, cylinders form a system of equipotential surfaces.

Now $\dfrac{F''(\phi)}{F'(\phi)} = -\dfrac{1}{\phi}$

Integrating, we get

$$\log F'(\phi) = \log A = \log \phi$$

$$= \log \frac{A}{\phi}$$

$$F'(\phi) = \frac{A}{\phi}$$

Integrating again with respect to ϕ, we get

$$F(\phi) = A \log \phi + B$$

But $V = F(\phi) = A \log \phi + B$

This gives us law of potential.

EXERCISES

1. Show that $(x - c)^2 + y^2 = \lambda \{(x + c)^2 + y^2\}$ represents a family of equipotential surface and that $V = A \log \lambda + B$ where V is the potential function and A **and** B **are** arbitrary constants. [T.M.B.U. 94H, 99H]
2. Show that the family of surfaces defined by $x^2 + y^2 =$ constant can be a family of equipotential surfaces in **free** space, and find the law of potential. [T.M.B.U. **96H,** 2001H, 2003H; B.B.A.B.U. 96H, 98H, 2004H; M.U. 2005H]

   [**Ans.** $V = A \log \phi + B$, where $\phi =$ constant and A, B are arbitrary constants]